WILD ITALY

A TRAVELLER'S GUIDE

TIM JEPSON

SHELDRAKE PRESS

LONDON

Published in 2005 by Sheldrake Press
188 Cavendish Road
London
SW12 0DA

Tel.: 020 8675 1767
Fax.: 020 8675 7736
E-mail: mail@sheldrakepress.demon.co.uk
Web-site: www.sheldrakepress.co.uk

Second edition
First published in 1994 by Sheldrake Press in association
with Aurum Press Ltd

Copyright © 1994, 2005 Sheldrake Holdings Ltd
Main text copyright © 1994, 2005 Tim Jepson

British Library Cataloguing in Publication Data
Jepson, Tim
Wild Italy: a traveller's guide. - 2nd ed. - (Wild guides)
1. Italy - Guidebooks
I. Title II. Rigge, Simon
914.5'0493

Printed in China

ISBN 1 873329 35 0
ISSN 1351-329 X

EDITOR: Simon Rigge
Managing Editor: Malcolm Day
Art Direction: Ivor Claydon
Picture Editor: Karin B. Hills
Assistant Editors: Mandy Greenfield, James Harpur,
Chris Schüler
Editorial Assistants: Sarah Bercusson, Annabel
Blatchford, Charlotte Cox, Alex Fazzari, Sinead
Fottrell, Tom Fox, Annabelle Jones, Nikki Macmichael,
Thomas Maguire, Matt Milton, Katie Morton, Aileen
Reid, Tracey Stead
Researchers: Elena Giovannini, Michele Howe, Anna
Motzo, Katia Muscarà, Eugenia Nuti, Isabelle Rigolo,
Tania Trosini
Picture Researcher: Elizabeth Loving
Line Illustrations: Syd Lewis
Production Assistants: Helen Reeve and Nikki Skowron
Maps: Swanston Publishing Ltd
Index: Sarah Hobbs

THE GENERAL EDITOR

DOUGLAS BOTTING was born in London
and educated at Oxford. He has travelled to the
Amazon, South Yemen, the Sahara, Arctic
Siberia, the rarely-visited Arabian island of
Socotra, to many parts of Africa and to many
European wild places.

Douglas Botting's travel books include *One
Chilly Siberian Morning*, *Wilderness Europe* and
Rio de Janeiro. He has also written biographies
of the great naturalist and explorer Alexander
von Humboldt, entitled *Humboldt and the
Cosmos*, the naturalist Gavin Maxwell and, most
recently, the author and conservationalist,
Gerald Durrell.

THE CONSULTANTS

TERESA FARINO is an ecologist with a
Master's degree in Conservation from University
College, London. She has travelled widely in
southern Europe and has a detailed knowledge
of the habitats, flora and fauna of the area. She is
the author of several books on wildlife, including
The Living World, Sharks – the ultimate predators
and the *Photographic Encyclopedia of
Wildflowers*. Having lived in northern Spain since
1986, she contributes regularly to *BBC Wildlife*
magazine about the environmental problems of
that country and is also joint author of *Wild
Spain* in the Wild Guides series.

MASSIMILIANO CALLIGOLA was born in
Bologna, and graduated with a dissertation on
Landscape Studies. His area of special interest is
north-eastern Italy, particularly the region of
Cadore, in the Dolomites, on which he has
written both for his degree and for the Italian
Touring Club (TCI). Keenly interested in
botany and conservation issues, he is moving
into environmental journalism as well as
completing an MA in photography.

Front cover: The rugged Zingaro coast offers some
of the best of Sicily's wild scenery.

CONTENTS

ABOUT THE SERIES

What would the world be, once bereft
Of wet and of wildness? Let them be
 left,
O let them be left, wildness and wet;
Long live the weeds and the wilderness
 yet.

Gerard Manley Hopkins: *Inversnaid*

These books are about those embattled
refuges of wildness and wet, the wild places
of Europe. But where, in this most densely
populated sub-continent, do we find a truly
wild place?

Ever since our Cro-Magnon ancestors
began their forays into the virgin forests of
Europe 40,000 years ago, the land and its
creatures have been in retreat before *Homo
sapiens*. Forests have been cleared,
marshes drained and rivers straightened.
Even some of those landscapes that appear
primordial are in fact the result of human
activity. Heather-covered moorland in
North Yorkshire and parched Andalusian
desert have this in common: both were
once covered by great forests which
ancient settlers knocked flat.

What then remains that can be called
wild? There are still a few areas in Europe
that are untouched by man — places
generally so unwelcoming either in terrain
or in climate that man has not wanted to
touch them at all — and these are
indisputably wild.

For some people, wildness suggests
conflict with nature: a wild place is a part of
the planet so savage and desolate that you
risk your life whenever you venture into it.
This is in part true but would limit the
eligible places to the most impenetrable bog
or highest mountain tops in the worst
winter weather — a rather restricted view.
Another much broader definition considers
a wild place to be a part of the planet where
living things can find a natural refuge from
the influence of modern industrial society.
By this definition a wild place is for wildlife
as well as that portmanteau figure referred
to in these pages as the wild traveller: the
hill-walker, backpacker, bird-watcher,
nature lover, explorer, nomad, loner, mystic,
masochist, *aficionado* of the great outdoors,
or permutations of all these things.

This is the definition we have observed
in selecting the wild places described in
these books. Choosing them has not been
easy. Even so, we hope the criterion has
proved rigid enough to exclude purely
pretty (though popular) countryside, and
flexible enough to include the greener,
gentler wild places, of great natural
historical interest perhaps, as well as the
starker, more savage ones where the wild
explorers come into their own.

These are not guide-books in the
conventional sense, for to describe every
neck of the woods and twist of the trail
throughout Europe would require a library
of volumes. Nor are these books addressed
to the technical specialist — the caver, diver,
rock climber or cross-country skier; the
orchid-hunter, lepidopterist or beetle-
maniac — for such experts will have data of
their own. They are books intended for the
general outdoor traveller — including the
expert outside his own field of expertise (the
orchid-hunter in a cave, the diver on a
mountain top) — who wishes to scrutinize
the range of wild places on offer in Europe,
to learn a little more about them and to set
about exploring them off the beaten track.

One of the greatest consolations in the
preparation of these books has been to find
that after 40,000 years of hunting, clearing,
draining and ploughing, Cro-Magnon and
their descendants have left so much of
Europe that can still be defined as wild.

WILD ITALY: AN INTRODUCTION

The Italy of popular imagination is scarcely a wild country at all. Its familiar landscapes are those of Tuscany and Umbria — pastoral vignettes of vines, olives and cypress-topped hills melting into the haze of a summer afternoon. Its countryside is the ordered work of centuries, tilled and tamed by peasants since the dawn of history. Yet behind this benign veneer lie vast areas of wilderness, from the glacier-carved cirques of the Dolomites to the sun-scorched mountains of the Sardinian interior. Vultures and eagles wheel in southern skies, lynx pad the Tarvisian forests, brown bears still roam the mountains of the Abruzzo and wolves have reappeared in much of the Apennines.

It is something of a miracle that so much has survived. Even ten years ago, Italy's natural heritage was one of Europe's most threatened, damaged not so much by the draining of wetlands, felling of woodlands and cutting of grasslands, as elsewhere, but by the effects of industrialization, which in fifty years turned Italy from an agricultural backwater into one of the world's leading economic powers. In the course of this transformation Italy's coast was ravaged, the Po poisoned by the effluent of northern cities and the countryside blighted by building projects that proceeded virtually without planning controls. Campaigns to limit hunting consistently failed in the face of opposition from one of the world's most powerful gun lobbies.

Progress to halt the environmental carnage was painfully slow until the end of the last century. In 1991 there were still only eight national parks, which it had taken 70 years to create. Since then the number has risen to 21. Adding in the regional parks and various types of reserves that have been set up alongside them, the proportion of the country that enjoys a measure of protected status has risen from 3 to 11 per cent. Italy now ranks fifth in Europe after Austria (19 per cent of land protected), United Kingdom (18 per cent), Norway (14 per cent) and Germany (13 per cent). The quality of protection has gone up with the quantity, and it is now generally accepted that in protected areas at least, there is no longer any possibility of hunting.

So take heart. Much has survived the onslaughts of developers and hunters. Wildlife is as varied here as anywhere in Europe. Although Italy covers only 1/80th of the continental land-mass, it hosts a third of the fauna (more than 57,000 species) and more than half the flora — 5,559 species (13 ½ per cent of which are endemics).

Italians in the rural areas are invariably friendly and hospitable, and few are likely to mind you tramping across their land. Many continue to enjoy the traditional Italian way of life, which is generally encouraged and preserved by park authorities. Living in small market towns and villages, consuming local produce and building with local materials, they are one with their history and proud of what they have to offer.

Do not be surprised to find yourself addressed in a language other than Italian; Italy is less a country than a federation of regions. Walkers in Valle d'Aosta and some parts of Piedmont will be confronted with a French patois; in the mountains of the South Tyrol they will find themselves dealing in German; and in the Dolomites they might come across Ladin. The Sard language of Sardinia is rivalled in its impenetrability only by Welsh, and in Sicily and Naples the dialects are so strong they might as well be from another continent.

Foreigners wishing to explore the wilder parts of Italy have been hamstrung by lack of a concise source in English for paths, areas of natural interest and regional flora and fauna. *Wild Italy* is the first one-volume guide to meet this need, describing Italy's finest walks and landscapes, as well as its immense natural variety and scarcely known protected places. It cannot be encyclopaedic, but it will give you a taste of the country's wild places and, I hope, a desire to explore them for yourself.

WILD ITALY

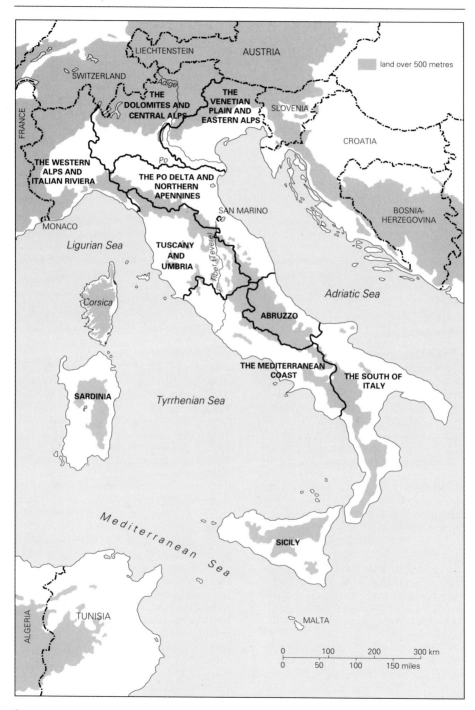

land over 500 metres

LIECHTENSTEIN   AUSTRIA

SWITZERLAND

Adige

THE DOLOMITES AND CENTRAL ALPS

THE VENETIAN PLAIN AND EASTERN ALPS

SLOVENIA

FRANCE

CROATIA

Po

THE WESTERN ALPS AND ITALIAN RIVIERA

THE PO DELTA AND NORTHERN APENNINES

SAN MARINO

BOSNIA-HERZEGOVINA

MONACO

Ligurian Sea

TUSCANY AND UMBRIA

Tiber (Tevere)

Adriatic Sea

Corsica

ABRUZZO

THE MEDITERRANEAN COAST

THE SOUTH OF ITALY

SARDINIA

Tyrrhenian Sea

M e d i t e r r a n e a n   S e a

SICILY

ALGERIA

TUNISIA

MALTA

| 0 | 100 | 200 | 300 km |
| 0 | 50 | 100 | 150 miles |

THE KEY TO ITALY'S WILD PLACES

WILD HABITATS

An appreciation of habitats is useful to anyone interested in seeing wild species in their natural environment. In turn, to understand the variety of habitats it is necessary to look at the major influences of climate and geology. What follows is a thumbnail sketch of the forces that have shaped the Italian landscape.

Geology: simply put, Italy divides into the Alps, Apennines and Po valley (with a separate mountain system in Sardinia). The Alps were formed as a result of continental drift, when a fragment of Africa collided with the European land-mass. They combine different rock types, the central core being granitic while the flanking ranges are of more varied composition (eroded Hercynian rocks dominate in the west, dolomite in the east). The Apennines are generally older and more weathered, and consist mainly of sandstone and limestone marl (clay) in the north, limestone in the centre and limestone and Hercynian granite in the south. On either side of the Apennines' main ridge are the sub-Apennines, lower ranges built up of generally softer and more recent rocks. The Po valley is a mixture of loams, gravels, permeable sands and silts brought down by glacial meltwaters after the Ice Ages. All over Italy, however, geological anomalies intrude; the most famous is the volcanic chain that extends south of Monte Amiata in Tuscany down to Etna in Sicily.

Soils: rock type has a profound influence on soils and, in turn, on vegetation. In Italy differences in climate, altitude and geology have produced a wide variety of soils. Most common are the dark-brown podzols, typical of mountains with a lot of flint and heavy rainfall, such as the Alps. Similar soils occur in the Apennines, together with rendzinas, humus-carbonate soils characteristic of limestone mountain pastures and of many Apennine meadows and beech forests. Red earth, the famous terra rossa, derives from limestone rocks: after weathering, only the clay minerals are left. This distinctive residue occurs most notably in Tuscany and Puglia, where it is the favoured soil of vineyards and olive groves.

Drainage: Italy's rivers are relatively short; the longest, the Po, which drains the western Alps, runs for only 650 kilometres (400 miles) before it empties into the Adriatic. The country's second longest river, the Adige, which drains the eastern Alps and the Dolomites, reaches only some 400 kilometres (250 miles). Other rivers flowing into the Adriatic from the Apennines, the peninsula's main watershed, tend to be even more modest. Those flowing west into the Tyrrhenian Sea are comparatively complex, including the Tiber, which flows through Rome, and the Arno, Florence's great river. Southern rivers are often dry in the summer but experience sometimes devastating flash floods in spring and autumn.

Climate: Italy lies essentially in a temperate zone, but because it is affected by continental Europe in the north and by the Mediterranean in the south it experiences a huge range of weathers.

Generally, the Alps have cold snowy winters and short mild summers, but like the Apennines, they also produce complex micro-climates, and partially shield the peninsula from the colder and wetter weather of the north and west. The Po valley has a typically continental climate, with stifling hot summers and cold damp winters. Cooler 'Balkan' weather is felt at times in the east as a result of more marked continental effects, including the bora, a wind which blows across the Adriatic from the north-east at up to 160 kph (100 mph).

Peninsular Italy and Sardinia are characterized by hot dry summers and mild short winters, but can be influenced by the moister and cooler Atlantic climate. In Sicily and the extreme south, North African weather often prevails, most obviously manifest in the droughts and high summer temperatures which may be intensified by the fierce scirocco wind blowing up from the Sahara.

Mountains and uplands: Italy is largely moun-tainous; 35 per cent of its area is covered by ranges of over 700 metres (2,300 feet) and 42 per cent by hills. The Alps and Apennines are the two main mountain ranges, their vast extent producing a variety of landscapes that range from Arctic ice and tundra in the highest part of the Alps to hot Mediterranean slopes in the south. Between these two extremes, more temperate conditions allow a wide range of flora and fauna to flourish.

Forest and scrubland: the largest remnants of Italy's great primeval forests, most of which have been cleared by centuries of cultivation, survive in the Sila in Calábria and in the Casentinesi forests of Tuscany. Elsewhere, precious relics testify to long-vanished areas of former woodland, in Piedmont's Gran Bosco di Salbertrand, the

Abruzzo's Bosco di Sant'Antonio and the Gran Bosco della Mésola on the edge of the Po Delta.

The Alps support magnificent fir forests, with larch and Norway spruce giving way at higher altitudes to green alder and dwarf varieties of pine, willow and juniper. Great forests of beech and sweet chestnut blanket much of the Apennines; in the higher parts of southern Italy, the Apennines also support clumps of ancient mountain forest, boasting trees such as Neapolitan maple, Italian alder and flowering ash. Harsher, cooler parts of the range in the Abruzzo and Calábria also support various pines, such as Balkan and Calabrian pine.

In lower areas of the peninsula, and especially in Sicily and Sardinia, trees typical of the Mediterranean flourish, principally olive, holm oak, cork oak and aleppo pine. In such areas, and where original vegetation has been partially cleared, a vigorous layer of thick scrub, known as *maquis*, is common. This is typically between two and four metres (seven and fourteen feet) high, formed by aromatic species such as lentisk, myrtle, cistus and Spanish broom. Drier stunted scrubland only half a metre (eighteen inches) in height, known as *garrigue*, may also develop, often on limestone or extremely thin soils. Steppes of tough drought-resistant plants and feather grasses grow in Puglia, replacing olive trees and shore vegetation which have been cut down, and in Sardinia, where the removal of carob forests has had the same effect.

Wetlands: lakes, swamps, marshes and rivers are of great interest for the richness of their plant and bird life. The Po delta, among Italy's best bird-watching areas, is the most famous. Some of the country's great areas of ancient marsh, such as Tuscany's Maremma and Lazio's Pontine, have been drained, but small slivers of wetland such as the Circeo national park still offer rich rewards. Italy also has some 1,500 lakes, from glacially scoured tarns in the Alps and the grand lakes of the sub-alpine region (Maggiore, Como, Lugano and Garda) to coastal saline lagoons such as Lésina and Varano in Puglia.

Coasts and islands: where it is free of commercial development, the Italian coast offers a spectacular variety of sea shores, cliffs, estuaries and coastal dunes. In addition Italy has 32 islands, ranging in size from Sicily and Sardinia to the coronet of wild islands around Sicily — the Eolie, the Égadi and the Pelágie — which include the naturalist's haven of Maréttimo and the volcanic islets of Stromboli and Vulcano.

On the Ligurian Sea close to the French border, the littoral is a succession of level gravels and high rocky cliffs. Along the Tyrrhenian, south through Tuscany as far as Campania, it turns to dunes and long sandy beaches, interrupted by bold promontories. Calábria's coast is again high and rocky, while Sicily's is mainly flat. Around most of Puglia, and almost all the way up Italy's Adriatic coast, the shore remains either flat or slightly terraced. Only the craggy Gargano and Cónero peninsulas and the bulge of the Po delta disturb its ruler-straight line. Lagoons characterize the area around Venice, before the coast picks up the limestone uplands of the Carso, close to Trieste.

PROTECTED WILD PLACES

Italy's system of environmental protection has undergone dramatic changes over the last ten years, starting as one of the most fractured and slipshod and ending as one of the most comprehensive in Europe.

The course of conservation in Italy never did run smooth. The story started early, in 1922, when 70,000 hectares (170,000 acres) of a former royal hunting ground gained state protection and became the country's first national park *(parco nazionale)*, the Gran Paradiso. A year later came the Abruzzo national park, in the central Apennines, at which point the process stalled. Two more national parks were created in the 1930s — Circeo (1934) and Stélvio (1935) — after which a much longer pause ensued. With the post-war addition of Calábria (1968), the heartland of Italy's protected areas was complete, but it still covered less than three per cent of the country and for another ten years resolutely resisted expansion.

The key to opening more parks was fresh legislation. The first significant change came in 1977, when Italy's 20 regions were granted power to designate their own protected areas. Most of the regional parks *(parchi naturali regionali)* were set up soon afterwards, and today they account for a third of the country's protected land, but the enthusiasm for creating and administering parks varies greatly among the regions. (The most prolific and positive are Piedmont, Lombardy, Trentino-Alto Adige and Tuscany.) Even more influential was the new state law on park organization enacted in 1991, which led to the creation of 16 new national parks, bringing Italy's total to 21, with three more on the way.

It is worth adding that in Italy, and in southern Europe as a whole, the park is seen not so much as an enclosed sanctuary for nature, as in the Anglo-Saxon world, but as a laboratory for the future, whose aim is to achieve a balance between conservation and sustainable development, mainly through encouraging organic farming and protecting local products.

Alongside the national and regional parks has sprung up a network of state, regional and provincial nature reserves as well as reserves and oases run by the World Wide Fund for Nature (WWF), the Lega Italiana per la Protezione degli Uccelli (LIPU) and other non-governmental bodies. The total area covered by some form of national protection has risen to 3 million hectares from the 1.3 million of 1988 (to 7.5 from 2.5 million acres). To this must be added the areas designated by the European Union under the Birds Directive of 1979 as Zone di Protezione Speciale (ZPS) and under the Habitats Directive of 1992 as Siti di Importanza Comunitaria (SIC). Key zones are also protected by international classifications such as Ramsar, World Heritage Site and Biosphere Reserve. All the main categories are defined in the Glossary (p214).

EXPLORING WILD ITALY

Italy is criss-crossed with ancient paths and mule-tracks. The highest concentration is in the Dolomites and the best-known parts of the western and central Alps, where tracks are clearly marked by the Club Alpino Italiano (CAI), the parks or local associations, and may be followed on several excellent series of maps. Planning and executing a hiking trip is probably made easier in these areas than anywhere else in Europe. Liguria and most northern and central Apennine regions are also well served by maps and trails.

Long-distance trails are also generally found in the north, notably the Alte Vie in the Dolomites and the Grande Traversata delle Alpi in Piedmont. Friuli in the north-east has the Traversata Cárnica. The Alpi Apuane have two long paths, Apuane Trekking and Garfagnana Trekking, and Liguria boasts the Alta Via dei Monti Líguri. The Grande Escursione Appenninica (GEA) runs through Tuscany and Emilia-Romagna as far as Umbria.

The longest of the long-distance trails is the European Trail E1, which when completed will cross the continent from North Cape to Sicily, a distance of 6,000 kilometres (3,700 miles). The Italian part, known as the Cammino dell'Alleanza, covers the whole country from the Swiss border at Porto Cerésio to Capo Pássero in Sicily, each section described in a guide available from Alleanza Assicurazioni (see Useful Addresses). South of Castellúccio di Nórcia in the Sibillini some sections may still be unmarked.

TO THE READER

Organization: each chapter is divided into exploration zones containing a narrative description, written in the first person singular and illustrated with personal anecdote, followed by a fact-pack which gives practical information on how to get there, when and where to go, where to stay and what to do, backed up with postal, e-mail and web-site addresses, contact numbers and lists of maps and further reading. This hybrid arrangement avoids cluttering the author's personal narrative with tedious guide-book detail, but at the same time ensures that you can find practical references instantly when you want them.

Eagle symbols: the eagle symbols used in this book indicate the wildness of the exploration zone to which they refer. This scale is based on a number of factors, including remoteness, ruggedness, spaciousness, uniqueness, wildlife interest, natural beauty and the author's subjective reactions. Three eagles is the highest rating, no eagles the lowest.

Maps: Kompass contour maps cover most of northern Italy, usually on a scale of 1:50,000, and open up parts of Tuscany, Umbria and the Monti Sibillini to the walker. The Istituto Geografico Centrale (IGC) produces 24 contour maps covering north-west Italy. The Tabacco 1:25,000 and 1:50,000 contour maps specialize in the Dolomites and north-eastern Alps. South of Rome, especially in Calábria, Sicily and Sardinia, you must rely on the old military maps produced by the Istituto Geografico Militare (IGM). You may also find the national parks' own maps useful.

Updating: while everything possible has been done to ensure the accuracy of the facts in this book, information does gradually become outdated. For this reason we would welcome readers' comments and corrections for incorporation in subsequent editions. Please write to The Editor, Wild Guides, Sheldrake Press, 188 Cavendish Road, London SW12 0DA, or send an e-mail to: mail@sheldrakepress.demon.co.uk.

Non-liability: both author and publishers have gone to great pains to point out the hazards that may confront the traveller in certain places described in *Wild Italy*. We cannot under any circumstances accept any liability for any mishap, loss or injury sustained by any person venturing into any of the wild places listed in this book.

CHAPTER 1

The Western Alps and Italian Riviera

The Alps sweep across northern Italy in a great arc that reaches from France to the Slovenian border. Europe's highest and most extensive mountains, hostile near their peaks to all but the best-adapted plants and animals, they have been partly tamed by centuries of human habitation. Their valleys are threaded with roads and railways or scattered with towns and industry. Ski resorts and hydro-electric schemes desecrate otherwise virgin territory. Wildlife has been beaten back or, in the case of bears and wolves, harried and hunted to the point of virtual extinction. Hordes of summer walkers pound the tracks and trails, whether pushing through meadows ablaze with flowers or braving the remoter citadels of ice and rock.

Bar a few stretches of Ligurian coastline, however, it is the Alps which yield north-west Italy's finest natural rewards. Most of the wildest places are crammed into the Valle d'Aosta, one of the country's smallest administrative regions, yet home to its most spectacular scenery and to Europe's three highest mountains: Mont Blanc (Monte Bianco), Monte Rosa and the Matterhorn (Monte Cervino). The rest of the wild places are spread across Piedmont, the 'foot of the mountains', whose mountainous borders with France and Switzerland are chequered with numerous parks, including Europe's highest nature conservation area (the Valsésia regional park) and

Pine forests frame the peaks and glaciers at the head of the Valnontey, one of the loveliest valleys in the Gran Paradiso.

one of its finest national parks (the Gran Paradiso).

For a first visit, leave these beautiful yet busy areas for later and opt instead for the Alpi Maríttime in south-west Piedmont. Here you will find landscapes where wilderness is still uncompromised — and perhaps the one walk you should tackle in the Alps if you tackle no other.

The hike in question follows part of the Grande Traversata delle Alpi (GTA), a long-distance footpath that meanders from the Alps' southern border with France to their first great climax in the Gran Paradiso. Head for the little hamlet of Sant'Anna, close to Valdieri, and drive to the Terme di Valdieri where you will find the Grand Hotel Royal. It was built around a hunting lodge once owned by the Savoys, dukes of Piedmont and later Italy's royal family. The road ends here, fading into a beautifully engineered and scenic mule-track, created to allow royal parties a graceful approach to the hunting grounds beyond.

The track climbs along the side of a valley and gives spectacular views down on to an ice-clear river fringed by strands of fir and pine. At the head of the valley stand the pinnacles of the main Alpine ridge. Beyond lies France. Sunlight filters through trees shading the track, which hairpins ever higher and tests your lungs, just as the higher, more precipitous paths will test your nerve. This steep climb is typical of virtually all excursions in the Alps: you have to get up early and climb the mountains' looming glaciated valleys before finding the flower-strewn meadows hidden at greater heights.

Pausing for breath, as I did one heavenly October morning, I caught a glimpse of the wildlife for which the Alpi Maríttime are renowned. In this case it was the face of a startled chamois

and, a little later, the contented, nibbling figure of a marmot soaking up the sunshine. Later still, for the first time, I heard the marmot's distinctive warning whistle, a piercing high-pitched shriek that echoed around the mountains as if from another world.

Reward for this climb, if reward were needed, is the appearance of the Valle di Valasco, a glacial valley containing perhaps the Alps' most idyllic upland meadow. After hours engaging with the path, its busy winding, its traverse of jumbled boulders, its arbour of yellow-tinted larches, you come to a series of waterfalls which heralds a change of mood, emerging eventually into a vast natural amphitheatre. Mountains gird it on three sides, craggy and snow-capped, and across the meadow at its centre meanders a lazy stream. Water is everywhere, coursing from the surrounding slopes and gushing from moss-damp hollows among the nearby rocks. The mule-track picks its way towards a single stone building, the Casa di Caccia, a romantically ruined hunting lodge, quiet and overgrown, giving no hint of the days when it sheltered the Savoys in all their splendour.

Beyond the tumbled stones and downcast timbers of the lodge the track peters out into a marshy stream-side path. A little later it picks up, curving round the head of the meadow to resume its climb towards the high ridges now crowding the skyline. It continues above the tree-line through a typically Alpine setting of splintered pinnacles and plunging rock walls. Often this stage of a trek is cut short by sheer cliffs, glaciers and other obstacles in the impenetrable armour of the high Alps. Here, though, you can crest the mountains, should you wish, by scrambling up to a knife-edge ridge that looks down into France and across a sweep of pastoral countryside stretching to the Riviera.

On this occasion, I decided to forgo the ridge and head for a beautiful trio of lakes, each cradled in a dramatic cwm and linked by a tortuous path that threads its way back to the meadow far below. The only sign of life up here was a tiny refuge, the Rifugio Questa, shuttered and forlorn at this time of year, but one of dozens open in season for walkers and skiers and invaluable on longer excursions.

A leisurely return to the Terme di Valdieri marked the easy end to a perfect day's walk, the sun catching the snow as it set behind the mountains. Any one of hundreds, perhaps thousands, of Alpine walks offers similar experiences: the early-morning slog from the valley, the stroll across upper meadows and the drama of the high country above the tree-line.

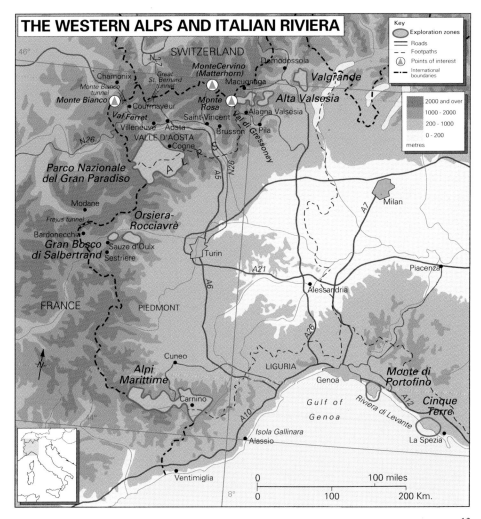

THE WESTERN ALPS AND ITALIAN RIVIERA

Key
Exploration zones
Roads
Footpaths
Points of interest
International boundaries

2000 and over
1000 - 2000
200 - 1000
0 - 200
metres

SWITZERLAND
Domodossola
MonteCervino (Matterhorn)
Chamonix
Great St. Bernard tunnel
Macugnaga
Valgrande
Monte Bianco tunnel
Monte Bianco
Courmayeur
Monte Rosa
Alta Valsesia
Val Ferret
Saint Vincent
Alagna Valsesia
Villeneuve
Aosta
Brusson
Pila
VALLE D'AOSTA
Cogne
Parco Nazionale del Gran Paradiso
Milan
Modane
Frejus tunnel
Orsiera-Rocciavrè
Bardonecchia
Gran Bosco di Salbertrand
Sauze d'Oulx
Sestriere
Turin
Piacenza
A21
Alessandria
FRANCE
PIEDMONT
Cuneo
LIGURIA
Monte di Portofino
Alpi Marittime
Genoa
Riviera di Levante
Cinque Terre
Carnino
Gulf of Genoa
Isola Gallinara
Alassio
La Spezia
Ventimiglia
0   100 miles
0   100   200 Km.

GETTING THERE

By air: international flights go to Genoa (for Liguria), T: (010) 60151, and Turin (for Piedmont and the Valle d'Aosta), T: (011) 567 6361.

By car: the main routes from France are through the Mont Blanc tunnel (T1) from Chamonix to Courmayeur (re-opened in 2002), the Fréjus tunnel from Modane to Bardonécchia (T4) and the A10 from Ventimiglia and the Riviera to Genoa. From Switzerland use the Great St Bernard tunnel (T2).

By rail: main-line services link Paris to Turin via Modane, the French Riviera to Genoa, Geneva to Domodóssola and Turin to Aosta. For details, contact Ufficio Informazioni dei Treni, freephone T: (1478) 88088 within Italy, otherwise visit www.fs-on-line.it or www.trenitalia.com.

WHEN TO GO

Piedmont and the Valle d'Aosta are primarily summer destinations; the Gran Paradiso and better-known parks can be crowded in July and Aug. Sept and Oct are best for walking; June is usually OK, though snow can linger on higher ground. The Ligurian coast is fine all year, except perhaps the busy months of July and Aug.

WHERE TO STAY

Hotels: there are plenty in the area's towns and cities, and in the villages and ski resorts of Piedmont and the Valle d'Aosta.

Refuges: mountain refuges, brick buildings that often provide food as well as shelter, are dotted over the popular hiking areas and are usually open June–Sept and Dec–Apr. There are also many smaller bivouacs holding up to 10 people, unmanned and frequently made out of corrugated iron.

Outdoor living: in Liguria most camp-sites are near the sea; in the mountains they tend to be near rivers or lakes. Most open only June–Sept.

ACTIVITIES

Walking: there are several excellent long-distance paths. The best known is the 55-day Grande Traversata delle Alpi (GTA) from Carnino on the Piedmont/Liguria border, which strikes north through the Alpi Marittime to the foothills of the Gran Paradiso. Two famous high-level routes in the Valle d'Aosta are the 10-day Alta Via I and the 7-day Alta Via II. Other trails include a 4-day tour of Monviso and the 11-day Tour du Mont Blanc (2 stages in Italy).

Fishing: sea fishing from boats or the shore is possible almost everywhere without a permit; to fish in freshwater you need an annual permit from Federazione Italiana Pesca Sportiva e Attività Subacquee (FIPSAS) offices; addresses are given in the exploration zones.

Skiing: major resorts include Courmayeur, Breuil-Cervinia, Saint-Vincent, Brusson, Pila and Cogne (in Valle d'Aosta); Sestriere, Sauze d'Oulx, Alagna Valsésia and Macugnaga (in Piedmont). Summer glacier skiing is available.

FURTHER INFORMATION

Tourist offices: the main offices of the Azienda di Promozione Turistica (APT) are (in Piedmont) Via Bogino 9, Turin, T: (011) 818 5011; Piazza Castello 161, Turin, T: (011) 535 181; Corso Nizza 21, Cuneo, T: (0171) 445 362; (in Valle d'Aosta) Piazza Chanoux 45, Aosta, T: (0165) 33352; (in Liguria) Via Roma 11, Genoa, T: (010) 576 791; Viale Mazzini 47, La Spézia, T: (0187) 770 900.

CLUB ALPINO ITALIANO (CAI)

The Italian Alpine Club was founded in 1863. It now has over a quarter of a million members, with 280 branch offices and nearly 400 local groups. The club's activities include mountaineering, climbing, caving, hiking, trekking, survival and mountain rescue. In addition to approximately 750 refuges and bivouacs, it runs 200 rescue stations, 150 avalanche, rescue and research centres, employs 400 instructors and recognizes 1,000 registered guides.

You can join the club at any of its branch offices (see fact-packs), though often they are open for only a couple of hours each week, so call in advance or check their times with the local tourist office. Take two passport photographs for registration.

Membership entitles you to insurance cover, access to local CAI groups, the use of club equipment and a discount of up to 50 per cent on overnight fees in CAI refuges. Not all refuges are owned by the club. Private huts are about twice as expensive.

Do not expect much for your money: bunks in unheated rooms and one cold tap are the norm in more spartan outposts. Most refuges have a bar and serve meals, on which members receive a discount of 10 to 15 per cent. Many are open only in July and August (June to October in a few cases) and over winter weekends. For a full list of huts, contact CAI at the address given on page 215.

Val Grande

Deserted valleys hidden away in Piedmont's most northerly corner, close to Lago Maggiore; parco nazionale
14,598 ha (36,072 acres)

The Val Grande is the largest uninhabited area in the Alps. A circle of peaks surrounded by deep valleys, it has no buildings, no cars and few tourists. The valleys are empty and mysterious, the peaks barren, the ancient tracks that cross the park overgrown. Between 1915 and 1918 military roads were built to counter a German invasion through Switzerland, but they are now largely ruined, leaving the burial mounds of primitive tribes on the Alpi di Sassolado and Alpe Pra di Cicogna as the most visible signs of human presence.

These mountains are low compared with the peaks of Monte Rosa ranging across the skyline to the west. Strictly speaking, they are only pre-Alps, their ring of summits at Tógano, Pizzo Mottác, Pizzo Proman and Cima di Laurasca barely rising above 2,000 metres (6,500 feet). Nevertheless, they present impressive views of Alpine scenery.

At the heart of the park runs the Val Grande river itself. Rising amid a wasteland of rock walls and high ridges, where golden eagles and chamois may be glimpsed, it twists southwards, fed by innumerable small streams and waterfalls that crash through steep-sided gorges. Chestnut and maple trees, as well as beech and the occasional yew, clothe the slopes. A plentiful supply of spring water also provides perfect conditions for many alpine flowers, including the rare white alpenrose, mountain tulip, martagon lily, gentian and edelweiss.

One of the most arduous of Alpine treks, a two-day assault course, follows the valley from Malesco in the Val Vigezzo to Colloro. The challenge should be considered only in the best conditions: on cool dry days in early spring or late autumn. Those looking for a gentler outing can depart from Cicogna and make for the Pogallo mountain pasture.

BEFORE YOU GO
Maps: IGM 1:25,000 Nos 73 I *Verbánia*, 52 II *Gurro* and 73 IV *Gravellona Toce*; Kompass 1:50,000 No. 97 *Omegna, Varallo, Lago d'Orta*.
Guide-book: P. Crosa Lenz, *Parco Nazionale della Val Grande* (Grossi, 1997).

GETTING THERE
By car: take A8 and A26 from Milan to Gravellona Toce, then SS33 to Domodóssola or SS34 to Verbánia. There is minor-road access from the south and Lago Maggiore, and the north via S. Maria Maggiore and the SS337.
By rail: trains run from Milan, Novara and Locarno to Domodóssola, T: (0324) 242 533 (Domodóssola station). A scenic line from Domodóssola to Locarno cuts across the northern edge of the Val Grande, with stations at S. Maria Maggiore and Malesco. Contact Ferrovia Vigezzina at Domodóssola, T: (0324) 242 055, or at S. Maria Maggiore, T: (0324) 94212.
By bus: services run twice a day from Verbánia to Cossogno, Rovegro, Miazzina and Caprezzo in the south of the park; contact A.S.P.A.N., Verbánia, T: (0323) 556 633. In the north, best go by train.

WHERE TO STAY
Hotels: there are many places around Lago Maggiore or at Domodóssola. Closer to the park, try La Jazza (2-star), Via la Jazza 4, S. Maria Maggiore, T: (0324) 94471.
Refuges: Rif. CAI Fantoli, Alpe Ompio, S. Bernardino Verbano, T: (330) 206 003; Rif. CAI Pian Cavallone, Loc. Pian Cavallone, Intragna, T: (0323) 402 852.
Outdoor living: free camping is prohibited.

ACTIVITIES
Walking: many hikes are long and demanding. Easier options include the climb from Miazzina to Rif. Cavallone in the south, and the traverse from the Valle Loana to In La Piana via the Bocchetta di Vald in the north. Guides are available May–Oct; contact the park office for details (see below).

FURTHER INFORMATION
Tourist offices: Via Romita 13 bis, Domodóssola, T: (0324) 248 265; Via Domodóssola 3, S. Maria Maggiore, T: (0324) 95091; Via Canonica 8, Stresa, T: (0323) 30150; Corso Zannitello, Pallanza, T: (0323) 503 249.
Park office: Ente Parco Nazionale Val Grande, Villa S. Remigio 19, Verbánia, T: (0323) 557 960, or visit www.parcovalgrande.it.

15

Alta Valsésia

Glacier-topped mountains on the border with Switzerland, Piedmont's highest and most spectacular Alpine massif; parco naturale regionale 6,511 ha (16,089 acres)

So wild are some parts of the Alta Valsésia that you can almost believe the legends linked with them: that hidden lakes brim over with liquid silver, and that the spring waters above Macugnaga issue from a lost valley, home to the Valle d'Aosta's earliest tribes.

The Alta Valsésia is a little bit of the Himalayas in the Alps. It rarely drops below 2,000 m (6,500 ft) and on Monte Rosa — Europe's second highest mountain, surpassed only by Mont Blanc — it climbs to 4,633 m (15,200 ft). Flanked by the Matterhorn (4,478 m/14,691 ft) immediately to the west, this awe-inspiring collection of high peaks and glaciers epitomizes the Alps at their iciest and grandest.

Rosa's name comes not from its colour — though it glows rosy-pink under a sinking sun — but from *roese* or *roisa*, which in the local patois means 'ice-covered'. Students of glacial effects should take their cue from this, for Monte Rosa allows you an unparalleled close-up of ice-formed features such as cirques, moraines, tarns and cwms as well as the creaking progress of its present glaciers: the Locce, Vigne, Sésia and Piode.

The highest peaks are all in the west, hard up against the Swiss border. The rest of the Alta Valsésia spreads across a disjointed area reaching from the base of the Rosa glaciers to the lower ridges that lie to the east across the heads of the Sésia, Sumenza, Egua and Mastallone valleys. Much of the area is ice, scree and boulder-covered pasture, a nursery for rare high-altitude plants. Thanks to Piedmont's fine conservation work, for which Alta Valsésia is one of the showcases, 57 species of plants have been recorded above the snow-line and many more below it. Animals, being unsuited to the upland tundra, are found mainly lower down.

If you should venture into the rocky terrain above the tree-line, though, you will no doubt be stricken with a sense of terrible inadequacy by the agility of chamois racing down precipitous slopes at breakneck speed as you approach. Perhaps the easiest of all creatures to encounter in the high mountains today, they were once hunted relentlessly for their soft skins (much prized as chamois leathers), as well as for meat and marksmen's trophies. Marmots too can be found, although you are more likely to see only the black tips of their tails disappearing into their burrows, accompanied by a chorus of high-pitched whistles warning of your approach. Among the more predatory creatures of Alta Valsésia are stoats and foxes, while four or five pairs of golden eagles rear their young on inaccessible crags.

The Alta Valsésia has a superb network of paths and nine well-equipped refuges, including Europe's highest, the Capanna Regina Margherita at 4,559 m (14,958 ft). The paths are crowded in summer, especially those from Macugnaga to Rifugio Zamboni-Zappa, where you will find the best view of the colossal walls of the Gnifetti (4,554 m/14,940 ft), the eastern flank of Monte Rosa.

A short stroll above Alagna (towards Rifugio Pastore) brings you to the Acqua Bianca waterfall, with stunning views on to the massif and across the River Sésia's mighty canyon. To be alone, head for the lower and more solitary peaks in the east, such as Pizzo Montevécchio, Pizzo Tignaga,

The majestic golden eagle, with its 2-m (6-ft) wing span, can be seen soaring over Alpine meadows and forests in search of unwary ptarmigan or mountain hares.

Cima Lampone, and their tranquil valleys, the Sermenza above Rima and the Egua above Carcóforo.

Despite a litter of ski lifts, much of the area has kept its traditional appearance, including the park's busy resorts at Macugnaga and Alagna. Wooden, geranium-hung houses, surrounded by flower-filled meadows, hark back to the area's famous Walser traditions. The Walser were medieval settlers who drifted here from other Alpine valleys further north, bringing their language and customs with them. Today, most of the villages in this area speak the predominant Walser language, German.

In Italy the stoat is confined to the Alps. It is supremely well adapted to its high mountain habitat. At the onset of winter, its coat turns pure white, providing camouflage when it ambushes prey and also preventing valuable heat escaping.

Before you go *Maps:* Kompass 1:50,000 No. 88 *Monte Rosa*; IGC 1:50,000 No. 10 *Monte Rosa, Alagna, Macugnaga*; 1:25,000 *Parco Naturale Alta Valsésia* — a hiking map.
Guide-book: Ente Parco Naturale Alta Valsésia, *Parco Naturale Alta Valsésia: Itinerari e notizie utili* (De Agostini, 1999).
Getting there *By car:* for Alagna Valsésia take A4 to Agognate (between Milan and Turin), then SS299 along the Sésia valley via Varallo. For Macugnaga take A4 via Novara and then A26 and SS33; at Piedimulera branch left on SS549 along the Valle Anzasca.
By rail: 7 trains daily to Varallo on the branch line from Novara (Milan–Turin line), T: (0163) 835 222. Nearest station to Macugnaga is at Piedimulera, 30 km (18 miles) away on the Novara–Domodóssola line, T: (0324) 242 533.
By bus: services to Alagna run all year from Novara, Varallo and Milan. Contact Autolinee Baranzelli, T: (0163) 834 125. Seasonal service from Milan to Macugnaga, T: (0324) 240 333.
Where to stay *Hotels:* a variety of options at Macugnaga, Carcóforo, Rima, Riva Valdóbbia and Alagna. In Macugnaga try

the Girasole (3-star), T: (0324) 65052.
Refuges: Capanna Regina Margherita, T: (0163) 91039; Rif. Abate Carestra, T: (0163) 91901; Rif. Pastore, T: (0163) 91220; or contact CAI, Via Durio 14, Varallo, T: (0163) 51530.
Outdoor living: camping prohibited in park, but organized camp-sites outside; try Val Sesoa, Varallo, T: (0163) 52307; Alagna, Riva Valdobbiana, T: (0163) 922 947, or Sporting Centre, Macugnaga, T: (0324) 65489.
Activities *Walking:* many options, but some involve rock climbs or ice-traverses (even in summer). Cable-cars and ski-lifts (summer and winter) provide a leg-up to ridges from Alagna and Macugnaga; one at Alagna climbs to Punta Indren (3,260 m/10,695 ft). Long-distance hikes across the park possible (unmarked, 2/3 days). The classic walk, for a view of Rosa's east face, is from the belvedere above Macugnaga (chair lift from Pecetto) to Rif. Zamboni-Zappa, then onwards to Lago delle Locce (red-white markings) and back to Burki via Rosareccio (4 hrs, blue markings). Another scenic walk

is the ascent from Rif. Pastore to Rif. Barba Ferrero (4 hrs). Guides are available for novices who wish to climb challenging high peaks involving ice-traverses; the most famous is the ascent from Punta Indren cable station to Punta Gnifetti via Mantova and Gnifetti refuges. Contact Corpo Guide Alpine, T: (0163) 91310 (Alagna)/(0324) 65170 (Macugnaga).
Skiing: cross-country, alpine and summer glacier skiing at Alagna and Macugnaga. Contact Funivie Monrosa, Alagna, T: (0163) 922 922.
Museums: at Alagna you can visit a 1628 Walser house, T: (0163) 91326.
Further information *Tourist offices:* Pro Loco, Piazza Grober, Alagna, T: (0163) 922 988; Ufficio di Informazione e Accoglienza Turistica (IAT), Piazza del Municipio, Macugnaga, T: (0324) 65119; APT, Corso Roma 38, Varallo, T: (0163) 51280; Comunità Montana Valsésia, Corso Roma 35, Varallo, T: (0163) 51555.
Park office: Parco Naturale Alta Valsésia, Corso Roma 35, Varallo, T: (0163) 54680.

Gran Paradiso

*Massif on the border of Valle d'Aosta and
Piedmont, boasting glaciers, high pastures
and wild valleys;* parco nazionale
*ZPS
70,000 ha (173,000 acres)*

Gran Paradiso is just what it purports to
be: a great paradise. Breathtaking views
of distant snow-capped peaks appear at
almost every turn in this landscape graced
with 57 glaciers. The mountain after which
the park is named is over 4,000 metres (13,000
feet) high, surrounded by dozens of other
peaks of over 3,000 metres (10,000 feet). Fir
forests, mountain tarns and snow-bound
upland plateaux provide magnificent settings
for numerous ibex, chamois, marmots and
virtually every other animal of the high Alps;
bears and wolves are the only absentees. It is
this abundance of wildlife, along with the ease
of seeing it, that puts the Gran Paradiso in a
league of its own among European parks.

Within the Alps the Gran Paradiso acts
like the pivot of a huge hinge. To the west,
north and east the other Alpine ridges swing
around it in a great arc, taking the French
and Swiss borders with them. In height as
well as layout the Gran Paradiso has most in
common with the central Alps, its peers being
the massifs of Mont Blanc and Monte Rosa.
Like theirs, its valleys run north and south
from a huge central ridge. This arrangement
divides the park neatly in two: the more open
and developed northern valleys that feed into
the Valle d'Aosta (Rhêmes, Savarenche, Valnontey, Cogne), and the narrower southern
valleys of Piedmont (Locana, Orco, Piantonetto, Eugio and Soana).

Received wisdom has the northern valleys
as the more beautiful. Their grandeur is
beyond dispute, certainly, but commercializa-
tion has taken its toll. Hotels and refuges
located in the heart of the mountains are

convenient, but in places have turned the spectacular Alpine scenery into more of an urban playground than a wilderness. Part of the reason is their position: close to Turin and, more importantly, to the Valle d'Aosta, which, after the building of the Mont Blanc tunnel and associated motorways, has been transformed into one of Europe's busiest crossroads. You will find the less dramatic southern valleys wilder and more deserted.

Gran Paradiso is the oldest of Italy's national parks. A royal ordinance forbade hunting in these mountains as early as 1821. By 1856 the Gran Paradiso had joined King Victor Emmanuel II's long list of personal game reserves. In 1919 the House of Savoy ceded 2,000 hectares (4,940 acres) to the state, a nucleus from which the park was born three years later.

The game reserve was set up for the purpose of hunting and husbanding the ibex. Now the symbol of the park, this hefty mountain goat with its massive saw-toothed horns can be seen on the craggy heights at over 3,000 metres

(10,000 feet). Quick and agile despite its layers of fat and heavy build, it can feed on plants found at the very edge of glaciers and moraines.

Once common throughout the Alps, ibex have been threatened with extinction since the 18th century. They were hunted not only for food and their horns, but also for a little bone near their hearts reputed to have magical properties. As a result their numbers had declined to only a hundred by the advent of royal protection. After a revival, numbers fell again in World War II. Since then, concerted efforts have taken the population up to about 4,000. Ibex colonies in Italy's Stélvio and Tarvísio parks, as well as the herds in France and the former Yugoslavia, have been bred from the Gran Paradiso's original nucleus.

The present ibex population is too large, claim some authorities, arguing that since they lack predators they are no longer fully exposed to the rigours of natural selection. Partly to rectify this imbalance, an attempt was made in 1975 to reintroduce lynx into the park (the last of the original population was shot in 1898). Glorious as it would be to see this large spotted cat, sometimes more than a metre in length, once again in the Alps, the attempt was a half-hearted and less than scientific affair: only two animals were released and both were male. Neither was heard of again.

The 10,000-strong army of marmots — again considered too many — is a further argument for reintroducing the lynx. The park's only other large predators, the fox and golden eagle, cannot keep them in check. Pressure to reintroduce the hunters instead, which the authorities know would be the thin end of the wedge, has so far been resisted. Similarly widespread are the chamois, now numbering an estimated 8,000. With the agility and speed of gazelles, they can leap distances of six metres (20 feet), reaching heights of four metres (13 feet). They can be seen in summer grazing on the more succulent grass of the high pastures, while in winter they descend to the forests and warmer south-facing slopes.

A wide range of butterflies flourishes in the

The Nivolet lakes lie in heavily glaciated terrain, with the summit peaks around Monte Gran Paradiso (4,061 m/13,068 ft) towering to their east.

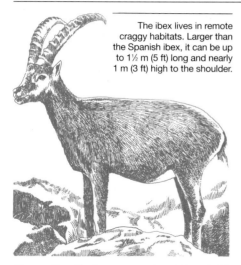

The ibex lives in remote craggy habitats. Larger than the Spanish ibex, it can be up to 1½ m (5 ft) long and nearly 1 m (3 ft) high to the shoulder.

enough to cloak the lower valley sides in green, thus completing the classic alpine trinity of colours: white of snow, green of tree and blue of sky. Autumn, and the turning of the larch, adds an equally vivid flash of yellow to nature's palette.

The Paradisia botanical garden at Valnontey contains many former alpine and pan-European species, as well as hosting a collection of the Gran Paradiso's rare plants. One of the most famous is the twinflower, *Linnaea borealis*, the only plant named after the great Swedish taxonomist Carl Linnaeus. Its pale pink petals and delicate perfume belie the harsh environment of its origin in the Arctic circle. The Gran Paradiso is now its southernmost limit.

Many of the other rare species are also distant from their genetic forebears. One legume, the central Alps milk-vetch *(Astragalus centralpinus)*, has Asian origins, while the cinquefoil *Potentilla pensylvanica* — no prizes here — has its nearest relative in America.

Thanks to the network of mule-tracks made for the Savoys and the several hundred kilometres of marked trails, it is easy to find walks, most of which should reward you with an ibex — trek from Valnontey to the Colle Lauson if you want to make sure. The ascent of the Gran Paradiso itself is the least arduous 4,000-metre (13,000-foot) climb in the Alps, and for long-distance walkers, the Alta Via II crosses the park from east to west. Cogne is probably the best base for first-time visitors, being close to some fine walks, to the Gran Paradiso's biggest glaciers and to the Valnontey valley, one of the prettiest.

Gran Paradiso's apparently inhospitable environment of rock, ice and snow. The apollo thrives at up to 2,000 metres (6,500 feet), while fluttering even higher, at up to 3,000 metres (10,000 feet), is *Parnassius phoebus sacerdos*, especially common in the mountains above Cogne.

Some 1,500 plant species grow in the park, including many Ice Age relics which have evolved in isolation and are unknown elsewhere. This magnificence has several causes: partly the area's varied geology, a mixture of schists, gneiss and limestone; partly the diversity of habitats ranging from moist meadow to Arctic tundra; and partly an altitude range of over 4,000 metres (13,000 feet).

Trees are mainly pines and though the forests are comparatively thin, there are

---

BEFORE YOU GO
Maps: Kompass 1:50,000 No. 86 *Gran Paradiso – Valle d'Aosta*; IGC 1:50,000 No. 3 *Parco Nazionale del Gran Paradiso*.
Guide-books: G. Novaria, *Quattro passi in Paradiso* (Priuli e Verlucca, 2004); M. Oviglia, *Rock Paradise* (Versante Sud, 2000)

GETTING THERE
By car: take the A5 from Turin to Aosta and then the SS507 to

Cogne, or one of 3 unclassified roads from Aosta to the Grisenche, Rhêmes and Savarenche valleys. Approach the southern valleys on the SS460 from Turin via Rivarolo Canavese and Pont Canavese to Ceresole Reale. You can reach the southern valleys from the north by crossing Gran Paradiso's main ridge, over the spectacular Nivolet pass (2,612 m/8,569 ft) on the Savarenche road from Aosta, but this route

is not always open.
By rail: regular services run from Turin and Milan to Aosta (change at Chivasso). Trains from Turin go to Rivarolo Canavese (for the southern valleys), with connecting buses to Pont Canavese, Locana and Noasca, T: (0124) 453 530.
By bus: S.V.A.P. and S.A.V.D.A. run services from Turin to Aosta, though some routes are seasonal; 5/7 buses daily go to Cogne, Valsavarenche, Pont and

villages *en route;* summer minibuses go from Cogne to Lillaz, Valnontey and Gimillian. Contact S.V.A.P., Chaversod, T: (0165) 41125 and S.A.V.D.A., Aosta, T: (0165) 361 244. Satti run services from Turin to Pont Canavese, Valprato Soana, Noasca and Ceresole Reale, freephone T: (800) 217 216.

WHEN TO GO

Best from May to Oct, though snow can linger until July and reappear as early as Oct. In June and July the flowers are at their best, but on mid-summer weekends paths and refuges are just too crowded. From Nov to Dec you can see both male ibex and chamois doing battle, though at this time of the year most of the park is closed to casual walkers. For a multilingual weather forecast, call T: (0165) 236 627.

WHERE TO STAY

Hotels: usually you can just turn up and find something, but in Aug it is wise to book. Standards are generally high and prices fair. Even hamlets in the northern valleys have rooms; there is no need to stay in busy Aosta, Cogne or Valnontey. Lillaz is quieter and near relatively untramped country. Dégioz is the key village in the Val Savarenche and there are also hotels in Eaux-Rousses and Pont. Rhêmes-Notre-Dame is the main centre in the Val di Rhêmes. In the southern valleys try at Ceresole Reale, Noasca and Valprato Soana.

Refuges: these range from stone huts to high-altitude hotels. There are 8 refuges and 26 bivouacs on the Valle d'Aosta side, details from the IAT Gran Paradiso (address below); 8 refuges and 6 bivouacs on the Piedmont side, details from the Segreteria Turistica, T: (0124) 901 070. Aosta tourist office publishes a list of all refuges

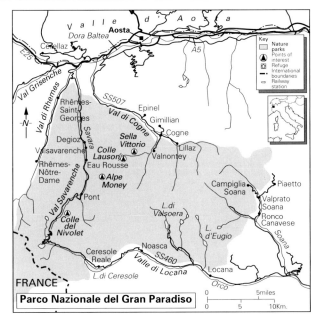

Parco Nazionale del Gran Paradiso

and bivouacs.

Outdoor living: free camping is prohibited, but there are many camp-sites in the park; for a complete list contact Associazione Valdostana Centri Turismo all'Aperto, Aosta, T: (0165) 44008, e-mail: info@campingvda.com, or visit www.campingvda.com.

ACTIVITIES

Walking: with 450 km (280 miles) of trails, there is a wide choice. Some of the best include: Valnontey to Rif. Vittorio Sella (2 hrs), then onwards to Herbetet (3,778 m/12,395 ft) via the Lauson lakes, returning to the village along the Valnontey valley (5 hrs, with views of the Tribolazione glaciers); Valnontey to the Alpe Money for great views of the main ridge of the Gran Paradiso (4 hrs); Cogne to Lillaz, a gentler walk with views of the Lillaz waterfall (1 hr); Pont to Rif. V. Emanuele (2 hrs) and onwards to the Gran Paradiso massif (5

hrs); from Introd in the Val Savarenche to Orvieille (3 hrs, with views of the Gran Paradiso massif); the southern valleys of Valsoera and Piantonetto. For guides, contact Parnassius Apollo Club Trekking, T: (0124) 700 023; Guide Alpine Aosta, T: (0165) 44448; Associazione Guide Naturalistiche, T: (0165) 74282; Esprit Montagne, T: (0165) 852 526; Co-op. Habitat, T: (0165) 363 851.

Pony-trekking: try Azienda Agricola Arpisson, Cogne, T: (0165) 74200.

Climbing: there are many excellent opportunities, with mainly rock and ice itineraries in the northern valleys (especially the Becco della Tribolazione) and rock walls in the southern valleys (on the Caporal, Sergent and Becco di Valsoera); Co-op. Interguide d'Aosta, T: (0165) 40939.

A chamois *(overleaf)* braves the perpetual snow which lies in the high Alpine cwms of Piedmont and the Valle d'Aosta.

Watersports: contact Grand Paradis Emotions, Aymavilles, T: (328) 976 1645, or Onda Selvaggia, Aosta, T: (347) 376 7729.

Ballooning: contact Nello Charbonnier, Aosta, T: (0165) 40205/765 525.

Skiing: the pistes at Cogne and Rhêmes-Notre-Dame are modest, but there are numerous cross-country runs (indicated on maps), hundreds of traverses and the GHRV long-distance route for alpine skiers; contact Sci Club Gran Paradiso, Cogne, T: (0165) 74072.

FURTHER INFORMATION

Tourist offices: Piazza Chanoux 3, Aosta, T: (0165) 33352; Piazza Chanoux 36, Cogne, T: (0165) 74040; Ceresole Reale, T: (0124) 953 121; IAT Gran Paradiso, Loc. Champagne, Villeneuve, T: (0165) 95055.

Park office: Ente Parco Nazionale Gran Paradiso, Via Umberto I 1, Noasca, T/F: (0124) 901 070.

Visitor centres: Rhêmes-Notre-Dame, Loc. Chanavey, T: (0165) 936 193; Pro Loco Valsavarenche, Loc. Dégioz, T: (0165) 905 816.

Ecology: Giardino Alpino Paradisia, T: (0165) 74147.

Gran Bosco di Salbertrand

Ancient broad-leaved and conifer wood in the Valle di Susa, Piedmont's western gateway into France; parco naturale regionale
ZSC
3,775 ha (9,328 acres)

'As grand, beautiful and mysterious as the hand of God', says a local ballad of Salbertrand's great wood. Covering the Valle di Susa's southern flanks between Oulx and Salbertrand, this is the largest forest in Piedmont and one of the most important stretches of primeval woodland in the Alps.

Trees cover a good two-thirds of the area, an arboreal mantle thrown over a shallow basin in the valley side above Salbertrand village. The remainder consists of pastures and flower-filled meadows, which break up the seemingly impregnable green fortress of the forest, making it easier to explore than it first appears.

The large azure flowers of the trumpet gentian (*Gentiana acaulis*) are a feature of rocky pastures in the Alps, appearing in late summer.

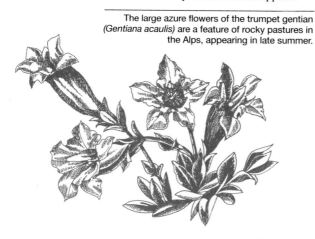

One approach is to follow the old military road which twists and turns through innumerable hairpins up through the west of the wood to the high pastures and summit ridges. Five minutes on, you might divert on to the Sentiero Sersaret, part of the GTA long-distance path that curves through the wood and round the head of the basin to rejoin the military road at the summit. Myriad other tracks dip and weave through the forest, the eastern parts less dense and more frequently interspersed with meadows.

As you climb, the trees change from the broad-leaved ash, beech and birch of the valley floor to the predominant pine and larch of the upper forest. Dozens of tiny streams accompany your panting ascent, twinkling and splashing as they spill through rocks and mosses, watering glades that offer excellent cover for wildlife.

Turin province introduced red deer to the Gran Bosco in 1962, having acquired them from Triglavski park in Slovenia. There are now just over a hundred deer in the park, but that does not mean you will be able to see them easily. The best chance of a sighting is at dawn on the high pastures before they return to the dark sanctuary of the woods.

Chamois and marmots are also visible at the highest altitudes, as are roe deer, a comparative rarity in the western Alps, reintroduced some ten years ago. Other typical forest creatures, such as badgers and wildcats, are also found, although being largely nocturnal they are much more elusive. Wildcats mate in early March and give birth to between two and four kittens in early May. At this time of year the adults may be seen in broad daylight. Presumably their need to find food quickly, so as not to leave their young undefended for too long, makes them less wary than normal.

Like other thick ancient forests, Salbertrand is home to a wide variety of birds, including the magnificent black woodpecker, the largest in the region at 45 cm (18 in) from head to tail. Clothed in funereal black, at first sight this bird might be mistaken for a crow; however, its distinctive undulating flight and scarlet crown will soon clarify its identity. Middle spotted woodpeckers are also found, the adults being easily distinguished from the similar greater spotted woodpecker by their red crowns and white cheeks.

Pairs of eagle owls inhabit these forests, along with breeding short-toed eagles, honey buzzards and goshawks. Above the tree-line it is not unusual to spot golden eagles soaring on high; rock partridges and black grouse are less visible, spending most of their time foraging on the ground. In winter you might be lucky enough to catch a glimpse of a merlin, Europe's smallest bird of prey, although most sightings consist of a blurred kestrel-like silhouette, dashing erratically past at ground level in pursuit of dragonflies and small birds.

Autumn is an obvious time to enjoy the Gran Bosco, but early summer rewards those who climb to the high meadows with an intense carpet of wild flowers; not rich in rarities, but gloriously coloured with yellow mountain saxifrage, deep-purple, yellow and white pasque-flowers and countless others.

Before you go *Map:* IGC 1:50,000 No.1 *Valli di Susa Chisone e Germanasca.*
Guide-books: I parchi del

Piemonte (L'Arciere, Regione Piemonte, 1998); Gubetti, Perotto and Pulzoni, *Occhi aperti sul parco* (Parco del Gran Bosco, 1996).
Getting there *By car:* SS25 and SS24 from Turin along Valle di Susa to the village of Salbertrand, from where a winding road leads up into the forest. *By rail:* 10 to 12 trains daily to Salbertrand on the Turin–Bardonécchia–Modane line. *By bus:* 2 buses daily from Turin to Fenestrelle, T: (0121) 322 032. Services also to Susa.
Where to stay *Hotels:* in Salbertrand, Oulx and Sauze d'Oulx. Try Macondo (3-star), Fraz. S. Marco, Oulx, T: (0122) 831 588, or La Torre (4-star), Via Della Torre, Sauze d'Oulx, T: (0122) 850 020, F: 850 888. *Refuges:* Rif. Arlaud, Salbertrand, T: (335) 401 624. *Outdoor living:* camping at Gran Bosco, Loc. S. Romano 75 towards Monginevro, Salbertrand, T: (0122) 854 653; other sites at Oulx and Pragelato.
Activities *Walking:* on Sentiero Sersaret walk (6 hrs), follow GTA (red-white dashes) on the ascent (850 m/2,800 ft) from Salbertrand village; orange forest signs on the return (on the military road). The circuit can be extended using the GTA to include Monte Gran Costa and Colle Blegier (2,381 m/7,812 ft). Contact CAI, T: (0122) 854 669, or ANA Alpini, T: (0122) 854 707 (both in Salbertrand).
Further information *Tourist offices:* Salbertrand's tourist office doubles as the park office, Parco Naturale Regionale del Gran Bosco di Salbertrand, Via Monginevro 7, Salbertrand, T: (0122) 854 720. APT offices are found at Piazza Garambois 2, Oulx, T: (0122) 831 786 and Piazza Assietta 18, Sauze d'Oulx, T: (0122) 850 700.

Orsiera-Rocciavrè

Mountains and meadows in western Piedmont, on the watershed between the Susa and Chisone valleys; parco naturale regionale ZPS
10,953 ha (27,065 acres)

It is hard to believe that Turin's city limits are just 30 km (20 miles) away from this magical wilderness where the metallic creep of the ski-lifts has been held at bay, roads are confined to the valleys and only ancient mule-tracks and farms testify to the presence of man.

The area is quintessentially Alpine, all high peaks and glacier-tortured crests draped with high meadows. Water everywhere enlivens the panorama, a tumbling and gurgling pattern of springs, waterfalls and streams. Twelve lakes dot the mountains, the best of which is Ciardonnet, a mirror of rock and sky clasped high in Orsiera's jagged ridges.

Centred on the pyramid peaks of Monte Orsiera (2,878 m/9,442 ft) and Monte Rocciavrè (2,778 m/9,114 ft), this is the largest regional park near the Susa and Chisone rivers. Forest cover accounts for about a fifth of its area, but is patchy in comparison with the Gran Bosco di Salbertrand (an easy morning's walk away to the west). Flowers, however, run rampant through the meadows in spring and summer, mainly mountain lilies, edelweiss, narcissi and trumpet gentian. A business enterprise that has been set up at Usseaux to cultivate aromatic and medicinal plants (such as the gentian) for export has partly persuaded local

25

people of the park's value.

The park's name sadly relates to wild animals that are no longer in evidence. Orsiera refers to the *orso*, or brown bear, and Rocciavrè to the 'mountain of goats', a nod to long-vanished herds of ibex. Red deer and wild boar, however, roam here from the woods of Salbertrand and golden eagles are known to patrol the highest hunting grounds. Chamois, too, are present, but in small numbers, along with the Alps' typical lesser mammals: badgers, foxes, mountain hares, squirrels, marmots and stoats.

A network of paths now supplements the old mule-tracks, making exploration easy, and a scattering of refuges saves going down to the bustle of the Susa and Chisone valleys for accommodation.

Before you go *Maps:* IGM 1:25,000 Nos 154 I *Condove*, II *Coazze*, III *Fenestrelle* and IV *Susa*.
Guide-books: G. and R. Ribetto, *Che uccello è ?* (Melli, 1995); *Guida naturalistica al Parco Orsiera-Rocciavrè* (Melli, 1993).

Getting there *By car:* SS25 from Turin to Susa, then, if vehicle permits, the dramatic road to Fenestrelle over the Finestre pass (2,176 m/7,139 ft). Alternatively, drive from Bussoleno to Rif. Toesca. Minor roads to Giaveno, Forno and Alpe Colombino on the park's east side, SS23 from Chisone valley and the south.
By rail: to Bussoleno on the Turin–Modane line, with hourly connections to Susa.
By bus: 2 buses daily from Turin to Fenestrelle, Autolinee S.A.P.A.V., T: (0121) 322 032. Services also to Susa.

Where to stay *Hotels:* numerous options in Susa, Prà Catinat, Fenestrelle and many villages in the Valle di Susa.
Agriturismo: try Fattoria Pian dell' Alpe, Usseaux, T: (0121) 842 672 (open June–Sept).
Refuges: Toesca, Pian del Roc, T: (0122) 49526, Geat-Val Gravio, Vallone del Gravio, S. Giorio, T: (011) 964 6364, Balma, Alpe della Balma, Coazze, T: (011) 934 9336, and Amprimo, Pian Cervetto, Bussoleno, T: (0122) 49353.

Outdoor living: nearest camp-site to the park is Serre Marie, Loc. Sagne, Fenestrelle, T: (0121) 83982 (all year). There is also Arcobaleno, Fraz. Fraisse, Usseaux, T: (0121) 83864. Free camping is permitted in the park from dusk till dawn.
Activities *Walking:* plenty of long, often demanding tramps. The park is crossed by the GTA long-distance path; the Valle di Susa by the Sentiero dei Franchi. *Pony-trekking:* Il Mulino – Centro di Turismo Equestre, Via Giordano 52, Mattiè, T: (0122) 38132.
Further information *Tourist offices:* APT, Viale Giolitti 7/9, Pinerolo, T: (0121) 794 003/795 589; IAT, Piazza del Popolo 6, Avigliana, T: (011) 968 650. *Park offices:* Ente di Gestione Parco Naturale Orsiera-Rocciavrè, Via S. Rocco 2, Bussoleno, T: (0122) 47064/49398, F: 48383, e-mail: orsiera@libero.it. The new visitor centre, an ideal departure point for walkers, is at Prà Catinat, 8 km/5 miles north of Fenestrelle, T: (0121) 83757/(0122) 47064, e-mail: rocciavre@libero.it.

Alpi Maríttime

Glorious and little-visited area in south-west Piedmont, straddling the French border; includes the Parco Naturale delle Alpi Maríttime (27,945 ha/69,055 acres) and the Parco Naturale Alta Valle Pésio e Tánaro (6,637 ha/16,401 acres)

I once hitched a lift with three pensioners on their way to walk in the Alpi Maríttime. Did they know these mountains well? 'Yes, very well, too well', they replied, with some unease. We drove on, admiring the scenery and discussing the prospects for a fine day's walking. Then the car slowed and the old

people fell silent. After a pause one old lady pointed to a snow-covered peak and said, 'Quella è la montagna dov'è morto mio figlio' — 'That is the mountain where my son died'. After another pause we drove on. The remark now beats a salutary tattoo whenever I walk in the high wilderness.

Despite this touch of doom, the Alpi Maríttime are probably my favourites among all the Alpine massifs. If you have been to the south of France you will undoubtedly have seen them. They form a spectacular backdrop to the sun-drenched shores of the Riviera, yet are quite different from their tourist-ridden French neighbours. Tucked away in Piedmont's south-west corner they are some of the wildest and least-known mountains in the Alps, with peaks of over 3,000 metres (10,000 feet), the Alps' most southerly glaciers,

An ice-clear mountain stream meanders through meadows in the Valle di Valasco.

high meadows, crystal-clear streams and dense forests. In short, the Alpi Maríttime offer the whole panoply of Alpine landscapes despite being the southernmost link in Europe's greatest mountain chain.

It takes no special skill to spot the features that set the Alpi Maríttime apart from the icy grandeur of the central Alps. Their proximity to the warming Mediterranean lends a distinctly southern flavour to the lower slopes, which are dotted with pockets of Phoenician junipers. The higher slopes are more verdant than in the central Alps, the scenery more enclosed, the rocks more chaotic, the valleys narrower, the peaks more heavily glaciated. Forests are thicker, trees more numerous, and everywhere there is more variety, less habitation and — above all — more solitude.

The area plays host to more than 2,600 species of plants and 250 species of mammals and birds. Such a wealth of wildlife is the result not only of climatic range but also of geological variation, the crystalline gneiss of the Argentera massif (3,297 metres/10,817

feet) in the west contrasting with the limestone of the Valle Pésio to the east. Here the Marguaréis (2,651 metres/8,697 feet) boasts precipitous walls of pallid limestone often described as dolomitic in their splendour. They tower dramatically over the huge karstic plain of the Conca delle Carsene, which is riddled with yawning sink-holes and caves up to 500 metres (1,600 feet) deep.

Among the Alpi Maríttime's floral riches, the star must be the ancient king (*Saxifraga florulenta*), a bizarre long-lived plant which is found only in rock crevices high in the gneiss cliffs of the Argentera. Because of the paucity of nutrients and the climatic extremes of the high mountains, the many-leaved rosettes of this saxifrage grow very slowly, taking years to accumulate the strength to reproduce. Finally, at the very end of its life, a spike of pale pink flowers appears, after which the whole plant dies.

The Valle Pésio is renowned for its

ALPINE BUTTERFLIES

A wealth of butterflies can be found in the Alps' flower-filled meadows and high mountain pastures. Among the better known species are: the small apollo, with its marble grey wings displaying beautiful scarlet 'eyes'; the mountain clouded yellow, whose dark grey upper wings contrast vividly with its bright yellow underside; and the alpine grayling, a large pale yellow butterfly which has small, white-centred black 'eyes' on the upper wings.

Dozens of ringlet butterflies inhabit the high pastures above the tree-line, but you need to examine them at close range to tell them apart. The blind ringlet, characteristic of the Dolomites, is medium brown with conspicuous yellowish arcs on the wings. The Pruner's ringlet, more typical of the Trentino Alps and Alto Adige, has rich chocolate-brown wings, each with an orange band containing small 'eyes'. Among the species which occur only in the Alps are Mnestra's ringlet, with orange-brown unmarked wings, and the sooty ringlet, whose males have velvety black wings.

Among the smaller, jewel-like Lycaenidae butterflies (of which most are blues, coppers or hairstreaks) the males are generally the more eye-catching, the females for the most part being drab, brown and almost indistinguishable. In July and August the high Alpine meadows are resplendent with the shimmering violet-blue wings of the Osiris blues; the pale turquoise of the Glandon blues; and the almost luminous turquoise wings, bordered by a narrow black band, of the Eros blues. The vivid blue wings of the alpine argus are a perfect match for the summer sky.

extensive forests of ancient firs and broad-leaves, both of which have benefited from centuries of care by the valley's Cistercian monks. Its alpine meadows teem with vibrant wild flowers. Orange lilies, with their upright, cup-shaped flowers of fiery vermilion, contrast spectacularly with the dull magenta turk's-cap bloom of the closely

The small apollo butterfly is easily identified by its red 'eyes' or ocelli. These prominent markings are designed to deter potential predators.

related martagon lily, while great yellow and spotted gentians stud the summer grasslands with spikes of gold. An uncommon type of fritillary, *Fritillaria tubaeformis* ssp. *moggridgei*, grows in the valley and can be identified by its brown-specked yellow bells. The Alpi Maríttime are a good place to see some alpine columbines. Among the more attractive species are Bertoloni's columbine (*Aquilegia bertolonii*), with its dark violet-blue flowers, and the dark columbine (*A. atrata*), distinguished from all others by its velvety deep-purple flowers with protruding yellow stamens.

In these mountains the maritime influence brings ample and refreshing rain, a bounty squandered by the eastern limestone (except for one splendid waterfall, the Pis del Pes), but utilized to wonderful scenic effect on the Argentera. I remember an idyllic day I spent walking to the Valle di Valasco, the walk I love above all others in the Alps, accompanied by the constant rippling and gushing of water. It flowed from cracks, from rocks, cascaded down waterfalls, ran in tree-shaded streams, lay mirror-still in lakes — all under a blazing sun and cloudless sky. I drank and drank, scooping up handfuls at every turn, unable to resist water which seemed to me the iciest and most wonderful I had ever tasted. At one twist in the path I found a shrine, a tiny Madonna and Child in terracotta keeping watch over a mossy spring. Jesus, poor soul, was missing his head and someone had tacked on a pebble with chewing gum in its place. Yet this comic sacrilege detracted not a jot from a place where generations had obviously honoured the water for what it was, in Byron's words 'the sweetest wave of the most living crystal'.

The walk to the Valle di Valasco takes a full day, but is well worth it. It forms part of the GTA route and starts in Valle Gesso at Terme di Valdieri where a road-like mule-track leads you up through rocky outcrops and verdant larch forests, with views of the snow-dusted peaks of the French border to lure you on. A steep haul past a shady waterfall and you reach the Valasco plain, the glacier-scraped bed of some ancient lake set in an amphitheatre of huge mountains that now stand revealed in their full glory. At the centre of this plain lie the remains of a royal hunting lodge built following the visit of King Victor Emmanuel II in 1855 when the area was declared a royal hunting reserve. A renewed attack on the now rocky trail brings you to Lago Inferiore di Valscura (2,274 metres/7,461 feet), just one of a dozen small rock-cradled tarns in the park.

The region is criss-crossed with hundreds of less-engineered trails. All are well marked and backed up by excellent maps and superbly situated refuges. Further exploration of the GTA will lead you eastwards into the Bosco e Laghi di Palanfrè and the Valle Pésio. Other tracks lead towards France, and the Bronze Age rock engravings of Mont Bégo and the Vallon des Merveilles.

Wildlife in the Alpi Maríttime is as rich and varied as the scenery. There have been sporadic sightings of the lynx, and the wolf, well suited to isolated areas such as this, seems to have made a spontaneous comeback, but generally carnivores are rare. With few predators to threaten them, large herbivores such as chamois and ibex are able to flourish. You should have no difficulty spotting at least one of the 4,500 chamois that live in the park. They can be easily distinguished from the ibex by their smaller size, slimmer structure and darker colour, and by the small backward arching horns set close together between their ears. Ibex, with their robust curling horns, were reintroduced into Valle Gesso in the 1920s from the former royal hunting reserve of Gran Paradiso. Their population has grown steadily since

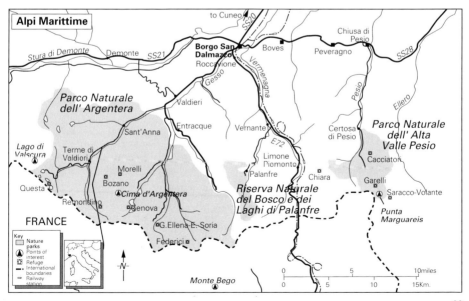

then and now numbers a healthy 500.

Alpine marmots abound above the tree-line and though you may not actually see one, their piercing whistles will confirm their presence. Far more elusive are the mouflon. These heavy-set sheep are Mediterranean rather than Alpine natives and were introduced to the neighbouring former French hunting reserve, now Mercantour national park, in the middle of the 19th century. In summer they tend to stray across the border to nibble at Italian grass.

Classic alpine birds that inhabit the harsh world above the tree-line include rock partridges and ptarmigan. Bearded vultures, otherwise known as lammergeiers, were reintroduced into the park in 1993 and have since steadily increased in number. Golden eagles soar above the peaks, while black grouse forage among the rocks, the males unmistakable with their glossy black plumage and lyre-shaped tails. Flocks of choughs are a common sight, their wheeling antics and rifle-shot calls as distinctive as their scarlet beaks and legs. If you are extremely lucky you might spot a wall creeper fluttering up one of the sheer rock walls and looking as much like a huge grey and crimson moth as a bird.

In the forested valleys of the Alpi Marittime you can find a quite different fauna. Black woodpeckers and eagle owls, both the largest European representatives of their families, breed here, as do nutcrackers, honey buzzards and short-toed eagles. Wild boar, once rare in the Alps, can occasionally be seen snuffling through some of the lower woodlands at dusk or dawn.

BEFORE YOU GO
Maps: IGC 1:50,000 No. 8 *Alpi Maríttime e Liguri*; Blu/PNAM 1:25,000 *Parco Naturale Alpi Maríttime – Carta dei Sentieri* (walking routes).
Guide-books: *La guida del Parco Alpi Maríttime* (Blu, 2000); *Le riserve naturali della provincia di Cuneo* (L'Arciere, 1998); B. Charpentier, *Montagne senza frontiere* (L'Arciere, 1995).

GETTING THERE
By car: from Genoa and the Ligurian coast, take the A10 and A6, exit at Mondovi, then take SS564 to Cuneo; from Turin and the north take A6, exit at Fossano, then follow SS231. For Argentera take SS20 from Cuneo south-west to Borgo S. Dalmazzo (8 km/5 miles), then a minor road to Valdieri, where small lanes diverge to major valleys in the park. For Palanfrè follow SS20 beyond Roccavione to Vernante and take the lane to Palanfrè village. For Valle Pésio follow SS564 from Cuneo or Mondori to Beinette, then a minor road to Chiusa di Pésio and take the valley road south to Certosa di Pésio.

By rail: trains from Turin to Cuneo leave approximately every hour, with connections to Vernante (for Palanfrè), Nice and the French coast. Contact stations at Cuneo, T: (0171) 634 965, or Turin, T: (011) 669 2825.

By bus: 5 buses a day go from Cuneo station to Valdieri and Entracque; in summer (June–early Sept), two a day run to S. Anna and Terme di Valdieri, but none the rest of the year. Contact Nuova Benese, Cuneo, T: (0171) 692 929.

WHERE TO STAY
Hotels: accommodation is concentrated in Cuneo and the skiing resort of Limone Piemonte, but you can stay in Terme di Valdieri at the luxurious Grand Hotel Royal (3-star), T: (0171) 97106 (open June–Sept), or the more basic Turismo (1-star), T: (0171) 97334 (summer only). In S. Anna di Valdieri (best base for those on foot), try the Regina (2-star), T: (0171) 977 840 (open June–Oct). For rooms in Valdieri, Entracque, Certosa di Pésio and elsewhere, contact Conitours, Via Senatore Toselli 1, Cuneo, T: (0171) 698 749, or visit www.cuneotourism.com (you can book on-line).

Refuges: there are 10 in the park, with 4 in or close to the Valle Pésio (most are open June–Sept). Try Rif. Questa, T: (0171) 97338, or Rif. Balma Meris, T: (0171) 977 835. There are in addition 7 bivouacs, for which contact CAI, Corso IV Novembre 14, Cuneo, T: (0171) 67998.

Outdoor living: Entracque has 2 camp-sites, the Valle Gesso, T: (0171) 978 247, and Il Bosco, T: (0171) 978 396 (both open all year).

ACTIVITIES
Walking: some of the most beautiful itineraries are Terme di Valdieri to the Valasco plain (3 hrs), and onwards to Valscura lakes and Rif.

Water cascades down the side of a steep valley in the Argentera, set off by the grey-black of the crystalline bedrock and the bronze of the autumn larches.

Morelli; Terme di Valdieri to Lourousa (3 hrs); Palanfrè village on the GTA to the Laghi degli Alberghi (2 hrs). In Valle Pésio, the walk to the foot of the Marguaréis rock walls is an Alpine classic. Start from the head of the road above Certosa and walk to Rif. Garelli (red and white markings, Trail H8), then continue south on the GTA to the Laghi di Marguaréis and descend on H1 to your starting point (5 hrs). Other options include the walk to the Pis del Pes (Trail H10) from the road above Certosa (2½ hrs), and from Certosa to Punta Pellerina and/or Cima Cars (5 hrs, Trail H4/5). Guides are available for walking, rock and ice climbing, cross-country skiing, nature and photography excursions. Contact Scuola Italiana Alpinismo-Scialpinismo, Arrampicata Alpi Maríttime, T: (0171) 955 094, or Accompagnatori Naturalistici Alpi Occidentali, Via Madonna dei Boschi 76, Paveragno, T: (0171) 338 156.
Pony-trekking: for organized treks, contact Gruppo Escursionisti Equestri Monregalesi, T: (339) 355 7942.
Caving: there are excellent opportunities in some of Piedmont's deepest caverns around the Marguaréis (in Valle Pésio). Contact CAI Mondovi, Via Beccaria 26, T: (0174) 46776.
Fishing: contact FIPSAS, Corso Dante 21, Cuneo, T: (0171) 681 422.
Canoeing: contact Federazione Italiana Canoa e Kayak, Loc. Gaiola, Circolo Stiera, T: (0171) 74204.
Skiing: aim for Limone Piemonte, with Entracque as a more modest back-up. Cross-country routes start at Entracque. Contact Scuola di Sci Entracque, T: (0171) 978 675, or Limone 1400, T: (0171) 928 134.

ALPINE GRASSLANDS

Meadows and grasslands are among Italy's most common mountain habitats and vary hugely according to soil, climate and altitude. Many are extremely interesting for the rare and endemic species they host, and in spring most have breathtaking displays of wild flowers. They can be divided broadly into calcareous and acid grasslands.

Calcareous meadows thrive on rocky and exposed slopes at altitudes of between 2,000 and 2,800 metres (6,500 and 9,000 feet). One grass is dominant, *Kobresia myosuroides*, found also in the Arctic and thus a relic of tundra plant communities that were once more widespread. Associated species include: snowy cinquefoil (*Potentilla nivea*), unbranched lovage (*Ligusticum mutellinoides*) and one-flowered fleabane (*Erigeron uniflorus*).

On lower and south-facing slopes the blue moor-grass *Sesleria albicans* predominates, found alongside milk-vetches, avens and that most famed of alpine flowers, the edelweiss (*Leontopodium alpinum*). Two common sedges find favour in damper soils between about 1,700 and 2,000 metres (5,500 and 6,500 feet): *Carex ferruginea*, found on fresher slopes, and *Carex firma*, concentrated on steeper and stonier ground. Alongside the first you might commonly find the alpine pasque flower (*Pulsatilla alpina*), alpine thistle (*Carduus defloratus*), leafy lousewort (*Pedicularis foliosa*) and the mountain hawk's-beard (*Crepis pontana or C. montana*). The second hawk's-beard keeps company with moss campion (*Silene acaulis*), blue saxifrage (*Saxifraga caesia*), gentians, alpine bistort (*Polygonum viviparum*), orchids and alpine rockrose (*Helianthemum alpestris*).

The acid grassland spreads over slopes at anything between 1,400 and 3,000 metres (4,500 and 10,000 feet). It develops well even under heavy grazing, the key elements being the mat-grass *Nardus stricta* and, at greater height, the sedge *Carex curvala*. Against this backdrop thrive species such as tormentil (*Potentilla erecta*), golden cinquefoil (*Potentilla aurea*), trumpet gentian (*Gentiana acaulis*), arnica (*Arnica montana*), bearded bellflower (*Campanula barbata*) and alpine meadow grass (*Poa alpina*).

Bird-watching: contact LIPU, Viale degli Angeli 81, Cuneo, T: (0171) 491 772.
Ecology: a nature reserve has been created to protect the rare Phoenician junipers that grow on the lower slopes. Access is by guided tour only. Contact the park office in Valdieri for a leaflet.

FURTHER INFORMATION
Tourist offices: APT, Corso Nizza 21, Cuneo, T: (0171) 445

362; IAT offices at Entracque, T: (0171) 978 616, Limone Piemonte, T: (0171) 929 515 and Chiusa di Pésio, T: (0171) 734 990.
Park offices: Corso Dante Livio Bianco 5, Valdieri, T: (0171) 97397, e-mail: parcalma@tin.it; Via S. Anna, Chiusa di Pésio, T: (0171) 734 021; and (for Mercantour national park) 23 rue d'Italie, B.P. 1316, F-06006 Nice Cedex 1, T: (00 33 493) 167 888; alternatively, visit www.parcnationaux-fr.com.

Monte di Portofino

Promontory on the Ligurian coast with dramatic cliffs and coves; includes parco naturale regionale *(2,500 ha/6,200 acres) and* area marina protetta *(372 ha/919 acres)*

One of Italy's most beautiful stretches of coastline, the Portofino promontory is not exactly a pristine wilderness; the day-trippers and yachts of the rich and famous have seen to that. But it remains the most important natural habitat between La Spézia and the French border — one, say ecologists, that deserves the protection of a national park — and it does have spectacular scenery.

Sailing is the best way to explore this most romantic of coasts. The stretch from Portofino to the aptly named Golfo Paradiso is an unforgettable odyssey of high cliffs, turquoise seas, silver olives, green pines and rock-perched pastel villages.

On *terra firma* Portofino promontory is almost equally stunning. A spine of limestone hills divides its jumble of valleys, crossing the headland from east to west and rising to Monte di Portofino (610 m/2,001 ft). On warm herb-scented days walking here is a gentle and unmitigated pleasure; the views are stupendous, the vegetation luxuriant and the paths excellent. Tracks start from most of the villages around the promontory — Portofino, Camogli and S. Margherita Ligure — and push into an interior still unscarred by roads.

Seven hundred species of plants grow here, courtesy of mild temperatures, a mixed geology of marls, limestones and conglomerates, and the dividing ridge of hills, which creates opposing micro-habitats of Mediterranean, montane and middle-European vegetation. This combination yields peculiar inversions: chestnut trees reach down to the sea, and coastal *maquis* can be seen sprouting on hilltops. Though species are bizarrely mixed, the north-facing slopes tend to support trees and shrubs associated with a more continental climate, while the southern slopes, which face the sun and sea, give rise to the more usual Mediterranean varieties.

One of the most interesting plants is the white-flowered saxifrage *(Saxifraga cochlearis)*, the Latin epithet referring to its spoon-shaped leaves. Its rosettes are typically found on shady rock walls, usually of limestone, in a small section of the Alpi Maríttime. Their occurrence on the Portofino promontory, some 130 km (80 miles) further east, is remarkable.

Growing in similar habitats is the knapweed *Centaurea apoplepa*, a pink-flowered species found only in western Italy and on a few small islands in the Tyrrhenian Sea. There are numerous subspecies of this plant, many of which are confined to a very small area; here on the coast around Portofino it is *Centaurea apoplepa,* ssp. *lunensis.*

The promontory is on a major bird-migration route between Europe and Africa, a key resting place for spring and autumn travellers situated between the urban bleaknesses of Genoa and La Spézia. Colourful migrants include: redstarts, conspicuous with their rusty rumps and constantly flickering tails; willow warblers, quickly picked out by their bright yellow plumage; garganeys, the males sporting a bluish-shoulder patch and a white stripe on their heads; and little egrets, small white birds with distinctive yellow feet.

Breeding birds include wrynecks, small brownish relatives of the woodpecker, as well as many more typically Mediterranean species, including alpine swifts, green woodpeckers, blue rock thrushes and three types of warblers: melodious, Sardinian and subalpine. The peregrine falcon is perhaps the most awe-inspiring of all the birds in this area. Feeding mainly on other large birds, it swoops on its prey almost vertically at speeds of up to 320 kph (200 mph).

The park is also home to a wide range of reptiles and amphibians, including the bright green stripeless tree frog with its harsh deep croak, often compared to a duck's quack; the Turkish gecko, a pink nocturnal reptile that tends to skulk between stones, rocks and walls, but can occasionally be spotted soaking up the sun; and the striking green lizard, over 40 cm (16 in) in length.

The sea around Portofino is reputed to support virtually every form of Mediterranean aquatic life, including sea sponges, anemones and red, orange and yellow soft coral.

Before you go *Maps:* Multigraphic 1:25,000 No. 6/8 *Appennino Ligure*; Studio F.M.B. 1:25,000 *Tigullio – Carta dei Sentieri*; Del Magistero 1:25,000 *Val Fontanabuona, Monte di Portofino – Carta dei Sentieri.*
Guide-books: A. Girani, *Guida al Monte di Portofino* (Sagep, 1997); A. Rosso, *Itinerari naturalistici del Parco di Portofino* (3 vols, Ente Parco di Portofino, 1997).
Getting there *By car:* A12/SS1 from Genoa and La Spézia (exit at Recco, Rapallo or Chiavari). *By rail:* to Camogli or S.

Margherita Ligure, both excellent exploration bases, on the Genoa–Livorno line, T: (0185) 286 630 (S. Margherita Ligure station).
By bus: to Portofino and elsewhere from S. Margherita Ligure; contact Tigullio Trasporti, T: (0185) 231 108.
Where to stay *Hotels:* at Recco, Camogli, Portofino, Paraggi and S. Margherita Ligure. Some hotels, especially in Portofino, are busy and over-priced in summer. Try Mediterraneo (3-star), Via della Vittoria 18/a, S. Margherita Ligure, T: (0185) 286 881.
Agriturismo: try La Madre, Léivi, T: (0185) 319 529, or Gnocchi, S. Margherita Ligure, T: (333) 619 1898.
Outdoor living: tents forbidden on the promontory; nearest camp-sites are Miraflores, T: (0185) 263 000, and Camping

Rapallo, T: (0185) 262 018, both at Rapallo, and Camping al Mare at Chiavari, T: (0185) 304 633.
Activities *Walking:* dense network of marked and well-kept paths. Most popular is the easy stroll from Portofino to S. Fruttuoso (2 hrs, red markings). The next coastal stretch, from Torretta to Punta Chiappa, the littoral's most spectacular, requires expertise and a head for heights. From S. Fruttuoso you can also cross the impressive little gorge of Pietre Strette and climb to Monte di Portofino and the summit ridge. The full traverse of the promontory (4 hrs) is best from Camogli to Portofino. From Portofino another fine path runs to S. Margherita via Olmi and the ruins of Madonna di Nozarego (2 hrs). For guides, contact Associazione Guide

Naturalistiche, T: (0185) 772 318/(368) 442 987.
Boating: failing a yacht, book a *de rigueur* boat trip along the Portofino coast through Trasporti Marittimi Turistici Golfo Paradiso, Camogli, T: (0185) 772 091, or Servizi Marittimi del Tigullio, S. Margherita Ligure, T: (0185) 284 670.
Further information *Tourist offices:* Via Roma 35, Portofino, T: (0185) 269 024; Via XX Settembre 33, Camogli, T: (0185) 771 066; and Via XXV Aprile 4, S. Margherita Ligure, T: (0185) 287 485.
Park offices: Ente Parco di Portofino, Corso Rainusso 1, S. Margherita Ligure, T: (0185) 289 479, www.portofino.com; Area Marina Protetta di Portofino, Via XX Settembre 33, Camogli, T: (0185) 776 700.

Cinque Terre

Richly varied stretch of Ligurian coastline; parco nazionale (4,226 ha/10,442 acres) and riserva marina (2,784 ha/6,879 acres) World Heritage Site

The *cinque terre*, or 'five lands', are pretty villages dotted along a stretch of Ligurian coastline between Lévanto and Por-tovénere: Monterosso al Mare, Vernazza, Corniglia, Manarola and Riomaggiore. Each lies at the end of a steep wooded valley that dissects the cliff-edged coastline, sur-rounded by slopes tightly terraced for vines and backed by beautifully picturesque and occasionally wild pockets of countryside.

Once the villages were accessible only by sea or on foot, and known only for a wine, the Vernaccia delle Cinqueterre, quaffed and praised in verse by Dante, Petrarch and

Boccaccio. Early man carved terraces here, exploiting a mild local climate to grow vines, figs, olives and capers. These terraces are still cultivated, and are thought to be some of the oldest in the Mediterranean.

The mountainous hinterland and difficult terrain, described by one medieval writer as too steep not only for goats, but even for the flight of birds, has been partly invaded by towns and tourism. With Portofino, however, the Cinque Terre still form the wildest parts of the Ligurian littoral, unblemished by a coastal road and especially unspoiled around Punta Mesco and near Portovénere. Here the mountains fall to the sea in the great rock walls of the Muzzerone, favourites of La Spézia's climbing fraternity.

The best way to explore the Cinque Terre is to walk the coastal path that links the villages, the Sentiero Azzurro, an excursion that will take a robust pair of legs eight hours. Though busy in summer, and only intermittently wild, it is one of Italy's most rewarding walks and one you could stretch to three days, allowing time for bathing and gastronomic excess in the villages en route.

The best-known section, the Via dell'

Aleppo pines are characteristic of the steep seaward slopes of the Portofino promontory.

Amore, links Riomaggiore and Manarola. Undoubtedly beautiful, it is also overcrowded, and lined with handrails and concrete balconies. More solitary are the sections from Corniglia to Vernazza, and Vernazza to Monterosso, where the terracing is especially impressive and the path turns into a series of steep steps cut into the stone.

In these quieter sections all is harmony and natural balance: a sun-warmed alternation of headlands, rugged cliffs, lush vegetation, tree-shaded coves, cultivated slopes and consistently lovely sea views. Even the tourist-filled villages have retained their charm, tiered on the cliff-sides and riddled with mazes of tiny alleyways. While you walk along this coast, look for the alternation of sandstone and unique variegated limestones. Most famous is the Portoro marble, found at Portovénere and on the island of Palmaria, renowned for its gold veining and grey lustre.

The most popular route after the coastal walk follows the mountain ridge that runs parallel to the sea. Taking in ten peaks — the highest Monte Malpertuso (812 metres/2,664 feet) — the path runs the length of the summit ridge between Portovénere and Lévanto, a haul of at least 12 hours.

Perfumed belts of *maquis* and *garrigue*, stands of aleppo pines and a huge variety of wild flowers grow along the Cinque Terre coast, and also on Palmaria island and its outliers, Tino and Tinetto. Part owned by the navy, and only half inhabited and cultivated as a result, the islands have a particularly rich and specialized flora and fauna, which has been helped to survive by the exceptionally mild climate. Orchids such as the common

The secretive, largely nocturnal, leaf-toed gecko has distinctive splayed feet with adhesive climbing pads at the tips of the toes. It is the smallest of all European geckoes, usually measuring only about 6 cm (2 in) from head to toe.

spotted *(Dactylorhiza fuchsii)*, burnt-tip *(Orchis ustulata)* and toothed *(Orchis tridentata)* can be found. A rare butterfly, the gloriously coloured two-tailed pasha *(Charaxes jasius)*, can occasionally be spotted, as can the Tinetto lizard *(Podarcis muralis tinettoi)*, unique to the island and numbering only about 200.

Rare fauna on the mainland include the freshwater crab *(Potamon edulis)*, celebrated on coins minted by the people of Agrigento in southern Sicily and thought to be the crab represented in the constellation of Cancer, and the Italian cave salamander *(Hydromantes italicus)*, found on the Portovénere promontory.

The coastal margins from Punta Mesco to Montenero have been designated a protected marine area, rich in submarine sea-life and distinguished by rarities such as black coral.

BEFORE YOU GO
Map: CAI 1:40,000 *Carta dei Sentieri delle Cinque Terre.*
Guide-book: S. Vivaldi, *Favole delle Cinque Terre* (L'Autore Libri Firenze, 2003).

GETTING THERE
By sea: boats go from La Spézia to Palmaria island and the Cinque Terre villages. There is also an expensive crossing of the 400 m (440 yds) of water separating Portovénere and Palmaria. Contact Navigazione Golfo dei Poeti, La Spézia T: (0187) 732 987/967 676.
By car: take the A12 to La Spézia, then the SS530 to Portovénere (best southern base); the SS370 to Manarola or unclassified roads off the SS1 to the four other Cinque Terre villages; alternatively, exit from the A12 at Carrodano, then take the SS566 direct to Lévanto and Monterosso (the most commercialized of the villages).
By rail: a better option is the La Spézia–Genoa line, which has stations at all the Cinque Terre villages with frequent services from La Spézia, T: (0187) 817 458 (Monterosso station) or (0187) 920 633

(Riomaggiore station).
By bus: impossible.

WHERE TO STAY
Hotels: the biggest range is at Lévanto and Monterosso. Manarola has the Marina Piccola (3-star), T: (0187) 920 103. Rooms are available at Portovénere, Corniglia and Riomaggiore.
Agriturismo: try Villanova, Loc. Villanova, Lévanto, T: (0187) 802 517.
Outdoor living: free camping is forbidden in the park. Among camp-sites, try Acquadolce, Lévanto, T: (0187) 808 465.

ACTIVITIES
Walking: La Spézia's CAI branch has seen to it that all the Cinque Terre area is criss-crossed by marked trails. The two main ones are the coastal path from Riomaggiore to Monterosso, marked in blue (8 hrs); and the ridgeway path from Portovénere to Lévanto, which involves a hefty 900-m (3,000-ft) climb and is marked in red (12 hrs). Minor tracks descend to the sea at several points along the ridgeway path. Contact CAI, Via Amendola 196, La Spézia, T: (0187) 22873; Comunità Montana, Lévanto, T: (0187) 807 290.
Climbing: Monte Muzzerone offers excellent opportunities. Contact Davide Battistella, T: (336) 619 525.
Fishing: contact FIPSAS, Via V. Véneto 173, La Spézia, T: (0187) 511 026.
Skin-diving: there is plenty of scope around the islands and from hired boats along the coast. Contact Coopsub Cinque Terre, Riomaggiore, T: (0187) 920 011.

FURTHER INFORMATION
Tourist offices: APT Cinque Terre e Golfo dei Poeti, Viale Mazzini 47, La Spézia, T: (0187) 770 900; Pro Loco

MEDITERRANEAN REPTILES

Italy boasts a great selection of reptiles — tortoises, marine turtles, lizards and snakes — which are found only on the sun-baked Mediterranean coast. The most characteristic are three species of tortoise: the Hermann's, its domed shell rarely exceeding 20 centimetres (8 inches) in length (see p116); the slightly larger spur-thighed tortoise with pronounced tubercles, or 'spurs', on the thighs; and the marginated tortoise which can reach 30 centimetres (12 inches) in length and has a flatter shell, flared at the rear. Much larger, but closely related to tortoises, are marine turtles. The only species of marine turtle seen regularly in Italian waters is the loggerhead, with its unmistakable heart-shaped horny carapace up to 110 centimetres (3 feet) long and a proportionally massive head.

Outstanding among Italy's lizards are the geckoes; all four European species are found here. They are small soft-skinned creatures with large heads and, unlike other lizards, eyes with vertical pupils. All except the leaf-toed gecko have tubercles on the upper part of the body and all are nocturnal except in cooler weather when they occasionally emerge during the day. Kotschy's gecko is the only species to lack adhesive pads on the toes, instead having characteristically kinked digits, but it is an agile climber nevertheless. Both the dark, flattened Moorish geckoes and the pale, almost translucent Turkish geckoes are common on most of Italy's coasts. The leaf-toed geckoes, on the other hand, are largely confined to islands in the Tyrrhenian Sea, Corsica, Sardinia and the north-western coast of the mainland.

Other typically Mediterranean reptiles include the eyed, or ocellated, lizards, now confined to the north-west coast. They are the largest European lacertids — some are reported to be over 80 centimetres (2½ feet) long. The males are magnificent creatures, with massive broad heads and vivid green bodies, frequently with prominent blue 'eyes' along the flanks. A rather different creature is the ocellated skink, a fat, almost snake-like lizard with small limbs which can burrow rapidly into loose sand if threatened.

Several species of snake are also found on the coastal lowlands, including the Montpellier snake, an aggressive creature up to two metres (six feet) long; the western whip snake of southern Italy and Sicily, a predator with a diet of lizards, small birds, mammals and other snakes, even vipers; the southern smooth snake, which does not usually exceed half a metre and emerges mainly in the evening to prey on geckoes and other small lizards; and the metre-long leopard snake, which feeds mainly on rodents, killing its prey by constriction.

offices at Monterosso, T: (0187) 817 506, Lévanto, T: (0187) 808 125 and Portovénere, T: (0187) 792 380.
Park office: Ente Parco delle Cinque Terre, Via Telemaco Signorini, Riomaggiore, T: (0187) 920 113, F: 920 866, www.parks.it/parco. porto.venere.
Ecology: WWF, Via Génova 58, La Spézia, T: (0187) 713 181.

CHAPTER 2

The Dolomites and Central Alps

Venture into the Dolomites and you will find yourself in one of the most surreal landscapes on the planet: a Gothic fantasy of crenellated spires and splintered peaks, saw-tooth ridges and fearsome chasms; of screes and steep rock faces to challenge the most experienced climber; of forests, streams, waterfalls and high meadows covered in wild flowers. Plastered over chocolate boxes everywhere and featured in the paintings of Titian, who was born in the area, at Pieve di Cadore, these are some of the most famous and extraordinary mountains in the world.

The Dolomites consist of twenty or so individual but closely packed massifs, each with at least one peak of more than 3,000 metres (10,000 feet). Separated from the main body of the Alps by the valleys of the Adige, Isarco and Rienza rivers, they form one of the largest self-contained areas in the Alpine chain, stretching about 100 kilometres (60 miles) north-south and nearly as far east-west. Their characteristic rock was named — fortunately not in full — after Dieudonné Sylvain Guy Tancrède de Gratet de Dolomieu, the French mineralogist who first identified it as calcium magnesium carbonate in 1801. He wrote his treatise in the margins of his Bible while languishing in prison at Messina on his way home from Napoleon's Egyptian campaign.

The massifs divide into two groups, the western and eastern Dolomites, each formed and weathered under

The unmistakable jagged peaks of the Dolomites form a spectacular backdrop to the forests of larches around Cortina d'Ampezzo.

slightly different conditions. To understand their origins, first imagine a tropical sea, something like the present-day Caribbean, which covered the region in the middle of the Triassic period, around 230 million years ago. Huge banks of marine invertebrates, algae and coral accumulated over many millennia, creating islands and tidal mud-flats which find their present-day equivalents in the Bahamas or the Maldives. From these deposits emerged the rock known as Sciliar dolomite which today forms the core of the main western massifs — former tropical islands all — of Sciliar, Catinaccio, Odle, Sella, Putia and Pale di San Martino. In the same period, lava that was spewed into the sea by erupting volcanoes settled and cooled in the gaps between the developing islands to leave the dark brown volcanic rock visible today in Alta Val Cordévole, Valbóite, Val di Fassa, Val Gardena and Val Badía.

As the Dolomite story unfolded during the late Triassic, the region — by now a vast tidal flat — was covered with layer upon layer of marine detritus which, when compressed, became the so-called Dolomia Principale, a rock that characterizes the peaks and ranges of the eastern Dolomites: Cristallo, Tofane, Pelmo, Civetta and Dolomiti di Sesto. Of all the layers in the complex dolomitic geology, it is the most evident to the naked eye, as it often constitutes massive banks of rock 1,000 metres (3,000 feet) thick.

In the subsequent Jurassic and Cretaceous periods the area was covered by yet more marine sediment. The entire sludge remained undisturbed until some 60 million years ago when Africa and Europe collided, producing the uplifting and buckling that gave birth to the Alps, and with them the Dolomites. In a further twist to the tale, not all the terrain reacted in the same way. The western Dolomites, supported by thick underlying layers of ancient rock, rose more or less as a single block. The eastern Dolomites, lacking this protective substructure, bore the full brunt of the impact, suffering massive folding and faulting as a result. In places this upheaval brought the old Sciliar deposits to the surface. All that remained to complete the story was for the agents of the weather, chiefly ice and water, to scour away the newer sediments (now residing in the Po Valley) and, over the millennia, to expose the original Triassic coral reefs — the magnificent saw-tooth mountains we see today.

The Dolomites cover a vast area and would take many lifetimes to explore in all their scenic variety. In certain places, in the right season, you may feel you have the mountains to yourself. Yet no one could pretend that these are places of uncharted wilderness. They attract probably more skiers, walkers and coach parties than all the other Italian mountains put together. Places of escape from cars and coaches do exist, of course, but there is no escape from paths and trails so well worn and well marked they might as well be roads.

The accessibility of the wild places was brought home to me one autumn morning in the Dolomiti di Sesto, an area renowned as one of the quietest and most breathtaking of the eastern Dolomites. On a grey inauspicious day I set off expecting to see wild windswept mountains — real mountains, not the blue-skied tourist attractions shown in travel brochures, all spectacle and no substance. All went well for a time. Mist swirled around the summits, and I had the damp dripping forest path to myself. After a couple of hours of solitude, and by now in awestruck reverie, I turned a corner to find three little old ladies sitting on a tree trunk. Dressed in their Sunday best and chattering away like small birds, oblivious to me and the mountains, they might as well have been playing a hand of bridge. They could not have been more unexpected had they been sitting on their trunk stark naked.

When you have had your fill of the Dolomites, retreat north to the Valle Aurina. This is part of the main Alpine ridge, and Italy's most northerly point. It is a supremely peaceful area of the utmost splendour.

Alternatively, visit the other mountains of Alto Adige, the German-speaking heart of the Trentino-Alto Adige region, west of the Adige river. Here the wilderness is of a more familiar Alpine cut, and often less frequented than the Dolomites. The Stélvio and Adamello-Brenta parks combine to form the largest protected area in the Italian Alps. Both parks, and the nearby Tessa massif, support all the fauna you could wish for, in contrast to the Dolomites, where — for all the splendid spring flowers and the phenomenal scenery — animals are scarce.

Geology made this a frontier zone, and throughout the millennia of human occupation it has remained the meeting place of central Europe and the Mediterranean. The Alpine passes were in use as early as the Neolithic period and amber from the Baltic found its way through here to Italy. Strange statue menhirs — flat slab-like human figures — have been found in the upper Adige valley; nobody knows for certain who made them, or when, but they probably date from the early Bronze Age. The Celts invaded around 500 BC, but suffered sustained attacks, and eventual defeat in 15 BC, at the hands of the Romans. After the fall of the Roman Empire, the area was again invaded, this time by Germanic settlers who pushed the Romano-Celtic inhabitants up into the remoter valleys, where their language, Ladin, has survived to this day. In the Middle Ages the Habsburgs took control of the region. It remained part of Austria until 1918, and to all intents and purposes is still so today. Its indigenous inhabitants universally refer to it as Südtirol, the South Tyrol. The onion-domed churches, wooden houses, even the brown bell-clanging cows are all thoroughly Mitteleuropean.

As a footnote, I would add that you can find the odd wilderness highlight

The western Dolomites *(below)* rose as un undeformed block; by contrast, the eastern Dolomites *(below right)* underwent severe buckling and folding when the European and African continents collided during the Tertiary period and rose as elongated humps. They weathered to produce the saw-tooth appearance for which the Dolomites are famous.

even in Lombardy, an industrialized and intensively farmed region prospering from the wealth of Milan. North of the city, Italy's money capital, the lakes of Maggiore, Lugano, Como and outlying Garda still have their moments, though tourism and pollution have taken a heavy toll of their once legendary beauty. For truly unspoiled country, you have to go higher, into the Orobie and Retiche mountains of the central Alps. Here, the scenery can still make you catch your breath, as can the parts of the Stélvio and Adamello-Brenta massifs that overlap the region's eastern border.

GETTING THERE

By air: the main international airports are at Munich, T: +49 8997 500; Milan Malpensa, T: (02) 748 5220; and Venice, T: (041) 541 5570. Smaller airports include Verona, T: (045) 8095 666, and Innsbruck, T: +43 5122 25250.

By car: the A8 and A9 link Milan to the lakes. The A22 (Verona–Bolzano–Brennero) serves the western Dolomites, Stélvio and Adamello. The A27 and SS51 from Venice lead through the eastern Dolomites to Cortina d'Ampezzo.

By rail: the Verona–Bolzano–Munich main line and the Bolzano–S. Candido branch line give rapid access to the Dolomites. International services from Milan serve the lakes. Slow lines link Venice to Belluno and Trento. Contact Ufficio Informazioni dei Treni, freephone T: (1478) 88088 within Italy, otherwise visit www.fs-on-line.it or www.trenitalia.com.

By bus: services in Trentino-Alto Adige link most centres large and small. In Bolzano province, contact S.A.D., freephone T: (800) 846 047 within Italy, or visit www.sii.bz.it. In Trento province, call Atesina, T: (0461) 821 000, or visit www.atesina.it.

WHERE TO STAY

For value and quality, accommodation in the Dolomites is almost unsurpassed in Italy. Rooms to rent in private houses can be found in even the smallest hamlets. Often you can arrive and hope for the best, but it is always worth checking with tourist offices to see if hotels and *pensioni* are open; many close Oct–Dec and Apr–June. Booking is strongly advised July–Aug and Jan–Mar. Useful addresses can be found on the Alto Adige tourism web-site, www.hallo.com.

Refuges: hundreds are scattered over the region, many privately owned and effectively run as hotels. Some are on trails, others can be reached by road or cable-car. In theory no one is turned away, which means huts can be very crowded in summer; you may end up on the floor. Call in advance.

Many Trentino huts operate through the Società degli Alpinisti Tridentini, Via Manci 57, Trento, T: (0461) 981 871. For huts in Lombardy, call CAI in Milan, T: (02) 8646 3516. Otherwise contact tourist offices; CAI, Piazza Erbe 46, Bolzano, T: (0471) 978 172; or Ufficio Informazioni Alpinistiche, Piazza Parrocchia 11, Bolzano, T: (0471) 413 809.

Outdoor living: camping is prohibited in the parks, but you will have few problems pitching a tent outside their borders. Most organized camp-sites are open only during the summer.

ACTIVITIES

Walking: thousands of well-worn and well-marked trails are on offer. As most paths are extremely busy in the summer, the best periods to visit are late spring and Sept–Oct. Do not be deceived by pictures of good paths or mountains in fine weather — the Dolomites can turn as nasty as any wilderness; go as well equipped as you would for any upland trek.

There are 7 *alte vie*, or high-level paths, in Trentino-Alto Adige and the Véneto. Most are 60–80 km (40–50 miles) in length, and are designed to take about 1 week, though allow extra time for rests and diversions. All are marked on Kompass and Tabacco maps.

The trails are: Lago di Bráies to Belluno (the most popular); Bressanone to Feltre (the Legends trail); Villabassa to Longarone (the Chamois); S. Candido to Pieve di Cadore (the Grohmann); Sesto to Pieve di Cadore (the Titian); Pieve to Vittório Véneto; and the Dolomiti Bellunesi to Alpago.

Oft-overlooked trails in Lombardy include: Via dei Monti Lariani to Lake Como (130 km/80 miles, 7/8 days); Sentiero delle Orobie (50 km/30 miles, 6 days); Sentiero Roma (52 km/32 miles, 7 days) and Alta Via della Valmalénco (110 km/70 miles, 10 days), both in the Badile and Disgrazia mountains. Contact

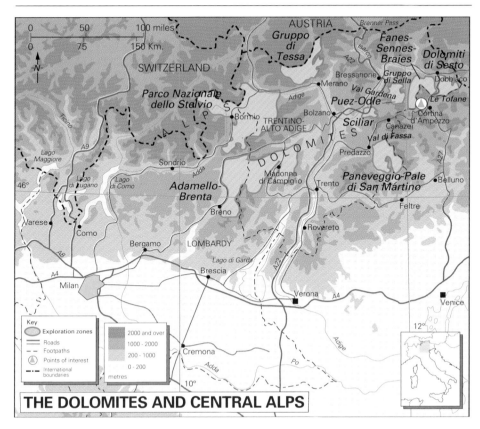

THE DOLOMITES AND CENTRAL ALPS

CAI (see Refuges above) and Federazione Italiana Escursionismo, T: (02) 205 7231.

Climbing: there are thousands of routes with numerous *vie ferrate* or 'iron paths', climbs with permanent rope-and-ladder fixtures. Call Società degli Alpinisti Tridentini (see Refuges above)

Fishing: FIPSAS, Piazza Verdi 14, Bolzano, T: (0471) 975 332; Passaggio S. Benedetto 8, Trento, T: (0461) 232 293; Via Abruzzi 79, Milan, T: (02) 2043 952.

Canoeing: many fine runs can be had on the Adige, Noce and minor rivers. Contact the Federazione Italiana Canoa e Kayak, Via Linfanno 27,

Trento, T: (0461) 506 059, or the Club Sportivo di Merano, Via Delle Corse 115, Merano, T: (0473) 232 126.

Skiing: there is a large choice of winter resorts. Summer skiing is possible at Passo dello Stélvio, Tonale, S. Caterina Valfurva, Marmolada and Val Senáles; there are cross-country itineraries in the Alpe di Siusi, Val di Bráies, Alta Pusteria, Val di Anterselva and Canazei. Tourist offices provide pamphlets for planning ski trips. The Superski Dolomiti pass gives access to most Dolomite slopes.

Bird-watching: for tours, advice and courses contact LIPU, Via Portici 51, Bolzano, T: (368)

500 777; Via S. Caterina 14, Trento, T: (0461) 260 913; Via Montegrappa 18, Milan, T: (02) 2900 4366.

FURTHER INFORMATION
Tourist offices: Via C. Battisti 12, Sondrio, T: (0342) 512 500; Piazza Walther 8, Bolzano, T: (0471) 307 000; Piazzetta S. Francesco 8, Cortina d'Ampezzo, T: (0436) 3231; Via Alfieri, Trento, T: (0461) 983 880.

FURTHER READING
M. Collins, *High-Level Walks in the Dolomites* (Cicerone, 1996); G. Price, *Walking in the Dolomites* (Cicerone, 2000); and K. Tempe, *Flora e fauna nelle Dolomiti* (Athesia, 1998).

43

Gruppo di Tessa

Rugged Alpine massif in Alto Adige, north-west of Merano; parco naturale regionale
33,430 ha (82,609 acres)

High above the Adige valley lies a stretch of wilderness graced with an extraordinary richness of forest, fauna, glaciers, lakes and mountain scenery. Covering a substantial area, and comparatively unvisited, the Tessa massif is one of the most splendid in the central Alps. The local language and culture are Teutonic — Austria is just over the border — and so too is the appearance of the foothills, where characteristic castles and wooden houses are dotted among the pine woods and close-planted vineyards.

In the higher reaches the scenery is on a grand scale, rocky and glacier-scarred. There are dozens of peaks over 3,000 metres (10,000 feet), the highest, Cime Nere, reaching 3,628 metres (11,903 feet). There are also numerous glaciers — Similáun, in the north-west, is the biggest — huge moraines and great tracts of forest such as the Val di Senáles, often known by its sobriquet as the Valley of the Larches.

The lakes of the Tessa are famous, especially the Sopranes group, some of which are named after their colouring: Nero, Latte and Verde ('black', 'milky' and 'green'). This is one of the loveliest spots in the mountains. Also famous — among geologists, at least — are the rock types of the higher reaches. Granite, gneiss and mica schists predominate, with rogue intrusions such as the ortogneiss on Monte Gigot and the marble of the Cima Fiammante. The upper Val Seeber is a hunting ground for minerals.

While the flora is limited by the ruggedness and acid bog of much of the area, the Tessa has surprisingly high concentrations of animals, given the non-observance of a law restricting hunting to local inhabitants. About 400 chamois roam the slopes and are easily seen, along with numerous marmots, if you climb high enough. The young chamois, known as lambs or kids, are born between April and June — one to each female — some six months after the autumn rut. Red and roe deer inhabit the forests at lower levels.

The best place to go for fauna is the Val di Fosse in the west, an intimate valley where wildlife, scenery and local culture all seem to reach their apogee. Eagles and lesser raptors inhabit the colossal rock walls that fall to the valley floor from the encircling peaks, especially the face of the Cima Bianca.

One of the quintessentially alpine birds of the Tessa is the ptarmigan, a plump, short-winged member of the grouse family which changes its plumage with the seasons. In the summer its upper body, head and breast are mottled brown, to blend with the ground cover. In autumn the brown fades to grey, and then in winter,

The marmot betrays its presence by an unearthly and extremely loud shriek, a defence mechanism that can terrify you out of your wits when you first hear it. It is about the size of a bulky cat. A lover of sunshine and gregarious in its habits, it spends up to five hours a day feeding off plants.

when the snow lies thick on the ground, to the pure white of its surroundings.

Other members of the grouse family found in the Tessa include hazel hens, also known as hazel grouse, and black grouse. Both are more typical of forested areas and keep their plumage unchanged in winter. The closely related capercaillie, the largest of the European grouse, is another species of the forest, resembling a clumsy turkey in flight. All these birds may be spotted in the Val di Senáles.

BEFORE YOU GO
Maps: Kompass 1:50,000 No. 55 *Merano*; IGM 1:50,000 Nos 12 *Silandro* and 13 *Merano*.
Guide-book: G. Barducci, *Parco Naturale Gruppo di Tessa*, available from tourist offices and park centre.

GETTING THERE
By car: the SS38 from Bolzano runs the length of the Venosta valley, with stunning side roads into the park (turn off at Naturno for Senáles and the Val di Fosse) and the mountains along the Austrian border further west. The SS44 from Merano serves the park's eastern edge, along the Passiria valley.
By rail: from Verona take the main line to Bolzano and change on to the Bolzano–Merano branch line (trains hourly).
By bus: services run from Merano to most towns and villages, including S. Caterina in the Val di Senáles and Ulfas in the Val Passiria, T: (0473) 221 702.

WHERE TO STAY
Hotels: Salvatoriana (2-star), Via Belvedere 6, Merano, T: (0473) 235 049; Tannenhof (1-star), Via Platt 34, Moso in Passiria, T: (0473) 649 575; Jägerrast (1-star), Loc. Val di Fosse 6, Val di Senáles, T: (0473) 679 230; Lärchenheim (2-star), Via Certosa 152, Certosa, Val di Senáles, T: (0473) 679 132.
Agriturismo: Fleckingerhof, Via Ceves 54, Vipiteno, T: (0472) 632 669.

Refuges: the 5 run by CAI are Monte Neve, T: (0473) 647 045; Plan, T: (0473) 646 709; Bellavista, T: (0473) 662 140; Similáun, T: (0473) 669 711; Petrarca, T: (0473) 643 545.
Outdoor living: camping is prohibited except at organized camp-sites. Try Adler, T: (0473) 667 242, and Wald, T: (0473) 667 298, both at Naturno, or Merano, at Merano, T: (0473) 231 249.

ACTIVITIES
Walking: the high- and low-level sections of the Meraner Hohenweg long-distance path both start from S. Caterina in the Val di Senáles and go east, crossing the Tessa massif to Ulfas in the Val Passiria. The high-level route, marked as Trail 24, leads to Rif. di Plan via Val di Fosse, Masogelato and Rif. Stettiner (the full circuit, Naturno to Merano, takes 4/5 days). Many farms offer bed and breakfast *en route*. Other fine walks include the ascent of L'Altissima (3,480 m/11,417 ft) on the Hans Grutzmacher Weg (5 hrs); Val di Fosse to Rif. Petrarca (5 hrs); Parcines to Rif. Cima Fiammante (7 hrs), a walk that can be linked to hikes in the Val di Fosse; and the Velloi–Plan traverse (12 hrs, using Riomolino chair-lift).
Climbing: enquire in Merano (best base) at CAI/Südtiroler Alpenverein, Corso Libertà 188, T: (0473) 237 134, or call Ufficio Informazioni Alpinistiche, T: (0471) 413 809.
Skiing: there is a huge and rather ugly complex in the Val di Senáles, T: (0473) 662 171, and another at Merano 2000, T: (0473) 279 457.

FURTHER INFORMATION
Tourist offices: Via Certosa 42, Certosa, Val di Senáles, T: (0473) 679 148; Via Municipio, Naturno, T: (0473) 666 077; Corso Libertà 45, Merano, T: (0473) 272 000.
Park office: Via dei Campi 3, Naturno, T: (0473) 668 201 (Apr–Oct).

MOUNTAIN SAFETY

The Alps and the Dolomites are genuinely wild places and present real dangers to those who venture into them without taking sensible precautions. The weather can change quickly in the mountains; even in summer, it is possible to get stranded by mist and fog, and exposure can be a serious hazard.

Always take a waterproof and some warm clothing; walking boots with moulded rubber soles (smooth soles can be lethal); food, map and compass; and a whistle to attract attention in case you get into difficulties.

Always tell someone where you are going and how long you intend to be, especially if walking alone.

Stélvio

*Huge Alpine range on the border with
Switzerland, in Trentino-Alto Adige and
Lombardy;* parco nazionale
ZPS
134,620 ha (332,659 acres)

The Stélvio is a landscape that invites superlatives. Choose a positive adjective
— large, grand, high — shift up through
the grammatical degrees, and you will have
a fair impression of its importance. Often
called the park of rock, ice and snow, it is
the largest protected area on the Italian
Alpine ridge, and the second largest in the
country (after Pollino in the south). Three-
quarters of it lies above 2,000 metres (6,500
feet); 25 peaks exceed 3,000 metres (10,000
feet), with the main ones edging closer to
4,000 metres (13,000 feet). The Passo dello
Stélvio on the Swiss border is Europe's second highest mountain pass, at 2,758 metres
(9,048 feet) only a hundred metres lower
than the Col du Midi de Bigorre in the
Pyrenees. A tenth of the park is permanently covered in ice — a hundred separate
glaciers in all, including Italy's (and one of
Europe's) largest, the Ghiacciaio dei Forni.
Ortles and Cevedale are the main summits,
edged around with dozens of lakes and
tens of thousands of hectares of enchanted
forests — a mountain kingdom worthy to
rival the Gran Paradiso, the Matterhorn or
Monte Rosa.

The park has more than 1,500
kilometres (1,000 miles) of marked paths.
If this sounds daunting, you could do

worse than start in the Valle dello Zebrù, a perfect introduction to the Stélvio. Due east of Bórmio, the valley cuts to the heart of the Ortles and Cevedale massifs, with views of glaciers and, in the rutting season, a good chance of witnessing the courting antics of red deer. Other glorious valleys lie on the park's northern fringes; one of the favourites with climbers and trekkers is the Val di Martello above Silandro. Many trails and cross-country ski routes start from the cluster of refuges at the head of the valley.

If you are seduced by the appeal of glaciers, you could join other devotees on a pilgrimage to the foot of the huge Ghiacciaio dei Forni ice sheet. Take a bus from Bórmio to Santa Caterina Valfurva and then hike up the Val di Forni. After an hour or so's Alpine idyll — all streams, lakes and forest — you clamber on to the

terminal waste of the glacial moraine and eventually reach the Branca refuge, from where you can view the deeply fissured ice. There is s something faintly ominous about a glacier, its creaking progress, its erosive power over the landscape, its habit of swallowing and spitting out, perhaps aeons later, anything that falls into its frigid grasp. In these mountains a further element of the macabre is added by the remnants of battle from the Great War, fought here up to heights of 3,000 metres (10,000 feet). Guns, shell casings, barbed wire and assorted sad detritus are still entombed in the glacial ice.

Lombardy and Trentino-Alto Adige share the management of the park, and both have robust conservation policies, including a hunting ban. In 1977, the two authorities extended the park to the Swiss border and linked it to the Engadina National Park in Switzerland, an initiative that inspired Piedmont's twinning of the Alpi Maríttime and Mercantour parks ten years later. In the huge combined parks of the Stélvio-Engadina and the nearby Adamello-Brenta the authorities have created a strategic conservation zone for the central Alps.

Though often surprisingly busy with walkers, the vast wilderness of the Stélvio still has plenty of space for large mammals to roam away from paths, bridleways and visitor centres. Ibex were introduced from the Gran Paradiso in 1967 and now number a few hundred, most of them in the Valle dello Zebrù. The red deer originally drifted across from Switzerland, forming a colony that has grown to about 800. Roe deer number 1,600, chamois 3,000. Most exciting of all has been the reintroduction of the brown bear from the Adamello.

For birds, the Stélvio offers a vast array of habitats ranging from lowland meadows and scrublands to thick alpine forests and bare wind-swept slopes above the tree-line. The avian population is

Frosted with permanent snow, the central Alps are known for their razor-sharp arêtes, hanging valleys and hundreds of miles of waymarked walks.

A nocturnal bird of Italy's coniferous forests, the long-eared owl is distinguished by its slim upright stance and conspicuous vertical ear tufts. The ears proper are concealed lower down on each side of the head.

correspondingly varied. More than 130 species have been recorded in the park, most of which breed here. In the forests are found a wide range of owls, including both pygmy and eagle owls, the smallest and largest of their species in Europe. Pygmy owls measure only 16 centimetres (6 inches) from head to tail and nest in old woodpecker holes, while eagle owls can be anything up to 70 centimetres (27 inches) long. Both hunt by day as well as by night. Only a little larger than the pygmy owl is Tengmalm's owl, a genuinely nocturnal species whose raised brows give it a quizzical expression. Equally unmistakable are the elongated face and conspicuous ear tufts of the long-eared owl.

No less than five species of woodpecker breed here. In the lower forests live wrynecks, so called because of their supposed ability to twist their heads through 360 degrees, and great spotted woodpeckers, probably the commonest members of the family in Europe. In the dense montane forests higher up are grey-headed woodpeckers, similar to their green cousins but with less red on the crown, and the much larger black woodpeckers.

Perhaps most distinctive are the three-toed woodpeckers, the only ones with no red in their plumage; the black-and-white-barred males sport yellow crowns.

Above the tree-line you will find a wealth of small birds such as alpine accentors and alpine choughs, dwarfed by the silhouettes of golden eagles, of which at least 10 pairs breed here — evidence of how wild this area still is. Even more striking evidence is provided by the return of a species that had been considered extinct in the Alps since the early 20th century, the majestic lammergeier. By 1986 it had started to breed again at isolated points in the Alps, and an international project was launched to reintroduce it along the whole of the Alpine ridge. It reached the Stélvio in June 2000 when the first pair was released in the Val di Martello. Three pairs are now nesting in the Lombard part of the park.

The Stélvio also scores well in plants — 1,200 species recorded so far, and the census still unfinished. The diversity stems from a rich mixture of soils, which in turn owe their origin to a jumble of rock types: ancient dolomites and other limestones in the east; crystalline schists rich in quartz, mica and feldspar in the west; magnetite on the slopes of Monte Péio; and deposits of manganese in the Valle di Solda. One of the more uncommon plants to grow in these soils is the unassuming but attractive chickweed wintergreen *(Trientalis europaea)*, which hides in the depths of Stélvio's conifer woods. A member of the primrose family, it has a single whorl of smooth, shiny green leaves near the top of the stem, from which emerges a solitary, star-like white flower.

Other appealing flowers include rare yellow gentians, which do not flower until their tenth year, deep azure trumpet gentians, which bloom at the height of summer, and smaller gentians with violet-blue fringes, which come out in autumn. Equally spectacular are the red and martagon lilies, sweet-scented black vanilla orchids, mountain avens (also a plant of the Arctic tundra) and alpine clematis, whose large purplish flowers would look familiar on any garden trellis.

BEFORE YOU GO

Maps: Kompass 1:50,000 *Parco Nazionale dello Stélvio*; IGM 1:50,000 Nos 11 *Malles Venosta*, 24 *Bórmio* and 25 *Rabbi*.

Guide-books: P. Turetti, *Escursioni nel Parco dello Stélvio, itinerari* (Cierre, 1997) and *Alpi Retiche, Passo dello Stélvio* (Multigraphic, 2002).

GETTING THERE

By car: no approach to the Stélvio is particularly quick. From the north, take the A22 to Bolzano and then the SS38 and SS40 to Malles Venosta (via Merano). From the SS38, minor roads lead into two wonderful valleys, the Val d'Ultimo (turn off at Lana, south of Merano) and the Val di Martello (turn off at Láces, near Silandro). Alternatively, leave the A22 at S. Michele all'Adige and join SS43 and SS42 along the Val di Sole, where minor lanes lead off into the Rabbi and Péio valleys. Coming from Milan, take the SS36 and SS38 via Lecco and Sondrio to Bórmio.

By rail: for access to the north of the park, use the Verona–Bolzano main line, then the Bolzano–Merano branch line (hourly services). For the south, use the Milan–Sondrio–Tirano line or the Brescia–Édolo branch line (10 daily). For train times, call Bórmio tourist office, T: (0342) 903 300.

By bus: services operate to most centres from Merano. Winter schedules are restricted. Useful routes include Merano to Silandro (8 daily) and S. Gertrude (5 daily, excellent for the Val d'Ultimo); Silandro to Rif. Genziana, in the Val di Martello (2 daily, summer only); Tirano to Bórmio (several a day connecting with trains from Milan); Bórmio/Merano to Passo dello Stélvio (summer only); Bórmio to S. Caterina Valfurva. Contact S.T.I., freephone T: (800) 846 047, or S.A.D. Merano, T: (0471) 450 111; alternatively, visit www.sii.bz.it.

WHEN TO GO

Most of the alpine flowers are in bloom June–Aug, but lovers of solitude should avoid the more popular trails then.

WHERE TO STAY

Hotels: in Bórmio try Adele (2-star), Via Monte Braulio 38, T: (0342) 910 175, or Stella (2-star), Via Roma 101, T: (0342) 910 397. Alternatives include Helvetia (2-star), Via Plan 173, Livigno, T: (0342) 970 066; Alle Tre Baite (3-star), Via S. Caterina 24, S. Caterina Valfurva, T: (0342) 935 545; Genziana (1-star), Via del Santo 2, Péio, T: (0463) 746 050; Alpenrose (2-star), Via S. Bernardo 171/1, Rabbi, T: (0463) 985 098.

Agriturismo: try Fischerhof, Via delle Sorgenti 5, Láces, T: (0473) 623 258; Niederhof, Waldberg 222, Martello, T: (0473) 744 534; Rumwaldhof, Solda di Sopra 9, Solda, T: (0473) 613 141; or La Baita, Loc. S. Bernardo, Sóndalo, T: (0432) 820 233.

Refuges: among about 30 CAI and private refuges, the most popular are Payer, T: (0473) 613 010, at 3,000 m (10,000 ft) a base for the ascent of Ortles; Corsi (in the Val di Martello), T: (0473) 744 785; Pizzini, T: (0342) 935 513; and Branca, T: (0342) 935 501.

ACCESS

You may learn to hate the 4-wheel drives that plague remote bridleways and valley roads.

ACTIVITIES

Walking: recommended routes include Valle dello Zebrù to the Rif. Quinto Alpini (5 hrs); Valle dello Zebrù to Rif. Pizzini via the Passo dello Zebrù (and on to the Val di Forni, 8 hrs/2 days); and S. Nicolò to Alpe Solaz, dropping to the Valle dello Zebrù (3 hrs). There are also comparatively easy hikes over ice if you are properly equipped. Certain areas (for example, Valle di Péio) have chair-lifts high into the mountains.

Climbing: there are many routes, especially on snow and

Parco Nazionale dello Stelvio
[map: SWITZERLAND, Zemez, Malles, Sluderno, Santa Maria, Prato allo Stelvio, SS38, Lasa, Silandro, Lasa, Stelvio, Punta di Cascata, Laces, Livigno, Trafoi, Solda di Fuori, Martello, Passo dello Stélvio, Ortles, Gran Zebrù, Passo dei Cevedale, Val d'Ultimo, Bórmio, Valfurva, Pizzini, Monte Cevedale, Aldergo Ghiacciaio del Forno, del Cevedale, Rabbi, Santa Caterina, Branca, Bagi di Rabbi, Sondalo, Passo di Gavia, Val del Monte, SS42, Pelizzano]

Key
Nature parks
Points of interest
Refuge
International boundaries
Railway station

0   5   10miles
0   5   10   15Km.

ice. Simple ascents of Cevedale are open to hikers with ropes and crampons; Ortles and Gran Zebrù are more demanding. For guided climbs, contact the Guide Alpine, Bórmio, T: (0342) 910 991 or Solda, T: (0473) 613 004.

Skiing: pistes can be found at Solda, T: (0473) 613 244/613 047; Trafoi, T: (0473) 611 577; and also Bórmio, S. Caterina Valfurva, Péio, Rabbi and Ponte di Legno. Cross-country skiing options exist in Bórmio, Valfurva, Valdidentro, Livigno, Ponte di Legno, Péio, Solda and Trafoi. Summer and alpine skiing possibilities are excellent.

FURTHER INFORMATION

Tourist offices: (Trentino-Alto Adige) Via dei Cappuccini 10, Silandro, T: (0473) 620 480; Via Principale 29, Prato allo Stélvio, T: (0473) 616 034; Via Marconi, Malè, T: (0463) 901 280; (Lombardy) Via Roma 131/b, Bórmio, T: (0342) 903 300; Piazza Migliavacca, S. Caterina Valfurva, T: (0342) 935 598; Via Verdi 2/a, Sóndalo, T: (0342) 801 816; Via Milano 41, Ponte di Legno, T: (0364) 91122.

Park office: Via Roma 26, Bórmio, T: (0342) 910 100.

Visitor centres: Via Roma 28, Cógolo di Péio, T: (0463) 754 186; Loc. Rabbi Fonte, near Rabbi, T: (0463) 985 190; Piazzale Europa, Ponte di Legno, T: (0364) 900 721.

Ecology: the right bank of the Adige, in the north-west of the park, is known for its flower-strewn meadows. The Rezia alpine botanical garden at Rovinaccia, near Bórmio, has 2,500 species under cultivation, 900 of them local.

Adamello-Brenta

Major Alpine and Dolomite massifs in Trentino-Alto Adige and Lombardy; parco naturale regionale
112,860 ha (278,888 acres)
Includes Ramsar, ZPS

The Adamello-Brenta park is the meeting point of two great mountain chains. The central Alps reach their eastern limit in the Adamello, the Dolomites their western limit in the Brenta, which is the only Dolomite massif west of the Adige. The park bridges the two, marrying the crystalline and sedimentary creatures by means of a thin strip of protected land north of Madonna di Campiglio.

Beneath the town — a hugely popular resort — runs the Guidicarie fault, a major Alpine fracture that marks the divide between the two ranges and between two strikingly disparate landscapes. To the west, the Adamello is rolling granite country, its crystalline rock formed a relatively recent 50 million years ago. To the east, the Brenta presents a far more complex picture of overlapping sedimentary layers thrown into dramatic confusion by powerful tectonic forces. Its bedrock is Dolomia Principale overlaid with 300 metres (1,000 feet) of Rhaetic black shale. This unique formation makes the Brenta appear similar to the saw-tooth mountains of the eastern Dolomites, yet without the benefit of Sciliar-dolomite tips — an anomaly that underlines just how twisted and contorted the story of the Alps' development can be.

For anyone seeking wilderness there is no question of which area to make for: the Adamello, rich, hugely varied and one of Italy's key wild places. At its heart rises eponymous Adamello, 3,539 metres (11,611 feet) high, girdled by a further dozen summits each exceeding 3,000 metres (10,000 feet) and draped with glaciers. Two massive ridges run south from this heartland, divided by the Val di Fumo. To the north stands an outlying wall of mountains, the Presanella, whose six peaks also rise above 3,000 metres, and beyond that the southern edge of the Stélvio.

Between the Adamello and the Presanella lies the beautiful Val di Génova. Italia Nostra has described this ice-scoured valley as 'the Alps' ultimate paradise'. It is a small nook of delightful scenery with fine walks and numerous opportunities for encountering wildlife. Above the village of Carisolo is a fairy-tale waterfall, the Cascata di Nardis. Two parallel streams drop 100 metres (300 feet), guarded by a pair of granite slabs which legend says are two demons turned to stone. Similar falls further up the valley crash over four successive rock steps,

known locally as *scale* or 'stairs'.

The scenery at the head of the valley is breathtaking, all high mountains, snow and deeply fissured glaciers — 'so ugly as to seem beautiful', say locals. In places this wilderness has been compared to the tundra of Alaska. Lower down, in the splendid forests that clothe the valley, devils are said to wander, supposedly the spirits cast out by the Council of Trent in the 16th century; so too the legendary King of Génova, a hunter of bear and chamois, who can be heard howling on nights when the moon is full. You may also hear the hooting of the eagle, pygmy and Tengmalm's owls or the rhythmical drumming of wood-peckers, the grey-headed, black and three-toed, as they signal their presence to one another. Among the trees are all the firs

The plunging rock walls and soaring pinnacles of the Dolomiti di Brenta catch the sun's dying rays, above Madonna di Campiglio.

and pines you could hope to find, along with hazel, beech, birch and wild cherry. Wonderful colours splash the mountain-sides in autumn when the leaves turn, complemented by the distinctive blood-crimson of the local lichen that covers the granite boulders.

Moving over to the Brenta is like crossing the Great Divide of the Rocky Mountains, tumbling into a still more spectacular world, but one whose wilderness is compromised by the sheer weight of visitors. One of the most popular of the Dolomite massifs, close to Trento, it is a notable skiing area and is embraced by a ring of roads that bring the trippers flooding in. The scenery, however, is likely to prove irresistible to any outdoor enthusiast: immense rock faces, jagged pinnacles, jumbled screes, fantastic peaks, all linked by excellent paths. The most famous of Italy's *vie ferrate*, the Via delle Bocchette, ranks among the world's ultimate footpaths and is unforgettable for those with the equipment — and the head for heights — to follow it.

The central ridge in the Brenta is lower than that of the Adamello, running at about 2,400 metres (7,900 feet) and peaking on Cima Tosa at 3,159 metres (10,364 feet) — not that you will be able to reach any of the isolated turrets that are the summits in the Brenta. They are just a scenic backdrop for all but the most experienced climbers. But as such they offer many highlights, including the Crozzon, a vast wall of grey rock, and the Campanile Basso, a perfect square tower 400 metres (1,300 feet) high, the grandest rock formation in the Dolomites.

In summer, the central area around the Brentei and Tuckett refuges (Tuckett was one of several Englishmen to pioneer climbs in the Brenta in the 1860s) is perhaps the busiest region in the Alps. The

The beautiful lady's slipper orchid *(Cypripedium calceolus)*, its lip shaped like a ballet shoe, is found in European montane woods and thickets. Increasingly scarce, it is protected by law in most countries.

tramp of the tourist's boot has driven away much of the local fauna, though in the northern parts there is still evidence of alpine brown bears. Perhaps two or three survive between the Adamello and the Brenta, and more are being reintroduced, though all you are likely to see of them are the signs of their passage: droppings, disturbed bees' nests and scarred trees. You have a better chance of coming across other typically alpine mammals, including chamois, deer and marmots.

The alpine flora is surprisingly abundant and includes mountain varieties such as edelweiss, lady's slipper orchid, Rhaetian poppy and black vanilla orchid. There are also more unusual species such as the spectacular primrose *(Primula spectabilis)*, brightening the rocks with its large pinkish-red flowers; the scarce *Paederota bonarota* of the figwort family; and *Campanula raineri*, a beautiful bellflower that grows in cracks in the rock, its short stems supporting deep blue flowers, while a low carpet of grey-green foliage spreads out below.

The most famous of the Brenta's natural landmarks is the Lago di Tóvel. For years, under certain conditions, the lake took on a deep red tint, coloured by the presence of a rare alga, *Glenodinium sanguineum*. The effect was unknown anywhere else in the world, at least with such intensity. Sadly, pollution has seriously upset the lake's delicate natural balance, causing the colour to wane. Until efforts to reduce this damage start to have an effect, tourists will be denied the sight their own curiosity has destroyed.

Elsewhere the record of conservation in the park is more encouraging. In the Adamello, the Val di Génova was saved by a whisker from a hydro-electric scheme (though not the Val Rendena, which was turned over to uranium mining). Special reserves have been set up, as at Matarot on the Vedretta della Lóbbia glacier, to protect land newly exposed by the retreat of the ice and to study its recolonization by plants and animals. Similar glacial retreats are protected around the peri-glacial lakes of Láres and Pozzoni, and near the Nardis waterfall.

BEFORE YOU GO

Maps: IGM 1:50,000 Nos 41 *Ponte di Legno*, 42 *Malè*, 57 *Malonno*, 58 *Monte Adamello*, 59 *Tione di Trento*, 78 *Breno* and 79 *Bagolino*.

Guide-books: H. Menara, *Escursioni ai rifugi del Sudtirolo* (Athesia, 2003); *Dolomiti di Brenta* (Cierre, 2003).

GETTING THERE

By car: the SS42 is the main artery for the Adamello from Brescia, Bergamo and the west. The Brenta is reached from Trento on the A22 and SS43 to Cles, then SS42 and SS239 to Madonna di Campiglio. A summer-only road runs to the Val di Génova from Carisolo, 12 km (7 miles) south of Madonna on SS239.

By rail: go to Trento on the Verona–Brénnero main line and take the branch line to Malè, 22 km (17 miles) north of Madonna (10 trains daily). For access to the Adamello from the west, there is a slow branch line from Brescia to Édolo (10 daily).

By bus: services go from Trento to Madonna and other towns via Stenico and Tione (4 daily, 2 hrs); from Milan to Madonna; and from Brescia to Breno, Édolo and other western towns; Atesina, Trento, T: (0461) 983 627.

WHERE TO STAY

Hotels: Madonna di Campiglio and Pinzolo are the best bases. Try Oberosler (3-star), Via Monte Spinale 27, T: (0465) 441 136, or Fontanella (2-star), Via Dolomiti di Brenta 125, T: (0465) 443 399, both in Madonna; Pinzolo Dolomiti (3-star), Corso Trento 24, T: (0465) 501 024, or Centro Pineta (3-star), Via Matteotti 43, T: (0465) 502 758, both in Pinzolo.

Agriturismo: Agritur Renetta, Via di Campo, Tassullo, T: (0463) 450 794.

Refuges: of the scores in this region the Città di Trento hut at the head of the Val di Génova is invaluable for the Adamello, T: (0465) 501 193; the Brentei is popular in the Brenta, T: (0465) 441 244, as is the Tuckett, T: (0465) 507 287.

Outdoor living: free camping is permitted in much of the Adamello. Organized camp-sites include Camping Faè, S. Antonio di Mavignola, T: (0465) 507 178; Camping Parco Adamello, Magnabò, near Pinzolo, T: (0465) 501 793.

ACTIVITIES

Walking: there are hikes to suit every ability, with some 20 ski lifts to take you to starting points high in the mountains. Most walks in the Brenta from Madonna are classics. The best known takes the chair-lift from Madonna to the Rif. Grostè (2,442 m/8,012 ft) and proceeds first to the Rif. Tuckett (Trail 316) and then to the Rif. Brentei (Trails 328/318). Here you can descend to Vallesinella and Madonna (Trail 317) or press on to the Rif. Pedrotti (7 hrs).

Routes in the Adamello tend to be longer. Well known are the hikes in the Val di Génova, especially those to the foot of the glaciers at the valley head, and the long trek from the Valle del Cáffaro to Ponte di Legno (6 days).

Cycling: bikes can be hired at Cinque Laghi, Via Campanil Basso 1, Madonna di Campiglio, T: (0465) 440 355.

Pony-trekking: contact the Brenta Club horse-riding centre, Andalo, T: (0461) 585 377.

Watersports: call the Surf Centre Marco Segnana, Lido di Molveno, T: (0464) 505 963/(338) 730 2377.

Skiing: contact the Consorzio Adamello, Via Presanella 12, Madonna di Campiglio, T: (0465) 447 744; Via Circonvallazione, Passo del Tonale, T: (0364) 92066; Via Corno d'Aola 5, Ponte di

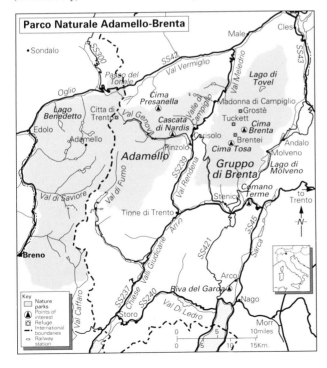

Parco Naturale Adamello-Brenta

53

Legno, T: (0364) 92097/42369.

FURTHER INFORMATION
Tourist offices: Piazza Alpini
2/a, Tuenno (for Lago di Tóvel),
T: (0463) 454 023; Corso
Milano 41, Ponte di Legno, T:
(0364) 91122; Via Pradalago 4,
Madonna di Campiglio, T:
(0465) 442 000; Via del Sole,
Pinzolo, T: (0465) 501 007;
Piazza Marconi 1, Molveno, T:
(0461) 586 924; Via Alfieri 4,
Trento, T: (0461) 983 880.
Park offices: (Trentino-Alto
Adige) Via Nazionale 12,
Strembo, T: (0465) 804 637;
(Lombardy) Piazza Tassara 3,
Breno, T: (0364) 324 011.
Visitor centres: (Trentino-Alto
Adige) Lago di Tóvel, Val di
Non, T: (0463) 451 033, and Via
Brescia 62, Daóne, T: (0465)
901 217 (summer only);
(Lombardy) Via Nazionale 91,
Vezza d'Oglio, T: (0364) 76131,
and Via Adamello 10, Saviore
dell'Adamello, T: (0364) 634 145.

Sciliar

*Dolomite massif and high
karstic plateau in Alto
Adige; partly protected by a
parco naturale regionale
(5,850 ha/14,456 acres)*

The Sciliar may well be your
first sight of the Dolomites,
their splintered peaks rising in
a huge rampart behind the
provincial capital of Bolzano.
Alongside, sentinel-like, stand
the rock pinnacles of the
Dente dello Sciliar, the 'tooth
of the Sciliar'.

Unseen from the town is the
Alpe di Siusi, an undulating
plateau of tree-dotted meadows
which intermingle with the
peaks. At 2,000 m (6,600 ft),
this green jewel set in a casket
of mountains is one of Italy's

largest and most beautiful
areas of high meadow.

Once the snows have melted,
fields of orchids, gentians, white
crucifers and buttercups come
into bloom. Other parts of the
plateau are turned into marshland by rain and meltwater.

Some of the Siusi plateau
has been spoiled by ski resorts
and roads, which have sprouted
despite protests from conservationists. Most of the development is concentrated in the
north, however, leaving plenty
of wilder scenery to explore in
the southern Val di Tíres.

The rocks of the Sciliar are
the oldest in the Dolomites and
contain an abundance not only
of fossils but also of minerals,
the fruits of past volcanic activity. Near Cima di Terrarossa
(2,655 m/8,710 ft), in the east,
stand bizarre towers of volcanic
rock known as the Denti di
Terrarossa, 'teeth of red earth'.

If the Sciliar's plateau
sounds tame by Dolomite
standards, it offers pastoral
walks beside verdant streams
and opens up superbly
panoramic views to the nearby
massifs of the Sella, Sasso
Lungo and Catinaccio.
Spectacular, too, are the gorges
that scythe down towards the
villages of Fiè and Siusi.

The Sciliar is also a place of
historical interest, known
locally as 'the mountain of
destiny' and populated since
ancient times. Prehistoric
remains have been found in its
caves (most interesting is the
Buco dell'Orso) and near
Albergo Frommer, probably a
site of pagan worship, at heights
of up to 2,500 m (8,000 ft).
Before you go *Map:* Kompass
1:50,000 No. 54 *Bolzano.*
*Guide-book: Parco Naturale
dello Sciliar*, available from
tourist office in Bolzano.
Getting there *By car:* take A22
to Bolzano Nord, then SS12
and minor roads to fringes of

Grasses and alpine flowers find shelter in the weathered limestone of
the Fánes-Sénnes-Bráies massifs.

park. Access also from Val Gardena, where several ski lifts operate to Alpe di Siusi.

By rail: station at Bolzano on Verona–Brénnero main line.

By bus: services from Bolzano to Siusi, and from Siusi to Saltría in heart of Alpe wetlands (summer only), S.A.D., freephone T: (800) 846 047.

Where to stay *Hotels:* around edge of park, Sciliar (2-star), Via Santner 6, Castelrotto, T: (0471) 706 177; Belvedere (2-star), Via O. Von Wolkenstein 49, Tíres, T: (0471) 706 336; Frommer (1-star), Via Compatsch 4, Siusi, T: (0471) 727 917. In Alpe di Siusi, Bellavista (3-star), Via Compatsch 50, T: (0471) 727 972; Santner (2-star), Via Joch 6, T: (0471) 727 913. Alternatives in Fiè, Saltría and many isolated hamlets. Check off-season opening with tourist offices. *Refuges:* most used, Rif. Bolzano, T: (0471) 612 024 (June–Sept).

Outdoor living: only at organized camp-sites such as Alpe di Siusi, S. Costantino, near Fiè, T: (0471) 706 459 (open all year).

Activities *Walking:* moderately demanding 1-day hike from Compaccio car park in Alpe di Siusi via Malga Saltner and Rif. Bolzano to Monte Sciliar, followed by descent to foot of Cima Terrarossa and on to Rif. Alpe di Tires; variety of return routes.

Other climbs to summit, often busy in summer, from Tíres, Siusi and Fiè. Hikes over Alpe di Siusi all extremely simple, with many refreshment points.

For full-blown traverse of park start at Hotel Bellavista in Alpe di Siusi, climb to Rif. Bolzano and descend to Fiè (6 hrs). Wilder hikes on offer near Tíres in Valle Rosarian and Valle Ciamin. Five paths marked by park authorities as nature trails.

Pony-trekking: centres throughout, with horse-drawn sleighs for hire in winter. Contact tourist offices or Noleggio Cavalli Trocker, T: (0471) 727 807.

Climbing: few testing climbs, unlike elsewhere in Dolomites. Most routes on western slopes of Sciliar: Punta Santner, Punta Euringer and Piccolo Sciliar. Contact Scuola di Alpinismo Sciliar, Via Siusi 25, Siusi, T: (0473) 706 285.

Skiing: most centres found on Alpe di Siusi, less crowded than some, with numerous lifts; Ortisei Ski, T: (0471) 799 022. Also skating and sledging. Some 80 km (50 miles) of renowned and spectacular cross-country routes, mainly on Alpe di Siusi.

Further information *Tourist offices:* Castelrotto, T: (0471) 706 333; Alpe di Siusi, T: (0471) 727 904; Siusi, T: (0471) 707 024; Fiè, T: (0471) 725 047; Piazza Walther 8, Bolzano, T: (0471) 413 808.

Panevéggio-Pale di San Martino

Virgin forest and savage Dolomite massif in Trentino; parco naturale regionale 19,711 ha (48,708 acres)

South of the main Dolomite massifs, near San Martino di Castrozza, lies a stretch of open country — some of Italy's most enchanting — that divides into two contrasting areas: Panevéggio, a huge area of primeval forest, and the Pale, some of the Dolomites' wildest and most dramatic mountains.

Most of Panevéggio's 2,700 ha (6,700 acres) of forest is an unspoiled wilderness of larch, silver fir, Arolla and mountain pines and Norway spruce. From its solemn expanse came some of the timber for the Venetian fleet of the 17th century, and the maple and pine that Stradivarius and his fellow Cremonese craftsmen made into violins. Today commercial logging demand has been relieved by a separate plantation that produces 120,000 trees a year, but less than four per cent of the total area of the forest is given over to cultivated woodland and roads.

Panevéggio contains comparatively modest mountains, dominated by the rounded heights of Colbricón (2,603 m/8,540 ft) and has an abundance of streams and waterfalls, many of which are well stocked with trout. Away to the west stretch the granite ridges of the Lagorai, an immense emptiness unvisited by the hordes of Dolomite trekkers heading further north.

Larger mammals have been hunted to virtual extinction, although red deer, reintroduced 40 years ago, have formed a viable colony, and smaller mammals, including pine martens, have recovered since the park's foundation in 1967. Birds of prey, however, have all but vanished.

Paths and surfaced bridleways are ideal for walking, mountain-biking and cross country skiing. Walks around Tognola (which can be quickly reached by a chair-lift) are especially appealing, confined to easy meadow and woodland tracks.

As a constant backdrop to forest walks you have stupendous views of the jagged

The yellow daisy-like flowers of arnica have long been used in central-European country medicine, both externally for bruises, wounds and sprains, and internally as a stimulant and febrifuge.

peaks of the Pale, one of the most breathtaking of all the Dolomite massifs. Distinct from neighbouring groups, the Pale boasts the major glaciers of Travignolo and Fradusta; its upper ridges, moraines and karstic plateaux are a barren wilderness, a landscape where comparisons with the surface of the moon are for once apposite. So pallid is the rock that it glows even in the first light of dawn.

Hiking itineraries vary greatly in degree of difficulty. Although all paths are well marked, some are extremely challenging, with much scrambling and the occasional *via ferrata*. Plan your walks and know your strength before setting out.

A little to the south of the main peaks of Vezzena and Cimón della Pala (both over 3,000 m/10,000 ft) lies the Val Canali, a more intimate and undemanding area. Reached from Fiera di Primiero, in whose mineral-rich hills silver has long been mined, it embraces the peaks of Sass Maór and the Cima d'Oltro. A 19th-century traveller described it as the most 'lonely, desolate

and tremendous scene... to be found this side of the Andes'.

The montane pastures of the Pale contain many of the classic alpine species. The star-like silvery flower-heads of edelweiss nestle side by side with the tiny dark purple spikes of the black vanilla orchid, and the orange-yellow flowers of arnica contrast with the pale lemon blooms produced by swathes of Rhaetian poppies. Lady's slipper orchids thrive in the seclusion of the least disturbed woodlands, while globeflowers flourish in the wetter grasslands.

Among the rarities found in these mountains are the lilac-flowered primrose *Primula tyrolensis*, a plant confined to the Dolomites, and devil's claw *(Physoplexis comosa)*, a bizarre member of the bellflower family which looks like a cross between a hedgehog and a cluster of Chinese lanterns. It is usually restricted to limestone and dolomitic rock crevices here and elsewhere in the southern Alps.

Before you go *Maps:* Kompass 1:25,000 No. 622 and Tabacco 1:25,000 No. 22 *Pale di San*

Martino; Tabacco 1:50,000 Nos 4 *Dolomiti Agordine – Pale di San Martino* and 7 *Val di Fiemme – Lagorai – Val di Cembra*.

Guide-book: S. Scalet, *Pale di San Martino. Arrampicare, camminare, volare* (Versante Sud, 2002). Also leaflets and trail itineraries from park and tourist offices.

Getting there *By car:* from Trento and west, leave A22 at Egna-Ora exit and take SS48 via Predazzo; from Feltre and south, follow scenic SS50 which bisects park, reaching 1,980 m (6,496 ft) at Passo di Rolle.
By rail: alight at Ora on Verona–Brennero main line or Feltre on Padua–Belluno–Calalzo branch line. *By bus:* frequent buses go to Panevéggio every day from Ora via Predazzo, and from Feltre via Fiera di Primiero and S. Martino. Services also to S. Martino from Venice (3 hrs, once a day, summer only), Trento (3 hrs, 3 times a day) and Bolzano (4 hrs, once a day); Atesina, T: (0439) 64165.
Where to stay *Hotels:* Biancaneve (2-star), Via Dolomiti 14, T: (0439) 68135, and Suisse (2-star), Via Dolomiti 1, T: (0439) 68087, both in S. Martino. Alternatives include Albergo Antico (3-star), Via Prai dei Mont 19, Bellamonte, T: (0462) 576 122; La Bicocca (1-star), Panevéggio, T: (0462) 502 093; Aurora (2-star), Viale Piave 8, Fiera di Primiero, T: (0439) 62386.
Agriturismo: Agritur Malga Canali, Loc. Malga Canali, Toradico, T: (368) 741 3582.
Refuges: most useful are Treviso, T: (0439) 62311, in Val Canali; Pedrotti-Rossetta, T: (0439) 68308/62567, and Pradidali, T: (0439) 64180, both on Pale plateau; Malga Ces, T: (0439) 68145, and Tognola, T: (0439) 68026, both near Colbricón.
Outdoor living: only at

organized camp-sites such as Sass Maór, S. Martino, T: (0439) 68347 (summer only); Castelpietra, Val Canali, T: (0439) 62426; or Calavise, Fiera di Primiero, T: (0439) 67468.

Activities *Walking:* recommended walks in Panevéggio include Passo di Rolle–Colbricón lakes (3 hrs), with possibility of descent to Rif. Malga Ces and S. Martino (3 hrs); S. Martino (use chair-lift)–Tognola–Punta Ces–S. Martino (7 hrs); in the Pale, classic hikes are Rif. Rosetta (cable-car from S. Martino)–Rif. Pradidali (6 hrs, Trails 701/702) and Malga Fossa–Rif. Col Verde (3 hrs, descend by lift or Trail 701). For guided walks into the Pale in July–Aug, Gruppo Guide Alpine S. Martino, T: (0439) 768 795. *Skiing:* S. Martino, resort south of Cortina d'Ampezzo, a favourite with Italians. Lifts and pistes at Tognola, Punta Ces and Passo di Rolle; call Skipass office, T: (0439) 68505. At least 30 km (20 miles) of cross-country routes available at S. Martino, Passo di Rolle, Val Canali and Passo di Cereda. *Museum:* a worthwhile excursion might be made to Museo Geologico, Piazza Santi Filippo e Giacomo 1, Predazzo, T: (0462) 502 392.

Further information *Tourist offices:* Piazza della Chiesa, Predazzo, T: (0462) 501 237; Via F.lli Bronzetti 60, Cavalese, T: (0462) 241 111; Via Passo di Rolle 175, S. Martino, T: (0439) 768 867. *Park office:* Villa Welsperg, Via Castelpietra 2, Tonadíco, T: (0439) 64854. *Visitor centres:* Villa Welsperg (see above, open all year); Panevéggio, T: (0462) 576 283, S. Martino di Castrozza, T: (0439) 768 859, and Prá de Mádego, near Caoría, T: (0439) 710 049, June–Sept only.

Puéz-Odle

Twin Dolomite peaks in Alto Adige; parco naturale regionale
10,196 ha (25,195 acres)

If mountains were awarded commemorative plaques like houses, the Puéz-Odle would carry the name of Reinhold Messner, one of the world's greatest climbers, who was born and started his career in these mountains — his 'garden', he called them. He is the latest and most celebrated in a line of Puéz-Odle enthusiasts going back to the 1930s when pioneers established some of Italy's most difficult routes here.

If the Puéz-Odle are above the common run of Dolomite massifs in the eyes of climbers, it must come as little surprise that they also rate highly for their scenery. The skylines are as spectacular as any in the Dolomites, dominated by the huge saw-tooth peak of the Odle and the massive block-like Puéz to the south.

Many kinds of rock formation are on view. The main Val Badía running down from the north marks a boundary between the eastern and western Dolomites and displays Tertiary folding resulting from the collision of the African and European continents. As well as showing evidence of Quaternary glaciation, it boasts the San Cassiano Formation, a fossil-rich seam south of Pedráces which draws collectors from all over Europe. Also to be seen are works of natural erosion such as the yawning natural arch of the Stevía, the Col della Sonea (shaped like a volcanic cone) and any number of bizarre atria, towers and pinnacles.

Many are the other highlights: the wild Vallunga in the south, known as the most unspoiled glacially carved valley in the Dolomites; the tiny ice-cold lakes of Crespeina and Ciampac; and the immense forests on the skirts of the Odle, which once grew much higher up the mountain, as fossilized trunks in local glaciers testify.

SIRENS OF THE ROSE MOUNTAINS

Amid the peaks and forests of the Dolomites linger ancient *dramatis personae*, traceable in place names such as Sasso di Stria, the 'rock of the witches', and the Fánes plateau, supposedly named after the Regno dei Fánes, a mythical kingdom. Other intriguing local characters include the *anguane*, women of beautiful aspect but with goat's hooves, who bewitch the senses of passers-by. In some valleys they are said to be not so fair, and to frighten the shepherds. Their menfolk are the *salvans*, literally 'wild men', who sometimes come down into the villages to perform good deeds. The best way to unearth these legends is to talk to the elderly in the remotest areas, especially the Ladin-speaking valleys of Fassa, Gardena and Badía. You may hear them tell how to dusk their *monti pallidi*, pale like the moon, take on a pink tinge they call *enrosadira* — the colour, so it is said, of petrified rose gardens.

The mountains of Tofane, south of Fánes-Sénnes-Bráies, have the massive folded-block appearance typical of the eastern Dolomites.

Though centrally placed in the Dolomite region, the Puéz-Odle mountains are mostly quieter than surrounding massifs. The best approach — and starting point for many peaceful walks — is in the west: Messner's own valley, the Val di Funes. It is far wilder than the southern Val Gardena where crocodiles of walkers crowd the slopes and caterpillar coach tours grind along the so-called Grande Strada delle Dolomiti, the 'Great Dolomite Road'. A verdant mix of meadows, huge larch woods and tranquil, wooden-housed hamlets, the Val di Funes will instantly take you back to the Dolomites of a century ago.

Before you go *Maps:* Kompass 1:50,000 No. 59 *Gruppo di Sella-Marmolada*; Tabacco 1:50,000 No. 5 *Val Gardena* and 1:25,000 No. 30 *Val di Funes*.
Guide-book: Meciani, *Odle-Puéz – Dolomiti tra Gardena e Badía* (TCI, 2000).
Getting there *By car:* Val Gardena and Val di Funes from A22 (Chiusa exit); Val Badía and east from Brunico (SS244) and Cortina (SS48).
By rail: stations at Chiusa and Bressanone on Verona–Brénnero main line; also at Brunico on Fortezza–S. Candido branch line.
By bus: services from these and other centres to most villages; S.A.D., freephone T: (800) 846 047.

Where to stay *Hotels:* Grohmann (2-star), Via Sacun 12, S. Cristina, T: (0471) 793 443; Sonja (2-star), Via Meisules 59, Selva, T: (0471) 795 198; Serena (3-star), Pedráces 32, Pedráces, T: (0471) 839 664; La Villa (3-star), Str. Boscdaplan 176, La Villa, T: (0471) 847 035.
Refuges: Génova, T: (0472) 840 132; Firenze, T: (0471) 796 307; del Puéz, T: (0471) 795 365.
Outdoor living: no free camping; site at Strada Sorega 15, Corvara, T: (0471) 836 515.
Activities *Walking:* in Val di Funes, Sentiero delle Odle and (with fine views of Odle) Sentiero dei Signori; superb climb to Rif. del Puéz from Selva via Vallunga (5 hrs); traverse of massifs on Alta Via II delle Dolomiti; Alpe di Gampen to Alpe Medálghes (5

hrs); ascent of Sass de Putia from Passo delle Erbe (5 hrs). Lifts from Val Gardena useful for starting walks in south, but paths, especially S. Cristina–Rif. Firenze, often crowded.
Pony-trekking: Country Club Sankt Ulrich, Via Vidalong 2, Ortisei, T: (0471) 796 904.
Climbing: many quiet routes, some dangerous. North face of Furchetta on Odle most difficult in region; Ufficio Guide Alpine, Selva, T: (0471) 794 133.
Hang-gliding: Helmut Striker, Pedráces, T: (0471) 847 592.
Skiing: at Bressanone-Plose, T: (0472) 833 905, and Val Gardena, T: (0471) 795 397. More modest options in Val di Funes and Val Badía. Excellent cross-country in Odle forests.
Further information *Tourist offices:* Via Rezia 1, Ortisei, T: (0471) 796 328; Via Chernun 9, S. Cristina, T: (0471) 793 046; Via Meisules 213, Selva, T: (0471) 795 122; Via Micurà 24, S. Cassiano, T: (0471) 849 422. *Park office:* Via S. Pietro 11, Funes, T: (0472) 840 180.

Fánes-Sénnes-Bráies

Dolomite massifs cut by deep valleys, near Cortina d'Ampezzo; Parchi Naturali Regionali di Fánes-Sénnes-Bráies in Alto Adige (25,680 ha/63,458 acres) and delle Dolomiti d'Ampezzo in the Véneto (11,200 ha/27,676 acres)

The Fánes plateau is one of Italy's finest tracts of limestone scenery. Guarded by a ring of peaks, it nestles at the heart of the eastern Dolomites, and is one of the region's wilder areas, ignored by the Gadarene herd of tourists which presses on to Cortina, one of Italy's foremost ski resorts. Certain pockets of

astonishing scenery, such as the Lago di Bráies, caught in a cwm on the northern slopes, have their share of summer coach parties but elsewhere the roads are few and the ski resorts — lumped together at Plan de Corones — unseen.

The mountains offer stunning panoramas, especially around the Croda Rossa (3,146 m/10,321 ft), Conturines and Picco di Vallandro. Paths can be some of the Dolomites' loveliest and least travelled. The Alta Via I, the most famous of the high walks, starts at Bráies, and for less energetic hikers there are the old military tracks of the Prato Piazza, also popular with mountain-bikers. Apart from Bráies, lakes worth visiting are clustered around the Fánes refuge, for example the tiny Lago di Fánes and the Lago di Limo, dwarfed by the huge crags of the Cima Scotoni.

Although hunting is

The craggy glaciated heights above Val Comelico contrast with flower-strewn meadows lower down in the Dolomiti di Sesto.

permitted, you will still encounter shy groups of deer on some of these walks, particularly on the long silent trails through the Val di Foresta. In the high solitary wastes of the Croda Rossa, you may see sure-footed chamois leaping up impossibly awkward crags. The secret of their agility lies in their flexible cloven hooves which separate on landing, providing both shock-absorption and the grip necessary to jump on to rock ledges only 30 cm (12 in) wide without slithering off.

Another creature supremely adapted to life in these barren uplands is the mountain hare, also known as the blue, variable or Arctic hare. Similar in appearance to the brown hare, but slightly stockier and with shorter ears, it changes its coat with the seasons. During the summer its woolly fur is a brownish grey, but in winter moults to pure white — except for the black tips of the ears — helping it to blend into its surroundings.

In the higher mountains you will be accompanied by groups of alpine choughs, their yellow beaks and high-pitched whistles distinguishing them from the closely related red-billed choughs. You may also see golden eagles soaring high above the peaks, immediately recognizable by their size alone.

Before you go *Maps:* Kompass 1:50,000 Nos 57 *Brunico* and 617 *Cortina d'Ampezzo*; Tabacco 1:25,000 No. 3 *Dolomiti Ampezzane.*
Guide-book: S. Ardito, *Dolomiti di Cortina — A piedi sulle Dolomiti, vol. 1* (Iter, 2001).
Getting there *By car:* the Fánes wilderness is ringed clockwise by the SS49 from Brunico to Dobbiaco, the SS51 to Cortina, the SS48 to Passo di Falzarego and the SS244. Unclassified roads penetrate the interior from

several points on this ring.
By rail: stations at Brunico, fax only, F: (0474) 554 284, and Dobbiaco, T: (0474) 72113, on Fortezza–S. Candido branch line.
By bus: frequent buses between Brunico and Corvara, for west; between Brunico and Dobbiaco, for north (and Lago di Bráies); and between Dobbiaco and Cortina, for east (and Prato Piazza and Croda Rossa); S.A.D., freephone T: (800) 846 047.
Where to stay *Hotels:* Alte Goste (2-star), Via Goste 3, Valdáora di Sopra, T: (0474) 496 171; Fiames (1-star), Loc. Fiames 13, Cortina d'Ampezzo, T: (0436) 2366.
Refuges: Sénnes, T: (0474) 501 092; Fodara Vedla, T: (0474) 501 093; Fánes, T: (0474) 501 097; and La Varella, T: (0474) 501 069.
Outdoor living: free camping permitted for 1 night, otherwise try Camping Al Plan, S. Vigilio di Marebbe, T: (0474) 501 694.
Activities *Walking:* trails in rugged Vallone di Lagazuoi; traverse from Pederu to hamlet of Armentarola via Passo Tadega (2,157 m/7,077 ft) and trails in Val di Fánes and Val Travenánzes. Summits of peaks, unlike many in Dolomites, accessible to average walker.
Climbing: massive rock walls of Scotoni and west face of Conturines; Scuola di Alpinismo Mountain Soul, Brunico, T: (335) 213 842.
Skiing: cross-country trails in Val di Foresta and Valle di S.Vigilio; large resort in Cortina, contact tourist office for details (see below).
Further information *Tourist offices:* Via Europa 22, Brunico, T: (0474) 555 722; S. Vigilio di Marebbe, T: (0474) 501 037; Via Bráies di Fuori 78, Bráies (for Lago di Bráies), T: (0474) 748 660; Piazza S. Francesco 8, Cortina, T: (0436) 3231. *Visitor centres:* (Alto Adige) S. Vigilio, T: (0474) 506 120; (Véneto) Cortina, T: (0436) 2206.

Dolomiti di Sesto

Dolomite massif of exceptional beauty, in eastern Alto Adige; parco naturale regionale *11,635 ha (28,751 acres)*

The last of the Italian Dolomites before the Austrian border, the Dolomiti di Sesto are a small but spectacular massif close to the skiing razzmatazz of Cortina d'Ampezzo. They provide a wide variety of Dolomitic scenery and habitats within a compact area and make a fine introduction to the Dolomites if you are starting in the east.

Their highlight, the three-peaked mountain Tre Cime di Lavaredo (2,998 m/9,836 ft), is one of the most photographed sights in the Dolomites. A road to the Auronzo refuge on its southern flanks, which conservationists want closed, delivers hordes of hikers to a mass of trails and some of the region's rockiest landscapes.

For more solitary exploration head for the Val di Sesto in the north-east, often claimed to be the prettiest in the Dolomites, and its two exquisite subsidiary valleys, the Fiscalina and Campo di Dentro. You can explore the mountains equally well from Sesto or Moso. The climb to the Locatelli refuge is a Dolomite classic, while from the Comici refuge you get one of the best views in northern Italy, looking over the Cima Dodici, the 'midday summit'. One of five peaks in the Meridiana di Sesto named after hours of the day, it is so called because locals took it to be noon when the sun came over it. Other peaks in this local meridian mark 9, 10, 11 and 1 o'clock.

Two of the Dolomites' high-level paths, the Grohmann and Titian routes (Numbers 4 and 5), start in the valley, from the villages of San Candido and Sesto respectively. Either of these, indeed any trail within the Dolomiti di Sesto, quickly leaves civilization as it wends its way into the mountains. Further pastoral spots are found in the west, around the steep-sided Val di Landro, and to the south at the Lago di Misurina, one of the prettiest lakes in the region, noted for its shimmering colours, but overcrowded in summer.

The mountains of Sesto mark an evocative watershed: the Rienza drains west to the Adige and the Adriatic, the Drava east to the Danube and the Black Sea. Given the strategic importance of these mountains, close to the Austrian border, it is no surprise to come across World War I battle debris, left over from the old 1915 front. Many walks — to Monte Piana, around the Tre Cime and near the Pian di Cengia refuge — pass scenes of savage fighting.

Before you go *Maps:* Tabacco 1: 50,000 No. 1 *Cadore – Cortina d'Ampezzo* or 1:25,000 No. 10 *Dolomiti di Sesto*; Kompass 1:50,000 Nos 57 *Brunico – Dobbiaco* and 58 *Dolomiti di Sesto*.
Guide-books: P. Bonetti & P. Lazzarin, *Il grande libro dei sentieri selvaggi* (Zanichelli, 2000); *Guida vacanze Alto Adige estate inverno* (TCI, 1998).
Getting there *By car:* A22 from Bolzano (Bressanone exit) and then SS49 along Val Pusteria to Dobbiaco and S. Candido. From Cortina, SS51 to Dobbiaco or SS48 for Misurina and Rif. Auronzo.
By rail: at Fortezza on Bolzano–Brénnero line take branch to S. Candido; stations at Dobbiaco, T: (0474) 72113, and

S. Candido, T: (0474) 731 334 (12 trains daily, 7 direct from Bolzano).
By bus: from Bolzano to Brunico, then on to Dobbiaco. From here, to Cortina (5 daily) or S. Candido, Sesto and Moso (8 daily); S.A.D., T: (0474) 554 600.
Where to stay *Hotels:* Villa Stefania (3-star), Via Duca Tassilo 16, S. Candido, T: (0474) 913 588; Wiesenhof (3-star), Via Monte Elmo 6, Sesto, T: (0474) 710 381.
Agriturismo: Villa Waldruhe, Loc. Carbonin Vecchia 2, Dobbiaco, T: (0474) 972 354; Hirschenhof, Loc. Valle S. Silvestro 57, Dobbiaco, T: (0474) 979 079.
Refuges: Locatelli, T: (0474) 972 002; Comici, T: (0474) 710 358; Auronzo, T: (0435) 99179.
Outdoor living: only at organized sites, such as Olympia, 2 km (1 mile) from Dobbiaco, T: (0474) 972 147, and Sesto camp-site in Moso, T: (0474) 710 444 (May–Oct).
Activities *Walking:* Valle Fiscalina–Rif. Comici (Trail 103)–Rif. Locatelli (Trail

101)–Valle Fiscalina (Trail 102, 7 hrs); Rif. Auronzo–Rif. Locatelli (Trail 101)–Rif. Auronzo (Trail 105, 4 hrs), Lago di Misurina–Rif. Fonda Savio (Trail 115 and difficult descent by Trail 117, 4 hrs); Lago di Landro–Monte Piana (2,324 m/ 7,625 ft), with superb views of Sesto and Cristallo massifs (Trail 6, 4 hrs).
Cycling: numerous trails, including amazing Alta Via della Pusteria, Dobbiaco–Lienz (43 km/27 miles). Hiring points: Strobl, Dobbiaco, T: (0474) 979 065, or Papin, S. Candido, T: (0474) 913 450.
Skiing: Alta Pusteria has Dolomites' finest cross-country routes (200 km/125 miles), including disused railway from Dobbiaco to Cortina (35 km/22 miles); lifts and pistes in Alta Pusteria, T: (0474) 710 355. Valle Fiscalina and Campo di Dentro provide more routes.
Further information *Tourist offices:* Dobbiaco, T: (0474) 972 132; S. Candido, T: (0474) 913 149; Sesto, T: (0474) 710 3100.

The mountain hare is well adapted to conditions in the Alps and Dolomites; at the onset of winter its brownish grey fur turns white.

CHAPTER 3

The Venetian Plain and Eastern Alps

Italy's north-eastern corner is a naturalist's dream and a politician's nightmare. The country's most extensive lagoons make it a bird-watching Mecca, and inland, where the Alps make their final bow, you can uncover some of the wildest, most beautiful parts of Italy.

For centuries this whole area has been the hottest of political hot potatoes. Today the meeting point of three international borders, it has been a crossroads of trade and peoples since prehistory. Italy, Austria and Slovenia meet at a point of passage used in the past by Celts, Romans, Avars, Istrians, Lombards, Slavs, Byzantines, Venetians, Friulians, Hungarians and, most unhappily for the Italians, by the Barbarians — the Goths and Vandals — who poured through a breach in the eastern Alps to close the book on the Roman Empire.

All these peoples left their mark on the landscape, the Austrians most noticeably in the Véneto and Friuli, which they ruled until 1866, and the Slavs in Venezia Giulia, where a border settlement with Yugoslavia was not reached until 1975. Walkers will find the most obvious evidence of past political passions in the area around the Italian skiing capital of Cortina d'Ampezzo, which remained in Austrian hands as late as 1919. This part of the northern Véneto contains some of the great Dolomite massifs —

Remote and picturesque, the Laghi di Fusine create open vistas among the forests of the Alpi Giulie.

Cristallo, Marmolada, Civetta — and during World War I it saw some of the most savage fighting that can ever have taken place in an area of high wilderness. The front line ran along the highest ridges, traces of it still visible, and stories are told to this day of the extraordinary feats performed by men condemned to fight on rock, ice and snow.

Today the wild traveller can ride freely over borders that have tested and exposed the folly of politicians for centuries. A trip from west to east will take you round to the Balkan peninsula and down to Trieste, no passport required. From north to south, you will pass in a few miles from the mountains of central Europe to the lagoons of Venice, crossing not only cultural boundaries but also four different landscape zones.

A backdrop of mountains curtains the whole of north-east Italy. As the Alps taper off towards Slovenia and the Hungarian plains, they share out their final ridges between the Véneto and Friuli-Venezia Giulia. The northern Véneto claims the last and highest of the Dolomite massifs, the old World War I battlegrounds invaded now by winter holiday-makers. Friuli picks up the thread where the Dolomites give way to the lower and narrower chains of the eastern Alps. The most extensive of these are the Cárniche which run for some 200 kilometres (120 miles) along the Austrian border. They take their name from the area in which they rise, the Cárnia, a wilderness largely devoid of roads or habitation. Tacked on to the very end, as Italy's scenic finale, are the Alpi Giulie.

One level down from the Alps lies a landscape zone known as the pre-Alps, a bland misnomer that does little justice to the gorgeous and almost entirely overlooked pockets of wilderness that you can find there. In the Véneto, the Belluno Dolomites are lower but also quieter and wilder than their northern counterparts. Together with the botanically rich Baldo and Lessini mountains to the south-west and the Cansíglio plateau — the region's largest area of ancient woodland — just to the east, these areas provide much needed protection for the local fauna, which is some of the most impoverished in the country.

Between the mountains and the coast lies an area that is something of a vacuum for foreign visitors. Few people have any idea what happens between Venice and Trieste. The answer is huge areas of flat land, which in Friuli have been compared to the American Mid-West, and which in the Véneto count as one of the most densely populated parts of Italy.

Running to the sea over the plains of both regions are the rivers that have done so much to shape the Adriatic coastline: the Po, Adige, Brenta, Piave, Tagliamento and Isonzo. Vast areas around the mouths of these rivers, the Po particularly, have been progressively lost to land reclamation and poisoned by effluent, but a surprising amount of wild country remains.

Along the great arc of coastline shared by the Véneto and Friuli-Venezia Giulia stretches an almost unbroken belt of marsh and lagoon. From the Po delta, this flat wind-swept landscape takes you across the famous Venetian lagoons, through the lesser-known and less-polluted Marano wetlands, and then curves round the northern Adriatic before rising to modest cliffs on the last leg down to Trieste. For birds in their millions, these lagoons and wetlands continue to be aquatic stepping stones on the Adriatic migration route to and from central Europe.

For the most exciting wildlife you must go to the Alpi Giulie and the Tarvísio forests in the farthest-flung corner of north-east Italy. If truth be told, the richness of fauna here has less to do with Italy than with Slovenia, for it is from the wilderness over the border that most of the finest animals have strayed. Something similar can be said of another area of Venezia Giulia, the Carso. This tongue of limestone connecting Trieste with the rest of Italy provides a fantastically complex habitat for flora and fauna that owe their characteristics as much to central Europe and the Balkans as to Italy.

BEFORE YOU GO
Guide-books: E. Cipriani, *A piedi nel Véneto* (Iter, 1999); *Guide dei monti d'Italia* (CAI, 2000).

GETTING THERE
By air: the area is well served by international airports including Venice's Marco Polo, T: (041) 260 6111, and Trieste's Ronchi dei Legionari, T: (0481) 773 224, as well as Verona, T: (045) 809 5666, and Treviso, T: (0422) 315 131/315 331.
By car: motorways link Verona, Vicenza, Padua and Venice. For the northern wilder parts of the Véneto the main routes are the A27 (Venice–Belluno) and the SS51 (Belluno–Cortina d'Ampezzo and the Dolomites), in Friuli-Venezia Giulia the A4 (Venice–Trieste) and the A23 (Udine–Tarvísio). The SS52 joins the northern halves of the two regions.
By rail: the main lines are Milan–Verona–Venice, Venice–Udine, Venice–Trieste and Udine–Tarvísio–Vienna. Useful branch lines from Padua and Venice to Belluno and Calalzo serve the northern Véneto; contact Ufficio Informazioni dei Treni, freephone T: (1478) 88088 within Italy, otherwise visit www.fs-on-line.it or www.trenitalia.com.

WHERE TO STAY
You should have no accommodation problems except in remote areas of

Europe's most famous alpine wild flower, the edelweiss grows in limestone pastures at up to 3,400 m (11,000 ft), flowering in late summer.

northern Friuli, such as the Alpi Giulie and the Cárnia wilderness.

ACTIVITIES
Walking: La Grande Traversata Cárnica runs from S. Candido in Alto Adige to Tarvísio. There are 12 other long-distance routes linking Cárnia with Carinthia in the Austrian Alps, collectively known as the Via delle Malghe Cárniche.
Caving: CAI, Via S. Toscana 11, Verona, T: (045) 803 0555, Galleria S. Bernardino 5, Padua, T: (049) 875 0842 and Via Battisti 22, Trieste, T: (040) 635 500.
Fishing: FIPSAS, Via Mezzaterra 96, Belluno, T: (0437) 944 854

and Via dei Macelli 5, Treviso, T: (0422) 40695.
Bird-watching: LIPU, Via Isonzo 10, Treviso, T: (0422) 260 162, or visit www.lipu.it.

FURTHER INFORMATION
Tourist offices: Via Psaro 21, Belluno, T: (0437) 940 083; Piazza Primo Maggio 7, Udine, T: (0432) 295 972; Via Diaz 16, Gorizia, T: (0481) 533870; Piazza Erbe 38, Verona, T: (045) 806 8680, www.verona-apt.net; Riviera Mugnai 8, Padua, T: (049) 875 2077; Via Rossini 6, Trieste, T: (040) 365 152.
Ecology: WWF, Via Chiodi 6, Verona, T: (045) 594 872 and Via Barini 11, Udine, T: (0432) 507 895.

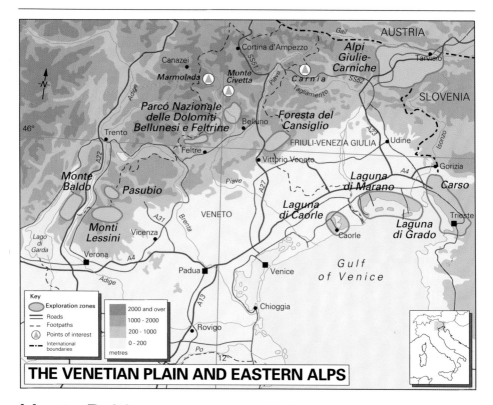

THE VENETIAN PLAIN AND EASTERN ALPS

Monte Baldo

Limestone range on the border of Trentino and the Véneto, renowed for its flora and exceptional views; includes five small riserve naturali (5,414 ha/13,378 acres)

Monte Baldo's ridges run for nearly 40 kilometres (25 miles) along the eastern coast of Lake Garda, cutting a fine profile as they rise sheer from the lake shore to Cima Telegrafo and Cima Valdritta, both over 2,000 metres (6,500 feet). The summits form a natural belvedere on to much of north-east Italy, with heart-rending views across the lake (camp here just for the sunsets) and broad panoramas stretching to the distant Adamello massif and the Brenta

Dolomites. Yet it is not for these dramatic heights that the area is renowed, nor even for the shimmering plays of light over the lake, but for the immense botanical diversity which, as early as the 16th century, had earned it the title Hortus Italiae, the 'garden of Italy'.

Monte Baldo owes its tremendous range of species to two main factors. The first is its wide geological variation. Baldo is mostly limestone, but this is broken up by basaltic lavas, fossil-rich seams and more than 60 different types of marble, which around Brentonicó, in the north-east, have weathered to produce famous red, yellow and green soils. The other factor is Baldo's broad range of microclimates. While the highest peaks have a distinctively alpine feel, covered in snow in winter and scorched by the sun in summer, the lower slopes are subject to the benign influence of Lake Garda. The lake, which has frozen over only once in

66

recorded history (in 1701), acts as a natural greenhouse, its shores a sun-warmed mix of olive and lemon trees, palms, cypress and cedars.

Baldo's morphology is also highly varied: the slopes facing east to the Adige river are rounded and pastoral, whereas the lake-side slopes are steep and cut by glacial cirques. During the Ice Ages the highest ridges stood out above the huge glacier that enveloped the area and as a result remained unmodified by ice. Their plant populations survived, isolated from their nearest neighbours for several millennia. Not surprisingly, endemic species evolved, many of which bear the epithet *baldense* or *baldensis* to indicate their status: the bedstraw *Galium baldense*, the reddish-purple flowered scabious *Knautia baldensis* and the distinctive sedge *Carex baldensis*, whose flattish silvery heads are surrounded by two or three leafy bracts.

Other plants are labelled with this specific name because they were first discovered on Monte Baldo. Perhaps the best known of these is the Monte Baldo anemone *(Anemone baldensis)*, whose blue-white flowers, up to 4 centimetres (1½ inches) in diameter, were later found in other parts of the Alps and in the mountains of former Yugoslavia.

From spring onwards, the grassy slopes of Monte Baldo display a variety of alpine flowers. Some of the rarest include the spectacular primrose *(Primula spectabilis)*, easily identified even when not in flower by the white horny rim round each leaf; the single-flowered cushion saxifrage *(Saxifraga burserana)*, with tiny cushions of pin-like, blue-green leaves and solitary white flowers up to three centimetres (one inch) across; the beautiful reddish-purple blooms of the large-flowered catchfly *(Silene elisabetha)*; and the gracious, yellow-white spherical heads of the rock bellflower *(Campanula petrea)*.

Monte Baldo possesses trees reputed to bring luck and springs said to have aphrodisiac qualities. Such myths may have a basis in the mountain's many medicinal plants, a natural pharmacy which attracts herbalists from all over the world. The violet-flowered monkshood *(Aconitum compactum)* contains many alkaloids that, although poisonous, have found use in homoeopathic medicine to reduce fever and rheumatism. Mezeron *(Daphne mezerum)* bark has been used effectively in the treatment of snake-bite and chewing slices of the root is said to cure toothache.

The range of animal life to be found on Monte Baldo, like the plants, reflects the variety of habitats. The summits are home to typical mountain birds such as black grouse, rock partridge, alpine choughs, ravens and water pipits; local naturalists have reported the return of the golden eagle. The thick vegetation that clothes the sunnier slopes is alive with bird-song in the spring, its more notable inhabitants including melodious warblers, wrynecks, red-starts and red-backed shrikes. Conifer woods provide a haven for nutcrackers, nightjars and tawny owls, while thousands of common and alpine swifts gather over Lake Garda during migration, providing food for the occasional passing hobby.

Substantial herds of roe-deer inhabit the more thickly vegetated areas, while brown bears occasionally stray into the region from the Trentino parks in the north. Marmots were reintroduced thirty years ago and are now widespread on the higher ridges, together with around 400 chamois. Plans are also under way to reintroduce red deer to the woodlands; so far they have only been sighted when migrating. Green lizards, wall lizards and slow-worms are typical denizens of the warmer slopes, while small pools and slow-moving streams near the summits contain populations of alpine newts, distinguished from those found in the rest of Europe by their heavily spotted throats and bright red bellies.

With its lake views, its spring and summer flowers and its rich variety of animal life, Baldo is one of the Véneto's most popular pre-Alpine chains. In summer the Malcésine funicular brings hordes of tourists and walkers up from the lake shores to tramp the well-worn ridge path. But if you come off-season, or avoid this black-spot altogether, you will have only the views and blustery wind for company.

The elegant green lizard, most at home in dense vegetation, climbs expertly in search of large invertebrates, fruit and even the eggs and young of small birds. The male are bright green, the females usually brownish.

BEFORE YOU GO

Map: Kompass 1:50,000 No. 102 *Lago di Garda – Monte Baldo*.
Guide-book: E. Turri, *Il Monte Baldo* (Cierre, 1999).

GETTING THERE

By car: from Verona, leave the A4 at Peschiera del Garda and take the SS249 up Lake Garda's eastern shore to Malcésine; minor roads lead into the interior. For the eastern side of Monte Baldo, take the A22 towards Bolzano and turn off at Avio for the Lastoni-Selva Pezzi reserve, or Lago di Garda Nord for the Gardesana Orientale reserve (see Ecology below).
By rail: there is a station at Peschiera del Garda, T: (045) 755 0028, on the Milan–Verona main line; for stations along the Adige valley, take stopping trains (every hour) on the Verona–Bolzano line.
By bus: services run all round Lake Garda and up the Adige valley from Verona to Rovereto. Contact Garda tourist office (see below).

WHERE TO STAY

Hotels: you have a vast choice on Garda, or try Leon d'Oro (4-star), Via Tacchi 2, Rovereto, T: (0464) 437 333 (closed Feb); if you prefer smaller towns, aim for Zeni (3-star), Via Roma 16, Brentonico, T: (0464) 395 125; Al Cacciatore (1-star), Loc.

Cambrigar, Ferrara di Monte Baldo, T: (045) 624 7163.
Refuges: try Telegrafo, T: (045) 773 1797 (summer)/724 1531 (winter); Novezza, T: (045) 624 7022 (summer)/724 1481 (winter, no overnight stays); Fiore del Baldo, T: (045) 686 2477. For others, contact tourist offices or CAI, Stradone Maffei 8, Verona, T: (045) 803 0555.
Outdoor living: Mamma Lucia, S. Zeno di Montagna, T: (045) 728 5038 (open May–Sept); La Rocca, Bardolino, T: (045) 721 1111 (open Apr–Sept); or visit www.aptgardaveneto.com.

ACTIVITIES

Walking: steep climbs from Garda can be avoided by using the funicular at Malcésine, although in summer you won't be alone. The most popular walk is the ridge path overlooking the lake. It runs south from the Malcésine funicular, via Cima Valdritta (2,218 m/7,277 ft) to Rif. Telegrafo (5 hrs, red-white markings). There are quieter trails on Baldo's northern and eastern flanks. Walks from the east side go from Ferrara di Monte Baldo to Punta di Náole (2 hrs); from Rif. Novezzina to Rif. Telegrafo (3 hrs); from Avio in the Adige valley to Rif. Telegrafo via the Cavallo di Novezza pass (5 hrs).
Cycling: many old military

roads offer excellent routes. Bikes can be rented from Due Ruote, Corso Italia, Garda, T: (045) 627 0420; or Scooter Bike, Via Don Gnocchi 36, Garda, T: (347) 894 4605 (open Apr–Oct).
Watersports: Tórbole at Garda's northern tip is the lake's main wind-surfing centre. Try Surf Centre Lido Blù, T: (0464) 506 349, or Surf Segnana, T: (0464) 505 963 (both open Apr–Oct).
Skiing: Brentonico has a small resort. Contact the tourist office, T: (0464) 395 149. Another is above Malcésine; contact Monte Baldo cable-car, T: (045) 740 0206. Cross-country routes exist around Prada and Ferrara di Monte Baldo.
Ecology: the only environmental protection on Monte Baldo is afforded by five tiny reserves, including Gardesana Orientale, a sanctuary for Mediterranean relict plants near the shore of the lake; Bes-Cornapiana, near Navene; and Lastoni-Selva Pezzi, which protects the mountain species. Elsewhere, in the view of some experts, tourists have upset the natural equilibrium. WWF, Via General A. Cantore, Caprino Veronese, T: (045) 623 0084, runs excursions and work camps on Monte Baldo.

FURTHER INFORMATION

Tourist offices: Giardini di Porta Orientale, Riva del Garda, T: (0464) 554 444; Via Capitanato 6, Malcésine, T: (045) 740 0044; Via Don Gnocchi 37, Garda, T: (045) 627 0384.

Monti Lessini and Pasubio

Small massifs in the Véneto, just north of Verona; includes parco naturale regionale *(10,368 ha/25,620 acres)*
7PS

I first saw the Lessini mountains, or *le piccole Dolomiti* as they are nicknamed, while travelling north from Verona to Bolzano. Primed as you are on this journey to reach the Dolomites, it comes as a surprise to encounter Dolomitic-looking mountains while still no further north than Lake Garda. If you stop off here, you will find an area of tortuous ridge and valley relief and complex geology. The natural bridge at Veja, the ravines at the Spluga della Preta and the Valle delle Sfingi (the 'valley of the Sphinxes'), strewn with massive blocks of

red limestone, are some of the exhibits on view in this giant open-air museum of erosion.

Of similar, though wilder, character is the adjoining little massif of Pasubio to the north-east, which reaches a respectable height of 2,235 m (7,332 ft). There are many who would like to see this extraordinary karstic landscape made into a national park; it is already a *zona sacra*, a sacred memorial to the dead of World War I — like the main Dolomite massifs further north, the territory was a bitterly contested battlefield.

Mixed in among these dramatic rock-scapes are meadows alive with wild flowers including Alpine lilies — the red and the martagon — and narcissi and edelweiss. There is also a great range of woodlands, home to the black woodpecker, pygmy owl, rock partridge, golden and short-toed eagles, ptarmigan, black grouse, honey buzzard and the eagle owl.
Before you go *Map:* Kompass 1:50,000 No. 100 *Monti Lessini – Recoaro Terme.*
Getting there *By car:* minor

roads feed north from Verona into Lessini. For Pasubio, take A22 to Rovereto, then SS46 across massif; Pasubio is also accessible from the east, via A31 from Vicenza.
By rail: stations at Ala, T: (0464) 671 063, and Rovereto, T: (0464) 433 644, on Verona–Bolzano line.
Where to stay *Hotel:* Croce (1-star), Via Croce 2, Bosco Chiesanuova, T: (045) 705 0042. *Outdoor living:* several camp-sites, including Fanton, Via Recoaro Mille 43, Recoaro Terme, T: (0445) 77139; Branchetti, Bosco Chiesanuova, T: (045) 678 4029; and Camposilvano, Velo Veronese, T: (045) 783 5658.
Activities *Walking:* many footpaths, old military roads and marked trails; contact CAI, Via S. Toscana 11, Verona, T: (045) 803 0555 or C.da Porta S. Lucia 95, Vicenza, T: (0444) 513 012.
Further information *Tourist offices:* Via Dante 63, Rovereto, T: (0464) 430 363; Piazza della Chiesa, Bosco Chiesanuova, T: (045) 705 0088.

Dolomiti Bellunesi e Feltrine

Most southerly and least known of the Dolomites, in the Véneto and within striking distance of Venice; parco nazionale
32,000 ha (79,075 acres)
Includes ZPS

Belluno's Dolomites are a disjoint group of massifs that form the Alps' final rocky curtain before the Véneto plains and 'civilization' to the south. They have been described as a living nature encyclopaedia,

and are protected by a national park that runs in an arc above the Piave valley between Feltre and Belluno.

In a coronet above Feltre lie the peaks of the Vette Feltrine, gathered around Monte Pavione (2,334 metres/7,657 feet). Moving north-eastwards you come to the upland plateaux of the Piani Eterni, the 'eternal plains'; and finally the wildest areas, the Monti del Sole, the 'mountains of the sun', and the Schiara Occidentale, dominated by Monte Schiara (2,563 metres/8,409 feet). Each of these heights is divided from the next by a series of deep valleys: the Valle di Canzoi, the Canale del Mis and the Canale di Ágordo.

Although they are the lowest of the outlying ranges, definitely a notch below their cousins to the north, the Bellunesi are not a poor man's Dolomites. They are full of wild places for those in search of mountain respite, and they are only an hour or two from the beautiful bedlam of Venice. Some parts may share the circus atmosphere of the northern playgrounds, around Monte Schiara's busy VII Alpini refuge, for example, but mostly these mountains are wild and unvisited. Roads rarely venture on to high ground, too busy linking the little villages in the Piave valley below. Paths are long and lonely, free from the over-zealous route-marking that directs the regimented hordes in the Dolomite heartlands. When you want them, you can find cosy refuges like the Feltrine's Dal Piaz hut, a throwback to the Dolomite hiking traditions of a century ago. And if you miss the refuges, you may yet stumble across the ancient sheep-pens known as *pendane*, long-standing memorials to the area's pastoral tradition, and the *malghe*, former dairies and animal shelters now used (if at all) by stranded walkers.

These paths and huts allow unlimited excursions into the high mountains: to the wild valleys in the Schiara, for those with a passion for the worst nature can throw at them; to the limestone wastes and glacial cirques, or *buse*, of the Vette Feltrine; to Monte Pizzocco below the cave-riddled Piani Eterni, a peak whose 800-metre (2,600-foot) ramparts have been compared to the Matterhorn; to the Gusela del Vescovà, a rock needle below Monte Pizzocco, beloved of many Alpine climbers; to the great gorges of the Ardo and Orrido di Val Clusa; or to the tranquil, intimate Lago della Stua, hidden away in the Canzoi valley.

The Bellunesi are well endowed with wild flowers. The typical upland forests of fir and pine and the sunnier mixed woodlands of the south, interspersed with rich meadows, host more than 1,500 species of plants. Spring heralds the appearance of such delightful flowers as the *Iris cengialti*, endemic to north-east Italy and particularly abundant on Monte San Mauro; its close relative the grassy-leaved iris *(Iris graminea)*, with its distinctive peach-plum perfume; and the beautiful, highly scented yellow lily *Hemerocallis*

lilioasphodelus, which is found only in the foothills of the south-eastern Alps. Rarities include the Alpine bluebell *Campanula morettiana*, which was chosen as the park's symbol, or *Alyssum ovirense*, an endemic plant that grows in isolated crags and blossoms with cushions of tiny yellow flowers at the beginning of the summer.

Two characteristic amphibians, the alpine newt and the alpine salamander, are found here, together with several of peninsular Italy's 15 species of snake. Both adder and asp are poisonous, but there is no more chance of receiving a fatal snake-bite than of being struck by lightning. It goes without saying that you should avoid walking barefoot or in open shoes through areas inhabited by venomous snakes.

Eagle owls and pygmy owls haunt the forests, together with capercaillie, hazel grouse and grey-headed woodpeckers, while the more open areas above the tree-line support black grouse and rock partridges. Birds of prey include up to five pairs of golden eagles and five or six pairs of black kites, as well as honey buzzards. The lower slopes often attract short-toed eagles; they are the only large birds of prey (they have a wing-span of around 1½ metres/5 feet) to hover like kestrels while hunting. They feed mainly on snakes and lizards and can sometimes be seen flying along with the tail of one of these half-swallowed reptiles trailing from their beak.

Larger animals are enjoying something of a renaissance. Hunting, as always in Italy, was the problem in the past, as you will gather if you visit the Palazzo Crepadona in the centre of Belluno, where a locally found Roman sarcophagus depicts a hunting scene involving deer and wild boar. Both animals still survive; the bear and the lynx, which disappeared more than a century ago, have now returned from the north and east. Chamois and roe-deer are widespread; the red deer population is rising and mouflon numbers are stable. Ibex, which at the end of the 19th century survived only in the Gran Paradiso, have been reintroduced to many other parts of the Alps and it is possible that a number will be released in the Dolomiti Bellunesi as well.

BEFORE YOU GO
Map: Tabacco 1:25,000 Nos
23 *Alpi Feltrine – Le Vette* and
24 *Prealpi e Dolomiti
Bellunesi*.
Guide-books: T. Soppelsa,
*Escursioni nel Parco Nazionale
delle Dolomiti Bellunesi*
(Cierre, 2000); C. Cima, *Andar
per sentieri in Véneto* (De
Agostini, 1989); C. Lasen,
*Guida botanica delle Dolomiti
di Belluno* (Manfrini, 1977).

GETTING THERE
By car: for Belluno take A27
up from Treviso, or SS51
down from Cortina
d'Ampezzo. Feltre and
Belluno are connected by SS50
which runs parallel to the
park. Minor roads from this
serve the Valle di Canzoi and
Valle del Mis; take SS203 for
the Monti del Sole and
Schiara Occidentale.
By rail: Feltre and Belluno
stations are on the Padua–
Calalzo di Cadore line. From
Venice 5 trains a day run direct
to Belluno; otherwise change at
Conegliano on the Venice–
Udine line; contact Feltre
station, T: (0439) 2317.

By bus: you can reach all the
villages round the park (though
not the park itself) from Feltre
and Belluno. Contact Dolomiti
Bus, Piazzale della Stazione,
Belluno, T: (0437) 941 237/941
167.

WHERE TO STAY
Hotels: L'Albergo Nuovo (3-
star), Via Fornere Pazze 5,
Feltre (a lovely place to stay),
T: (0439) 89241; Mirella (3-
star), Via Don Minzoni 6,
Belluno, T: (0437) 941 860.
Agriturismo: Meneguz, Loc.
Arson 113, Feltre, T: (0439)
42136; Sass de Mura, Val
Canzoi, Cesiomaggiore, T:
(0439) 43143.
Refuges: contact CAI, Porta
Imperiale 3, Feltre, T: (0439)
9065 and Piazza S. Giovanni
Bosco 11, Belluno, T: (0437)
931 655.
Outdoor living: camp-sites
include Gaiole, Loc. Soravigo,
Arsiè (15 km/10 miles from
Feltre on SS50 towards
Trento), T: (0439) 58505
(Apr–Sept), and Park Camping
Nevegál, Via Nevegál 347,
Belluno, T: (0437) 908 143
(open all year).

A riot of wild flowers carpets the
Pian del Gat in the Dolomiti
Bellunesi.

ACTIVITIES
Walking: the most popular walk
is from Rif. Gioz to Rif. VII
Alpini in the Schiara (3 hrs);
otherwise the trails are some of
the quietest in the Dolomites.
Pony-trekking: there are stables
in many areas; contact the
Associazione Turismo Equestre
Feltrino at the tourist office in
Feltre, T: (0439) 977 011. Treks
are also organized by the
Comando Forestale at
Cellarda, T: (0439) 89520.
Bird-watching: LIPU, Via
Tempietto 128, Belluno, T:
(0437) 752 023.

FURTHER INFORMATION
Tourist offices: Piazza Trento e
Trieste 9, Feltre, T: (0439) 2540;
Via Psaro 21, Belluno, T:
(0437) 940 083.
Park office: Piazzale Zancanaro
1, Feltre, T: (0439) 3328, or
visit www.dolomitipark.it.
Visitor centre: Piazza I
Novembre 1, Pedavena, T:
(0439) 304 400 (open
weekends).

Bosco del Cansíglio

The Véneto's largest ancient forest, between Belluno and Vittório Véneto; contains six riserve naturali statali (6,570 ha/16,230 acres)
ZPS

Travelling south from Belluno, you quickly run out of wilderness. The forest of Cansíglio, stretched across the plateau east of the Lago di San Croce, is the last wild place you will encounter before reaching the sea. Nothing of note lies beyond it save the plains of the Véneto.

One of only a handful of big 'historic forests', as the Italians call their relict woodlands, Cansíglio was once much bigger. To the Venetians it was the 'wood of oars', the timber being used to equip the galleys of the Republic. From 1550 to 1830 it was reduced from 57,000 to 14,000 ha (140,800 to 34,600 acres), and under Austrian ownership it was further whittled down to barely half that. Though still run as a commercial forest, it happily enjoys a hunting ban and lavish conservation care.

Two-thirds of the trees are beech, pure forests of which are relatively rare in the Alps; the rest are pine. Peace can be found both in the forest and in the amphitheatre of Dolomitic mountains which cradle the plateau to the north, culminating in Monte Cavallo (2,250 m/7,382 ft). Over 600 roe-deer share this tranquillity, along with 450 red deer that have escaped forest 'acclimatization' reserves.

Long summer strolls should bring you in sight of many forest birds, including black woodpecker, black grouse and capercaillie. Raptors such as black kite, sparrow-hawk, buzzard and short-toed eagle live at the higher altitudes.

Being karstic terrain, the region is known for its caves. The Bus de la Lum (180 m/590 ft deep), the 'hole of the light' in local patois, takes its name from the flames that were seen flickering from its entrance, fuelled, it is believed, by rotting animal carcasses thrown into it during an epidemic. The Bus della Genziana (580 m/1,902 ft deep) is the only known home of the beetle *Consiliella toniello paoletti* and the millipede *Typhloiulus ausugi gentianae*. Partly because of the presence of these endemic species, it was made Italy's first speleological reserve in 1991.

Before you go *Map:* IGM 1:50,000 No. 64 *Farra d'Alpago.*
Guide-book: G. Spada & V. Tonniello, *Il Cansíglio* (Tamari, 1987); E. Sartor, *Il Cansíglio in bicicletta* (Tamari, 1996).
Getting there *By car:* from south, exit A27 at Fadalto-Lago di S. Croce. From north, minor roads lead to forest off SS51.
By rail: all trains on Venice–Calalzo line stop at Vittório Véneto, T: (0438) 57243, and Ponte nelle Alpi.
Where to stay *Hotels:* Locanda S. Lorenzo (3-star), Via IV Novembre 75, Puos d'Alpago, T: (0437) 454 048; All'Alba (3-star), Loc. Tambruz, Tambre, T: (0437) 439 700.
Agriturismo: Dal Borgo, Via S. Giustina 114, Pieve d'Alpago, T: (0437) 478 351; Malga Cate, Via Villanova, Chies d'Alpago, T: (0437) 454 199/(337) 214 508.
Outdoor living: Sarathei, Farra d'Alpago, T: (0437) 46996.
Activities *Walking:* marked nature trails.
Riding: Co-op. Monte Cavallo, Col Indes, near Tambre, T: (0437) 439 615.
Skiing: alpine and cross-country, Scuola Italiana Sci Cansíglio, Piano del Cansíglio, T: (0438) 585 398.
Further information *Tourist offices:* Via Psaro 21, Belluno, T: (0437) 940 083; Piazza XI Gennaio 1945, Tambre, T: (0437) 49277; Piazza del Popolo, Vittório Véneto, T: (0438) 57243; also visitor centre and botanical garden at Piano del Cansíglio, T: (0438) 585 301.

Alpi Giulie-Cárniche

Rugged mountain chains in the eastern Alps, where Friuli meets Austria and Slovenia; includes Parco Naturale Regionale delle Prealpi Giulie (9,400 ha/23,200 acres)

🐾🐾🐾

Mention the Alps, and most people think of Mont Blanc or the Matterhorn. Few would opt for the Julian or Carnic Alps. They may not be household names, but that does not stop them from being some of the finest ranges in Italy. The Cárniche to the north, running along the Austrian border, have the more rounded relief and humbler heights, at around 2,000

metres (6,500 feet). The Giulie to the south boast more familiar Alpine profiles and the more impressive heights, rising to 2,753 metres (9,032 feet) at Iôf di Montasio. But size is not their defining characteristic.

What sets them apart is something else. An ineffable air of romance hangs over these small, wonderfully explorable areas of wilderness, prompted in part by their Nordic appearance and in part by their geographical position. This is one of the most continental and thus coldest corners of the Alps, chilled by Siberian winters. Average snow-fall is 4 to 5 metres (13 to 16 feet) a year (10 metres in 1951!), and permanent snow lies as low as 2,000 metres, a thousand lower than in the western Alps, so walkers can expect the crisp crunch of snow underfoot.

An early morning mist *(overleaf)* hangs in the Alpi Cárniche, on Italy's north-eastern border with Austria.

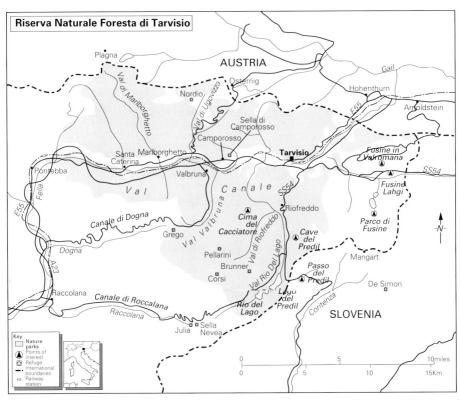

Riserva Naturale Foresta di Tarvisio

73

More, this romance comes from the proximity of the east, from the feeling that you are on the threshold of a divide far greater than international boundaries. Imagine that you are standing on the bridge at Tarvísio, the very centre of the region. In the time-honoured fashion of children everywhere, you drop a stick into the river. This stick, in childish imagination at least, will make its way down the Bártolo, the Gail and Drava tributaries to the Danube and eventually to the Black Sea. Now walk a short way up the road and drop another stick into the Fella. This small homage will float the other way, bobbing and weaving via the Tagliamento until it reaches the Adriatic and the Mediterranean.

Tarvísio is a dividing line in other ways. It lies in the Val Canale which not only separates the two mountain chains but is the gap through which the Barbarians entered Italy in the dying days of the Roman Empire. Here you are in frontier country politically as well as geographically, the inauspicious meeting point of four cultures where Friulians, Slavs and Austro-Hungarians have fought Italians for centuries.

Up in the mountains the tree cover displays frontier aspects too. The forests are some of the most famous in the Alps, huge and elemental seas of firs, often burdened with snow, which evoke the unfelled primal wilderness of Russia and the far north. Elsewhere sunnier montane species shine through, mixed broad-leaved woods which present a much more temperate European appearance.

In spite of the harsh winters, some marvellous varieties of flowers spring up here. They include alpine staples such as edelweiss and gentians, as well as more localized species such as the one-flowered cushion saxifrage *(Saxifraga burserana)*, the carnic lily *(Lilium carniolicum)* and the dainty figwort *Wulfenia carinthiaca*. Among Italy's rarest blooms, this blue-flowered wonder grows in the meadows of the Passo di Pramollo, the 'damp field pass', above Pontebba in the western Cárniche. To find it elsewhere you would have to visit Albania or the Himalayas.

If the Cárniche take the floral honours,

the Giulie have the edge when it comes to scenery. Their spectacular profiles bear the classic alpine hallmark of glacial friction, with knife-edge ridges of splintered limestone and towering rock walls like those at the north face of Mangart (2,677 metres/8,782 feet), where you will find some of the Alps' most demanding climbs.

Walks in the area, though short and simple, are some of Italy's most enchanting. Paths lead along the breathtaking U-shaped valley of the Dogna, a huge gash through the grandeur of the Giulie, or to the huge cwm at the head of the Valbruna. Another notable walk takes you to Masso Pirona and Masso Marinelli which are recognized as the Alps' largest erratic rocks. Nearby are the Laghi di Fusine, a draw for any lover of the wild and largely unknown even to Italians. A pair of glacial lakes, picturesque beyond words, they are framed by the soaring walls of Mangart and surrounded by forest stretching as far as the eye can see.

The Cárniche and Giulie mountains are wild enough to attract lynx and brown bears which have strayed from their prolific communities in the Triglavski National Park of neighbouring Slovenia. Your best hope of spotting these shy carnivores is to make for the highest reaches of the Val Uque, Val Bártolo or the barren windswept expanses above Cave del Predil.

Large herbivores are more readily seen, especially roe-deer and chamois. In the Foresta di Tarvísio, which clothes much of the area, there are thought to be 2,000 of each. Red deer can muster 800 and ibex, introduced from Piedmont's Gran Paradiso, number 120 on, of all places, Cima del Cacciatore, the 'mountain of the hunters'. Hunting has been all but consigned to history since 1980 when it was banned in 23,000 hectares (57,000 acres) of state forest. The change has benefited not only deer and chamois, but also wild boar and smaller mammals such as stoat, red squirrels and badgers, all of which have reached stable populations. Capercaillie and golden eagles breed in the forest, and there are sporadic visits from Balkan-based griffon vultures and even the occasional lammergeier.

Maps: Tabacco 1:50,000 No. 8 *Alpi Giulie*; IGM 1:50,000 No. 33 *Tarvísio*.
Guide-books: G. Buscaini, *Alpi Giulie* (CAI-TCI, 2001); G. Simonetti, *Il Parco Naturale delle Prealpi Giulie* (Résia, 1997).

GETTING THERE
By car: take A23 from the south or SS51 and SS52 from Cortina d'Ampezzo and the west. Minor roads lead to the Valbruna, to the Canale di Raccolana and to the Fusine lakes (off SS54 east of Tarvísio).
By rail: the Rome–Venice–Tarvísio–Vienna main line has stations at Malborghetto-Valbruna or Tarvísio-Boscoverde (4 stopping trains daily).
By bus: S.A.F. provides services from Tarvísio to Pontebba, Ugovizza, Valbruna and other towns, and a combined bus and train ticket from Udine to Tarvísio, T: (0432) 608 111.

WHERE TO STAY
Hotels: Al Cacciatore (2-star), Via S. Leopoldo 88, Pontebba, T: (0428) 90362; Al Camoscio (1-star), Via Val Uque, Malborghetto, T: (0428) 60076; Meublé Tarvis (2-star), Via Vittório Véneto 112, Tarvísio, T: (0428) 644 164.
Refuges: the most popular (open 20 June–20 Sept and winter weekends) are Nordio (Valle di Ugovizza); Luigi Pellarini (Valbruna); Guido Corsi (Iôf Fuart), T: (0428) 60035; Zacchi (above the Fusine lakes), T: (0428) 61195.

ACTIVITIES
Walking: the Fusine lakes trek is the most popular; from the lake shores follow the track up to Rif. Zacchi and then the path that climbs to the foot of Mangart. Complete the circuit by descending to the lakes (3½

hrs, red-white markings). Other fine walks in the Giulie include: the traverse of the Valbruna and ascent to Rif. Pellarini (2½ hrs); the magnificent climb from Sella Nevea to the Corsi hut (5 hrs); from Lago del Predil (9 km/6 miles east of Sella Nevea) to Rif. Brunner (5 hrs). In the Cárniche: from Rif. Nordio in the Val di Ugovizza to Monte Osternig (2½ hrs); from Coccau (above Tarvísio) to Monte Goriane (4 hrs). Contact the Scuola di Alpinismo, T: (0433) 2660, or for a guide, Fulvio Pisani, T: (0432) 985 784.
Skiing: the area has fine cross-country routes around Tarvísio and summer skiing above Sella Nevea. The main winter resorts are Passo di Pramollo, Valbruna and Sella Nevea, with Arnoldstein and Villacher Alpe in Austria. Contact Promotur, Tarvísio, T: (0428) 2967 or Sella Nevea, T: (0433) 54026.

FURTHER INFORMATION
Tourist offices: Via Roma 10, Tarvísio, T: (0428) 2135; Piazza Primo Maggio 6-7, Udine, T: (0432) 295 9721.
Park offices: Piazza del Tiglio, Prato di Résia, T: (0433) 53534; Ufficio Forestale, Via Romana, Tarvísio, T: (0428) 2786.

A pure white heron up to 1 m (3 ft) tall, the great white egret is a winter visitor to Italy's northern and eastern shores, flying in from its breeding grounds in central Europe.

Laguna di Cáorle

Wildest wetlands in the Véneto; parco naturale regionale
8,500 ha (21,500 acres)

Of all the lagoons in the Véneto, Cáorle is the most easterly and most exemplary. For years its four basins — Valle Zignago, Valle Perera, Valle Grande and Valle Nuova — were unknown except to hunters and fishermen, despite being immortalized by Ernest Hemingway in *Across the River and into the Trees.* They are still a world apart, far from the pollution and tourist fuss that is destroying the neighbouring natural habitats of Venice.

The Grande is the last of the Véneto's classic lagoons — the one closest to its natural state and the only one with a full complement of wetland birds and vegetation. Some 15,000 birds winter here, skimming over misty waters which are rarely more than 50 cm (1 ft 8 in) deep. Myriad species of geese, coots and duck (notably pochard) predominate in the cold months, giving way in

Little egrets congregate at the Laguna di Marano on the Gulf of Venice.

summer to large numbers of breeding water-birds, such as night and squacco herons, little egrets and marsh and Montagu's harriers.

A distinctive local feature is the survival of *casoni*, fishermen's huts made from reeds, which can be found in the lagoons' remotest reaches.
Getting there *By car:* A4, exit at S. Stino di Livenza or Porto-gruaro, then minor roads. *By rail:* stations at S. Stino di Livenza, T: (0421) 460 741, and Portogruaro, T: (0421) 71833.
Where to stay *Hotel:* Dolomiti (2-star), Viale Falconera 31, Cáorle, T: (0421) 81328.
Outdoor living: Pra delle Torri, Duna Verde, Cáorle, T: (0421) 299 063 (summer only). **Further information** *Tourist offices:* Borgo S. Agnese 57, Portogruaro, T: (0421) 274 230; Calle delle Liburniche 11, Cáorle, T: (0421) 81085, www.infocaorle.it. *Ecology:* WWF, Viale Cadorna 31, Portogruaro, T: (0421) 760 713.
78

Laguna di Marano and Laguna di Grado

Italy's second largest lagoon complex, in Friuli; includes four riserve naturali regionali *and* oasi WWF *Ramsar, ZPS*
4,182 ha (10,334 acres)

The Marano and Grado lagoons form a vast wetland complex between the Tagliamento and Isonzo rivers. Some 32 km (20 miles) long and 5 km (3 miles) wide, they are second in Italy only to the Venetian lagoons, but considerably less polluted. With their thick vegetation and marshy surrounds they form a natural haven for innumerable

resident and migratory bird populations, a major staging post on the Adriatic migration route to central Europe.

Five rivers and a series of canals flow into the Laguna di Marano. At the estuary of the westernmost river, the Stella, distinguished by its high proportion of fresh water, a Ramsar wildlife oasis has been created. Pride of the reserve are the 35 to 40 pairs of breeding marsh harriers and the 80 to 90 pairs of breeding purple herons. Gulls, cormorants and waders of all descriptions are present, along with birds rarely seen elsewhere, such as eider, scaup, long-tailed duck and velvet and common scoters.

The range of wetland flora is impressively wide. The deeper parts of the lagoon are covered with eel-grass, the mud-flats with cord-grass and tasselweed, and permanently

exposed banks with glassworts. The dunes are bound by marram-grass and couch-grass, while the freshwater channels entering the lagoon have areas of reeds, bulrushes and willows.

At the mouth of the Isonzo, mud-flats and sandbanks attract breeding marsh harriers and purple herons, though not in such numbers as at the Stella. There are also passage and wintering waterfowl, including red- and black-throated divers and red- and black-necked grebes. Flocks of mallard and teal abound, together with black tern, tufted duck and the rarer goldeneye, known as *quattrocchi* or 'four-eyes' in Italian. This is also one of the few sites in the Mediterranean where nesting eider duck can be seen in summer.

Before you go *Maps:* IGM 1:50,000 Nos 108 *Lignano Sabbiadoro* and 109 *Grado*. *Guide-books: La Riserva*

Naturale della Foce dell'Isonzo (Regione Friuli-Venezia Giulia, 1999) and *L'Oasi di Marano Lagunare* (WWF Italia, 1999).

Getting there *By car:* A4 from Venice, exit at Latisana, S. Giorgio-Porpetto or Palmanova. *By rail:* from Venice and Trieste to Latisana, T: (0431) 50306, S. Giorgio di Nogaro, T: (0431) 65178, and Cervignano del Friuli, T: (0431) 387 311. *By bus:* hourly from Udine to Grado, ½-hourly from Cervignano to Grado; call Grado, T: (0431) 80055, or S.A.F., Udine, T: (0432) 504 012.

Where to stay *Hotels:* Iolanda (3-star), Via Udine 7-9, Marano Lagunare, T: (0431) 67700; Aquila Nera (1-star), Piazza Garibaldi 5, Aquiléia, T: (0431) 91045; Ai Pini (3-star), Viale Andromeda 25, Grado, T: (0431) 80888. *Outdoor living:* Pinomare, Lungomare Riccardo Riva 15, Lignano Sabbiadoro, T: (0431) 424 424;

Puntaspina, Via Rotta Primero 9, Grado, T: (0431) 80732.

Access: WWF oasis at Foci dello Stella open all year, but only to organized groups in boats. **Activities** *Boating:* to Foci dello Stella, contact Marano visitor centre; to Marano lagoons, Saturno, Marano Lagunare, T: (0431) 67177; to Laguna di Grado (and Venice), Agenzia Viaggi Adriamare, Grado, T: (0431) 80187.

Further information *Tourist offices:* Via Latisana 42, Lignano Sabbiadoro, T: (0431) 71821; Piazza Capitolo 4, Aquiléia, T: (0431) 91087; Via D. Alighieri 72, Grado, T: (0431) 899 278. *Visitor centres:* Via delle Valli, Marano Lagunare, T: (0431) 67551. For Foci dell'Isonzo, contact Ecothema, Via Stuparich 15, Trieste, T: (040) 371 554, e-mail: ecothema @tiscalinet.it.

Autumn colours brighten a hillside in the vast Foresta di Tarvísio.

Carso

Wild-flower and caving paradise in the far east of Venezia Giulia, against the Slovenian border; includes five riserve naturali regionali *(2,021 ha/4,994 acres) and one* riserva marina *(127 ha/313 acres)*
Includes Biosphere Reserve

Y ou need little etymological skill to deduce *karst* from Carso. Believed to derive from *kar*, a word of Celtic origin meaning 'a rocky place' — also the root of Cárnia and Carinthia, two nearby mountainous regions — it now denotes a brand of limestone scenery of which this region is the archetype.

The Carso is a slender ledge of Italy that reaches down the east coast of the Adriatic to Trieste. It is the only part of the Istrian peninsula still belonging to Italy, the rest having been ceded to Yugoslavia after World War II; nonetheless, much of the hilly region is geologically, not to say culturally, a part of Slovenia. This is its chief appeal, bringing a little piece of the Balkans within the Italian traveller's grasp.

The Carso is one of Europe's great environmental crossroads: a mix of central European, Alpine, Mediterranean and Balkan habitats, with a correspondingly diverse range of flora and fauna. It contains one of the highest tallies of endemic plants in Italy, with no less than 1,900 distinct

species. One of the more remarkable native plants is the knapweed *Centaurea kartschiana*, whose solitary heads of tiny pink flowers refuse to grow anywhere but under a drenching sea spray along the Carso coast. Plants like this must be hardy enough to weather both the intense summer heat and the icy winter blast of the *bora*, a buffeting north-easterly wind so strong that railings are fixed along the steeper streets of Trieste for people to grab.

Every season carries its bounty: spring, delicate with the blossoms of hawthorn, plum and cherry; summer, ablaze with wild roses, gentians and more than 30 species of orchid; autumn, bringing cyclamens and much besides to add to the woodlands' riot of colour. The Carso is perhaps at its most photogenic at the fading of the year, when entire hillsides of red sumac blaze with the intensity of a deep sunset, the bushes tinted, so the locals say, with the blood of the 100,000 soldiers who fell here during World War I. The Carsiana botanical garden near Sgónico has been attempting the Herculean task of collecting at least a portion of the Carso's remarkable flora.

Flowers alone would be enough to justify a visit in most people's minds. The plethora of limestone features provides another compelling reason. The sights start on the coast, which is fringed by low cliffs, itself unusual on the Italian Adriatic which, give or take a Cónero or Gargano promontory, is all but flat. Many of the cliffs are sculpted into strange shapes, almost waves of stone; the best are at Duino, Sistiana and Miramare (which also has Italy's only underwater WWF reserve).

Inland, erosion of the permeable limestone has produced more than 2,000 caves with honeycombs of galleries and subterranean lakes, swallow-holes and dry

---

Up to 25 cm (10 in) long, the cave-dwelling aquatic olm has an ivory-coloured cylindrical body with poorly developed limbs and striking pink gills.

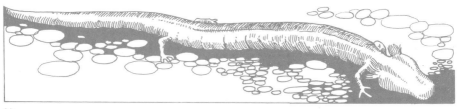

valleys. The baffling Timavo river rises across the border in Slovenia and then flows 40 kilometres (25 miles) underground to emerge in Italy with a volume 25 times as great as when it disappeared. Even more extraordinary is the Grotta Gigante, the largest cave in the world open to the public; 107 metres (351 feet) deep and 208 metres (682 feet) wide, it is big enough to swallow St Peter's Cathedral in Rome.

Bird-watchers cluster around three small areas of wetland on the Doberdò lake, best known for its eight-metre (30-foot) changes in water level, a fluctuation that yields a rich variety of aquatic flora and fauna. Many hundreds of terns are the main attraction, but other species occupy this and other habitats of the Carso in large numbers all the year round.

The Carso's other fauna are harder to spot but well worth looking out for. Herds of roe-deer are common in the remnant tracts of pine and oak forest and there have even been sightings of bears and lynx. Lower down the food chain, the range of climates and habitats yields scores of endemic invertebrates, as well as several typically Balkan reptiles which are unknown further west in Europe. These include the Balkan whip snake, the Dalmatian wall lizard and the Dalmatian algyroides (another lizard, the male distinguished by its orange-red belly and blue throat); Horvath's rock lizard is known only in the karst region of north-eastern Italy and Slovenia.

The most extraordinary creature of the area is the olm, a cave-dwelling amphibian similar to the salamander, and the only member of its family in Europe; its nearest relatives live in eastern North America. When fully grown, the olm retains larval characteristics, including prominent gills, but is still able to reproduce — a feature known as neoteny.

BEFORE YOU GO
Map: IGM 1:50,000 No. 110 *Trieste*.
Guide-books: D. Cannarella, *Escursioni storico-naturalistiche sul Carso Triestino* (Edizioni Italo Svevo, 2001); D. Cannarella, *Itinerari del Carso Sloveno* (Edizioni Italo Svevo, 2001).

GETTING THERE
By car: from the A4 Venice–Trieste motorway, exit at Trieste-Lisert for the Doberdò lake, Monfalcone for Duino and Sistiana. Miramare and the Grotta Gigante are both next to Trieste and can be reached by a short stretch of *superstrada* and minor roads.
By rail: fast trains on the main Venice–Trieste line stop frequently at Monfalcone; contact Trieste station, T: (040) 452 8111.
By bus: for services throughout the Carso, call Trieste Trasporti, Via dei Lavoratori 2, Trieste, T: (040) 77951.

WHERE TO STAY
Hotels: Al Pescatore (2-star), Via Duino 69, Duino, T: (040) 208 188; Milano (3-star), Via Ghega 17, Trieste, T: (040) 369 680.
Hostels: Ostello Tergeste, Via Miramare 331, Trieste, T: (040) 224 102.
Outdoor living: Marepineta, Loc. Sistiana 60/d, Duino, T: (040) 299 264, S. Bartolomeo, Strada per Lazzaretto 99, Múggia, T: (040) 271 275 (both summer only), or others along coast.

ACCESS
The land section of the Miramare reserve is open daily. To visit the underwater section you must book with WWF (see Park offices below); scuba-diving is available weekends, Apr–Oct.

ACTIVITIES
Caving: for the Grotta Gigante, and for climbing, contact CAI Commissione Grotte, Via Donotà 2, Trieste, T: (040) 630 464.
Boating: for services between Grado, Trieste and Pola (in Croatia), contact Samer & Co., Piazza dell'Unità d'Italia 7, Trieste, T: (040) 670 2711 (May–Sept); for trips to coastal resorts, Trieste tourist office.
Sightseeing: the Carsiana botanical garden, divided into 8 areas each replicating a different local habitat, is between Gabrovizza and Sgónico, T: (040) 327 312 (Apr–Nov).

FURTHER INFORMATION
Tourist offices: Via Principale 56/b, Sistiana, T: (040) 299 166; Piazza Unità d'Italia 4/e, Trieste, T: (040) 347 8312.
Park offices: WWF, Castello di Miramare, Viale Miramare 349, Trieste, T: (040) 224 147; Comunità Montana del Carso, Fraz. Sistiana 54/d, Trieste, T: (040) 291 460.
Ecology: Ambiente e Vita, Via Crespi, T: (040) 360 525, and WWF, Via Rittmeyer 6, T: (040) 360 551, both in Trieste.

CHAPTER 4

The Po Delta and Northern Apennines

It was in the Marche, or the Italian Marches, that I had my first taste of wilderness in Italy. Here I learned three sharp lessons which stood me in good stead for future sorties into the Italian countryside: do not trust the maps, do not take a short cut through the woods and remember that Italy can be as cold, damp and miserable as any desolate outpost of northern Europe.

Young, eager and chronically unhealthy, my friend and I had set off to see the Sibillini mountains in the south of the Marche. Plotting an easy course on the footpath, marked on our map with a thick red line, we struck off towards the hills, eager to avoid the roads and keen to pitch our tent before the advent of what promised to be a storm of biblical proportions. Panting in the muggy air, and mildly alarmed at my companion's observation that he was sweating brown sweat — a medical first — I soon realized that if the marked path had ever existed, which seemed unlikely, it certainly did not now.

Paths in these parts are mapped, it seems, from ancient hearsay or surveys carried out on behalf of Mussolini. A lot of vegetation can grow in fifty years, as we found out crashing through the woods in a desperate search for our destination. Various tracks tempted us to follow them but after a while they would peter out, leaving us to stagger blindly after the next false trail. At any

The snow-streaked slopes of Monte Vettore loom over Castellúccio, at 1,452 m (4,764 ft) one of Italy's highest and most remote villages.

other time I would have marvelled at nature's profusion, the densely packed trees, the wonderful thickness of the gorse bushes, the delicacy of the pink cyclamen pushing through the yellowing grass into which I was falling face first. Right then I was too busy cursing, bleeding and wheezing.

This is what Italian textbooks refer to lightly as *sottobosco*, the 'underwood' or undergrowth: fine-sounding on the page, but an impenetrable nightmare on the ground and a challenge never to be undertaken lightly. In the way of these things, the promised storm broke some thirty seconds before the last tent peg had been hammered in. This was just long enough for us to receive a fair old soaking and guarantee a long damp evening spent nursing wounds and cursing map-makers.

Our reward came the next day as we gazed down from the Sibillini peaks into the mist-filled valleys below. Such mountain-top views are rare in the Marche and Emilia-Romagna, which are both predominantly low-lying regions. To find high wilderness you must go to their margins: almost to Umbria for the Sibillini, or to the border with Tuscany for the Casentinesi forests and the Cimone.

A traditional stronghold of the left, Emilia-Romagna is a vast flat corridor across the country, almost linking the Adriatic with the Ligurian Sea, and marking the division between the cold north of the Alps and peninsular Italy, the warm, sunny land of popular imagination. Gentle pastoral hills stretch along the southern edge of the plain, creeping higher as you move south until they break 2,000 metres (6,500 feet) and can safely be described as the northern Apennines.

Modern-day Emilia-Romagna was once a handful of separate states. They were brought together during Italian unification but only given their present borders in 1947. Quite where one ends and the other begins is a cause of dispute. Common knowledge holds that it is more a question of character than of geography — and the criterion for finding out where you are is the kind of welcome that you receive. Pull up at any house, and ask if you might have a drink: while they give you water you are still in Emilia; when they give you wine you have crossed into Romagna. More prosaically, you could say that Bologna, the regional capital, sits in the middle, with Emilia to its left and Romagna to its right.

The first to cross this area with any thought of route-making were, of course, the Romans. They drew a line on the map and built the Via Aemilia (now spelled Emilia), a road running from north-west to south-east that has formed the region's axis ever since. In the Middle Ages pilgrims trudged along it on their way to Rome, as did the Crusaders heading for Ravenna and embarkation for the Holy Land. Agriculture thrived on the vast prairies that lay to either side, earning the region the titles of 'bread basket' and 'fruit bowl' of Italy. Pigs are still supposed to outnumber people here, and some of the famous Italian staples — salami, Parma ham, Parmesan cheese — help to make Bologna the culinary centre of the country.

So much for your stomach, but what is there to satisfy the wilderness-hungry traveller? Not terribly much in the tedious symmetry of the plains — fog-bound in winter, stifling in summer — but a great deal more in the Po delta, known as the Italian Camargue.

The Po is a strange and almost forgotten river, worthy rather than splendid. Few would deny its importance as the great divide separating the Alps from the Apennines or overlook the fact that its huge basin covers 15 per cent of the country's land area and supports a third of the population. What is in question is its drama rating, its lack of visual pyrotechnics. The Tiber, which drains only a quarter of its area and carries a sixth of the water, is far more evocative, still bubbling and cascading over rapids as it flows through Rome, emptying into the sunny Tyrrhenian in the shadow of St. Peter's and the magnificent ruins of Ostia Antica.

No fine city awaits the Po, nor any open seas, only the narrow Adriatic, a bleak delta and a view of the Balkans — a more dour and subdued prospect than the Tiber's promise of the Mediterranean and Africa. Where the Tiber is short and vigorous, the Po is mournful, laden with the nitrates which have been forcing it into a slow suicide and poisoning the sea into which it flows. Even the title of Italy's longest river can seem of little consequence when you consider that it is only 650 kilometres (400 miles) from end to end — half the length of the Rhine, and a modest fraction of the Volga's 3,700 kilometres (2,300 miles).

This is to be hard on the river, which excites loyalty in writers and painters and which, after time spent in its presence, begins to exert a subtle and slowly insidious charm; the charm of a dream landscape with rows of poplars rising from mist-covered fields, long empty views over gentle brown soils and the soft tints of autumn leaves and winter evenings. It draws the birds as well. For them the delta is a key stage on their migration route from Africa to central Europe.

This route also takes them over the Marche, a narrow region south of Romagna that takes up much of Italy's eastern coastline. Marche comes from *marka*, the German for a boundary, and the word is used here (as in the case of the Welsh Marches) to describe troubled frontier lands. In ancient times they marked the border area disputed by early tribes such as the Umbrians, the Piceni, the Gauls and the Sabines; and from about the 10th century AD they formed a border province of the Holy Roman Empire.

The topography of the Marche is wonderfully straightforward and has been well described as resembling one half of a herring bone. Its spine is the limestone Apennine range. From this, nine major and many minor valleys run

The Comácchio lagoons of the Po delta are rich with aquatic life, particularly the vast numbers of eels which have drifted here on ocean currents as larvae. Towards the end of their lives they will make the arduous return trip to their origins, 6,000 km (4,000 miles) away in the Sargasso Sea, where they will breed and then die.

down towards the sea, separated by ridges of hills — the bones — tapering to a coastal plain of clays and marls. This drab strip, dotted with seaside resorts, is pleasantly interrupted by one of the region's natural highlights: the rocky Cónero promontory. Here, just south of Ancona, named after the peninsula's jutting limestone 'elbow' (*agkon* in Greek), lies a feast of cliff scenery.

Away from the coast, the Marche are lovely to look on, the quintessence of pastoral Italy with olive groves, vineyards and green rolling hills as charming as any of the more famous parts of Tuscany and Umbria. Unassuming as they are, the Marche combine one of the country's most civilized corners with pockets of Apennine wilderness, where it is still possible to find wolves, golden eagles and marvellous, unvisited walking country.

GETTING THERE

By air: major internal and some international and charter flights go to Bologna's Guglielmo Marconi airport, T: (051) 311 576, and to Forlì airport, T: (0543) 474 990/1. Other flights go to Rimini, T: (0541) 715 711, and Ancona, T: (071) 28271.

By car: the A1 runs across Emilia-Romagna from Milan through Parma and Modena to Bologna, and thence to Florence and Rome. Other useful motorways include the A21 from France and Turin; the A13 from Venice to Bologna; the A14 linking Bologna to Rimini and Ancona on the Adriatic coast; and the A22 from Austria, through the Dolomites to Verona and Modena. East-west routes across the Marche are slow, the main axis being the coastal A14. Motorway spurs run from the A14 to Urbino, Tolentino and Ascoli Piceno. The main trans-Apennine route is the SS76 from Ancona to Fabriano.

By rail: Bologna is the junction for main lines, including Milan–Bologna–Rome, Venice–Bologna and Brénnero–Bolzano–Bologna.

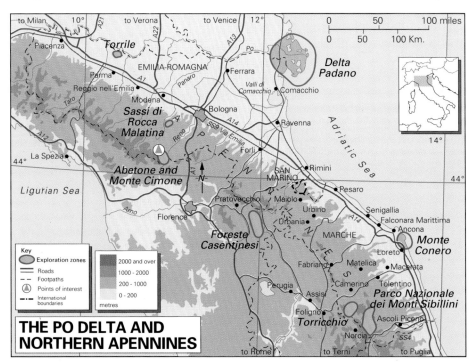

THE PO DELTA AND NORTHERN APENNINES

The main route through the Marche is the coastal line Rimini–Pesaro–Ancona, with a link from Ancona to Rome via Fabriano, Foligno and Terni. Contact Ufficio Informazioni dei Treni, freephone T: (1478) 88088 within Italy, otherwise visit www.fs-on-line.it or www.trenitalia.com.

WHERE TO STAY
Hotels: take your pick in the cities, but expect problems in the park areas out of season.
Agriturismo: contact Agriturist, Piazza dei Martiri 5, Bologna, T: (051) 253 880 and Corso Mazzini 64, Ancona, T: (071) 201 763.

ACTIVITIES
Walking: you will have low-level hill walking except in the Cimone and Sibillini mountains. A long-distance path in 11 stages, the Grande Escursione Appenninica (GEA), runs all along the northern Apennines.
Pony-trekking: contact tourist offices or, in Emilia, the Associazione il Gese, Via Jussi 126, S. Lazzaro di Savena, T:

(051) 625 1452; in the Marche, FISE, Via Monfalcone 6, Ancona, T: (071) 358 0316.
Fishing: contact local FIPSAS branches at Via Andrea Costa, Bologna, T: (051) 614 3836 and Via Ceci 7, Ascoli Piceno, T: (0736) 251 295.
Skiing: the best organized facilities in Emilia-Romagna are at Monte Cimone, T: (0536) 62350, and Corno alle Scale, near Lizzano in Belvedere, T: (0543) 51052. In the Marche there are excellent resorts in the Sibillini; try Sarnano, T: (0733) 651 101, and Ussita, T: (0737) 90224. Other centres are around Carpegna in the northern Marche; contact IAT, Pesaro, T: (0721) 69341.
Bird-watching: LIPU has its HQ at Via Trento 49, Parma, T: (0521) 273 043, and a branch at Bologna, T: (051) 432 020, e-mail: lipusezpr@interfree.it.

FURTHER INFORMATION
Tourist offices: IAT, Via Melloni 1/b, Parma, T: (0521) 218 889, or visit www.turismo. comune.parma.it; Piazza Maggiore 1/e, Bologna, T: (051) 246 541; Via Thaon de Revel 4,

The submerged leaves of the carnivorous greater bladderwort (*Utricularia vulgaris*) have small rounded bladders which catch tiny aquatic invertebrates by means of a trap-door mechanism.

Ancona, T: (071) 358 991 or freephone within Italy, T: (800) 222 111.
Ecology: WWF, Via Savenella 13, Bologna, T: (051) 332 233 and Via Cialdini 24/a, Ancona, T: (071) 203 634.

Delta Padano

Marshes, dunes, woods and islands at the mouth of the River Po, on the border of the Véneto and Emilia-Romagna; protected by two parchi naturali regionali
70,227 ha (173,538 acres)
Includes Ramsar, World Heritage Site, ZPS

The Po expires quietly, having enjoyed its youthful exuberance while tumbling through the Alps. Venerable in old age, it fans out into a delta worthy of the greatest rivers, forming a river-lagoon habitat with a curiously powerful appeal even to those

whose first love is not bird-watching. This unusual wilderness embraces dunes, swamp, freshwater marsh and strange formless areas — covering thousands of hectares — of shifting sands, islands and mud-flats in between. Winter brings the chilly desolation of windswept sands and grey scudding seas. Landscapes are flat and ethereal, skies huge. Lonely horizons stretch across mist-patched or shimmering sheets of water.

This silent and remote region where fresh and salt water meet is one of the most important wetlands for shore-birds and migrating waders in the Mediterranean. Yet for years, it was the only great European delta that did not have proper environmental safeguards: Spain's Guadalquivir was protected by the Doñana National Park as long ago as 1969; in France the Rhône formed part of a regional park, and even in Romania the Danube delta boasted reserves covering 40,000 hectares (100,000 acres). The Po, by comparison, was protected by a mere 6,000 hectares (15,000 acres) of reserves.

Starting in the late 19th century and continuing right through into the 1960s, vast areas of marshland were drained for farming. Drilling for natural gas proceeded unchecked, while the commercial extraction of sand and gravel caused subsidence and added to the already high risk of flooding along the river banks. In the early 1980s a power station was plonked down in the middle of the delta, despite widespread protest. As if this were not enough, industrial and agricultural effluent had by then turned the Po into one of Europe's most polluted rivers. It took the growth of huge

banks of algae in the Adriatic Sea, nurtured by the Po's contaminated discharge, to force the authorities to acknowledge the truth and do something about it.

At long last, in 1988, Emilia-Romagna declared a regional park covering the southern margins of the delta and a long section of littoral, dunes and marshes culminating in the salt-flats at Cérvia, south of Ravenna. The majority of the delta, which falls on the Véneto side of the regional border, remained unprotected until 1997, when it, too, was finally included within a regional park.

Plans are afoot to extend the protection up as far as Chióggia, on the southern tip of the Venetian lagoon, and to turn the whole area into an interregional park managed jointly by the Véneto and Emilia-Romagna. For now, the two regions are running their parks independently, but they have at least made a start on cleaning up the pollution and halting encroachment by agriculture and industry.

The Po's is a textbook delta, created in a region with the world's most perfect preconditions for delta formation. The Adriatic is a long sheltered gulf fed by a sea virtually free of tides and currents. Anywhere else, the river's silt might have been dispersed, but here it has settled undisturbed at its mouth. Numerous tributaries add enormous volumes of silt eroded from their upper reaches. The Po is estimated to deposit a ton of silt for every hundred tons of flowing water. Three other large rivers, the Adige, Brenta and Reno, also empty into the sea nearby, adding their silt to the coastal waters.

Such is the scale of deposition that following the Po to its mouth becomes a difficult task. Having drifted and weaved through different courses over the centuries, the river has formed a leaf-skeleton of streams and channels, creating land one year, removing it the next. As it meanders seaward it loses its identity to such an extent that it is rechristened as a series of branches: the Po di Levante, the Po di Venezia, the Po della Pila, the Po di Gnocca, the Po di Goro — and so forth.

Thousands of birds pass through here on their migration route, spending the winter among the lagoons and marshes. They are

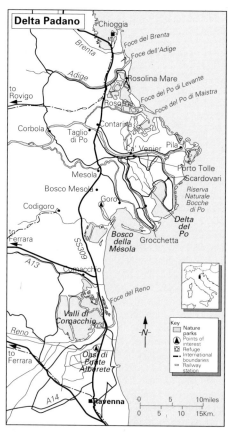

especially drawn to the Valli di Comácchio, so-called 'valleys' ranging from sea-linked lakes to deep still pools rich in aquatic activity, lined by solitary poplars and threaded by small canals. Until 1152, when the Po broke away from its original course, this used to be the delta; now the river struggles seaward to the north. The *valli* were formed as the sea retreated during the Middle Ages, and were much reduced by drainage projects after World War II. What survives, though, is a paradise for waterfowl. Most noticeable are the thousand or so greylag geese, easily identifiable by their yellowish legs and bills. Up to 10,000 coot congregate during the winter, when wood, common and green sandpiper, as well as dunlin, can also be seen. Pygmy cormorant number 3,000 to 4,000, while knot and sanderling, though present, are harder to spot.

Breeding birds are found in smaller numbers but what they lack in quantity they make up in sheer variety. The islands in the Po delta support squacco herons, which have some thirty nests along the banks of the Po di Maistra. The brackish lagoons at Valle Bertuzzi, Lago delle Nazioni and Foce del Po di Volano have large numbers of Mediterranean and black-headed gulls, a few slender-billed gulls, wintering diving ducks, such as tufted duck, and black, sandwich and gull-billed terns. Birds that had once vanished from Italy, such as the hen harrier, are reported to be returning; most remarkably, the greater flamingo has been nesting here since 2000.

There were once great forests south of the Po delta, on the coastal strip leading towards Ravenna. Today, only a few

The rare Italian spadefoot, or Padano toad *(Pelobates fuscus insubricus)*, was discovered in 1873 near Milan. It occurs in the Padano-Venetian plain, Switzerland and Slovakia.

remnants survive, including the Mésola woodlands with their red and fallow deer, the oldest populations in peninsular Italy. Hares, hedgehogs and weasels also thrive in this sanctuary.

North and south of Ravenna respectively are the *pinete*, or pine woods, of San Vitale and Classe. The pines are thought to have been introduced by the Etruscans in pre-Roman times, and were exploited by the Romans to provide timber for their fleet. Nature, left to its own devices, has since run riot. Mature oak, ash and holly, intermingled with various species of maritime pine, rise above a lush forest floor. The beauty and tranquillity of these woods, with their sun-dappled glades, have been praised by generations of poets from Dante to Lord Byron.

BEFORE YOU GO
Maps: IGM 1:50,000 Nos 187 *Codigoro*, 188 *Porto Tolle*, 205 *Comácchio* and 223 *Ravenna*.
Guide-books: *Zone umide del Delta del Po* and *Pinete di Ravenna* from WWF, Ravenna; M.Bonora, *Delta, The Wild Spirit* (Calderini, 2000).

GETTING THERE
By car: from Venice take the SS309; from Bologna, the A13 to Ferrara, then the spur to Comácchio and Porto Garibaldi; and from Ancona, the A14 to Ravenna.
By rail: for the Chióggia–Rovigo, Ferrara–Codigoro and Ferrara–Ravenna branch lines, contact Rovigo station, T: (0425) 33395, or Ferrara station, T: (0532) 55544.
By bus: to approach from

Padua, Rovigo, Ferrara and Ravenna, call S.I.T.A., Rovigo, T: (0425) 410 555, or A C.F.T., Ferrara, T: (0532) 599 492/490.

WHERE TO STAY
Hotels: try Bella Rosa (2-star), Rosolina Mare, T: (0426) 68044; Loco Novo (3-star), Lido degli Estensi, T: (0533) 327 520.
Agriturismo: Corte Papadopoli,

Via Cà Mello 46, Porto Tolle, T: (0426) 80090; S. Gaetano, Via Moceniga 20, Rosolina, T: (0426) 664 634/664 584.

Outdoor living: summer-only camp-sites on the coast include Rosapineta, Rosolina Mare, T: (0426) 68033, and Mare Pineta, Via delle Acacie 167, Lido di Spina, T: (0533) 330 194.

ACTIVITIES

Cycling: hire bicycles at Bosco della Mésola, T: (0533) 794 730.
Fishing: contact Compagnia Polesana di Navigazione, Isola Albarella, T: (0426) 340 019.
Boat-trips: traditional flat-bottomed boats ply the *valli* and canals in summer. Try Marino Cacciatori, Via Matteotti 304, Porto Tolle, T: (0426) 380 314.
Pony-trekking: try the Circolo Ippico Ravennate, Via Cerba 263, Ravenna, T: (0544) 451 043.
Bird-watching: you can see birds virtually everywhere, though the Bertuzzi, Comácchio and Campotto lagoons are outstanding; contact LIPU, Via Porta Catena 118, Ferrara, T: (0532) 772 077.

FURTHER INFORMATION

Tourist offices: Via Dunant 10, Rovigo, T: (0425) 361 481; Corso Giovecca 21, Ferrara, T: (0532) 209 370; Piazza Folegatti, Comácchio, T: (0533) 310 161; Via Salara 8, Ravenna, T: (0544) 35404. Smaller Pro Loco offices (most summer only) are at Adria, T: (0426) 21675; Contarina, T: (0426) 631 778; and Porto Tolle, T: (0426) 81150.
Park office: (Véneto) Via Marconi 6, Ariano nel Polesine, T: (0426) 372 202; (Emilia-Romagna) Via Buonafede 12, Comácchio, T: (0533) 314 003.
Ecology: Italia Nostra, Palazzo Gran Guardia, Piazza Vittório Emanuele II, Rovigo, T: (0425) 21260; Via Palestro 31, Ferrara, T: (0532) 207 262/212 145; WWF, Via Gordini 27, Ravenna, T: (0544) 33081.

Torrile

Tree-lined wetlands in the Emilia-Romagna plains, near the Po; oasi LIPU 35 ha (86 acres)

Whatever the merits of man-made scenery, returning cultivated fields to their original marshland state, as has happened here, creates a stretch of wilderness where none existed before. In the ecological desert of the central Po basin, opening a sanctuary for wildlife has even more to recommend it. At Torrile, close to the banks of the Po, LIPU has designed a maze of canals, islands and sand spits, lakes, marshes and low-lying basins which is home to more than 250 species of birds.

A special attraction is the black-winged stilt, named the Cavaliere d'Italia, the 'knight of Italy', for its elegant black and white plumage and slender, long red legs; 120 pairs breed here. The waters are stocked with eel and carp, and newts and lizards have been introduced. So has the rare *Pelobates fuscus insubricus*, a subspecies of the Italian spadefoot toad, native to the Padano-Venetian plain.

Specially planted trees of every description line the banks and ditches — willow, oak, ash, alder, birch, even fruit trees. Introduced plants include rarities such as the carnivorous greater bladderwort *Utricularia vulgaris*, which has bright yellow flowers, and the free-floating water-fern *Salvinia natans*.
Before you go *Map:* IGM 1:25,000 No. 181 I *S. Secondo Parmense.* **Getting there** *By car:* take SS343 north from Parma to Colorno (16 km/10 miles), then west on minor road to Torrile (4 km/2 miles).
Where to stay *Hotel:* Il Mulino, (1-star), Strada Asolana, Fraz. S. Polo Torrile, T: (0521) 819113. *Agriturismo:* Fondo Grande della Selva, Strada della Selva 12, T: (0521) 523 021, and Antica Grancia Benedettina, Corte di Sanguigna 136, T: (0521) 814135, both in Colorno. *Youth hostel:* Parco Cittadella 5, Parma, T: (0521) 961 434.
Access: open Thurs, Sat, Sun all year. Facilities for disabled.
Activities *Bird-watching:* LIPU in Torrile run courses and visits, T: (0521) 810 606.
Further information *Tourist office:* IAT, c/o Municipio, Via I Maggio 1, Torrile, T: (0521) 812917.

Italy's longest river, the Po, glides quietly to the Adriatic Sea between the marshes and islands of its complex delta.

Sassi di Rocca Malatina

Series of monolithic sand-stone tors and outcrops in Emilia-Romagna; includes parco naturale regionale (1,120 ha/2,770 acres)

Amid the soft-contoured hills south of Modena and Bologna you can find examples of nature at its most capricious. The *sassi* or 'stones' are a group of tors and rock outcrops that have been eroded into striking and often bizarre shapes. The most impressive have razor-thin outlines and one, the Sasso della Croce, has a staircase of ancient steps cut into it. From the top, which at 567 m (1,900 ft) is the highest point in the area, you can look down on some lovely views, with the Panaro valley before you — verdant, timeless countryside — or follow well-worn tracks that weave among the *sassi* and the surrounding thickets of oak and chestnut.

The tors are blocks of sandstone formed in the Tertiary period some 30 million years ago when Italy was still under water. Originally laid down like a layer cake in what is now the Ligurian Sea, they were conveyed here on shifting sediment over millions of years and eventually up-ended in a cataclysmic tectonic upheaval. Exposed to the elements, they were gradually delaminated until they acquired their present sharp profiles. They are nesting places for many birds, in particular peregrine falcons, which breed here undisturbed now that rock climbing is banned.

More spectacular even than the *sassi* is the Pietra di Bismantova which lies about 50 km (30 miles) to the west. Mentioned by Dante, and a sacred place since prehistoric times, this tableland rises 1,000 m (3,300 ft) sheer from the surrounding woodland. It is a landmark for miles around, swamped by trippers at weekends but nonetheless extraordinary enough to demand a visit. As are the Salse di Nirano, violently bubbling pools of volcanic mud known as *vulcanelli*, which create a spectacle near Ferrari's home town of Maranello.

Before you go *Map:* IGM 1:25,000 Nos 236 I *Pavullo nel* *Frignano*, 218 III *Castelnovo ne' Monti*.

Getting there *By car:* Modena Sud exit on A1, then SS623 via Vignola and Guiglia to Rocca Malatina. From Bologna, SS569 to Vignola via Bazzano. Salse di Nirano are between Sassuolo and Maranello, off SS467; for Pietra di Bismantova, exit A1 at Reggio nell'Emilia, then SS63. *By bus:* services to Sassuolo, Vignola and Zocca from Modena, A.T.C.M., T: (059) 416 711, and Bologna, A.T.C., T: (051) 290 290; to Castelnovo ne' Monti from Reggio nell'Emilia, A.C.T., T: (0522) 431 667.

When to go: in spring, when region around Vignola is covered with cherry blossom, or early autumn.

Where to stay *Hotels:* at Castelnovo ne' Monti, Foresteria S. Benedetto literally leans against Pietra di Bismantova, T: (0522) 611 752; Joli (3-star), Via della Pineta 1, Zocca, T: (059) 987 052. *Agriturismo:* Ca' di Marchino, Loc. Monteorsello, Guiglia, T: (059) 795 582. *Outdoor living:* Camping Montequestiolo, near Zocca, T: (059) 985 137 (open all year).

Access: ticket required to ascend Sasso della Croce, free elsewhere.
Activities *Walking:* fine ascent of Pietra di Bismantova via Casale from hermitage at foot of rock (3 km/2 miles from Castelnovo); short strolls around Malatina tors.
Climbing: spectacular *via ferrata* on Pietra di Bismantova; no climbing on *sassi*.
Further information *Tourist offices:* IAT, Via Roma 33/c, Castelnuovo ne' Monti, T: (0522) 810 430; Co-op. Promappennino, Via del Mercato 68, Zocca, T: (059) 98499. *Park office:* Pieve di Trebbio, Guíglia, T: (059) 795 721. *Ecology:* for guided tours, contact LIPU, Via Schedoni 27, Modena, T: (059) 222 161 (also WWF office).

Abetone and Monte Cimone

Limestone mountain chain in the northern Apennines between Emilia-Romagna and Tuscany; includes three parchi naturali regionali *in Emilia (44,036 ha/108,817 acres) and two* riserve naturali statali *in Tuscany (827 ha/2,044 acres) ZPS*

Mountains make good boundaries, and few are as emphatic as the linked ridges that mark the border between Emilia-Romagna and Tuscany. Known collectively as the Appennino Tosco-Emiliano, they curve gently eastward, dividing two regions and two worlds. To the north stretches the area known as the Frignano and beyond it the low worthy hills of Emilia, the plains of the Po and the country's industrial heartland — continental Italy;

to the south lie the Garfagnana and the sunny hills of Tuscany — Mediterranean Italy, a different country altogether.

Noble creatures, the mountains on the Frignano side are the loftiest and most rugged of all the jumbled ranges in the northern Apennines, their heights matching those of the more famous Abruzzi to the south: Monte Sillano, Monte Prato, Monte Alto and the Corno alle Scale, 'the horn by the stairs', all reach 2,000 m (6,500 ft) or close to it; Monte Cusna and Monte Cimone are a little higher.

Most of the year these mountains have few visitors. If they are known at all, it is by the skiers who crowd into Cerreto Laghi, Abetone and Séstola. The highest point, Monte Cimone (2,165 m/7,103 ft), is swarmed over by skiers, brutalized by a radio transmitter and scarred by a hideous road. Make instead for Monte Cusna, a long majestic crest west of Cimone, but connected to it by a rocky outlier, the Passo Lama Lite. Heavily wooded valleys — the Abetina Reale and the Bargetana — fall away to the north and south. Here you will find uncharted wastes: the air alpine-fresh, the roads scarce, the wilderness extreme.

Hikers should approach Cusna from the south, where the hamlet of Civago provides the most convenient base. Mountain huts are numerous and closely spaced; the Battisti refuge on the Passo Lama Lite (owned by CAI) is particularly welcoming. Ice-climbing and cross-country skiing are also possible on Cusna and nearby Monte Prato.

Further south, the area is distinguished by the Pistoiesi forests, the grandest of which are at Abetone. The trees are

mainly spruce, a species that enjoyed a huge expansion in Italy during the last Ice Age but has since retreated northwards. Fossils testify to its former southern extent at the Lago di Massaciúccoli near Pisa, nowadays an area of thoroughly Mediterranean character.

Wildlife, once ravaged by hunting, is scarce in the forests, though there are red and roe deer, boar, mouflon and an estimated 50 marmots — survivors of a colony introduced by foresters in 1954.

Further south still, as the mountains fade into hills, so the forests become smaller, the main ones being the Acquerino in the south-east and the beech woods of the nearby Cantagallo within sight of the domes and spires of Florence.

Before you go *Maps: Sentieri dell'Appennino Modenese* (CAI Modena) and Multigraphic 1:25,000 No. 18 *Appennino Reggiano-Modenese.*
Guide-book: M. Salvo and D. Canossini, *Appennino Ligure e Tosco-Emiliano* (TCI, 2003).
Getting there *By car:* from north, A1 to Modena Sud, then SS12 to Abetone. For Cimone area follow Séstola signs. For Cusna, SS63 from Reggio to Carpineti, then minor roads. From south, Pistoia exit on A11 and SS66/12 to Abetone.
By rail: station at Prácchia on Bologna–Pistoia line, T: (0573) 31192/2078, or main-line stations at Reggio, Modena and Pistoia, then bus.
By bus: on Emilia side, A.C.T., Reggio nell'Emilia, T: (0522) 431 667; A.T.C.M., Modena, T: (059) 416 711; on Tuscan side, Copit, T: (0573) 630 130.
Where to stay *Hotels:* in woods of Monte Cimone, Hotel Passo del Lupo, T: (0536) 62338; in Abetone, Miramonti (3-star), T: (0573) 60017, or Tosca (2-star), T: (0573) 60317.

B&B: Villa Fedora, Via della Pieve 19, Lizzano in Belvedere, T: (0534) 51122. *Agriturismo:* Il Feliceto, Via Ca' Zucchi 454, Ospitale di Fanano, T: (0536) 69525. *Refuges:* Battisti, T: (0522) 897 497 (open July–Sept and winter weekends), or contact CAI, address below. *Youth hostel:* Renzo Bizzarri, Abetone, T: (0573) 60117. *Outdoor living:* free camping permitted; otherwise, Via Tintoria 50, Séstola, T: (0536) 61208, or Pinguino, Pian di Novello, near Abetone, T: (0573) 673 008 (both open all year). **Activities** *Walking:* Grande Escursione Appenninica (GEA) runs along ridge of Appennino Tosco-Emiliano. Starting point at Prácchia, 15 km (9 miles) north of Pistoia on SS632. Trail's most rewarding stretch, through forests and marvellous Apennine scenery, is long haul between Abetone and Passo della Cisa. Recommended shorter walk is ascent of Monte Rondinaio (1,964 m/6,443 ft) from Lago Santo, 11 km (7 miles) south of Pievepélago, accessible by minor road. Take Trail 5 (marked red-white) to Foce a Giovo; then Trail 7 west to summit and for return to Lago Santo (4 hrs). **Further information** *Tourist offices:* Piazza Passerini 18, Séstola, T: (0536) 62324; Piazza Piramidi, Abetone, T: (0573) 60231; Via Villa Vittoria 129/1, S. Marcello Pistoiese, T: (0573) 630 145. *Park offices:* (Gigante) Via Nazionale Sud 3/1, Busana, T: (0522) 891209/891585; (Frignano) Via Roma 84, Pievepélago, T: (0538) 72134; (Corno delle Scale) Via Roma 1, Pianaccio, T: (0534) 51761. *Ecology.* CAI, Viale del Mille 32, Reggio nell'Emilia, T: (0522) 430 266; Via Altopascio 8, Prato, T: (0574) 22004.

Foreste Casentinesi

Largest forests in the northern Apennines, draped across mountain ridges on the Emilia-Romagna/Tuscany border; parco nazionale
36,000 ha (90,000 acres)
Includes European Diploma, ZPS

The seasons are fickle creatures. Sometimes autumn starts its courting of summer with weeks in hand, sometimes it crashes into wedlock in a single tempestuous night. Knowing that nature needs subtle timing, I had planned my trip carefully, hoping to catch the Casentinesi forests in their autumn splendour. As it happened, I was a week early, with summer wilting, but still resisting autumn's advances. The ground was a carpet of leaves and branches, untimely wrenched from the trees by a late summer storm. Most were still green. But higher up the mountains, where wintry winds were roaring off the Romagna plains, the leaves had started to turn. Their golden tints caught the evening sun, emerging at last after a day of grey scudding clouds. Grass and leaves were strewn with virginally shiny conkers; soft-down-covered sweet chestnuts lay everywhere, and underfoot the squelching of the forest floor released that distinctive wet-mulch smell of seasonal decay.

Even as the forests clung to summer, they were wild and chill, their scale breathtaking. As I looked out from ridge-top eyries, no field or rock interrupted the mantle of sun-tinted trees; just line after line of wooded hills reaching as far as the eye could see. All was breezy loneliness

The eagle owl, Europe's largest, lives in remote forested areas and hunts mainly at dawn and dusk. Although it feeds mostly on hares and game birds, such as capercailles, it can take prey up to the size of a young roe deer.

during a long and solitary walk, my only human encounter a furtive couple staggering under sacks of ill-gotten mushrooms.

These forests are among the most important in the Apennines, if not in Italy. They contain a huge variety of woodlands, some pure and some mixed, dominated by firs, beech and mountain ash, but richly interspersed with chestnut, elm, lime, yew and oak. Most of the woods have been untouched for centuries, and even now are only felled to meet the minimum requirements of good husbandry.

Though you will be hard pushed to find boundaries on the ground, the forests are loosely divided into a collection of reserves: Sasso Fratino, Campigna, Badía Pratáglia, Camáldoli and La Lama. Set up on land acquired by the State in 1866 and 1914, they are subject to rigorous ecological supervision, Sasso Fratino in particular: dating from 1959, it was Italy's first integral reserve, maintained without human interference as an ancient forest of immense scientific value. Its management team has been awarded the European Diploma for their outstanding conservation work. In these reserves, the woodland is kept as close as possible to its original state and casual visitors are discouraged from entering.

The area's earliest settlers were 12th-century Christian hermits, no doubt drawn by the woods' meditative tranquillity. Even today, three important monasteries survive deep in the park, one at La Verna and two in Camáldoli.

Later the forests passed to the Grand Duchy of Tuscany, which took the biggest and straightest trees to its arsenal at Pisa. To qualify as masts for ships — the trees' main use — the trunks had to be 6 metres (20 feet) in girth and at least 28 metres (90 feet) high. As many as 75 pairs of oxen were used to drag the biggest trunks to Pratovécchio, on the Arno, from where they were floated downstream to Florence. The journey took ten days, and another six if they were taken on to Pisa. You can still walk along the so-called *vie dei legni*, or 'wood roads', which

reached into the heart of the forests and along which the trees were transported. Although timber was later taken for railway building and charcoal burning (in Sasso Fratino alone there are ruins of 350 ovens), the terrain, even in the industry's commercial heyday, was always too rugged for wholesale exploitation, and so the forests survived.

The Apennines here are an unusual mixture of sandstone, schists and marls, creating the rich soils that nurture the trees, but also producing steep bluffs and stratified outcrops, most marked on the highest northern margins. The more gentle slopes on the Tuscan side, which ripple along as far as Vallombrosa, reveal an Arcadian play of streams and waterfalls in idyllic harmony with the woodland.

The careful management of foresters over the centuries has allowed not only trees and other plants to flourish but also animals, particularly birds. Amidst the communal chatter you may hear the desolate cry of the bullfinch or the bitter ring of the great spotted woodpecker and the near-hysterical laugh of the green woodpecker. Kingfishers dart over rocks splashed by streams, while kites and buzzards hover above. Golden eagles nest in the upper reaches of the park, but sightings are rare. Almost equally elusive are the goshawk, eagle owl and black woodpecker.

Many large mammals — rare in the Apennines — are found here, including 900 red deer and more than 5,000 easily sighted roe deer. You may see an occasional mouflon or fallow deer, but they are not natural residents, only survivors of a much criticized and now abandoned repopulation experiment, and their numbers are dwindling. The long-absent Apennine wolf, by contrast, has not only reappeared but increased to 40, the largest colony in a European protected area.

The lover of the wild will find few modern intrusions to criticize in these mountains; the work of the foresters has seen to that. Only at Camáldoli is there tourist fuss and bother, easily escaped. Roads have begun to replace mule-tracks, but even now they peter out in the higher reaches where tree cover is denser, such as on Monte Falco, Monte Falterona and

Musk thistles bring a touch of colour to the Val di Patino in the Monti Sibillini.

Poggio Scali, all around 1,500 metres (5,000 feet). The only real gripe is the vast Ridrácoli reservoir which is at odds with its surroundings in the wildest part of the forests to the north of the Romagna border.

The lattice of forest trails in the Casentinesi is ideal for easy strolls or mountain-biking and, in winter, provides perfect cross-country ski routes. Other walks follow mule-tracks and lumber roads or ancient paths between monasteries, whose buildings complement a landscape the monks helped to mould. If hiking among the trees becomes too claustrophobic, high ridges and views are never far away. For dedicated yompers there is the Grande Escursione Appenninica (GEA), a 25-day long-distance route that includes a four-day traverse of the forests. Pony-trekkers can follow it too, with slight variations.

Camáldoli has an alpine rescue call-out point, a salutary reminder that these are serious mountains; disorientation is a real danger if you lose the paths. This applies especially in winter, when snow lies in the valleys and on exposed ridges. Bear in mind, too, that in the dark depths of the forest, night falls early.

BEFORE YOU GO
Maps: TCI 1:70,000 *Parco Nazionale delle Foreste Casentinesi, Monte Falterona, Campigna* (available in English); SELCA 1:25,000 *Carta Escursionistica.*
Guide-books: *Parchi nazionali. Foreste Casentinesi, Falterona e Campigna* (L'Airone, 1998); M. Franceschi, *Una giornata tra i mammiferi del Parco Nazionale delle Foreste Casentinesi* (Anima Mundi, 2002).

GETTING THERE
By car: from Forlì take SS67 or SS310, a beautiful north-south traverse of the region; from Florence and the west, take SS67, then SS70 or SS556; from Arezzo and the south, SS71 to Bibbiena and Camáldoli.
By rail: an antiquated branch line runs from Arezzo, on the main line, to Stia. It has 10 trains daily, and useful halts at Bibbiena, Poppi and Pratovécchio.
By bus: services are run on the Romagna side by A.T.R. in Forlì, T: (0543) 27821; on the Tuscan side by S.I.T.A., T: (055) 47821, freephone T: (800) 373 760. In summer, there are free bus services within the park.

WHERE TO STAY
Hotels: the pretty towns in the area have the more comfortable accommodation; try Lo Scoiattolo (1-star), Via Campigna 7, Campigna, T: (0543) 980 052, or Bosco Verde (2-star), Via Nazionale 8, Badía Pratáglia, T: (0575) 559 017. For fascinating alternatives stay at Camáldoli monastery, T: (0575) 556 012, or at the Eremo di Camáldoli, which can accommodate up to 10 people, T: (0575) 556 021.
Refuges: Città di Forlì, Burraia di Campigna, T: (0543) 980 074/734 207, and Fangacci, Badía Pratáglia, T: (0575) 561 273, are open all year.
Agriturismo: try Castagneto Picci, Fraz. Romena 7, T: (0575) 583 836, or La Chiusa, Loc. Gaviserri 1, T: (0575) 509 066, both in Pratovécchio; or Fattoria di Marena, Bibbiena, T: (0575) 593 655.
Outdoor living: Vivaio, S. Sofia, T: (0543) 980 097; Camping Camáldoli, Camáldoli, T: (0575) 556 006/157; Capanno, Badía Pratáglia, T: (0575) 518 015.

ACCESS
Wander where you will, except into the *riserva integrale* at Sasso Fratino, which requires a permit.

ACTIVITIES
Walking: a 2-day portion of the GEA from Camáldoli to Castagno d'Andrea (red-white markings) crosses Monte Falterona and the best part of the forests. Favourite walks include the GEA from Camáldoli to Passo la Calla, passing Sasso Fratino (4¹/²hrs); the ridge circuit north of Badía Pratáglia via Passo dei Mandrioli and Passo Fangacci (5 hrs); the ascent of Monte Penna (1,333 m/4,373 ft) from the Eremo della Verna via Prato alla Penna (2 hrs).
Museums: the small Carlo Siemoni museum in Badía Pratáglia is devoted to the forests and their history, T: (0575) 559 155 (open Tue–Sun in summer, visits by arrangement in winter).

FURTHER INFORMATION
Tourist offices: Via Fiorentina 38, Bagno di Romagna, T: (0543) 911 046; Via Nazionale 14/a, Badía Pratáglia, T: (0575) 559 054/477, and Via E. Mattei, Pratovécchio, T: (0575) 504 584, are open every day Jun–Sept, weekends only in winter.
Park office: Via G. Brocchi 7, Pratovécchio, T: (0575) 50301.
Visitor centres: the centre at Via Nefetti 3, S. Sofia, T: (0543) 971 297, is open 9.30 am to 12.30 pm, Wed–Sun. There are nine others in the park.

Monte Cónero
Probably from the Greek
komaros, strawberry tree

*Mountainous promontory
with rugged coastal cliffs in
the Marche; parco naturale
regionale
6,000 ha (15,000 acres)*

During Italy's submersion in the
seas of the Pliocene, Monte
Cónero stood in wonderful
isolation, a diminutive Cos or
Capri. Stranded on its summit,
you could have looked south
and seen the tips of the Gran
Sasso and the Sibillini
mountains, stretched as islands
across the watery horizon.

Today this mighty
promontory is still something
of an island, its jagged
amalgam of marls, sandstones
and limestone clearly visible
from the sea and the low hills of
the Marche. The most
accentuated relief on Italy's east
coast, it is the only headland to
break the 700 km (450 miles) of
flat sandy beaches that stretch
from Trieste to the Gargano
peninsula in distant Puglia.

In form, Monte Cónero
resembles a cupola, thickly
wooded in places, barren in
others, a salient whose highest
point (572 metres/1,877 feet)
rears up spectacularly from the
sea. To the south and west it
falls away in gentle slopes,
largely covered in dense
vegetation. To the north and
east, its margins are a wild mix
of steep, rocky hills sliced
through by ravines and gullies,
which tumble into the sea in
cliffs, headlands and a series of
tiny sandy coves.

Offshore stand sea-lashed
steeples of rock, their soft marls
wave-sculpted and brilliant
white against the blue of the sea.

Most striking are the Due
Sorelle, the 'two sisters', home
to gulls, swallows and peregrines
poised to prey on migrating
birds attracted by the
promontory's plant cover.

The Cónero is best known as
an important repository for
flora; many plants find either
the southern or northern limits
of their distribution here. More
than a thousand species have
been counted, including several
extremely unusual ones. Among
the rarest are *Bellevalia dubia*,
which has blue-violet flowers in
cylindrical spikes, and is found
in grassy places; *Fumana
arabica*, the Mediterranean rock
rose with yellow flowers; and
Asphodeline liburnica, a member
of the lily family with yellow
flowers, which grows in rocky or
bushy areas.

Cónero did not get park
status until 1987, despite more
than 20 years of asking, and by
then holiday homes had started
their insidious creep up the
hillsides; yet it manages to be
among the wildest of Italian
promontories — miraculously,
given the proximity of some
horrendous beach resorts. It is
one of the few spots on the
Adriatic to retain broad swathes
of *maquis*, supporting tree
spurge (*Euphorbia dendroides*)
as well as the more usual
strawberry tree, oleander,
lentisk and alatern. Unusually
for a rocky littoral, the north-
east corner around Portonovo
contains an example of coastal
marsh rarely found on the
Adriatic; it harbours many
species of ducks and is a
favoured stopping point for
migrating birds.

Before you go *Map:* SELCA
1:20,000 *Carta Escursionistica*
(Consorzio del Parco del
Cónero).
Guide-book: F. Burattini, *Guida
del Monte Cónero* (Aniballi,
1993).
Getting there *By car:* Ancona

Sud or Loreto exits from the
A14; minor-road access from
the SS16.
By rail: stations at Ancona,
Ósimo and Porto Recanati.
By bus: from Ancona,
Conerobus, T: (071) 280 2092,
and Reni, T: (071) 804 6504/430.
Where to stay *Hotels:* Strologo
(2-star), Via Guasto 89,
Camerano, T: (071) 95190; Eden
Gigli (3-star), Via Morelli 11,
Numana, T: (071) 9330 652.
Agriturismo: Il Ritorno, Via
Piani d'Aspio12, Sirolo, T: (071)
933 1544. *Outdoor living:* La
Torre, Portonovo, T: (071) 801
257; Numana Blu, Marcelli, T:
(071) 739 0993.
Access: military zone near Monte
Cónero's summit closed off.
Activities *Walking:* many
panoramic routes, some sections
steep or overgrown. Dense scrub
and military zone make off-path
exploration difficult. Well-worn
trail, initially marked by yellow-
red-blue dashes, from Hotel
Internazionale, Portonovo, via
Badía di S. Pietro to Sirolo (4
hrs), part of unmarked long-
distance path to Visso in
Sibillini (8 days). *Pony-trekking:*
gentle riding on Cónero's
southern slopes; FISE, Via
Monfalcone 6, Ancona, T: (071)
358 0316. *Boating:* for trips, sea
fishing, contact tourist offices or
Compagnia Traghettatori
Riviera del Cónero, T: (071) 933
1795. *Skin-diving:* Ancona
Centro Sub, T: (071) 31991.
Further information *Tourist
offices:* Via Thaon de Revel 4,
Ancona, T: (071) 358 991; Via
Peschiera, Sirolo, T: (071) 933
0611 (June–Sept); Piazza del
Santuario, Numana, T: (071)
933 0612 (June–Sept).
Park office: Via Vivaldi 1/3,
Sirolo, T: (071) 933 0376/1161.
Visitor centre: Via Peschiera
30/a, Sirolo, T: (071) 933 1879.
Ecology: WWF, Via Cialdini
24/a, Ancona, T: (071) 203 634;
CAI, Via S. Cataldo 3, Ancona,
T: (071) 207 0696.

Monti Sibillini

Walking is a delight on the springy turf and open windy ridges of the Monti Sibillini.

High Apennine massif running north-south in the Marche; parco nazionale
71,437 ha (176,528 acres)
ZPS

In all my walks in the Sibillini mountains I have met only one person, and that was on a wild autumn day as I tried to escape the freezing mist swirling on a high ridge.

Sea stacks known as the Due Sorelle, 'two sisters', are a landmark on the spectacular coast of the Cónero peninsula, south of Ancona.

As I made my way down from the summit, a shepherd's hut emerged from the murk, followed by its tattered owner, an old weather-beaten man sporting a greasy white hat clearly fashioned — if that is the word — from the raw wool of his sheep. A cross between a dish-cloth, balaclava and a nurse's bonnet, it gave him the appearance of a shambling madman.

The hut was clearly his home. Dinner — half a sheep — hung inside. A small gas cylinder stood outside, the only visible concession to the modern world. His dogs sat patient, pure white, yellow-eyed, big as wolves. We were nearly 2,000 metres (6,500 feet) up, on a windswept and exposed crest

99

between two deep valleys. In one, mist rolled way below and thunder rumbled around an ominous sky. In the other the view was clear, with patches of evening sunlight casting rocks and gullies into pale orange shadow. It seemed for a moment like a glimpse of the end of the world, hell to one side and heaven to the other.

The Sibillini invite morbid speculation. I have always found it a little disturbing that the Kompass map of the area bears the devil's own number, 666. The mountains are renowned for black magic, and are said to be the home of one of the three sibyls of antiquity, after whom the mountains are named. According to legend, the mythical harridan was chased up here from the underworld, taking up residence on Monte Sibilla in the ominously entitled Grotta delle Fate, the 'cave of the Furies'.

It seems strange that the Lago di Pilato, one of the loveliest lakes in the Apennines, should have been the subject of so many dark and mythic musings. Nestled in a glacial cwm below Monte Vettore, it was here, legend says, that Pontius Pilate was interred, swallowed by the deep dark waters of the lake, after the oxen pulling his hearse refused to go any further. Said to have been a gathering place for wizards in ancient times, the lake has acquired a reputation for contemporary necromancy and devil worship.

The Sibillini are the only true mountains of the Marche, with more than 50 peaks of over 2,000 metres (6,500 feet) — the most precious natural environment for many hundreds of kilometres. Wilder, higher and steeper than many of the Apennines, they show flashes of majesty that would not disgrace an Alpine setting.

Italy perhaps has more dramatic mountains, but none like Monte Vettore — at 2,476 metres (8,123 feet) the third highest point on the peninsula — that give an impression of such size, of such overbearing whale-backed immovability. Immense, barren and smooth-sided on the western flanks, it is marked on its eastern slopes with the savage scars of glaciation. Elsewhere too the scenery is spectacular. Great walls of rock rear up with dolomitic pretensions on Monte Bove, the Palazzo

Borghese and Pizzo del Diavolo, 'the devil's beard'. The Ambro gorge and the Gole dell'Infernaccio, 'hell's canyon', carved into mountainsides pitted with caves and cwms, are two of the most spectacular gashes in the Apennines.

The Sibillini may have given me a rude shock on my first encounter, leaving me dowsed and bleeding, but they are still some of my favourite mountains. Exploring them is a joy despite, or perhaps because of, the scarcity of paths and waymarking. Climbs and descents are demanding, but easy to plan, the emptiness of the hills, uninterrupted by woods, walls or streams, allowing you to wander more or less at will. Only beware the eastern precipices. They have treacherous screes (especially so when wet), enshrouding mist and some of the steepest grass slopes imaginable. If you fall, you may never be found.

While offering some of the most beautiful and empty mountain landscapes on the peninsula, the Sibillini are renowned above all for their famous upland

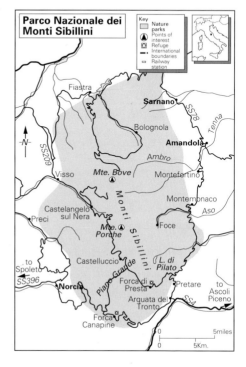

plains, or *piani*, which include the Piano Perduto, Piano Piccolo, Piano dei Pantani and, most memorably, the Piano Grande, one of the strangest and most eerie landscapes in Europe.

Some 1,300 metres (4,250 feet) above sea level, eight kilometres (five miles) long and five (three miles) wide, the Piano Grande is an enormous prairie without trees, hedges or houses, in fact without any individual feature at all, save sheep and the odd bedraggled haystack. The Sibillini rise sheer and sombre on all sides, a solemn amphitheatre formed by nature to gather the high-mountain mists. Gazing down on this waste from Castellúccio, a shepherds' hamlet, as the weather turns, it is easy to imagine the danger that lurks for the unsuspecting traveller. In the past, papal officials forbade the crossing of the plain during winter, and even today the bells of Castellúccio toll when the mist comes down, like a terrestrial fog-horn reaching out to guide solitary shepherds wandering the mournful plains.

Strange and compelling in any season, the *piani* are particularly splendid in spring, when they are ablaze with a varying feast of wild flowers. One week all 1,300 hectares (3,200 acres) of the Grande are radiant with buttercups; the next comes a sudden burst of poppies, burning an incandescent red that seems almost too intense to be natural. Snow-white daisies follow, dotted with wild tulips.

Botanists have busied themselves over the slopes of the Sibillini for more than two centuries, identifying many rarities. Among them is the Apennine edelweiss (*Leontopodion nivale*), which grows on the summit of Vettore, and elsewhere only in very restricted areas of the Maiella and Gran Sasso. Other discoveries include the martagon lily, bear-berry, Apennine cinquefoil (with white flowers and silvery leaves) and the alpine buckthorn. Woods are limited but beautiful; consisting mainly of beech, they are found at up to 1,700 metres (5,600 feet), dotted in sheltered hollows, making rare splashes of colour against the huge smooth sides of the mountains.

Since the Sibillini became a national park in 1990, the wolf, fox, wildcat and crested porcupine have returned, and roe deer have been reintroduced into the woodlands. Among the raptors to be seen are buzzards, kestrels and sparrowhawks, as well as, in the rockier highlands, peregrine falcons and a handful of golden eagles. Breeding birds include rock partridge, eagle owl, alpine and common choughs, chaffinch and wallcreeper.

As a curious footnote, it is worth mentioning a tiny endemic crustacean found at the Lago di Pilato. Orange, and just ten millimetres (less than $\frac{1}{2}$ inch) long, it is considerably shorter than its magnificent name, *Chirocephalus marchesonii*. The only living species that bears any relation to it is found in Asia.

BEFORE YOU GO

Maps: Kompass 1:50,000 No. 666 *Monti Sibillini*; Editor SER 1:25,000 *Carta dei Sentieri*. The Universo 1:25,000 *Monte Vettore, Carta dei Sentieri*, available locally, is extremely useful for the southern Sibillini. **Guide-book:** A. Alesi and M. Calibani, *The Loveliest Walks/Le più belle escursioni* (CAI Delegazione Marche, Ascoli Piceno, 1997).

GETTING THERE

By car: western bases are easiest to approach. Take SS395/209 from Spoleto for Visso, and SS320/396 to Nórcia for Castellúccio and the Piano Grande. Take SS4 from Ascoli Piceno and the east for Arquata del Tronto and the Forca di Presta (starting point for an ascent of Monte Vettore). Minor roads push into the eastern valleys from SS78 between Ascoli Piceno and Amándola. **By rail:** Spoleto is on the Ancona–Rome main line, T: (0743) 48516; Ascoli Piceno is on a branch from the east-coast main line, T: (0736) 341 004. **By bus:** 4 buses run daily from Spoleto to Nórcia and Visso, and 1 every Thurs from Nórcia to Castellúccio; Spoletina Trasporti, T: (0743) 2122. From Ascoli Piceno you can get to Arquata del Tronto, Foce, Amándola and Sarnano; Saspe, T: (0736) 663 137, and Contrame, T: (0736) 636 504.

WHEN TO GO

Mid- to late-June to catch the wild flowers on the *piani*.

WHERE TO STAY

Hotels: the simple Taverna at Castellúccio makes a perfect base for the Piano Grande, T: (0743) 821 158 (open all year). Alternatively, try Al Kapriol, (1-star), Forca Canapine, T: (0736) 808119. **Refuges:** the Zilioli hut on

Vettore is high, but in poor condition and solely for emergency use, T: (0736) 809 278 (15 beds). Road-side refuges include Città di Ascoli at Forca Canapine, T: (0736) 808 186, and another at Forca di Presta, T: (0736) 809 278. **Outdoor living:** camping is permitted everywhere, with many excellent pitches, but take plenty of water. Otherwise, try Camping Quattro Stagioni, Via Forseneta, Sarnano, T: (0733) 65114 / (open all year).

ACTIVITIES
Walking: here you will find some of the best hiking in central Italy, with walks of all standards and, unlike many Italian uplands, opportunities for long ridge walks. There are 50 paths on Monte Vettore alone, though few are marked and many are very minor tracks. CAI Trails 19, 18 and 1 will eventually link to run the entire length of the range, and each one is a day trip. The Grande Anello dei Sibillini trail (GAS) allows you to circle the whole park in 7 days, with 9 stops.

Classic hikes include: Forca di Presta to Vettore (4 hrs); traverse of the Gole dell'Infernaccio (3 hrs); the ridge walks from Vettore to Foce or Monte Porche (both 4 hrs); and Foce to Lago di Pilato (5 hrs) with spectacular views of the Valle del Tenna; Lago di Pilato is a favourite start for the ascent of Vettore. **Climbing:** popular routes with all degrees of difficulty exist on Monte Bove, the Pizzo del Diavolo (above Lago di Pilato) and nearby Gran Gendarme. You will also find many excellent winter challenges. Details from CAI, Corso

The Piano Grande, one of Europe's most beautiful upland plains, lies at an altitude of 1,300 m (4,250 ft), enclosed by the Sibillini's whaleback mountains.

Mazzini 81, Ascoli Piceno, T: (0736) 343 934 or Via della Gabbiaia 9, Perugia, T: (075) 573 0334.

Hang-gliding: Castellúccio has become one of the Italian centres for this sport; contact Fly Castellúccio Adventure, T: (0736) 255 630/(338) 604 5583, e-mail: flyliverotti@libero.it

Skiing: you can find lifts and pistes at Sarnano, Acquacanina, Bolognola and Ussita. For skiers seeking solitary runs, superb cross-country possibilities are everywhere, especially on the Piano Grande, with easy routes to Val Canatra (5 km/3 miles) and Piano dei Pantani (8 km/5 miles). Alpine skiing is also magnificent, with popular routes on Vettore reached from Foce and Forca di Presta.

FURTHER INFORMATION

Tourist offices: Largo Ricciardi 1, Sarnano, T: (0733) 657 144; Piazza XI Febbraio, Frontignano, T: (0737) 99124; Piazza del Popolo 7, Ascoli Piceno, T: (0736) 253 045; Via Solferino 22, Nórcia, T: (0743) 828 173.

Park office: Largo G. B. Gaola Antinori 1, Visso, T: (0737) 972 711, or visit www.sibillini.net.

Visitor centres: the 15 Case del Parco, exclusive to the Sibillini, act both as information points and park service centres; they include Casa del Parco di Amándola, Via Indipendenza 73, Amándola, T: (0736) 848 598, and Casa del Parco di Arquata del Tronto, Via del Mattatoio 2, Arquata del Tronto, T: (0736) 809 600 (both open all year); for the full list visit www.parks.it/parco. nazionale.monti.sibillini.

Ecology: Società Botanica Italiana, Via la Pira 4, Florence, T: (055) 275 7379; WWF, Via F. Crispi 113, Macerata, T: (0733) 230 485.

Torricchio

Classic Apennine landscape in the Marche; riserva naturale statale and oasi WWF
ZPS
317 ha (783 acres)

North of the Sibillini stretch range after range of middling limestone hills, some of central Italy's least-known countryside. Tempting secondary roads — the sort which habitually lead to the edge of wilderness — are the only means of access. Deep-cut valleys open on to rounded summits, notably Monti Torricchio and Fema, both around 1,500 m (5,000 ft). Gaunt intrusions into the wide sweep of more Arcadian country close by, they are magnificently wild, belvederes for far-reaching views of the Sibillini and, across in Umbria, the long shadowy-grey ridges of the Valnerina.

St Francis of Assisi tramped through this country, where high pasture alternates with mixed deciduous woodlands. In autumn, wild cherry colours the hills a glorious red. High beech forests, some with trees 400 years old, add russet and golden hues to the arboreal scene. Where woods have been cleared for the grazing of sheep, brought here from as far away as the Roman countryside, solitary beech have sometimes been left as shelter for shepherds and their flocks.

The Val di Tazza, a narrow cave-studded gorge on the flanks of Monte Fema, contains a reserve and WWF oasis from which sheep, whose nibbling used to decimate the meadow flowers, have been largely excluded. The flora is now rich and colourful, with

The rare mountain alcon blue *(Maculinea rebeli)* is found in the Val di Tazza in the northern Apennines. Other small isolated communities are scattered across western Europe, but they have declined almost to the point of extinction.

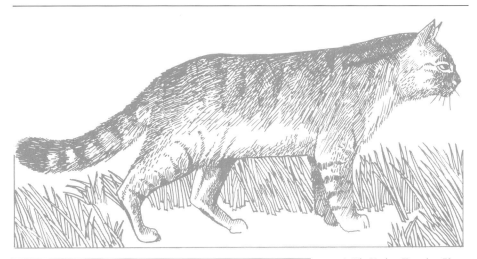

THE WILDCAT

Closely resembling a large tabby, the wildcat can be recognized by its broad head and thick bushy tail with black rings. The largest can weigh 10 kilograms (22 pounds). Although they feed mostly on small mammals and ground-dwelling birds, they are also capable of bringing down animals as large as roe-deer fawn, using stealth and surprise rather than speed. Evidence suggests that wildcats rarely attack livestock; occasionally they may take a sick lamb or kid, though people in rural areas are often convinced otherwise, and persecution of this magnificent feline persists in many parts of Europe.

---

white asphodels and orchids accompanying wild pear, wild strawberry, cyclamen and thickets of the unusual Neapolitan maple (*Acer obtusatum*).

This wealth of wild flowers attracts considerable numbers of butterflies, including metallic green hairstreaks, vivid orange scarce coppers and purple-shot coppers, whose vermilion wings have an iridescent, violet sheen. Perhaps the most distinctive butterfly of the reserve is the mountain alcon blue (*Maculinea rebeli*). The males have bright-blue upper sides with chequered fringes, while the less conspicuous females are predominantly chocolate-brown in colour.

Woodland is creeping forward on all fronts, giving refuge to wildlife that had previously been hunted to within a hair's breadth of extinction. Badgers, red squirrels and the occasional wolf from the Sibillini may be glimpsed, as may the elusive wildcat.

Before you go *Map:* IGM 1:25,000 No. 325 IV *Visso*.
Getting there *By car:* take SS395 and SS209 from Spoleto along Valnerina to Visso, best base. From Camerino head south on SS209; from here minor roads branch off into hills. Torricchio reserve is about 5 km (3 miles) from village of Pieve Torina; also high-level entry point at hamlet of Femate, on Valnerina side of reserve.

Where to stay *Hotels:* I Duchi (3-star), Via Varino Favorino 72, Camerino, T: (0737) 630 440; Del Cacciatore (3-star), Via Spinabello 13, Múccia, T: (0737) 646 121; Tre Monti (3-star), Loc. S. Antonio, Visso, T: (0737) 95427.
Outdoor living: camping permitted outside reserve. Camp-sites include Camping Estate Inverno, Loc. Calcara, Ussita, 5 km (3 miles) east of Visso, T: (0737) 99448, and Il Collaccio, Castelvecchio, near Preci, T: (0743) 939 084 (Apr–Oct).
Access: Torricchio reserve run by WWF, but to arrange visit contact Prof. Franco Pedrotti, Istituto di Botanica, Università di Camerino, T: (0737) 404 504/505.
Activities *Walking:* ascent of Monte Fema from Pian della Cuna (2 hrs), with superb views from summit. Also appealing, hike up and down Val di Tazza (3 hrs), starting at Casale Picini, lower entrance to reserve.
Further information *Tourist offices:* Piazza Cavour 2, Camerino, T: (0737) 632 534; Piazza Capuzzi, Visso, T: (0737) 9239 (seasonal).
Ecology: WWF, Via F. Crispi 113, Macerata, T: (0733) 230 485.

CHAPTER 5

Tuscany and Umbria

For many people, Tuscany *is* Italy. One view of a cypress tree, vineyard or stone farm-house and we are entranced, overcome by that longing for the warm south which Icelanders describe nicely as the 'need for figs'. Countryside here has a purity that to northern eyes is simply irresistible: enticing forests, sleepy villages, gentle hills, olive groves, winding lanes, terraced slopes, geraniums, orange-tiled roofs, all over-arched by the translucent pearly skies of a thousand Renaissance paintings.

Tuscany is a huge region, however, and far more complex than its beguiling pastoral image would suggest. The arc of the northern Apennines marks its borders to north and east, curving in an embrace around the great Renaissance cities of Florence and Siena. Within this broad sweep lie all manner of intriguing landscapes. From the high country of the Garfagnana, Mugello and Casentino in the east the wild traveller's interest shifts westward, skipping over the Tuscan heartland — the Chianti hills, the tourist-filled cities, the Sienese badlands — to the Apuan Alps, jagged, marble-veined mountains that belie any notion of soft-centred pastoralism. Further west still, attention alights on Tuscany's coast and offshore islands. In the last two hundred years, what was a malaria-infested desolation of marsh and forest has been transformed into a drained and prosperous agricultural area of almost unremitting tedium, but the few remaining relics of the earlier landscape

Cultivation over thousands of years has banished wilderness from much of Tuscany and Umbria. Today their vineyards, woods and gentle hills are a picture of pastoral repose.

— minus the malarial mosquitoes — are little Eldorados.

In the Maremma, for example, Tuscany can claim the finest piece of untouched coastline in the country: a pristine tract of *maquis*, hills, dunes and coastal pine woods (or *pinete*). Close by, protected by the Argentario peninsula, are the Orbetello and Burano lagoons, the finest bird-watching areas on Italy's western coast, and the WWF oasis at Bólgheri which is one of the few areas in Tuscany where mammals, particularly the indigenous boar, can roam safe from hunters' guns.

Guns are a threat to the birds and other animals of Umbria, too, as I found out when I lived in a little hamlet on the region's borders. An ear-shattering fusillade of shots under my bedroom window would disturb my slumbers every Sunday morning. Apart from disturbed sleep — nothing to what the poor birds were suffering — I have only fond memories of Umbria, a region which was my introduction to the why and wherefore of Italy. I was fed, looked after, taught Italian and educated by local people in a rural way of life that I imagined had disappeared. I was also introduced to a fiery home-made hootch, but that is another story.

You hear all sorts of things about Umbria: that it is Tuscany's 'gentler sister', that it is the country's 'green heart' or that it is Italy's 'mystical soul'. All have more than a grain of truth. Umbria is an insular and character-filled region, the only one in Italy without either a sea coast or a border with another country. Its timeless countryside and coronet of hill-towns are as beautiful as anything you can find in Tuscany. And it is certainly religious, the *terra dei santi*, the land of the saints, having given birth to Francis and Benedict, fathers of Western monasticism, and to more minor saints than probably any other patch of ground in Christendom.

There are those who say, and I would agree with them, that this surfeit of saints stems from some mystical quality inherent in the landscape. Whether this is something to do with the extraordinary light, soft and misty-edged, which suffuses the paintings of Raphael (who was apprenticed in the region), or to the gentle and ineffable beauty of its hills and woods, I don't think you can say. Strange and faintly unworldly it is, however. Come here for solitary retreat and respite for the soul.

Come here, too, to be roused from introspection by the rude blast of wind and rain. Umbria can be truly wild, and this side of its character becomes more pronounced the further east you go, towards the mountains that linger in the background. If the west is the domain of sheep and pasture, the east is the kingdom of wolf and wilderness. It is a little known side of the region, centred on the valley of the Nera — the Valnerina — and on the ridges of Monte Cucco in the north-east. These mountains mark the beginning of the central Apennines, Umbria's eastern margin. Depleted of fauna — the hunters again — they are superb for walking, caving, climbing and hang-gliding.

Given Umbria's associations with St Francis, noted above all, perhaps, for his divine love of nature and famous sermon to the birds, it is an ironic tragedy that for years its regional authorities had one of the worst environmental records in the country. In 1983, however, a mass demonstration in Assisi, Francis' birthplace, demanded a stop not only to the killing of local birds, but also to the huge slaughter that takes place all over Italy year after year. The aim of the so-called Assisi Bird Campaign was to restore bird-song to the hills above Assisi and to force Umbria to create a reserve to keep the hunters out. It is no reflection on the conservationists, rather a sad comment on the pathetic foot-dragging of Italian bureaucracy, that it took more than ten years before the authorities took note and finally — in 1995 — established the Parco Naturale del Subásio.

Seekers of figs should expect to feel a certain ambivalence about both Tuscany and Umbria. For all the timelessness of their rural scenery, the modern world has crept in and disfigured both regions with factories and new towns. Expect this desecration chiefly in the basins of the main rivers, the Arno and the Tiber.

Tuscany and Umbria are the buffer zones of central Italy, where the affluence and flavours of the north fade slowly to the relative poverty and Mediterranean manners of the south. Such meeting points have always brought friction — ever since the Romans dislodged the Etruscans. Today the battle is more insidious: the unresolved world struggle between progress and pastoralism.

Distinguished by its plumage of orange, yellow, green and blue, the bee-eater feeds on insects, which it catches on the wing. Its long thin bill also allows it to take bees and wasps from their nests.

BEFORE YOU GO
Web-sites: www.toscana.turismo.it and www.umbria.turismo.it.

GETTING THERE
By air: Rome's Fiumicino airport, T: (06) 65951, has good road and rail links to both Tuscany and Umbria. There are international flights to both Pisa, T: (050) 500 707, and Florence, T: (055) 306 1700.
By car: the A1 Rome–Florence motorway bisects Tuscany and Umbria, with spurs to Viterbo, Perugia, Siena and Arezzo. The SS3 (Via Flaminia) from Orte serves Terni, Spoleto, Gualdo Tadino and then, as the SS76, Ancona and the Marche. The SS2 (Via Cassia) runs from Rome through the heart of Tuscany to Siena and beyond. There is also a *superstrada* between Siena and Florence. On the coast, the SS1 (Via Aurelia) from Rome serves the entire western half of Tuscany. North-east Tuscany and eastern Umbria have slower but scenic roads.
By rail: the coastal main line from Ventimiglia to Genoa and Rome serves western Tuscany, including Pisa, Livorno and Grosseto. Branch lines run from Florence to Pisa and Siena, Grosseto to Siena, Lucca to La Spézia and La Spézia to Parma. In western Umbria, the main Rome–Florence–Bologna–Milan line heads for Orvieto and Castiglione del Lago; in eastern Umbria the Rome–Ancona line leads from Orte to Spoleto, Foligno and Gualdo; and branch lines run from Foligno to Assisi, Perugia, Terontola, Rieti and Terni, and from Terni to Perugia and Sansepolcro. Contact Ufficio Informazioni dei Treni, freephone T: (1478) 88088 within Italy, otherwise visit www.fs-on-line.it or www.trenitalia.com.

WHEN TO GO
Mid-April to late May is best for wild flowers, especially orchids, and has the best walking weather (late May–June in the higher parts of the Apuan Alps and Valnerina).

WHERE TO STAY
Hotels: virtually all towns in both regions have ample, high-quality accommodation.
Agriturismo: try Agriturist Grosseto, a farm-holiday booking centre serving all of Italy, T: (0564) 417 418.

ACTIVITIES
Walking: Tuscany has some of the most panoramic hill and mountain walks in Italy,

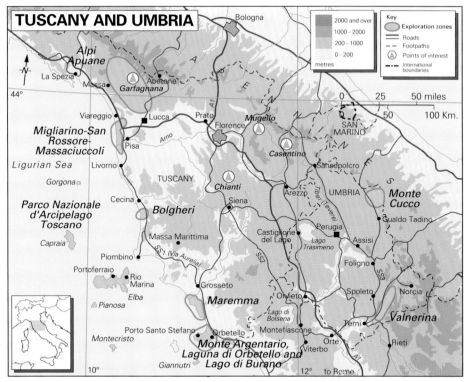

TUSCANY AND UMBRIA

Key

2000 and over	
1000 - 2000	
200 - 1000	
0 - 200	

metres

Exploration zones
Roads
Footpaths
Points of interest
International boundaries

Bologna

Alpi Apuane

La Spezia

Massa
Garfagnana
Abetone

44°

0   25   50 miles
50   100 Km.

Viareggio
Lucca
Prato
Florence
Mugello
SAN MARINO

Migliarino-San Rossore-Massaciuccoli
Pisa
Arno
Casentino

Ligurian Sea
Livorno

Gorgona

Parco Nazionale d'Arcipelago Toscano
Cecina
TUSCANY
Chianti
Siena
Arezzo
UMBRIA
Monte Cucco

Capraia
Bolgheri
Gualdo Tadino

Massa Marittima
Castiglione del Lago
Perugia
Assisi
Lago Trasimeno

Piombino
SS1 (Via Aurelia)
SS2

Portoferraio
Rio Marina
Grosseto
Foligno
SS3

Elba
Maremma
Orvieto
Spoleto
Norcia

Pianosa
Lago di Bolsena
Terni
Valnerina

Montecristo
Porto Santo Stefano
Orbetello
Montefiascone
Orte
Viterbo
Rieti

Giannutri
Monte Argentario, Laguna di Orbetello and Lago di Burano

Sansepolcro

Tiber (Tevere)

10°   12°   to Rome

including strenuous treks along the Apuan Alps, Tuscan/Emilian Apennines and in the higher zone of Garfagnana. Long-distance walkers will enjoy Apuane Trekking, Garfagnana Trekking and the stretch of the Grande Traversata Appenninica from Bocca Trabária to the Passo della Cisa, where the route interconnects with the Alta Via dei Monti Liguri. These take from 1–20 days, and you can break for refreshments in one of the many refuges in the lower valleys. Less demanding, though often solitary, walks can be taken in the Maremma and S. Rossore-Massaciúccoli regional parks, and the Monti dei Chianti, Monte Amiata and Metallifere hills. The islands of the Tuscan archipelago are perfect for excursions. Contact CAI at

Viale Mazzini 95, Siena, T: (0577) 270 666 and Via della Gabbia 9, Perugia, T: (075) 573 0334 (open only Tues and Fri evenings), or visit www.cai.it.
Pony-trekking: Tuscany has probably more riding centres than any other Italian region. Many organize treks with overnight accommodation. Contact FITETREC-ANTE, Piazza Mancini 4, T: (06) 3265 0230.
Caving: Tuscany and Umbria have the best caves in Italy, chiefly in the Apuan Alps and around Monte Cucco.
Fishing: rivers (Arno, Ombrone, Nera, Tiber, Clitunno), lakes (Trasimeno, Corbara Piediluco) and the Tuscan coast offer endless possibilities. Contact FIPSAS, Viale Tiziano 70, Rome, T: (06) 368 583 65.

Skiing: modest resorts are at Abetone, Cutigliano and Monte Amiata (in Tuscany) and around Nórcia, Forca Canapine and Spoleto (in Umbria); visit www.mtnresorts.com.
Bird-watching: LIPU at Via S. Gallo 32, Florence, T: (055) 474 013, run summer work camps in Tuscany.

FURTHER INFORMATION
Tourist offices: Via Cavour 1/r, Florence, T: (055) 290 832; Piazza del Campo 56, Siena, T: (0577) 280 551; Via Mazzini 21, Perugia, T: (075) 573 6458.
Ecology: WWF, Via S. Anna 3, Florence, T: (055) 477 876 and Via XX Settembre 134, Perugia, T: (075) 505 8506; Italia Nostra, Via Gramsci 9/a, Florence, T: (055) 247 9213. WWF run summer work camps in Umbria, T: (075) 914 9287.

Alpi Apuane

Dante's *Divine Comedy* mentioned the Procinto, a dramatic pillar of rock seen here with the summits of the Alpi Apuane in the background.

Mountains, valleys and hills of northern Tuscany; includes Parco Naturale Regionale delle Alpi Apuane (20,598 ha/50,900 acres) and, in the Orecchiella, three riserve naturali statali *and common land* Includes ZPS

The first time I saw the Apuan Alps, dusk was falling on the Tuscan coast. Dark waves were breaking on the shore and, to the east, the land was beginning to fall into shadow. The crests of a jagged mountain chain caught the sun's last rays, shining an almost luminous cream against a red-tinged sky. The forests below were already in darkness, twinkling with the lights of isolated farms. Long after they should have faded into night, the mountains continued to shine with a strange and unearthly glow.

It was marble that was catching the light — huge open mines of it, great jagged pinnacles and scars of it. The Apuan Alps, the most spectacular mountains of the northern Apennines, have for two thousand years been the marble capital of Italy. Some 180 quarries in and around the mountains

111

remove more than a million tons of stone a year, making this the single largest marble-producing area in the world. Innumerable factories and workshops line the coast near the town of Carrara.

There are those who bemoan the desecration and begrudge the quarriers their spoil. I am not sure I do. Maybe it is the marble's beauty — more noble than coal or slate — that causes one to reserve judgement. Or perhaps the grandeur and scale of the mining, or the fact that sculptors from Michelangelo to Henry Moore have always turned to Carraran marble. Whatever the reason, marble is an integral part of life in these mountains. Every shade and hue of stone is here, for although Carraran marble is mainly white — like that of Michelangelo's David — the skill of local craftsmen attracts unworked stone from as far as Brazil, India and China. Incredibly, this vast operation is invisible in all but the lower valleys, where the dust of workshops lies over every road and village. In the wild, wooded interior lies some of the finest country in Tuscany.

The 50-kilometre (30-mile) long ridges fully deserve the title of Alps, their jagged scenery as rockily spectacular as any of the Alps proper. Rising close to the sea, they appear vast, majestic and impenetrable but their highest point, Monte Pisanino, is only 1,946 metres (6,384 feet). Such modest altitude means you can reach the summits, which is often difficult in the Alps.

If you are not tempted by summits, you can find dozens of waymarked walks throughout the mountains. You might plump for the lower, more matronly foothills in the east, greener and more Apennine contours that drop gently to the Garfagnana valley and rise again to the Orecchiella mountains beyond, or you might be drawn towards the Alpine profiles in the west, sun-scorched and marble-rich, with marvellous views of the sea. The highlights are many, from the towering Monte Altissimo to the Pánia della Croce, known as the 'queen of the Apuan Alps', in the heart of a wild, quarry-free area.

A much-photographed feature is the *finestra*, or window, of Pánia Forata, an arch that looks like a huge Cyclopean eye cut into the

mountain's crest. Myth has it that for one moment each year the setting sun shines through the hole to cast a menacing beam on the already darkened villages in the east; you can actually see this phenomenon from one point or another nearly every day. The single most impressive feature of the Apuan Alps, however, is the Procinto, an isolated rock tower like some lost part of the Yosemite National Park or the Mojave desert. Its 200-metre (650-foot) rock walls, along with those of the Pizzo d'Uccello to the north, offer the finest of the many climbs in these mountains.

It was while marching back from the marvel of the Procinto, feeling rather self-satisfied after my walk, that I bumped into two cavers, exhausted and bedraggled after two days underground. They put my hike into perspective. How far had I walked — 20 kilometres (12 miles) perhaps? Under these mountains were an estimated 400 kilometres (250 miles) of caves and galleries. One cave, the Antro del Corchia, is the third deepest in Italy — 1,200 metres (nearly 4,000 feet), almost as far as I had *climbed* that day. Not surprisingly, this is the undisputed caving capital of Italy, with some of the greatest challenges in European speleology: the Tana dell'Olmo Selvatico, the Tana che Urla, the Abisso Roversi, the Grotta del Vento and many more.

These and nearby caverns support some rather unusual cave salamanders. They are agile climbers with partially webbed feet and short squarish toes. Only two species of cave salamander have so far been discovered in mainland Italy: *Speleomantes ambrosii* is confined to a very small area near Florence, while the Italian cave salamander *Speleomantes italicus* is more widespread.

Far more accessible to the average traveller is the huge range of wild flowers to be seen in the Apuan Alps. Because of their southerly location, height and varied topography, the mountains contain a wide range of habitats. Bleak upland moors resembling the Arctic tundra stretch down to alpine meadows with wild flowers galore, interspersed with colossal beech and chestnut forests as dense as any in the Apennines. Lower down still, the dry Mediterranean grasslands are enlivened by orchids and lilies in the early spring. About one quarter of all the plants found in Italy are known to occur in the Apuan Alps, including species such as the Irish spurge *(Euphorbia hyberna)*, which thrives on Apuan marble.

Centuries of hunting have left the larger fauna rather scarce, but snow voles, also known as alpine voles, are still found on the higher slopes. Delightful long-whiskered, pale-grey rodents, they can sometimes be seen basking in the sun on tussocks of grass, but more often than not, the only signs of their presence are the mazes of semi-circular channels which can be seen during a thaw — the bottom halves of the tunnels the voles have bored in the snow.

If you venture inland from the Apuan Alps you will find one of Italy's best-kept secrets: the Garfagnana valley. The bedrock here is mostly sandstone so there is no marble to be mined and none of the Alps' dusty commercialism as a result. The hills are greener and neater, the tree-line ruler-straight, the upper slopes wide and open-topped. To the north-west, in the limestone and sandstone mountains of the Orecchiella, lies a bolder landscape. Here, the spring carpets of colour are if anything more vivid than in the Alps. Magnificent swathes of heather and rhododendron bloom near the bare summits, mirrored in the lower meadows by quite glorious spreads of peonies, lilies, narcissi and wild orchids. A large part of the mountains is dominated by the Pánia di Corfino, a craggy limestone peak; other fine features include the Corte canyon near Sillano and the sandstone ramparts of Monte Prado and Monte Vecchio. Among these crags and on their wooded slopes, 165 types of bird have been recorded, 85 breeding here, including, in the most secluded forests, honey buzzards, goshawks and the magnificent eagle owl.

Graced with extensive lakes, the lower slopes of the Orecchiella and Alpi Apuane *(overleaf)* are clothed in deciduous woods dominated by sweet chestnut.

BEFORE YOU GO
Maps: Multigraphic 1:50,000 No. 511 *Parco delle Alpi Apuane* and (unnumbered) *Garfagnana*, 1:25,000 No. 505 *Parco dell'Orecchiella*.
Guide-books: F. Greco, *Le Alpi della Toscana – escursioni scelte* (Tamari Montagna, 1999); *Alpi Apuane* (Multigraphic, 2003); F. Ravera, *Garfagnana – La terra dei Parchi* (Multigraphic).

GETTING THERE
By car: take the A15 from Milan and Parma or A11/A12 and SS1 (Via Aurelia) from Pisa and the south. Minor roads thread into the Apuan Alps regional park from points around its border; one *strada provinciale*, from Massa to Castelnuovo di Garfagnana, crosses the park from west to east. To reach the Orecchiella (and the eastern Alps), take the twisting SS445 from Lucca to Castelnuovo di Garfagnana, which runs the length of the

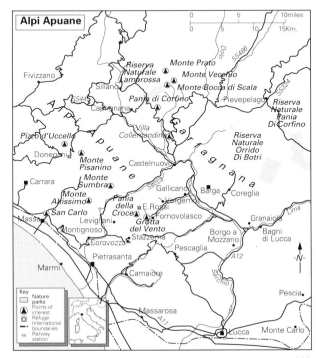

Garfagnana valley and on to Aulla. Minor roads east from this artery lead into the Orecchiella.

By rail: the Rome–Genoa line has convenient stations at Pietrasanta, Massa and Carrara, and a charming and useful branch line runs from Lucca to Aulla (10 trains daily), T: (0585) 793 499.

By bus: most towns and many remote villages are served by C.L.A.P. from Lucca, Massa, Pietrasanta and Castelnuovo di Garfagnana, T: (0584) 53704.

WHERE TO STAY

In the summer many small villages offer *pensioni* and B&Bs; off-season you may have to settle for the uglier coastal towns such as Forte dei Marmi, Massa and Carrara — all otherwise perfectly good bases — and then rely on the efficient bus network. The Garfagnana valley, and Castelnuovo di Garfagnana in particular, are prettier locations.

Hotels: Marquee (3-star), Via Provinciale 14/b, Castelnuovo di Garfagnana, T: (0583) 62198; Mediterraneo (3-star), Via Génova 24, Carrara, T: (0585) 785 222.

Refuges: the Alps have numerous refuges and high-altitude hotels, some run by the CAI branches at Lucca, Massa

and Carrara. The most popular are: Del Freo, T: (0584) 778 007 (Apr–Oct); Donegani, T: (0583) 610 085 (May–Oct); and Carrara, T: (0585) 841 972 (all year). There are 2 refuges in the Orecchiella, at Caparignana and Granaiola, as well as many shepherds' huts. Contact the excellent Comunità Montana della Garfagnana, Piazza delle Erbe 1, Castelnuovo di Garfagnana, T: (0583) 65169.

Outdoor living: camping is prohibited in the Apuan Alps regional park, but camp-sites can be found along the coast and in the Garfagnana valley (most summer only).

ACTIVITIES

Walking: the Alps' best walks are the climb to the Rif. Freo and Pánia della Croce (1,858 m/6,096 ft) from Levigliani (4 hrs); to the Procinto from Seravezza (2 hrs); and around the Pizzo d'Uccello mountain in the Val Seranaia (4 hrs). For details of long-distance treks (2–4 days) from Carrara, Massa, Castelnuovo di Garfagnana or Seravezza, contact the Comunità Montana della Garfagnana (see above) or park offices.

Climbing: here you can find some of the best on the Italian peninsula, including rock climbs on the Pizzo d'Uccello,

Procinto, Penna di Sumbra and Monte Nona; and excellent snow climbs on Pánia della Croce and the crests of Pisanino. Contact CAI, Via L. Giorgi, Carrara, T: (0585) 776 782 or Piazza Mazzini 13, Massa, T: (0585) 488 081 (both evenings only). Try also the Comunità Montana della Garfagnana.

Caving: contact CAI at the addresses above, or CAI Gruppo Speleologico Garfagnana, T: (0583) 65461. Non-experts can descend the Grotta del Vento, on the Garfagnana side of the Alps at Fornovolasco (17 km/11 miles from Barga). There are 3 different-length tours, all led by multilingual guides. The cave is open all year but tours are less frequent out of season, T: (0583) 722 024, or visit www.grottadelvento.com.

Skiing: few runs are to be found in the Alps, bar short cross-country routes on Campo Catino; better opportunities exist in the Orecchiella, which offer a resort at Foce delle Radici and cross-country excursions on forest paths.

Ecology: the Orecchiella contain a large swath of common land *(demanio regionale)* and three state nature reserves, administered by the Corpo Forestale:

HERMANN'S TORTOISE

One of southern Europe's most endangered reptiles, Hermann's tortoise is common along the Tuscan coast but can also be found a little way inland. It is equally at home in sand dunes, meadows and dense scrub. It feeds mainly on vegetation, but also eats carrion, molluscs and slow-moving insects. In the breeding season, male tortoises aggressively repel rivals and court their chosen mates passionately. The females lay around a dozen eggs which take several weeks to hatch, depending on the weather: the warmer, the quicker.

Riserva Monte Orecchiella (218 ha/539 acres), Riserva Biogenetica di Lamarossa (167 ha/413 acres) and Riserva della Pánia di Corfino (135 ha/334 acres). This last also contains a superb botanical garden, the Orto Botanico della Pánia di Corfino, T: (0583) 644 911 (open July–Sept).

FURTHER INFORMATION
Tourist offices: Piazza Menconi 6, Carrara, T: (0585) 632 519; Lungomare Vespucci 24, Massa, T: (0585) 240 063; Piazza Guidiccioni 2, Lucca, T: (0583) 919 931; Viale Carducci 10, Viareggio, T: (0584) 962 233.
Park offices: Castelnuovo di Garfagnana, T: (0583) 644 242; Seravezza, T: (0584) 75821, e-mail: info@parcapuane. toscana.it; and Massa, T: (0585) 315 300.

Migliarino-San Rossore-Massaciúccoli

Long stretch of Tuscan coast and relict woodland near Pisa; parco naturale regionale
14,245 ha (35,200 acres)

Between Viareggio and Livorno lies a stretch of beach, dunes, *maquis* and woodland that forms the largest surviving tract of traditional Tuscan littoral. Despite river pollution, rampant building development and drab urban surroundings, parts are still wild and beautiful.

In the north, squeezed between motorways, lies the Massaciúccoli lake, only 2 m (7

ft) deep but occupying an area the size of nearby Pisa. It is the lone survivor of many such lagoons long since lost to land reclamation. A LIPU oasis has been created here and more than 200 species of permanent, migratory and nesting birds have been recorded, among them grey and purple heron, little egret, marsh harrier and black-winged stilt. In spring, the lake teems with passage ducks, terns and gulls.

To the south lies the Mácchia di Migliarino, the main body of the park. Running for 32 kilometres (22 miles), it is a coastal band of dune, marsh and mixed woodland that contains some of the most enchanting colonnades of trees in Italy. For all that they are man-made, these long avenues, lined across empty countryside, provide one of the great Italian images, elegant rather than obviously formal additions to the landscape. The trees — pine, oak, ash, elder and poplar — were planted in the 18th century to consolidate the littoral and shelter the fields from the lash of winter storms.

Once, what was not *maquis* or marsh on the Tuscan coast was forest, and few of the woods were as grand as the ancient hunting reserve of San Rossore. Here, at the southern end of the park, you can still enjoy what remains of the Selva Pisana and Selva Palatina woods, with their protected colonies of red and roe deer, wild boar and smaller mammals. Some of the oaks are centuries old.

Numerous waterfowl migrate to Migliarino and San Rossore in spring, including the glossy ibis, greater flamingoes, bean and greylag geese, garganeys, ferruginous ducks, cranes and black and white-winged black terns.
Before you go *Maps:* IGM

1:25,000 Nos 260 II *Viareggio* and 272 II *Marina di Pisa*.
Getting there *By car:* from Pisa, take the minor road to Cascine Vecchie, a village situated near the centre of the park.
Where to stay *Hotels:* Cavallino Bianco (3-star), Viale Matteotti 26, Migliarino, T: (0533) 52023; Manzi (2-star), Via Repubblica Pisana 25, Marina di Pisa, T: (050) 36593. *Agriturismo:* Le Rene, Via Palazzi 40, Pisa, T: (050) 989 222. *Outdoor living:* Viareggio, Via Comparini, Viareggio, T: (0584) 391 012; Pineta, Via delle Mimose 12, Tirrenia, T: (050) 32038; Torre Pendente, Viale delle Cascine 86, Pisa, T: (050) 561 704; and Bosco Verde, Viale Kennedy 5, Torre del Lago, T: (0584) 359 343.
Access: LIPU restrict entry to parts of Massaciúccoli, but you may freely take minor roads leading to east and west shores, one by way of a lovely 2-km (1-mile) colonnade of trees. Access to some of woods at S. Rossore also restricted; contact visitor centre, T: (050) 530 101. Unrestricted entry to Pineta di Levante between Versilia and Bufalina river; best wood if you have little time.
Activities: guided tours, cycle trips and horse-treks organized by Ente Parco Regionale, Via Palazzi 21, Tenuta di Coltano, T: (050) 989 084.
Bird-watching: LIPU provide accompanied boat trips on Lago di Massaciúccoli, T: (0584) 975 567.
Further information *Tourist offices:* Via Pietro Nenni 28, Pisa, T: (050) 929 777; Viale Carducci 10, Viareggio, T: (0584) 962 233. *Park office:* Via Aurelia Nord 4, Pisa, T: (050) 525 500, or visit www.parks.it/ parco.migliarino.san.rossore. *Ecology:* WWF, Via Betti 1, Complesso C. Marchesi, Pisa, T: (050) 580 999; LIPU, Via del Porto 6, Massaciúccoli, T: (0584) 975 567.

Bólgheri

Tuscan patchwork of beach, dunes, marsh and woodland; oasi WWF Ramsar, ∠PS *518 ha (1,280 acres)*

This beautiful stretch of the Tuscan coast north of Piombino represents a milestone in Italy's conservation history. In 1959, a refuge for wildlife was set up by the owner, Marchese Mario Incisa della Rocchetta. Three years later it became the first of Italy's 105 WWF oases. Under the joint management of the Marchese and WWF the oasis has attracted an impressive list of birds, including many rarities.

In winter thousands of starlings wheel overhead and the marshes are crowded with ducks, including mallards, wigeons and shovelers. Also to be seen is the greylag goose, symbol of the oasis, and the elegant lapwing which nests here — its southernmost breeding point — along with peregrines (preying on the numerous starlings and woodpigeon) as well as the grey heron, crane, little egret and great white egret. The marsh and hen harrier hunt on the ponds and marshlands.

In spring the African migratory birds arrive: the bee-eater, Blyth's reed warbler, the sedge warbler, the white stork and the numerous types of shore birds including the black-winged stilt which first nested in Bólgheri in 1999. At night, you can hear the nocturnal tawny owl, scops owl and barn owl as well as the nightingale.

The loveliest corners of the sanctuary are the lakes and marshy grasslands, brimming with birds in winter, dry in summer and emerald green with lush grass in spring. All the elements of the traditional Tuscan shoreline are here as well, from exquisite pine groves to relict tracts of juniper and mixed scrub forest. Pioneer plants such as the spiny sea holly thrive on the dunes, as does the sea daffodil, whose flower of purest white breaks out in August, casting its creamy perfume over the shingle and upper beaches. Beyond the dunes unfolds a succession of *maquis*, marsh and hills, all dominated by some of the most ancient and celebrated stands of cypress in Italy.

Such is the Eden-like tranquillity of the reserve that many animals can be seen easily in broad daylight. Wild boar — the ancient Maremma breed — root in the undergrowth alongside equally pure-bred roe deer. The crested porcupine flourishes and you may glimpse Hermann's tortoise and the rare European pond turtle.

Before you go *Guide-books:* A. Canu, *Il libro delle oasi e dintorni* (ADN Kronos, 1997); WWF Toscana, *Le oasi del WWF in Toscana* (L'Erbolario, 2000). **Getting there** *By car:* SS1 (Via Aurelia) turning off at La California (from north) or Castagneto Carducci (from south), then follow signs to the oasis. *By rail:* station at Bólgheri on Rome–Pisa main line about 2 km (1 mile) north of oasis. *By bus:* Livorno to Piombino with a stop 500 m (550 yds) north of oasis, T: (0586) 884 262. **Where to stay** *Hotels:* Cécina is a modern town with functional hotels. Alternatives around Bólgheri and Castagneto Carducci or at historic towns of Volterra and Massa Maríttima. *Agriturismo:* Eucaliptus, Loc. Magazzino, Castagneto Carducci, T: (0565) 763 511. *Outdoor living:* no camping in reserve, but many sites up and down coast. **Access:** guided visits at 9 am and 2 pm every Fri and 1st and 3rd Sat mid-Oct–end Apr, T: (0565) 224 361. **Further information** *Tourist offices:* Piazza S. Andrea, Marina di Cécina, T: (0586) 620 678 (summer only); Piazza Cavour 6, Livorno, T: (0586) 898 111. *Ecology:* WWF, Via Pietro Gori 36, Piombino, T: (0565) 224 361, or visit www.wwf.it.

The adult osprey is a striking bird with a white head, a loosely crested crown and a dark stripe through the eyes. It is a fish hunter, equipped with large feet and long powerful talons for grasping its prey.

A damp autumn morning breaks over the Chianti hills, with the heights of the Pratomagno and Foreste Casentinesi in the far distance.

THE CRESTED PORCUPINE

One of Italy's most eye-catching mammals, the crested porcupine is not a native of the country. The Romans probably introduced it from Africa. It is quite common on hill slopes that give adequate cover. Generally nocturnal, it occasionally appears during the day near its hole. Predators are deterred by its loud grunts and the erection of its bristly white hairs and needle-like quills. Although resembling giant hedgehogs, porcupines are rodents, relatives of rats and mice, with teeth designed for gnawing.

Parco della Maremma

Virgin Tuscan coastline running from Principina a Mare to Talamone, near Grosseto; parco naturale regionale *European Diploma, ZPS 8,900 ha (21,993 acres)*

The Maremma probably takes its name from the Spanish word *marisma*, or marsh, the linguistic legacy of two centuries of Spanish rule. Dante described the region as running from Cécina near Pisa down to Corneto on the present border with Lazio. In his day it was an inaccessible mixture of forest, dune, swamp and scrub made practically uninhabitable by malarial mosquitoes. All that has now gone: the malaria was vanquished in 1950, the dunes have been levelled and the marshes drained. All gone, that is, except for this virginal remnant, saved largely by the owners' refusal to sell out to the gods of tourism and agriculture.

It is impossible to overstate the importance, or, for that matter, the beauty of this area. One looks at this remaining fragment with a mixture of wonder and sadness. Wonder that it has survived and sadness to know that even 50 years ago — until economic boom brought marinas, seaside hotels and the like — Italy boasted hundreds of kilometres of similar coastal wilderness.

The main point of entry to the Maremma regional park — strictly controlled — is not at the coast, but in the middle of the Monti dell'Uccellina, a long series of whale-backed hills that form the park's hinterland. These come as a surprise as you travel along the Tuscan coast, only 400 metres (1,300 feet) high, but suddenly dominating the coastal plain. Old Spanish watch-towers add a romantic touch to the wooded hilltops, except on cloudy days when, with the slopes in deep shadow, they add a dark menace to what are already strange, melancholy hills. On sunny days, however, this touch of the Gothic lifts, leaving the uplands a delight for the solitary walker.

From the official entry point the first of four marked paths, Trail 1, weaves into the rocky green hills. This is by far the least-used of the paths, most people preferring to head for the dunes and the sea. The markings are not easy to follow, but with the sea as a constant point of reference it is difficult to get lost for very long.

In the past the woods were exploited briefly by the Spanish and Sienese for cork and charcoal — the only time they have known even the most rudimentary population. Except, that is, for the monks who inhabited San Rabano, a monastery built in the 11th century and abandoned around 1650. Its ivy-covered ruins lie in the hills and are reached by Trail 1. The only other signs of human habitation are the prehistoric remains discovered in caves on the north-west edge of the hills, caves — the

Scoglietto, Fabbrica and Galino — which you can visit by following Trail 3.

If you are on a day trip and decide to explore the hills, you probably will not have time to explore the coast as well, so you may be tempted to confine yourself to the coastal option. This is an area where all nature's variety seems to have been compressed into a single small space: the beaches, pine forests, dunes and *maquis* are so rich and lush that they seem almost artificial. It is as if they started out as an ornamental park and then degenerated into wilderness.

It was the beach that I felt drawn to, but I tramped through several habitats before I was rewarded with the open sea. Below the hills came a sudden rush of grassy meadows and groves of ancient olive trees, their trunks gnarled and twisted, sometimes fused together in smooth whorls of wood. All around were rosemary bushes in bloom. Hillsides and path-sides were covered in light mauve flowers, the air alive with the constant busy humming of bees. One huge, vividly coloured, gold-banded bumble bee remains in the memory, bumbling heavily from bush to bush.

Beyond the olive groves came the park's crowning glory. I had seen pictures of the Maremma's pine forests, but climbing a low hill to look down on them for myself brought one of the loveliest views I have seen in Italy. A vast green spread of umbrella pines, like tightly packed emerald mushrooms, stretched almost as far as the eye could see. Here and there a rogue juniper or foreign pine interrupted the canopy, standing out in a sea of green limited only by the sky and the blue of distant waves.

Many of the pines were planted: the domestic variety for their pine nuts, which are still collected today, and the maritime variety, now spreading rampantly, in order to consolidate the Maremma's vast area of dunes. To wander through these woods is sheer bliss. The ground is a soft carpet of sand and dry needles, the branches alive with bird-song and the undergrowth rich with heathers and grasses. Occasionally you may hear the rustle of a wild boar snuffling away as you approach.

You can roam for hours along the coast,

your only limits the canals and areas of marsh at their edges. These, too, are a joy, with their fringes of reeds and trees, the plopping splash of frogs as you approach and crystal waters full of darting fish. Otters are on the increase, and birds are numerous, especially migrating winter species. Tiny reptiles, invertebrates and mammals, such as roe deer, badgers, foxes and crested porcupines, can also be seen. Together with the flowers and trees, all this wildlife proves, as Italia Nostra claims, that the Maremma is 'one of the last earthly paradises in Italy'.

There are those who come here simply to enjoy a beach without roads, bars or litter. You can walk for miles on the sand with scenery that would be a credit to Treasure Island. The Uccellina hills and *maquis*-covered hinterland provide a wonderful backdrop. To the south, dunes give way to cliffs and small bays (Trail 4); to the north, they stretch deserted to the river Ombrone.

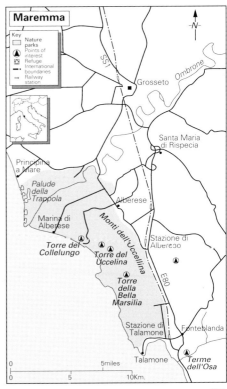

Some of the cliffs and interior country can be approached from the fishing port of Talamone, south of the park. Although access from here is less restricted than in the north, the best introduction remains along the beach, using Trail 4 as far as the headland at Cala di Forno (12 kilometres/7 miles in all). On this walk you may see the dwarf palm, Italy's only naturally growing palm, which reaches the northerly limit of its distribution in the park.

The mouth of the Ombrone, Tuscany's second longest river, is a flat alluvial plain. Some is dune which has been colonized by pine woods creeping up from the south. The rest is a mixture of marsh (the Palude della Trappola on the northern bank), lakes behind dunes and cultivated fields. Here, in season, you can see the rarest of the park's birds — the flamingo, osprey and peregrine — as well as the stone curlew, hobby, roller and bee-eater. The Maremma is famous also for its oxen and semi-wild horses. Sadly, the Maremma's legendary horsemen are nearly all gone, although the rounding up of the horses, with thirty or more animals galloping through lake and marsh, is still a spectacular sight.

BEFORE YOU GO
Maps: IGM 1:25,000 Nos 331 III *Alberese* and 342 IV *Talamone*.
Guide-books: *Maremma e Parco dell' Uccellina* (Multigraphic, 2003); *La Toscana dei parchi naturali — percorsi nella natura protetta* (Giunti Editore, 2003).

GETTING THERE
By car: from the south (Rome) or the north (Pisa) take the coastal SS1 towards Grosseto. Exit south of the town at S. Maria di Rispescia or Stazione di Alberese and follow the signs for Alberese.
By rail: plenty of trains on the Rome to Pisa line serve Grosseto, T: (0564) 22331; only a few stop at Alberese, T: (0564) 596 052.
By bus: there is a frequent service from Grosseto to Alberese, with extra buses in summer, T: (0564) 25215.

WHERE TO STAY
Grosseto is the nearest place, a modern, functional town with hotels to match. Talamone is more picturesque; try the Capo

---

For centuries the olive has been grown for its fruit and oil. The wild olive has thorns, but these are lost in cultivation.

---

d'Uomo (3-star), T: (0564) 887 077 (closed Oct–Mar).
Agriturismo: try Pian di Barca, Loc. Voltina, T: (0564) 25763, or Albarese Natura, Loc. Albarese, T: (0564) 407 100, both in Grosseto.
Outdoor living: camping is strictly prohibited within the park, and difficult in the intensely cultivated surroundings, but many camp-sites are available on the neighbouring coastline.

ACCESS
Entry to the park is by ticket only, and numbers of cars are strictly regulated. You take a special bus from the park office to the set-down point at Pratini. Once you have rattled through hills and scrub, you are herded from the bus and left to your own devices. The price of the ticket includes the bus and a printed guide. A summer timetable applies mid-June to end Sept. You can get straight to the sandy beaches from Marina di Alberese. Avoid public holidays as visitor numbers are limited.

ACTIVITIES
Walking: 2 trails start at Talamone, 4 (Trails 1–4) from the bus set-down point at Pratini, 2 from Alberese and 1 at the mouth of the Ombrone river from Marina di Alberese. A leaflet showing these itineraries is available from the park centre. Trail 1: Abbazia di S. Rabano, leads to the abbey through the woods and rocks of the Uccellina hills; demanding, but one of the most rewarding walks, with superb views over the Tuscan interior and the park's varied habitats (6½ km/4 miles, 5 hrs). Trail 2: Le Torri, links several of the towers on the lower hills, with views over the pine forests from Torre Castel Marino (5½ km/3 miles, 3 hrs), and can be joined to Trail 1 to make a good day's walk. Trail 3: Le Grotte, takes you to the prehistoric caves; flatter and more mundane than other walks, but follows a long stretch through the pine woods (8½ km/5 miles, 4 hrs). Trail 4: Cala di Forno, a long cliff-top, hill and coastal walk; has good views and is little frequented (12 km/7 miles, 6 hrs).
Pony-trekking: most rides are on the dikes and paths around the mouth of the Ombrone, but there are other options. Contact Le Canelle at Talamone, T: (0564) 887 020, or Il Rialto near Grosseto, which offers 3 itineraries, T: (0564) 407 102.

Great spotted cuckoos arrive in western Italy in early spring. They lay their eggs in magpie nests, thus avoiding the tiresome chore of raising their own young. With no parental duties to perform, the adults have usually left for Africa by June.

Fishing: you can fish on the right bank of the Ombrone before sunset 3 evenings a week, permit from Consorzio del Parco, T: (0564) 454 510.

FURTHER INFORMATION
Tourist office: Via Fucini 43/c, Grosseto, T: (0564) 414 304 (closed 1–4 pm), or visit www. grosseto.turismo.toscana.it.
Park office: Via del Fante, Alberese, T: (0564) 407 098.
Ecology: WWF, Via Mazzini 9, Grosseto, T: (0564) 26148. The WWF in Florence, T: (055) 477 976, runs summer work camps in the park. Carapax, the first Italian tortoise reserve, is near Massa Maríttima.

Monte Argentario

Mountainous promontory on Tuscan coast and two nearby lagoons; partly protected by state, regional and WWF reserves Includes Ramsar and ZPS

I have lounged on deserted dunes and watched the sun drop over the Argentario more times than I care to remember. Caught at dusk in rocky profile, it juts from the monotony of the Lazio and Tuscan coastlines, sheltering in its ample lee the largest lagoon on the Tyrrhenian seaboard, the Laguna di Orbetello.

Although Argentario is close to two busy resorts at Porto Ercole and Porto Santo Stefano, it has quiet and rugged corners, some fine stretches of coast and a high point of 635 metres (2,083 feet) which qualifies — emotionally at least — as a mountain. An island for thousands of years, it was eventually joined to the mainland by the three sand spits that enclose the 2,600-hectare (6,400-acre) Orbetello lagoon. With the smaller Lago di Burano immediately to the south, these shallow waters are the bird-watching capital of Italy, claiming 260 of the estimated 450 species that inhabit or visit the country every year.

Thirty years ago the lagoons were unknown except to hunters and a handful of hard-pressed ornithologists. In 1967 the WWF made Burano their second Italian oasis (after nearby Bólgheri) and quickly followed up with another oasis protecting part of Orbetello, including the northern corner where freshwater enters from Albegna. Birds have since taken to the waters in increasing numbers.

A census is impossible; suffice it to say that many rarities breed here. Among them are the little egret, stone curlew, Montagu's harrier and black-winged stilt, known as the knight of Italy, which otherwise breeds only in Sardinia and the lagoons of the Po delta. Other rare birds include great white egrets, velvet scoters, bluethroats, smew and in summer, with luck, the rare great spotted cuckoo. Storks and grey herons arrive in large numbers in the autumn, while the flamingo and garganey are common winter visitors. With the cold and damp come wigeon, shovelers and golden-eyed, chestnut-headed pochard. On the iciest days you might see geese on their way to milder wintering quarters.

One reason for the variety of birds is the general lack of refuge elsewhere on Italy's western coast. Another is the modest 1-metre (3-foot) depth of the lagoons, which provides an accessible mulch of fish, molluscs, crustaceans and algae as food; and a variety of wood, marsh, *maquis*, dune and reed habitats for nest-building.

On the Argentario itself are numerous short walks, coves and lonely shingle beaches. The higher crags are home to rapacious peregrines which join ospreys and marsh harriers hunting over the lagoons. On the promontory you will have the chance of seeing such unusual creatures as the red-rumped swift, which breeds only here and in Puglia; a rare African butterfly, the two-tailed pasha *(Charaxes jasius)*; and, especially on offshore rocks, a number of rare lizards, which include two subspecies of wall lizard, *Lacerta muralis beccarii* and *Lacerta muralis marcuccii*,

the second of which is distinguished by an extraordinary azure skin.
Before you go *Maps:* IGM 1:25,000 Nos 342 II *Orbetello* and 352 I *Porto Ercole.*
Guide-books: F. Pratesi, *Oasi d'Italia* (Musumeci, 1987). Local guides available from tourist office in Porto S. Stefano and bookshops in Orbetello and Porto Ercole.
Getting there *By car:* from north take either A12 from Pisa to Livorno, then SS1 (Via Aurelia) to Orbetello crossroads, or motorway from Florence to Siena, followed by SS223 to Grosseto and SS1. From south, A12 to Civitavecchia, then SS1. Link road to Orbetello can be congested July–Aug. Less traffic on road round south of promontory from Ansedónia. Lago di Burano is ½ km (⅓ mile) from Capalbio exit on SS1.
By rail: station at Orbetello Scalo with through trains from Rome, Pisa, Siena and Florence. Station at Capalbio (Rome–Grosseto line) for Lago di Burano. Train times from Grosseto station, T: (0564) 22331.
Where to stay *Hotels:* plenty of popular but expensive places at Porto S. Stefano, Porto Ercole and along coast at Ansedónia and Capalbio. Summer booking advised.
Agriturismo: try La Guglielmina, SS Aurelia km 145, Orbetello, T: (0564) 862 681.
Outdoor living: camp-sites on coast near Orbetello, with 2 on northern sand spit: Gianella, T: (0564) 820 049, and Il Voliero, T: (0564) 820 201 (summer only).
Access: WWF oases at Orbetello and Burano open 1 Sept–30 Apr, 10 am–2 pm Sun to Thurs (Burano Sun only). Unrestricted access to Riserva Forestale Duna Feniglia (470 ha/1,161 acres) on southern sand spit.
Activities *Walking:* short walks on Argentario, including climb

to summit (Il Telegrafo) up choice of tracks from Porto Ercole, and along Tómbolo di Feniglia, from where you can do a simple coastal walk via Ansedónia to WWF oasis at Burano (4 hrs).
Bird-watching: WWF oasis at Orbetello has 3 itineraries. 1, classic route with 9 observation points. Take SS1 south, turn off at Albínia and follow WWF signs; 2, Patanella route. Exit from SS1 at Patanella; 3, Casale Giannella route. Directions as for park office below. Birds can also be seen from many other points including pink flamingoes from Feniglia sand spit. At Burano, you can watch from minor road along north shore of lagoon or from coastal dunes at western end.
Further information *Tourist office:* Pro Loco, Piazza della Repubblica 1, Orbetello, T: (0564) 860 447.
Park offices: WWF Oasi di Orbetello, Strada Provinciale della Giannella km 4, T: (0564) 820 297; WWF Oasi di Burano, Bivio di Capalbio, T: (0564) 898 829.
Ecology: C.E.A. runs courses from another park office at Casale Giannella.

Arcipelago Toscano

Seven islands off Tuscan coast; parco nazionale *18,000 ha (44,480 acres) land area, 57,000 ha (140,853 acres) sea area — the largest European marine park*
European Diploma, ZPS

The islands of the Tuscan archipelago lie midway between the mainland south of Livorno and the French island of Corsica. Three require a permit to visit: Gorgona (a penal colony), Pianosa and Montecristo. Giglio is full of tourists and Giannutri is going the same way, but Elba and Capraia fully merit a visit. Elba, the best-known, is a rich field for the mineralogist and the third largest of the Italian islands.
Doubtless when Napoleon was exiled to Elba in 1814 — he chose it personally for its 'gentleness of climate' — it was

Among the summer visitors to Italy's wetlands is the black-winged stilt, a wading bird which is distinguished by its enormously long crimson legs.

a place of considerable wilderness. Today it is a holiday resort with more than a million visitors in August alone, so it is not exactly unspoiled. However, areas of untouched scrubland still exist in the west, the interior is green and pretty and the coast has its moments.

Along with the other islands, Elba forms part of a submerged granite range blessed with huge mineral wealth. Inhabited since 3000 BC, Elba produced copper, bronze and iron through the early ages of man. The Greeks named it Aethalia, or 'sparks', after its many forges, and it was with Elban iron in their swords that the Romans conquered an empire. Enthusiasts can pick over an A to Z of minerals, from andalusite to zircon, using Rio Marina's museum as an introduction.

Wooded Montecristo (1,040 ha/2,570 acres), home of Alexandre Dumas' fictional Count, supports the Montecristo viper, a variant of the asp viper, and numerous indigenous lizards and invertebrates. From time to time it provides a refuge for monk seals.

Distant Capraia is the best of the islands, unspoiled, varied and very beautiful. The credit for preserving the island must go to the local council which in 1979, helped by young volunteers, set up and actively supported a 1,926-ha (4,759-acre) regional park covering about 80 per cent of the island and extending $5\frac{1}{2}$ km ($3\frac{1}{2}$ miles) out to sea, all now part of the national park.

The island's volcanic origin has given rise to spectacular coastal cliffs, some of black contorted lavas, others of bright red rock as at Cala Rossa. Sea winds make for a mild, fresh climate, and there are several springs — even an idyllic lake, La Stagnone — to keep the rugged interior green.

Tracks criss-cross the entire island, and there are simple walks to the highest point, Monte Castello (447 metres/1,467 feet), as well as to the bay at Zuvletti and the headland at Punta dello Zenobito. Boats will take you round the 40 or so km (25 miles) of consistently spectacular coastline.

The isolation of these islands has favoured specialized endemics, which are similar to species confined to Sardinia and Corsica. Plants include the Capraia toadflax *(Linaria capraria)*, with its purplish-violet flowers, and the campion *Silene salzmannii*. Birds are of exceptional interest, with 40 resident species and many migratory visitors. Breeding

birds include at least 150 pairs of Audouin's gull (the rarest breeding gull in Europe), Manx and Cory's shearwaters, peregrines, gannets and warblers (notably Marmora's, spectacled and Dartford). Passage migrants include honey buzzards, Bonelli's and booted eagles, as well as ospreys.

Before you go *Maps:* IGM 1:25,000 No. 317 IV *Isola di Capraia*; IGDA 1:50,000 *Isola d'Elba e Arcipelago Toscano*; map of paths on Capraia (Agenzia Viaggi Parco, address below). *Guide-books:* M. Lambertini, *Capraia-Terra Mare* and G. Rinaldi, *La flora dell'Arcipelago Toscano* (Agenzia Viaggi Parco).

Getting there *By sea:* return trips from Livorno to Capraia daily (3 hrs), Toremar Lines, T: (0586) 896 113, or visit www.toremar.it. Numerous ferries and hydrofoils to Elban

ports (Portoferráio, Porto Azzurro and Rio Marina) from Piombino (1 hr), Toremar Lines, T: (0586) 31100, or Moby Lines, T: (0565) 928 101. Portoferráio ticket office, T: (0565) 918 080. Best to book cars in summer. For Pianosa, boats leave Tues from Elba (Porto Azzurro), foot passengers only; book with agency Arrighi, T: (0565) 950 000. Half-day trips round Capraia through island's tourist office (address below). To visit Montecristo, contact Corpo Forestale, T: (0566) 40611.

Where to stay: Capraia has 1 hotel, 4 *pensioni* and a camp-site, Le Sughere (open May–Sept), T: (0586) 905 066; Elba has hotels and camp-sites, many open Apr–Oct only.

Access: permits needed to visit Gorgona, Pianosa and Montecristo. Day trips only to Giannutri, a private island. On

Capraia, no access to Punta dello Zenobito during spring nesting season.

Activities *Walking:* paths and tracks on Capraia; marked trails on Elba, notably on and around Monte Capanne (1,018 m/3,340 ft). *Diving:* excellent around Capraia and Elba. Capraia Diving Service, T: (0586) 905 137.

Further information *Tourist offices:* Capraia, T: (0586) 905 138 (summer only); Portoferráio, Elba, T: (0565) 914 671, www.arcipelago. turismo.toscana.it. *Park office:* Via Guerrazzi 1, Portoferráio, Elba, T: (0565) 919 411, or visit www.islepark.it. *Ecology:* guided walks, bird-watching, botany and photography courses, boat trips and accommodation organized by helpful co-op., Agenzia Viaggi Parco, Via Assunzione 42, Capraia, T: (0586) 905 071.

Sea-birds wheel above Capraia's remote western coast, known for its numerous caves.

Monte Cucco

Limestone massif in north-east Umbria popular with walkers, cavers and hang-gliders; parco naturale regionale
10,480 ha (25,897 acres)

Monte Cucco, one of the highest points in Umbria (1,566 m/5,138 ft), is a robust and rounded mountain, a true wilderness far removed from the pastoral countryside for which Umbria is renowned. However, what is famous in this instance is not the mountain but what lies beneath: one of the deeper cave systems on the

Italian peninsula.

The Grotta di Monte Cucco was first explored as early as 1890, but has only recently been opened up by the hundreds of cavers that flock here from all over Europe. Known to have 30 km (20 miles) of galleries and to be at least 920 m (3,000 ft) deep, it prompted the formation of Italy's most energetic caving club at nearby Costacciaro. Only 780 m ($\frac{1}{2}$ mile) of the galleries are open to the public (entered down a well 27 m/89 ft deep) but the club organizes longer excursions for enthusiasts and offers guidance for visiting experts.

Above ground hundreds of hang-gliders find Monte Cucco's bare, blustery and grass-covered slopes the ideal launching pad, taking off mainly at the Val di Ranco. Monte Cucco is now Italy's foremost hang-gliding centre. Its smooth terrain also provides perfect piste and cross-country opportunities for skiers, with ample winter snow despite its modest height. The Pian delle Macinare, north-west of the summit, provides the best skiing.

The area has become a well-signposted and well-looked after destination for walkers and campers. It offers some of the loveliest medium-standard walking in central Italy, with all the woods, meadows, gentle grass slopes and rounded summits typical of the Apennines. In the less exposed valleys of the Ranco and the Macinare, magnificent beech woods relieve some of the smooth-sloped monotony beloved of the gliders.

There are plenty of walks, too, in the surrounding mountains, particularly near Valsorda. One of the most popular is the ascent made by pilgrims to the summit of the Serra Santa, 'holy mountain' (1,423 m/4,668 ft). A treat for anyone exploring by car is the SS360 north from Costacciaro which leads into the Gola del Corno, a magnificent gorge between Monte Cucco and Monte Catria.

Before you go *Maps:* IGM 1:25,000 Nos 300 I *Gubbio* and 301 III *Gualdo Tadino*; Kompass 1:50,000 *Gubbio–Fabriano* and *Sentiero Europeo E1*.

Getting there *By car:* A1 to Orte (from Rome), then SS204 and SS3 to Costacciaro via Foligno and Gualdo Tadino. Unclassified road leads from Sigillo, 12 km (7 miles) north of Gualdo, to Val di Ranco, best departure point for walks in the area. Alternatively, take A318 from Perugia to Gualdo Tadino via Valfábbrica. Approaches from east are more difficult, best being SS76 via Fabriano and Fossato di Vico. *By rail:* station at Fossato di Vico (southern edge of park) on Rome–Ancona main line. *By bus:* A.P.M. serve Gualdo Tadino, Sigillo, Costacciaro and Foligno from Perugia, T: (075) 506 781.

Where to stay *Hotels:* Da Tobia, at 1,048 m (3,438 ft) in Val di Ranco, is a renowned cavers' and hang-gliders' hotel and best base for walkers, T: (075) 917 7194 (open Apr–Oct, booking advised). Alternatives at Sigillo, Costacciaro, Scheggia, Sassoferrato and Fabriano, though you might prefer Gubbio, one of Umbria's prettiest hill towns. *Agriturismo:* Oasi Madre del Buon Consiglio, Costacciaro, T: (075) 917 0780; Azienda Bonomi, Loc. Montecamera, Gualdo Tadino, T: (075) 918 145. *B&B:* Il Castellare, Loc. Grello, Gualdo Tadino, T: (075) 914 8137. *Outdoor living:* camping permitted, organized sites at Rio Verde, Costacciaro, T: (075) 917 0138 (Jun–Sept), and Valsorda, Gualdo Tadino, T: (075) 913 261 (Apr–Sept).

Activities *Walking:* 31 marked trails in area. For ascent of Monte Cucco from Val di Ranco (4 hrs) follow Trail 1 (yellow/red signs) to Pian delle Macinare, then take Trail 2 heading for Valrachena to reach summit. Follow Trail 2, passing the Grotta and Pian di Monte, for descent. You might also try the walk from Casa il Sasso (near Pascelupo) through Valle delle Prigioni to Pian de Rolla (Trail 4, 2 hrs); the short, panoramic ascent from Pian delle Macinare to Monte le Gronde (Trail 8, 1$\frac{1}{2}$ hrs); or the walk to the austere Riofreddo canyon (equipment necessary). *Climbing:* routes at Le Lecce and Fossa Secca. Details from CAI, Via Piermarini 3, Foligno, T: (0742) 358 804, or C.E.N.S. (address below). *Caving:* the Grotta di Monte Cucco has 20 separate pots, the largest, Gizmo, 176 m (577 ft) deep. Non-cavers can explore the first pot with a guide; the rest are for experts only. Other local caves, again for experts, include Voragine Boccanera and Grotta Ferrata. Centro Nazionale di Speleologia (C.E.N.S.), Via Galeazzi 5, Costacciaro, T: (075) 917 0400, www.cens.it, provides guides and equipment and publishes 1:16,000 map of paths on and around Monte Cucco. *Hang-gliding:* main areas are south of Monte Cucco in Val di Ranco; 2 organized take-off points. Instructors from Università Volo Libero, Sigillo, T: (075) 917 7144, or Albergo Monte Cucco, T: (075) 917 7194.

Further information *Tourist office:* Piazza Oderisi 5/6, Gubbio, T: (075) 922 0693. *Park office:* Villa Anita, Sigillo, T: (075) 917 7025.

Valnerina

Umbrian valley running for 40 km (25 miles) between high limestone ridges; includes Parco Naturale Regionale Fluviale del Nera (2,120 ha/5,239 acres) Includes ZPS

Wilderness in Umbria cuts in east of Spoleto where a genuinely undiscovered corner of the region beckons the wild traveller. This is the Valnerina, the valley of the Nera river which forms one of the most important tributaries of the Tiber. It runs from above the bleak frontier town of Nórcia, tumbling through unkempt mountain scenery, and then turns south, youthful enthusiasm spent, to rejoin civilization at industrial Terni. All the vivid and turbulent beauty of the Apennines is here, and though the higher Sibillini make a tempting show to the east, the Valnerina gives ample cause to linger: an unending succession of rocky crags and forests, fortified villages, peaks and valleys, and the river itself — fast-flowing and ice-cold clear. Fishermen, presented with trout, eels, even crayfish, are in seventh heaven.

A road runs its entire length, but no matter, for stunning side valleys lead immediately into empty countryside where passable tracks lead up and up, climbing to pronounced ridges and finally to a high point at Monte Coscerno of 1,685 m (5,528 ft). Gloriously solitary to walk, the hills have wonderful views and meadows filled with wild flowers. Wild boar populate the clumps of beech forest, and wolves — the ultimate seal on any wilderness

— are known to prowl the higher slopes.

Until a few years ago a railway ran up the valley, linking Spoleto and Nórcia. In its day it must have been one of the most beautiful in Italy. Now its trackless route forms the basis for an increasingly popular walk. The best section starts midway down the valley at the road junction for the village of Sant'Anatólia di Narco. From here the route winds west through two km (one mile) of tunnels (take a torch) and over viaducts to Spoleto, a seven-hour walk through mountains and wooded gorges.

Close to Ferentillo lies the 9th-century abbey of San Pietro in Valle, resplendent in its isolation, and one of the most important monasteries in central Italy. Also close to Ferentillo are crags and overhangs popular with the free-climbing fraternity.

The waterfalls at Mármore with their 165-metre (540-foot) drop are also spectacular, though partly man-made. They were created by the Romans for drainage projects to the south, and boosted by the damming of local rivers for industry in the 1930s. It is a little disheartening to know that they can now be switched off and the water diverted to power hydro-electric turbines. Still, the setting is magical — verdant with vegetation and water-polished marble — and the falls majestic, loud with crashing water and spray as delicate as lace.

Before you go *Maps:* IGM 1:25,000 Nos 347 II *Rieti*, 346 I *Terni*, 337 IV *Nórcia*, 336 IV *Spoleto* (railway walk); Kompass 1:50,000 No. 666 *Monti Sibillini*. **Getting there** *By car:* SS209 runs the length of the Valnerina, reached either from Terni or on picturesque SS395 from Spoleto. Laborious approaches from east (Ascoli Piceno) on SS4 then SS396 via Nórcia. *By rail:*

stations at Spoleto, with frequent trains from Rome, Perugia and Ancona; Terni for southern valley; and Mármore on Terni–Rieti link. *By bus:* several buses daily from Spoleto station to Nórcia and villages *en route*, and from Terni station to Mármore, Ferentillo and Arrone. Società Spoletina d'Imprese e Trasporti, T: (0743) 212 208. **Where to stay** *Hotels:* modest places at Visso, Preci, Nórcia, Triponzo, S. Anatólia, Scheggino, Ferentillo; more luxurious at Spoleto and Terni. In Nórcia try Grotta Azzurra (3-star), T: (0743) 816 513, and in Scheggino, Del Ponte (2-star), T: (0743) 61131. *Hostel:* Il Tiglio, Via Abruzzo 10, Ferentillo, T: (0744) 388 710. *Outdoor living:* free camping permitted. Two camp-sites at Spoleto: Monteluco, T: (0743) 220 358; Il Girasole, T: (0743) 51335 (open Apr–Sept). **Activities** *Walking:* apart from railway walk, appealing outings include climb from Forca Castelmonte to Monte Fionchi (1,337 m/4,386 ft), ascent of Monte Coscerno (1,685 m/5,528 ft) from Gavelli (4 hrs), and Mármore Falls, T: (0744) 737 535 (open Mar–Sept and public holidays in winter). Spoleto's tourist office has walks leaflet. *Climbing:* for routes in Ferentillo, contact CAI, Vicolo Piancini 4, Spoleto, T: (0743) 220 433 (Fri 6–8.30 pm) or Via Fratelli Cervi 31, Terni, T: (0744) 286 500. *Watersports:* canoeing and rafting on Nera, Centro Canoa e Rafting, T: (0744) 67158. *Fishing:* Nera is heavily stocked and fished; permits from tourist offices and FIPSAS, Viale Turati 16, Terni, T: (0744) 285 327. **Further information** *Tourist offices:* Viale C. Battisti, Terni, T: (0744) 423 047; Piazza Libertà 7, Spoleto, T: (0743) 220 311. *Park office:* Via del Convento 2, Montefranco, T: (0744) 389 966.

CHAPTER 6

Abruzzo

Come to the Abruzzo and you will find some of the wildest and most beautiful country in Italy. You are just an hour away from Rome's Via Véneto and the famous Seven Hills, and yet you might as well be in a backwater from the 19th century. This is still a place that could provide settings for a dozen fairy tales, with its wolves and bears, sturdy country folk, woodsmen and shepherds; its mist-wreathed villages on lofty crags, deep valleys and dark forests; and ancient crafts practised for their own sakes, not just for the tourists.

Most of all, though, it is a wild place, the heartland of the Apennines. It is the most completely mountainous region in the country. Only 23 of its 261 *comuni*, the Italian equivalent of parishes, are below 500 metres (1,600 feet). Except for a sandy coastal strip, all is upland, with hills rising quickly to form three distinct groups of mountains: the Laga, the Gran Sasso and the Maiella.

The Abruzzo was for centuries the most isolated part of the country except for Calábria. Not many people made the effort to breach its defences. The English poet Henry Swinburne tried in 1779, and was forced back to Rome by 'as outrageous a blast of snow as any I ever faced, even in my own country'. Even now many an Abruzzese village is cut off for weeks in winter.

Only in the last half-century has the Abruzzo begun to open up. A motorway now runs across it, ferrying hikers and skiers to the burgeoning resorts of the Gran Sasso, while providing a gateway

In the high central Apennines, the limestone bedrock and cool climate provide perfect conditions for beech trees.

to Rome for the Abruzzo's young and dispossessed. Emigration has left villages full of old people and old ways, and not rewarded many of those who escaped. In winter almost every seller of roast chestnuts in Rome seems to be from the Abruzzo, and in the way of these things the Abruzzese have become the butt of every Italian joke that requires a dullard as protagonist.

The break with the past has been felt most in sheep farming, the mainstay of Abruzzese life for centuries. Local pasture was too poor to support animals through the winter; and since Puglia's land was scorched by summer sun, landowners came up with a system of transhumance that made the best of both worlds. They organized twice-yearly migrations along ancient *tratturi*, drove-roads up to 20 metres (66 feet) wide and as often as not filled with animals 12 abreast and in flocks that could number thousands. This army of grey wool advanced in divisions, each flock led by a shepherd and an old ram, the *manso*, meaning 'gentle' or 'trained'. Before the 19th century more than a million sheep a year were moved in this way. Now the flocks are smaller, the roads abandoned and movements, such as they are, made in articulated trucks. The old curse of the shepherds, however, the Apennine wolf, still prowls the Abruzzo's mountains. The sheep-dogs — huge white creatures — used to be equipped with spiked collars to protect them from attack.

Today the major stronghold for wildlife is the Abruzzo national park, the most important protected area on the entire peninsula. The Apennines' last bears roam here, as well as some of the tamest chamois. Excellent though the conservation is, for a taste of real wilderness I prefer the untended heights of the Maiella or the endless forests of the Monti della Laga.

All the Abruzzo mountains, save the Laga, provide classic examples of limestone scenery: high buckled massifs, the nonpareil of the Apennine landscape. Myriad species of plants flourish in their soils, and beech proliferates in huge mixed montane and Mediterranean forests. This rugged natural beauty comes at a price: the Abruzzo is earthquake country. The landscape's odd and distorted contours are a constant reminder of its geological origins, and of the great disaster of 1915 when 30,000 people died and 400 villages were razed to the ground.

You might want to avoid a January visit, since this is the month in which most earthquakes since the 14th century have occurred. Unless you are skiing, you will also want to avoid January for the sheer cold, the clouds swirling around the mountains and the grey-streaked rain that turns the hills into mires. That Italy might have its sub-Arctic moments was brought home to me in Pescasséroli, village capital of the national park. When I arrived there in October I found the back streets filled with wood stacks the size of houses, set up in preparation for the winter.

Little Molise, sandwiched on the east coast between Puglia and the Abruzzo, is often seen as an appendix to Abruzzo. Although it was only officially created as a region in 1963, Molise has had a distinct identity, with its own dialect, since medieval times. It also has some of the most neglected hill country in Italy. People here are the rural hard-working folk they have always been, and proud of traditions that were influenced by the arrival of Slavs and Albanians in the 15th and 16th centuries. Venture here and you will find one of the country's quietest and most charming corners.

GETTING THERE

By air: the capital, Rome, has excellent motorway connections with most centres in the Abruzzo and Molise; its Fiumicino international airport, T: (06) 65951, is as good a destination to fly to as any. Fly-drive deals are simple enough to organize, and enable you to be in the Abruzzo within 2 hours of landing. In the Abruzzo there is an international airport at Pescara, T: (085) 431 1962/432 4200. The nearest airports to Molise are Naples, T: (081) 789 6203, or Foggia in Puglia, T: (0881) 610 042/617 916.

By rail: for mountainous regions, the Abruzzo and Molise are both well served by railways, though the network is complicated and services can be slow. The main axis is the trans-Apennine Rome–Avezzano–Sulmona–Pescara line (for the Velino and the Maiella national park). There are branches from the Sulmona–L'Áquila–Rieti–Terni line (for the Gran Sasso and Monti della Laga national park); Vairano–Isérnia–Carpinone (for the Alto Molise); Sulmona–Castel di Sangro (for the Abruzzo national park and Molise); Avezzano–Roccasecca (also for the Abruzzo national park); and S. Vito–Archi–Castel di Sangro (for the Maiella). Contact Ufficio Informazioni dei Treni, freephone T: (1478) 88088 within Italy, otherwise visit www.fs-on-line.it or www.trenitalia.com.

By bus: the Società A.R.P.A. runs services throughout the Abruzzo; contact offices at L'Áquila, T: (0862) 412 808; Chieti, T: (0871) 348 613; Sulmona, T: (0864) 210 469. For Molise, contact Molise Trasporti,T: (0874) 484 360, Agenzia Larivera, T: (0874) 64744, or Autolinee S.A.T.I., T:

(0874) 94138 (all of them based in Campobasso).

WHERE TO STAY

Hotels: in Molise accommodation is scarce outside main centres such as Campobasso and Isérnia. The Abruzzo is better served, but again hotels are mostly in larger towns or ski resorts. L'Áquila, Sulmona and Amatrice are all well placed for the parks and have a wide variety of hotels. For full accommodation lists consult local tourist offices, or write to the main regional offices (addresses given below).

ACTIVITIES

Walking: the Abruzzo has the best walking in central Italy. The Gran Sasso-Monti della Laga and the Abruzzo national parks have numerous marked paths. Contact CAI offices listed in individual exploration zones for further information and maps. The Maiella national park and Velino, by contrast, lie virtually uncharted, offering ample opportunities for independent exploration by both amateur and experienced walkers. Molise provides equally unknown countryside. It is more suited to low-level hikes, but there are also occasional high mountain environments. There are 2 unofficial long-distance paths: from the Sibillini (see map, p86) to the Gran Sasso (3–4 days), and from the Simbruini (see map, p158) to the Abruzzo national park (10 days). Shorter treks are listed in the relevant exploration zones.

Fishing: contact the FIPSAS branches for permits, regulations and information on the best places to go. For the Abruzzo, offices are in Pescara, T: (085) 66200 and Avezzano, T: (0863) 412 880.

For Molise contact Isérnia branch, T: (0865) 451 004.

Watersports: the numerous lakes and rivers of the Abruzzo provide plenty of opportunities for rafting, boating and canoeing; contact Club Nautica di Pescara, Pescara, T: (085) 692 456, or A.S. Patrick Rafting, Pescara, T: (340) 890 0859.

Skiing: Gran Sasso has the best pistes in central Italy, with broad slopes perfect for family skiing, and the most advanced and extensive amenities as a result. Other massifs have very minor resorts, though cross-country skiing is outstanding in all areas. See relevant exploration zones for details of schools and ski-hire. In Molise there are small developments for cross-country skiing at Capracotta, T: (0865) 94232, and Campitello Matese, T: (0874) 784 114.

Bird-watching: the lack of major wetland habitats in the Abruzzo and Molise is compensated for by both the quantity and the quality of the mountain environments, where most high-level birds, such as eagles, choughs and falcons, can be seen. Extensive literature is available on these areas, particularly in the Abruzzo national park. Contact park offices listed in the relevant exploration zones for information, or try LIPU local branch at Caramanico Terme, T: (085) 922 291, e-mail: lipu_abruzzo@yahoo.it.

FURTHER INFORMATION

Tourist offices: for information on the Abruzzo, contact A.P.T.R. Abruzzo Promozione Turistica Regionale, Via N. Fabrizi 171, Pescara, freephone T: (800) 502 520 within Italy, or (085) 448 2301 from abroad. For information on Molise, contact IAT, Via G. Berta 4, Isérnia, T: (0865) 4411, or APT, Piazza Vittória, Campobasso, T: (0874) 415 662.

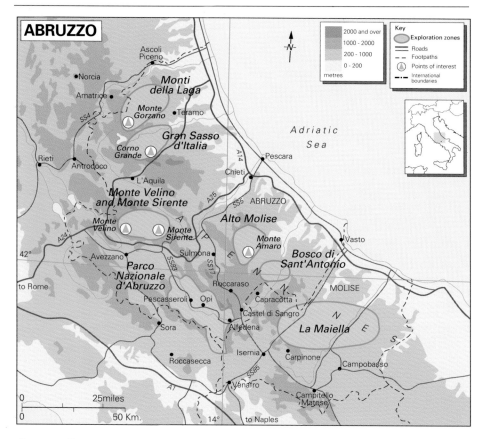

Gran Sasso and Monti della Laga

Contrasting massifs in the northern Abruzzo, the one hailed as Italy's finest outside the Alps for skiers and climbers, the other forested and comparatively unvisited; parco nazionale *150,000 ha (370,665 acres)* ZPS

Once into the Abruzzo the Apennines gather themselves for their greatest assault on the Italian altitude challenge. First off are the Monti della Laga, the northernmost of the Abruzzo's four colossal ranges,

touching 2,458 metres (8,064 feet) at Monte Gorzano, quickly followed by the Gran Sasso d'Italia, the 'big rock of Italy'. As the highest and most spectacular peak on the Italian peninsula, reaching 2,914 metres (9,560 feet) at Corno Grande, it attracts swarms of mountain-hungry hikers and offers hundreds of superb trails.

The Laga form the bridge between the Umbro-Marchigiano and Laziale-Abruzzese Apennines, with the Sibillini marking their boundary to the north and the Gran Sasso presenting a bold Himalayan profile to the south. The Laga are the lowest of the Abruzzo's massifs, but with the Maiella they are some of central Italy's most remote and unvisited mountains. Still too inaccessible, too far from the big cities to be tainted by tourism, safe from skiers and speculators alike, they have largely escaped the urban exodus from Rome and Naples.

They rise suddenly from the Amatrice plain in an unbroken scarp of between 1,000 and 1,500 metres (3,300–5,000 feet), and then ascend to solitary, rounded peaks in a south-running ridge of some 30 kilometres (20 miles). They differ from other Abruzzese massifs in being made of Miocene marls and sandstone rather than limestone. These less permeable rocks have a dramatic effect on the landscape: they allow rain-water to collect, so everything is greener, and they allow the formation of thousands of streams, brooks, lakes and above all waterfalls. Some of these water-falls are up to 80 metres (250 feet) high, and all tend to emerge at around 1,500 metres (5,000 feet). At this height they can freeze in winter, creating one of the most magical natural sights in Italy.

If an Abruzzo winter is too daunting a prospect, a good time for a visit is between May and June. Then the meadows are in flower, the rivers in spate and the falls a torrent of crashing, muddied meltwater. On days such as these you might have stumbled into the Alps. And if you are here at this time, make straight for the valley of the Acero in the Laga's south-east corner.

The valley lies above the village of Crognaleto off the SS80, just before this lonely, lovely road begins its climb up to the ridges of the Gran Sasso. Follow the unmetalled lane to the hamlet of Cesacástina, where a foaming abundance of water and a profusion of violets, buttercups and red and white orchids (including the rare, leafless *Epipogium aphyllum*) herald the region's highlight: the Valle delle Cento Cascate, the 'valley of a hundred waterfalls'. As you walk, the Gran Sasso stretches before you across the near horizon, its snow-covered peaks contrasting with the exuberant rushing of white water.

Forests are the greatest glory of the Laga. In the woods of the Martese, pines and silver firs grow in numbers greater than anywhere else in the Apennines. On the eastern slopes dense beech and pine forests roll on north towards the Marche for mile after impenetrable mile, while in the Valle Castellana, pride of place goes to mixed woodlands. In few parts of central Italy, save perhaps the Maiella, are you so lost in mystery, silence and the most utter solitude.

Walkers in the Laga are well served by paths. You might look into the still unresolved question of the ancient track that traverses the massif from Amatrice to Montagna di Fiori. The stretch to Pizzo di Sevo (2,419 metres/7,936 feet) is known by tradition as the *tracciolino di Annibale*, 'Hannibal's little track'. Locals say that the Carthaginian general, more famous for his Alpine crossing, tramped over these mountains on his march to the Adriatic.

The Gran Sasso used to be every bit as quiet as the Laga. Once, indeed, there were few places so inaccessible. In 1943 it was used as a prison, like a land-locked Alcatraz or Robben Island, for the deposed Mussolini, before German commandos in a daring raid took him north for a brief career as a puppet-ruler of the Salò Republic. The raid would not need to be nearly so intrepid today: a journey which could then only be made by light plane can now be made every day by car.

I have a slight and not irrational dislike for the Gran Sasso that stems from an August weekend when I shared my mountain track with a caravan of walkers that appeared to number several thousand. If this were not enough to compromise its wilderness, a motorway cuts to its heart, tunnels through its bowels and then leads to cable-cars that run straight to its once secret corners. For skiers, the Gran Sasso's limestone is among the world's best, its wide pistes depressingly perfect for family skiing. For me all this dulls the mountain's majesty and diminishes its dignity. That said, it remains an extraordinary place, often described as a small piece of the Dolomites brought south. Come here by all means, but remember that reservations about the Dolomites apply equally to the Gran Sasso: the mountains are magnificent, but you have to share them.

From other Abruzzo massifs, the Gran Sasso appears as a single mountain; from the Adriatic coast, however, its summits are visible as detached peaks, the 2,914 metres (9,560 feet) of the Corno Grande resplendent as a glorious free-standing pyramid. From its summit, and from that of the neighbouring Corno Piccolo (2,665 m/8,743 ft), both Adriatic and Tyrrhenian coasts are visible on clear days.

To escape humanity you must climb high, rather like the mountain's beleaguered wildlife. It is on high — many peaks are in excess of 2,500 metres (8,000 feet) — that the Gran Sasso presents its grand union of Alpine and Apennine scenery. It is a place of superlatives. It has one of Europe's southernmost glaciers, the Calderone, a modest area of six hectares (15 acres), as well as the highest spring in the Apennines, the Fonte Grotta (2,050 metres/6,726 feet). Campo Imperatore is the largest upland plain in the Apennines, 27 kilometres (17 miles) long and 8 kilometres (5 miles) wide, the mother of all Italy's flower-filled meadows. Gorgeous with colour in spring, in summer it becomes arid, sun-baked and monotonous.

Although much visited, the Gran Sasso does conceal corners of solitude. The more remote cliffs and crags provide nesting sites for a few pairs of golden eagles, lanner falcons and peregrines, as well as colonies of choughs, distinguished by their scarlet beaks. It was here that I once disturbed a feeding peregrine. When I reached the point on the path from which it had taken off, I found the neatly discarded head, feet and spinal cord of what had once been a chough. I was frankly amazed that such an aerial acrobat could have fallen prey to a bird that is only a little larger than itself.

Until recently, neither the Laga nor the Gran Sasso had much of an animal population. Their tally was small or limited to minor fauna such as Orsini's viper and the Italian newt, both typical of the high Apennines. Thanks to the efforts of the park authorities, however, there has been an upturn. Wildcats, foxes, badgers, snow voles, martens and ferrets are all present and correct. Chamois have been successfully reintroduced in a couple of places, wolves have returned to hunt in packs and marsican bears are occasionally sighted.

To make the most of the mountains it is best not only to go high but to arrive out of season. An ideal day would find you on the Gran Sasso in October, the crowds gone and the snow yet to fall. The refuges are still open, and the chair lifts get you off to a cracking start. The CAI branch in Ascoli has published a useful guide for walkers which lists over 60 routes in the Gran Sasso. Some are easy, some call for stout heart and stout boots, but all should be treated with respect. Some stretches require climbing skills, and in others the snow arrives early and stays long. Some areas are out of bounds because of the risk of avalanches. The rule is, stay on the trails. There is more high-level lodging here than anywhere else in the Apennines. Some huts are virtual hotels, others simply provide shelter for shepherds.

ORSINI'S VIPER

Orsini's viper, *Vipera ursinii ursinii,* is a thick-set, slate-grey snake with a black-bordered zigzag stripe down the centre of its back and a rather narrower head than most vipers. The smallest of the European vipers, it is rarely more than a metre (three feet) long when fully grown, seldom bites and carries relatively weak venom. It can be found in isolated groups in the mountains of France and in Italy where it has been recorded in the Monti Sibillini, the Monti della Laga, the Gran Sasso and the Velino; it probably also lives in the Abruzzo national park. Of all the Italian colonies, the one at Campo Imperatore in the Gran Sasso is by far the largest.

BEFORE YOU GO

Maps: IGM 1:25,000 Nos 338 IV *Acquasanta Terme*, 349 I *Montório al Vomano*, 349 IV *Campotosto*; CAI 1:50,000 *Monti della Laga*. For the Cento Cascate walk (see below) take IGM 1:25,000 No. 338 III *Monte Gorzano*. For the Gran Sasso the best single sheet is the 1:50,000 *Carta del Gran Sasso* (CAI L'Áquila).

Guide-books: E. Burri, *Parco Nazionale del Gran Sasso e Monti della Laga* (Carsa, 2002); A. Alesi, M. Calibani, A. Palermi, *Gran Sasso, Parco Nazionale Gran Sasso-Laga, 64 itinerari e la traversata del Gran Sasso in 6 giorni* (part of *Le più belle escursioni* series, CAI Ascoli Piceno, 2000).

GETTING THERE

By car: for the Monti della Laga take the SS4 from Rome to Rieti, Antrodoco and Amatrice; otherwise take the A24 to L'Áquila, the best base for the Gran Sasso. From Pescara and the north-east take A14 and SS80 to Teramo, where minor roads reach into the eastern side of the park, and for the Lago di Campotosto continue on the SS80 beyond Teramo. For the funicular to the Campo Imperatore take the A24 to Assergi, whence minor roads lead east and west across the national park.

By rail: go to L'Áquila on the Terni–Rieti–Sulmona line (9 trains daily), then take buses to towns and villages in the park. Information from the station at Sulmona, T: (0864) 55243.

By bus: buses regularly run between Teramo, Amatrice, Pescara, L'Áquila, Sulmona, Avezzano and Rome; a limited service is provided to mountain centres such as Cesacástina, Campotosto and Prati di Tivo from Teramo or L'Áquila. Contact A.R.P.A., Teramo, T:

(0861) 245 857, Pescara, T: (085) 421 5099, L'Áquila, T: (0862) 412 808, Sulmona, T: (0864) 209 133 or Avezzano, T: (0863) 26561.

WHERE TO STAY

Hotels: L'Áquila has accommodation in every category. On the northern edge of the Gran Sasso, Prati di Tivo is aimed primarily at skiers, but has places open all year: try Hotel Amorocchi (3-star), Piazza Amorocchi, T: (0861) 959 603, or Hotel Europa (2-star), T: (0736) 255 671 (open weekends only during the winter). For the Monti della Laga, try Hotel Valle (2-star), Via Roma 57, Campotosto, T: (0862) 900 119. Alternatives are at Amatrice, which is the best overall base for these mountains: Hotel La Conca (2-star), Via della Madonnella, T: (0746) 826 791; or at Acquasanta Terme: Hotel Terme (2-star), Piazza Terme 20, T: (0736) 801 263.

Agriturismo: for bases at the edge of the park try La Torre di Carapelle, Carapelle Calvisio, T: (0862) 930 305, or L'Aperegina, Corvara, T: (085) 888 9351.

Refuges: the hills are scattered with huts belonging to shepherds and the forestry authorities. CAI runs 5 huts in the Gran Sasso. The most popular are Duca degli Abruzzi, T: (0862) 606 657, and Franchetti, T: (0861) 959 634 (summer) and (06) 827 0047 (winter); both are departure points for climbs and walks on the Corno Grande and Corno Piccolo. The others are: Nicola D'Arcangelo, T: (0861) 413 637; Tito Acerbo, T: (085) 823 131; and Del Monte, at the northern foot of Monte Corvo, T: (0871) 331 198.

ACTIVITIES

Walking: highly recommended is the trek in the Valle delle Cento Cascate, with optional ascents of Gorzano and the Monti della Laghetta (6 hrs): it starts (and finishes) at the bridge on the road above Cesacástina, a hamlet 6 km (4 miles) south-east of Gorzano. The path follows an obvious route along the stream and then climbs in open country to the main ridge at the Sella di Gorzano. Another classic walk is the west-wall ascent of Corno Grande from Rif. Duca degli Abruzzi (there is a funicular from Assergi to 2,120 m/6,955 ft, 1 km from the refuge). From the summit you can continue to Rif. Franchetti, cross the Valle delle Cornácchie and descend to Prati di Tivo, with another chair lift, if required, for the final descent; yellow and red markings (6 hrs). To return to the Duca the following day, take the trail via the Val Moane. (Snow may linger on the route as late as July.) Other noteworthy walks include: the climb to Monte d' Intermesole (2,635 m/8,644 ft) from Capanne in Val Moane (3 hrs); the climb to Pizzo Cefalone (2,533 m/8,310 ft) from Passo della Portella (2 hrs); the panoramic ascent of Monte di Mezzo (2,136 m/7,007 ft) above Lago di Campotosto from Frattoli or Campotosto village (4 hrs); and the walk to Monte Gorzano from Amatrice via the Fosso di Selva Grande and Sella della Solagna (6 hrs). This walk starts at the hamlet of Capricchia, launch pad for several hikes.

Skiing: excellent scope for the alpine skier, with a noted traverse of the Monti della Laga range (10–12 hrs) as well as resorts at Campo Imperatore, T: (0862) 221 46, and Prati di Tivo, T: (0861) 955 104; cross-country options include the Tre Laghetti (16 km/10 miles) on the Campo Imperatore and the route along

the Valle del Chiarino (12 km/7 miles) as well as some high-quality routes in the solitary Bosco della Martese and the haul from Umito to S. Gerbone.

FURTHER INFORMATION
Tourist offices: IAT, Via Oberdan 16, Teramo, T: (0861) 244 222/247 304; APT, Via Cintia 87, Rieti, T: (0746) 201 146/7; IAT, Piazza S. Maria Pagánica, L'Áquila, T: (0862) 410 808. For walking, climbing and skiing information, contact CAI offices at Corso Umberto I, Amatrice, T: (0746) 826 344 (also Pro Loco office open weekends only during winter); Via Fedele Romani 5, Teramo, T: (0861) 245 262; or Via Sassa 34, L'Áquila, T: (0862) 24342.

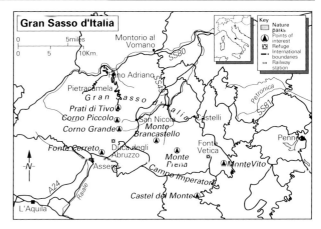

Park office: Via del Convento, Assergi, T: (0862) 60521, or visit www.gransassolagapark.it. **Visitor centre:** Comunità del Parco, Torricella Sicura, T:

(0861) 552 566.
Ecology: WWF, Via Gasbarrini 1, Teramo, T: (0861) 411 147; Via Collesapone 2, L'Áquila, T: (0862) 28274.

Sirente-Velino

Immense mountain ranges on the borders of the Abruzzo and Lazio, commanding the approach from Rome; parco naturale regionale
62,000 ha (153,000 acres)
ZPS

Climb to the top of St Peter's in Rome on a clear winter's day and you can see the snow-covered summit of Monte Velino on the eastern horizon. One of the most monumental and magnificent of all the mountains in central Italy, it is known as *la montagna morta,* the 'dead mountain', a mass of Mesozoic limestone whose vast areas of semi-desert from afar give the impression of total nakedness. In this unforgiving empty quarter you could walk from the Velino's northern foothills, crest

the central peaks and drop down the ridges of the adjoining Sirente — a distance of some 120 kilometres (75 miles) — crossing just one tarmac road.

The massif's heartland is Monte Velino itself (2,487 metres/8,159 feet) and its cluster of adjoining high peaks: Monte di Sévice, Monte Cafórnia and the Colle dell'Orso, all over 2,000 metres (6,600 feet). In the north-west the Velino mountains merge with the Monti della Duchessa, in the south-east with the Sirente, which are if anything quieter, broader and even more lonely. Their summits also break the 2,000-metre mark; more peaks, in fact, cross that barrier in the Sirente-Velino than in any of the more famous Abruzzo massifs.

The Sirente-Velino have the split personality of many Italian mountains, by turns harsh and unforgiving, gentle and life-giving. They display their most splendid character traits on their south-facing flanks. Pyramidal in profile, seemingly sheer cliffs and crags stare down at Avezzano and the Fúcino plain. Behind this imposing facade, the northern slopes are more discreet, punctuated by limestone plains, splintered ridges and ancient beech forests. Wildlife flourishes where the harshness ends.

The stark glacial grandeur of the Gran Sasso, the highest point in the Apennines (2,914 m/9,560 ft), attracts large numbers of hikers and climbers.

For all their classic limestone configuration, these mountains show the effects of glaciation to a degree rare in the Apennines. They have tumbling screes, moraines, hanging valleys, even rogue rocks carried from distant mountains by advancing ice. High on Monte Morrone, in the Duchessa, for example, is the famous Pietra Rosa , the 'pink rock', a huge, solitary boulder brought from who knows where during the last Ice Age. Birds of prey gather in this ice-carved scenery, happy to nest in its moraines and rocky clefts. The Murolungo, the 'long wall', towering hundreds of metres high, is home to buzzards, lanner falcons, peregrines, short-toed eagles and a colony of alpine swifts. At the cliff base nestles the Grotta dell'Oro, a cave kept moist, even in summer, by the dripping of water through the rocks above. It attracts evening conventions of birds, including redstarts from the surrounding broom scrub.

Elsewhere you will find scooped-out tarns, tiny glinting lakes in an otherwise barren wasteland. The loveliest is the Lago della Duchessa, cradled in crags at 1,772 metres (5,813 feet). It has no source, but is supplied simply by rain and meltwater, the spring and winter life-blood of visiting birds. Coot, teal, garganey and tufted duck cluster here at dawn and dusk. Alongside gather hundreds of wheatears and water pipits, in a constant search for shore-side insects and larvae.

The most spectacular glacial features are the gouged valleys of the Gole di Celano, Val di Teve and Valle Majelama. Easily accessible to walkers, the Gole di Celano, situated on the southern side of the Sirente, is perhaps the most majestic gorge in the Apennines. Between the villages of Ovíndoli and Celano it drops 600 metres (2,000 feet) over 10 kilometres (6 miles), narrowing to a corridor the width of outstretched arms and flanked by walls 100 metres (300 feet) high on either side. A magnificent track follows the gorge for its entire length. Walk it in September, before the rains make it dangerous or even impassable.

In among the more barren expanses of rock lie oases of green. Grassy uplands such as the Piana di Pezza and Campo Felice enjoy brisk summer breezes and a brief but exceptional riot of seasonal colour; buttercups, gentians, saxifrages, campions and toadflaxes are all too quickly snuffed out by sun or snow. Beech forms forests where it escapes the climatic extremes, usually in the shelter of the steeper valleys. Oak can be glimpsed here and there, but you have to drop from the beech's domain before reaching the mixed woodlands that harbour much of the Velino's wildlife. Wildcats and martens are on the prowl, and even wolves, which in the coldest winters have been known to scavenge on the outskirts of Ovíndoli.

The broad high plateau between the Velino and Sirente massifs, commanded by Ovíndoli, marks another break from bare slopes. Birdlife is well represented: common species, such as thrushes, blackbirds and woodcock, inhabit the fringes of the woodland, quail, crows, shrikes and rock partridges thrive in the meadows, and when heavy November rains turn the ground into a marshy bog, white wagtails, snipe, plovers and other waders make an appearance.

BEFORE YOU GO

Maps: IGM 1:25,000 Nos 368 I *Ovíndoli*, 359 III *Piano di Campo Felice*, 368 IV *Massa d'Albe*, 368 II *Celano*.
Guide-books: S. Ardito, *A piedi sul Sirente Velino* (Iter, 1995); S. Ardito, *A piedi in Abruzzo I* (Iter, 1996).

GETTING THERE

By car: approach on A24/25 from north, west and east (L'Áquila, Rome and Sulmona); take Valle del Salto exit for Duchessa; Magliano exit for Massa d'Albe and Monte Velino; Celano exit for Gole di Celano. One minor road, the SS5, bisects the Velino and Sirente massifs.
By rail: the Rome–Avezzano–Pescara line hugs the southern edge of the park with useful stations at Cappelle (for Velino), Celano (for the gorge) and Avezzano. The branch line from Sulmona to L'Áquila and Terni (Umbria) is moderately useful for northern access to the massifs. For further information contact tourist offices and the stations at L'Áquila, T: (0862) 419 290, or Sulmona, T: (0864) 55243.
By bus: A.R.P.A. runs services to all towns and villages. Main termini are at L'Áquila, T: (0862) 412 808, Avezzano, T:

(0863) 26561, and Sulmona, T:
(0864) 210 469.

WHERE TO STAY
Hotels: L'Áquila has a wide
range but if you want to stay in a
village, try Cristal (3-star), Via
Saas-Fee 2, Rocca di Cámbio, T:
(0862) 918 119; Cavallino Bianco
(2-star), Via O. Moretti,
Ovíndoli, T: (0863) 705 544; you
should be able to find rooms in
Róvere and Celano.
Agriturismo: try Sotto L'Aia,
C.da Sotto l'Aia, Gagliano
Aterno, T: (0864) 790 197.
Refuge: there is a single
mountain refuge, the Sebastiani
(2,100 m/6,900 ft), at the head of
the Piana di Pezza. Contact
CAI, Via Galvani 10, Rome, T:
(06) 5728 7143/574 7607.
Outdoor living: camping is
permitted, and can be the only
way of seeing much of the
region. Camp-sites without
services exist at Prati del
Sirente and Campo di Via, near
Ovíndoli. For fully equipped
camp-sites, either contact
tourist offices or visit
www.camping.it/abruzzo.

ACTIVITIES
Walking: walkers on high
ground can expect some of
Italy's most exposed and
gruelling outings. Local
weather has a reputation for
being changeable. Try the
superb traverse of the Celano
canyon; the ascent of Velino
from the Piana di Pezza (6 hrs);
the Valle di Teve from Cartore
(4 hrs); the Lago della
Duchessa from Cartore (2 hrs).
Longer ascents of Velino are
possible from Monte Cafórnia
and Massa d'Albe. In the
Sirente, explore the relict beech
woods at Anatella; the Prati del
Sirente and its tiny lake; and
the lesser peaks of Faito, Serra
di Celano and Pizzo di
Ovíndoli.
Pony-trekking: the mountains
will prove too much for all but
the keenest riders and hardiest
animals. The gentler terrain of
the Altopiano delle Rocche is
more suitable, and there are
numerous trekking centres on
the SS5 between Rocca di
Mezzo and Ovíndoli. Contact
Circolo Ippico Ponte Grosso,

Rocca di Mezzo, T: (0862) 917
135.
Climbing: winter snow and ice
climbs are excellent; summit
approaches to Velino, Sirente,
Cafórnia and Serra di Celano
are Italian classics, but there
are surprisingly few other
possibilities. Contact CAI, Via
Sassa 34, L'Áquila, T: (0862)
24342.
Skiing: alpine skiers head for
the resorts of Monte della
Magnola, Ovíndoli, T: (0863)
705 087, and Campo Felice,
Rocca di Cámbio, T: (0862) 917
803. Some classic cross-country
circuits are to be found at Rocca
di Mezzo, Puzzillo and the
Piana di Pezza.

FURTHER INFORMATION
Tourist offices: IAT, Piazza S.
Maria Pagánica, T: (0862) 410
808, L'Áquila; Pro Loco, Via
Duca degli Abruzzi 2, Rocca di
Cámbio, T: (0862) 918 100 and
Via IV Novembre 2, Rocca di
Mezzo, T: (0862) 916 125.
Park office: Via Orti di S. Maria
1, Rocca di Mezzo, T: (0862)
916 343, e-mail: sirvel@tin.it.

Parco Nazionale d'Abruzzo

*Straddling Abruzzo's southern border with
Lazio is a stretch of unspoiled Apennine
scenery famous for its spectacular flora
and fauna;* parco nazionale
*European Diploma, ZPS
44,400 ha (109,700 acres) with a buffer
zonc of 80,000 ha (198,000 acres)*

The Abruzzo national park is the last
major refuge in central Italy for the wolf,
bear and chamois, creatures that until the
20th century had roamed the Apennines for
thousands of years. In this model of good

conservation, Italy for once has done itself
proud, creating a park recognized as one of
the most important in Europe.

Not hugely well endowed with massifs, the
park clings mostly to the course of the
Sangro valley, garnering small mountain
groups to either side, the highest of these
being in the south-east, the Monti della Meta
(2,247 metres/7,372 feet). The rest reach a
respectable 1,800 metres (5,900 feet).

Mesozoic limestone underpins the
scenery in all but the Monti della Meta
where a slice of Dolomitic rock adds a
dash of Alpine spectacle, hoisting higher,
glacier-carved crests above the less-
modified slopes of its surroundings. Lakes,
albeit small ones, bring the glint of water

A meadow in the Sangro valley *(overleaf)* is brilliantly
illuminated by poppies, one of the 2,000 species of
flora in the Abruzzo national park.

The brown bear, Europe's most threatened carnivore, is represented in the Apennines by the subspecies *marsicanus*. About 100 remain in the Abruzzo.

to the landscape, natural-born Vivo, Scanno and Pantaniello competing with man-made creations such as the Lago di Barrea.

The park claims some 8,000 species of plants and animals, including 74 species of mammals, 44 reptiles, 230 birds and 267 fungi, one of the richest tallies in Italy. If this sounds like a shopping list, it is the only drawback to the park, which at times seems a little too tidied and tamed if you like your wilderness wild. Wardens patrol, animals are kept in semi-captivity and signs instruct and implore at every turn. All this, sadly, is the price of protection.

This state within a state, however, is neither a half-hearted wilderness nor just a wildlife park where human beings are reduced to visitors. It has mountains to satisfy even the most demanding walker and a centuries-old pastoral tradition that is still very much alive. It contains 24 towns and villages, the main ones — Pescassèroli, Opi and Villetta Barrea — ranged along the Sangro valley. All are fully integrated with the park, symbols of a way of life fused with an ancient landscape. Regional costume is sometimes seen, sheep farming still predominates, and you are as likely to encounter old men bringing firewood from the forests on donkeys as you are to meet tractors and cars.

The history of protection goes back a long way. The park was once a royal hunting reserve, like many of Italy's present-day parks. Although the reserve was discontinued in 1877, its tradition of caring for wildlife — albeit with a view to killing it

later — was carried on in a smaller reserve between 1900 and 1912. By 1922 an embryonic national park had been created by private initiative; and by 1923 it had a central authority and care of some 30,000 hectares (74,000 acres) of land. These measures are one reason for the particular abundance of fauna in the Abruzzo. Another is the area's central position, which has made it a natural assembly point for animals migrating to escape the summer heat of the south. Yet another is its inaccessibility: only one road crosses the park.

Bears are the rarest and most reclusive of creatures, and though you may find evidence of their presence, you will need the most enormous amount of luck to see one. It is exciting, though, just to know they are prowling the hills around you. The Abruzzo's bears are descended from Alpine ancestors, but over centuries of evolutionary isolation have developed enough different features to merit the status of a subspecies: *Ursus arctos marsicanus*, named after Marsica, the generic name for much of the park area, itself deriving from the Marsi, the area's earliest indigenous tribe.

Bears were common until the 16th century, when they were hunted almost to extinction. After a three-week hunting expedition with the King of Naples at the end of the 18th century, Sir William Hamilton, in a blood-sated post-mortem on the trip, wrote: 'We have been from morning to night without the least intermission persecuting bears, wolves, chevreuil and foxes, of which we have slain about one thousand.' As late as 1915 a bounty was still paid for every bear killed. About 100 bears are reckoned to have survived such brutal treatment, and in the absence of a latter-day Sir William, they are now managing to increase their numbers.

The Abruzzo's wolves evoke the same instinctive fascination as the bears, though your chances of seeing one are probably equally remote. Here, where about 60 Apennine wolves survive, they are the subject of local pride. Locals say the best time to catch a wolf's fleeting shadow is at dawn, when a few strays return to the forest after foraging in outlying farms. Because wolves increasingly cross-breed with domestic dogs, the park maintains a pack in a semi-liberated state at Civitella Alfedena, the idea — a noble one — being to preserve at least some of the species in a genetically pure state.

You are far more likely to come across the Abruzzese chamois. Like the bear, these animals are descendants of an Alpine strain now evolved into a distinct subspecies: *Rupicapra rupicapra ornata*. Sporting a summer coat of uniform brown, in winter they take on multicoloured tints which form a lovely contrast to the black and white markings on their face and neck. About 800 chamois lead a carefree existence in the park, tolerant of humans, but able to run at 85 kph (53 mph) when the occasion demands. They are easily seen in the Valle delle Rose, and there is a reserve at Opi to train specialists in the care of the animals (many are released from here into other parts of the Abruzzo). Completing the picture are a thousand red deer and 800 roe deer, all reintroduced during the 1970s.

Though large mammals take the plaudits, birds play fine supporting roles. Four to five pairs of golden eagles are the stars among the park's many raptors. In two areas, the Camosciara and around Monte Petroso, you might see the white-backed woodpecker, an extremely rare species associated with ancient Apennine forests. Also scarce, but more widespread, is the Apennine rock partridge, recently recognized as a subspecies.

About two-thirds of the park is dominated by forests of beech and maple. The beech here reaches apotheosis, especially on the highest slopes, where the cooler, moist conditions favour its growth. In few places will you see specimens of such magnificent height or colossal girth. The most striking feature of these forests is that they have trees of all ages: delicate striplings; fully grown, ramrod-straight giants; and gnarled veterans of 500 years or more, some of them growing directly out of the bedrock, others lodged among huge moss-covered boulders.

Interspersed with the beech are black hornbeam, ash and hawthorn, along with wild apple, pear, cherry and blackthorn, all trees with wonderful spring coats of blossom. Arboreal specialities include the *Pinus nigra*, which is endemic to Villetta Barrea, and the neighbouring Civitella Alfedena; Lobel's maple, endemic to the mountain woods of central and southern Italy; and *Acer obtusatum*, another maple found also on the Balkan peninsula and in Sicily. At Coppo Oscuro di Barrea there is even birch, an Ice Age remnant of the cold-climate flora that once covered the Apennines. Clusters of chestnut occasionally flourish, and on sunnier slopes the holm oak waves a reminder — for all the chill of the mountains — that we are still in the Mediterranean.

With its wild flowers, too, the park enjoys the best of two worlds: Alpine and Mediterranean. Although snow can linger until May, spring ushers in a riotous assembly of asphodels, crocuses, gentians and snowdrops. The park's pride and joy is the violet-flowered iris — the recently discovered *Iris marsica*, endemic to calcareous rocky hillsides in the central Apennines. Other notables shared with neighbouring mountains, though in equally small numbers, are columbines and lady's slipper orchids, with splendid brown, yellow and purple flowers.

BEFORE YOU GO

Map: the park's own 1:50,000 map is all you need. It is available from park offices.

Guide-books: the energetic director, Franco Tassi, who deserves much credit for the park's success, has written the definitive guide, *Nel Parco Nazionale d'Abruzzo* (Martello, 1985), available in English, French, Spanish and German. Both volumes of S. Ardito's *A piedi in Abruzzo* (Iter, 1996) are useful for Italian-reading walkers.

GETTING THERE

By car: from Rome take the A25, exit at Pescina, then follow SS83 to Gioia dei Marsi, Pescasséroli and Opi. From Naples use A1, exit at Caianello, then use SS85 just past Venafro before turning on to the SS158 to Alfedena.

By rail: the station at Alfedena on the Sulmona–Vairano line has connections from Rome and Naples, though the best approach from Rome or Pescara is by train to Avezzano and bus to Pescasséroli. Contact Rome station, T: (06) 4730 6559.

By bus: several buses run daily between Avezzano and Castel di Sangro (at opposite ends of the park) via Pescasséroli, Opi,

Civitella Alfedena and points *en route*. Contact A.R.P.A. at Avezzano, T: (0863) 26561 or Pescassèroli, T: (0864) 210 469.

WHERE TO STAY

Hotels: La Conca (3-star), Via Rovereto 2, Pescassèroli, T: (0863) 910 562, is central and open all year. Try also La Pieja (3-star), Via Salita la Croce 44, Opi, T: (0863) 910 756; Leon d'Oro (1-star),Via Roma 32, Alfedena, T: (0863) 87121.

Agriturismo: try Madonna degli Angeli, Tocco Casauria, T: (0862) 422 3813; La Torre di Carapelle, Carapelle Calvisio, T: (0862) 930 305.

Refuges: many in the park are

Winter is long in the high grasslands of the Abruzzo, where snow lies from October to June.

solely for study purposes and only a few open to the public; try Rif. dell'Orso, near Pescassèroli, T: (0863) 91955; Rif. del Diavolo, Gioia dei Marsi, T: (0863) 88152/(06) 445 7512.

Youth hostel: try the Tre Confini at Villavallelonga, T: (0863) 949 406.

Outdoor living: there are campsites at Scanno, Villavallelonga, Pescassèroli, Civitella Alfedena, Villetta Barrea, Barrea and — one of the most pleasant — Le Foci, Via Fonte dei Cementi, Opi, T: (0863) 912 233.

ACCESS AND CLOSURES

Forest roads are closed to motor traffic and in some valleys the number of visitors is restricted in the summer.

ACTIVITIES

Walking: you can choose from 150 numbered and well-marked

The western slopes of many Abruzzese massifs are often rounded and grassy, as here in the Gran Sasso, in contrast to the eastern flanks which are bare and glaciated.

trails of all standards. The most popular — avoid it during summer weekends — is Trail L1 from Civitella Alfedena to the Valle delle Rose, sightings of chamois almost guaranteed (5 hrs). Other favourites include: the climb from Barrea to Lago Vivo (2 hrs); the easy walk in the Camosciara valley to the refuge at Belvedere della Liscia (2 hrs); a variety of paths in the well-known Val Fondillo. Marked treks include the Alta Via Est-Ovest from Roccaraso to Sora (3 days) and the Alta Via Nord-Sud from Villavallelonga to Civitella (4 days). Obtain details from park offices

147

(addresses given below).

Pony-trekking: try Centro Ippico Monte Javuttaro, Via Cabinovia, Pescassèroli, T: (0863) 910 480; stables are also to be found at Opi, Scanno and Villetta Barrea.

Canoeing: the River Sangro east of Opi has one of the classic Italian routes, an 8-km (5-mile) run through fast-flowing water to the Lago di Barrea.

Skiing: G.I.S.P., Pescassèroli, T: (0863) 911 118, has cable-cars to Monte delle Vitelle (1,945 m/6,381 ft), where there are 5 lifts, a beginners' slope and 20 km (12 miles) of pistes. The best cross-country routes are north of the park at Scanno.

Bird-watching: the park's own map suggests the best points to see birds, and also other animals.

Museums: Museo Naturalistico in Pescassèroli, T: (0863) 910 405; Museo del Lupo Appenninico in Civitella Alfadena, T: (0864) 890 141.

FURTHER INFORMATION
Tourist offices: IAT, Via Piave, Pescassèroli, T: (0863) 910 461; Pro Loco, Via S. Giovanni, Opi, T: (0863) 910 622; Piazza Umberto I, Alfedena, T: (0864) 87394.

Park offices: Via Tito Livio 12, Roma, T: (06) 354 033 31; Via S. Lucia, Pescassèroli, T: (0863) 910 715; for queries on outdoor pursuits, refuges, guided tours and wildlife, contact Ufficio di Zona Pescassèroli, Via Consultore 1, T: (0863) 91955.

Visitor centres: Civitella Alfedena, T: (0864) 89170 (where you can also find the wolf centre); a modern international centre at Villetta Barrea, T: (0864) 89102; Villavallelonga, T: (0863) 949 261 (the best place to see bears both in captivity and in the wild); and others in minor towns during the summer.

Parco Nazionale D'Abruzzo

Bosco di Sant'Antonio

Ancient beech forest in the south-eastern corner of the Abruzzo; riserva naturale regionale, part of the Parco Nazionale della Maiella 550 ha (1,359 acres)

If you had to choose a particular microcosm of the Apennines — its woods, hills and wildlife — it would probably be this most perfect of beech forests. Beech is the characteristic tree of central Italy: verdant in spring and fiery in autumn, the almost constant companion of walkers in the Abruzzo.

The Sant'Antonio forest spreads over the Vera valley above Pescocostanzo, a short distance to the east of the Abruzzo national park. It is sheltered on either side by Monte Rotella and Monte Pizzalto, resting in the perfect 'V' of a valley that lies between them, overshadowed by crags and surrounded by tranquil grassy meadows.

Some of the trees are a thousand, and most many hundreds of years old. Certain gigantic specimens on the valley floor at Piano del Ceraso have trunks over 3 m (10 ft) in diameter. In modest contrast, during the spring little bursts of colour, peonies and narcissi, push through the forest floor. The mood here alternates between cathedral-like solemnity and the bird-filled chatter of stately sun-washed branches. Sharing the forest glades you may glimpse woodpeckers, tits, chaffinches, blackcaps, cuckoos and golden orioles. The sharp scent of fox pervades the air, and hungry wolves sometimes abandon the shelter of the trees to hunt the sheep grazing in neighbouring meadows.

As so often, the wood owes its survival to the care of monks, here based at the medieval hermitage in nearby Sant'Antonio. It still came within a hair's breadth of destruction 40 years ago, and it was as late as 1985 that a binding order was put on the area. It is now part of the Maiella national park.

Some 130 ha (321 acres) of the reserve are primary woodland, a precious fragment that survives just kilometres from Roccaraso and Rivisóndoli, two of the Abruzzo's most developed tourist resorts.

Before you go *Map:* IGM 1:25,000 No. 379 III *Roccaraso*.
Getting there *By car:* most visitors make for Pescocostanzo, a traditional lace-making village as appealing as the forest itself. It lies 5 km (3 miles) north of Roccaraso, just off the SS17 between Isérnia and Sulmona.

From the village a lovely unclassified road runs for 20 km (12 miles) up the Vera valley to Cansano.
By rail: stations at Cansano and Pescocostanzo on the (slow) Sulmona–Isérnia–Carpinone line (5 trains daily). Contact Società Sangritana, T: (0872) 7081. *By bus:* services run to Castel di Sangro and Roccaraso from Avezzano, Sulmona, Pescasséroli and Isérnia. Contact A.R.P.A., Avezzano, T: (0863) 26561 or Sulmona, T: (0864) 210 469.
Where to stay *Hotels:* there is a rather ugly hotel on the edge of the wood, S. Antonio, T: (0864) 67101. Alternatively, try Le Torri (4-star), Corso Roma 21, Pescocostanzo, T: (0864) 642 040; Calypso (3-star), Via G. Marconi 93, Rivisóndoli, T: (0864) 641 910; or Fonte Romana (2-star), Via Caramanico 9, Campo di Giove, T: (0864) 40111.
B&Bs: try Faggeto at S. Antonio, T: (0864) 67100, or

Archi del Sole at Pescocostanzo, T: (0864) 640 007. *Outdoor living:* in the hills to the south is Del Sole, Piana del Leone, T: (0864) 62532.
Activities *Riding:* try the *maneggio* at Bosco S. Antonio, which organizes treks through the woods from spring to autumn, T: (0864) 67136.
Pony-trekking: try Centro Ippico Il Casale delle Querce, C.da Casali 85, Nocciano, T: (085) 847 625.
Skiing: try Scuola di Sci Alpino, Piazzale degli Sciatori, Pescocostanzo, T: (0864) 641 436; or the Bosco S. Antonio school, T: (0864) 67135/6 (ski hire available). You will also have ample opportunities for cross-country skiing through the woods.
Further information *Tourist offices:* IAT, Vico delle Cárceri 4, Pescocostanzo, T: (0864) 641 440, Via Roma 60, Roccaraso, T: (0864) 62210 and Piazza Municipio 6, Rivisóndoli, T: (0864) 69351.

La Maiella

Abruzzo limestone massif cut by deep canyons; parco nazionale *74,095 ha (183,096 acres)*

The mystery and spirit of a place are qualities as hard to account for as personal charm. The Maiella, the *madre montagna*, or 'mother of mountains' in Abruzzese tradition, has both, along with the sort of wilderness that is found elsewhere in Italy only on Etna, Pollino and in the Sardinian interior. Its name derives from Maia, mother of the god Mercury (Hermes in classical Greece), whose bountiful gifts as the Earth Mother were at one time widely worshipped in the Adriatic.

But to call the Maiella a mountain is to oversimplify. It is a fantastically complicated massif of 61 peaks and 75 hills whose highest point is Monte Amaro (2,793 metres/9,163 feet), the 'bitter mountain', second in height on the Italian peninsula only to the Gran Sasso. The main ridge runs north-south for 30 kilometres (20 miles). To the east spreads a labyrinth of spectacular valleys. To the west lies a foreboding jumble of lower hills, broad plains and finger-like crests that curl up towards the summits.

If any range symbolizes the grandeur of the central Apennines, to my mind it is the Maiella, more so than either the Velino or the Gran Sasso, from whose heights to the north it appears as a great bowed shield. It needs to be courted as a stranger — slowly and warily. Distances are long, and the walks in the foothills laborious. Road, rail and civilized comforts are far away. Exploration should be gradual, with time spent in the lower valleys

Towering above its girdle of rocky grassland, the Maiella remains one of Italy's most forbidding natural redoubts, even set against neighbouring wild massifs.

before moving onwards and upwards.

The eastern, more inaccessible approaches are the best. The ancient tracks of brigands, monks and shepherds climb through dark, almost Nordic, forests, solemn places which from afar appear as a coarse blanket of fuzz cast over the mountains — a single intense green in which it is hard to discern individual trees. Under its mantle, invisible streams have cut deep fissures into the valley sides, showing up as etched lines which reach up until the green fades to rock and the rock, in its turn, to the white of summit snows.

On summer days there is nothing but an immense silence in these valleys; silence and the stately passage of clouds over monochrome green. You may choose from several such valleys: the Fara San Martino or Santo Spírito, Selvaromana, Taranta

Peligna, Tre Grotte, Fossato, Mandrelle or the ominous Vallone di Fémmina Morta, the 'valley of the dead woman'. To confound neat categories, the most spectacular valley is not in the east but on the northwestern slopes of the Maiella above Caramánico, the Valle d'Orfento.

The forests of the Maiella valleys are some of Italy's grandest, and contain important relict woodlands. The best of the many huge beech forests grow on the slopes of the Maielletta and in the valleys of the Orfento and Valico di Forchetta. Gessopalena harbours colossal oaks, and on the Blockhaus ridge on the Maielletta grow groups of dwarf pine which, in the central Apennines, are found only here and in the Abruzzo national park.

As famous as the valleys are the high plains above them. Here are some of the wildest meadows in the Apennines, vast areas of rocky grassland that give a wonderful sense of solitude and remoteness. Higher still, above 2,500 metres (8,000 feet), come barren plateaux that seem to support nothing but a covering of stones As far as the eye can see there appears neither tree, water nor blade of grass. Views are outstanding, embracing the Gran Sasso, the Matese hills and the Trémiti islands, visible only as pinpricks in the distant Adriatic.

In among these godforsaken and apparently lifeless spots flourish the wild flowers that have made the Maiella famous. The most scented meadows lie on the massif's western shoulders, heady with dozens of herbs: thyme, lemon balm, wormwood, sage and so on. There are rare alpines such as the Icelandic moss *Cetraria islandica*, a white poppy, *Papaver sendtneri*, and a cornucopia of endemics that include Apennine edelweiss, Matilda's rock-jasmine and Apennine pheasant's eye, *Adonis distorta*.

Under these floral treasures lies the limestone that nurtured them, a rock as riddled with karstic quirks as it is in the rest of the Abruzzo. The sink-holes in the Vallone di Fémmina Morta and the Valle Cannella have an extraordinary grandeur, but nothing to match the famous cave system at Cavallone. Its entrance, hidden beneath the slopes of the Taranta valley, is reached by 174 rock-hewn steps and guarded by bats and flocks of darting alpine swifts. The Galleria della Devastazione, a fantastic jumble of fissures and fractured rock, provides evidence of major subterranean upheavals in the past. Stacks of fallen stalactites lie on its floor, some piled high like heaps of unicorn horns, others regenerating in bizarre and mutant forms. Lakelets, springs and waterfalls complete a highly theatrical effect.

The story of the Maiella's fauna is a not entirely happy one: a century's impoverishment followed by a period of repopulation under the watchful eyes of conservationists. Wolves, bears and wildcats abounded until the 19th century; the last bear was killed in 1899 by gypsies, who offered it to the natural history museum in Florence. Now bears, wolves and even otters have reappeared of their own accord, while other species are being reintroduced, including chamois, of which there are now about 70, together with red and roe deer. The biggest success story, however, has been the spread of the wild boar, which is now protected, like the other mammals, from hunting.

Birds found here are species typical of high rocky habitats, for instance alpine swifts, alpine choughs, jackdaws and the lovely wallcreeper — a gorgeous red and grey in flight. Raptors, including golden eagles, lanner falcons and peregrines, are numerous, though it is the presence of the dotterel *(Eudromias morinellus)* that establishes the Maiella's special place among Italian wildernesses. The bird was not discovered here until 1952. A handful of pairs nest 2,500 metres (8,000 feet) up on Monte Amaro, where they find conditions similar to their normal Arctic tundra. As far as is known, this is the bird's southernmost breeding site in Europe.

The Maiella's designation as a national park follows a history of attacks on its wilderness. At the end of the 1960s, in stories that made front-page news, it seemed as though the mountains were to become the latest sacrifice to the great god of skiing. In the end the developers were held at bay, though some resorts were built and traces of other aborted construction projects — lifts and roads — still survive as a reminder of hard-fought battles.

The wallcreeper's long curved bill, its grey and crimson plumage and butterfly-like flight belie its close relationship with the stumpy nuthatch.

BEFORE YOU GO

Maps: CAI at Chieti produce an invaluable 1:50,000 *Carta Turistica della Maiella*, generally more useful than the IGM 1:25,000 sheets: Nos 370 I *Guardiagrele*, 370 II *Fara S. Martino*, 370 III *Campo di Giove*, 370 IV *Caramánico Terme*, 379 III *Roccaraso*, 379 IV *Palena*.

GETTING THERE

By car: approaching from the east, take A14 to Pescara and then A25 to Sulmona-Prátola Peligna; from Rome take A24 then A25. Minor roads leave A25 at Alanno and Torre de' Passéri for the west. The east is served by SS81 and SS84 from Chieti to Roccaraso. Unclassified roads also thread through the park.

By rail: Sulmona is a busy junction on the Pescara–Rome, Sulmona–L'Áquila–Rieti–Terni and Sulmona–Isérnia lines. The station at Campo di Giove on the Isérnia link is useful for access to the south. Contact stations at Sulmona, T: (0864) 55243, or Isérnia, T: (0865) 50921.

By bus: for services to Pretoro, Fara S. Martino, Palena, Roccaraso, Pescocostanzo, Campo di Giove, Caramánico Terme and the other towns in the park from Pescara, Chieti, Lanciano, Guardiagrele and Sulmona, contact A.R.P.A., Pescara, T: (085) 421 5099, Chieti, T: (0871) 348 613 or Sulmona, T: (0864) 210 469. For buses to Taranta Peligna, contact the Società Sangritana, T: (0872) 7081.

WHERE TO STAY

Hotels: try Garibaldi (2-star), Chieti, T: (0871) 345 318, or Armando's (2-star), Sulmona, T: (0864) 210 783. Alternatives are Scoiattolo (2-star), SS Maielletta 7, Pretoro, T: (0871) 898 123; La Maielletta (3-star),

Passo di Lanciano, T: (0871) 896 141; Hotel del Parco (3-star), Pennapiedimonte, T: (0871) 897 147; Camerlengo (3-star), Fara S. Martino, T: (0872) 980 136; Pineta (1-star), Palena, T: (0872) 918 135; Scoiattolo Nero (3-star), Campo di Giove, T: (0864) 408 461; Celidonio (2-star), Pacentro, T: (0864) 41138; or Viola (3-star), Caramánico Terme, T: (085) 92332.

Agriturismo: try De Angelis, Caramánico Terme, T: (085) 922 267, or Masseria Verlengia, Taranta Peligna, T: (333) 769 5355.

Refuges: CAI operates several refuges and bivouacs. The most useful are: Pelino (bivouac) at the top of Monte Amaro; Pomilio (manned refuge serving food and drink) on the Maielletta, T: (0871) 83408; Manzini (unmanned refuge) in the Val Cannella below Monte Amaro; Fusco (bivouac) on the Cima delle Murelle. Obtain keys and information on times and facilities from local CAI branches: Via Fedele Romani 5, Sulmona, T: (0864) 210 635; Piazza dei Templi Romani 3, Chieti, T: (0871) 331 198.

Outdoor living: Valle dell'Orfento, Caramánico Terme, T: (085) 922 251 (summer camp-site); La Maielletta, Pretoro, T: (0871) 896 132 (open all year).

ACTIVITIES

Walking: the key hike, only for experienced walkers, is the

THE WILD BOAR

The boar was one of Italy's most prized mammals. Hunted almost to extinction by those seeking its huge-toothed head as a trophy, it has been persecuted since antiquity.

Despite loss of numbers through hunting and deforestation, the boar can still be found in the Maiella, the Tuscan Maremma and the Calabrian Apennines, as well as in Alto Molise and parts of the Alto Tarvísio and Alpi Maríttime. Traditionally shy animals, boars are only vicious if wounded or cornered, especially females with young. The furrows scooped as they dig for bulbs and tubers are the easily identifiable marks of their passage.

ascent of Monte Amaro (2,795
m/9,163 ft) from Fara S.
Martino via Vallone di S.
Spirito (9 hrs); also to Monte
Amaro from either Block Haus
(6 hrs) or Campo di Giove (7
hrs); and from Campo di Giove
across Monte Porrara to
Stazione di Palena (5 hrs).
There are shorter walks in the
Valle di S. Spírito (1–2 hrs) and
from Block Haus to Scrima
Cavallo (1–2 hrs). Contact Co-
op. Tre Portoni, Caramánico
Terme, T: (085) 922 085, or
CAI, Guardiagrele, T: (338)
543 5854.
Climbing: people go mainly to
the walls of Monte Focalone,
the Dea Maia at
Pennapiedimonte and the Valle
di S. Spírito at Roccamorice.
Noted are the Paretone on the
north-east Cima delle Murelle,
the abseil after the Val Serviera
and the winter routes on
Morrone and Monte Porrara.
For guides, contact Giampiero
di Federico, T: (0871) 64853, or
CAI Chieti, T: (0871) 331 198.
Skiing: alpine pistes can be
found on the Maielletta at
Passo Lanciano, Passo S.
Leonardo and Campo di
Giove. Excellent cross-country
routes are also available on the
Maielletta; contact Sci...volare,
T: (0871) 408 310.

FURTHER INFORMATION
Tourist offices: IAT, Via B.
Spaventa 29, Chieti, T: (0871)
63640/65967, Corso Ovidio
208, Sulmona, T: (0864) 53276,
Piazza S. Maria della Valle 12,
Scanno, T: (0864) 74317 and
Piazza Municipio, Rivisóndoli,
T: (0864) 69351.
Park offices: Via Occidentale 6,
Guardiagrele, T: (0871) 80713;
Piazza Duval 1, Campo di
Giove, T: (0864) 408 51.
Visitor centres: among several
in the park are those at
Caramánico Terme, T: (085)
922 343 and Fara S. Martino,
T: (0872) 980 034.

Alto Molise

*Lonely peaks surrounded
by gently rolling hills in
Molise's north-west corner;
includes three small* riserve
naturali statali
*Includes Biosphere Reserve
and ZPS*

Alto Molise is a timeless
countryside of lazy rivers, soft
valleys and lonely peaks.
The area's capital is Isérnia,
recently identified as one of the
oldest settlements in Europe.
Bones, evidence of fire and traces
of a permanent camp suggest
human activity going back
750,000 years. No human
remains have been found, but the
ghostly inhabitants have been
given the name Isernian Man.
Sheep farming is the
principal activity. To the south
runs one of Italy's great
medieval sheep roads, used for
centuries for the seasonal
movement of flocks.
Massive overhanging crags
are typical, as at Monte Campo
(1,746 m/5,728 ft), which is
some 500 m/1,600 ft higher
than the bulk of Molise's hill
country. Views from these
mountains reach to the
Adriatic, the valleys of the
Maiella and the hillocks that
stretch unbroken to the plains
of Puglia. Walks are short and
energetic, and never far from
roads, the exception being the
lonely, lake-dotted country
around Frosolone.
The mildness of Molise's
landscape can be deceptive.
Capracotta is one of the highest
villages in Italy (1,421 m/4,662
ft) and is often buried in 7 m (23
ft) of snow.
Alto Molise is the region's
only proposed park, and it is
still unprotected except for

three state reserves at
Montedimezzo, Collemeluccio
and Pesche, to the south. Among
breeding birds, it can lay claim to
honey buzzards, black and red
kites, peregrines and occasional
golden eagles. Montedimezzo,
an ancient Bourbon hunting
reserve, provides a haven for
wild boar and lynx.
Before you go *Maps:* IGM
1:25,000 Nos 405 IV
Macchiagódena, 392 I *Carovilli*,
379 II *Capracotta*, 380 III
Agnone, 393 I *Trivento*.
Getting there *By car:* from A1
exit at S. Vittore or Caianello,
then SS85. From L'Áquila and
the north take SS17; from the
east, SS650 and SS652.
By rail: from Rome change at
Cassino, from Naples at
Vairano; take line to Isérnia, T:
(0865) 50921, and on to
Alfadena and Sulmona,
connections for Abruzzo.
By bus: from Campobasso to
Agnone and Pescopennataro,
Agenzia Larivera, T: (0874)
64744; from Agnone to
Capracotta, Agenzia Siti, T:
(0874) 94738; otherwise, Molise
Trasporti, Campobasso, T:
(0874) 493 080.
Where to stay *Hotel:* Capracotta
(3-star), Via Vallesorda,
Capracotta, T: (0865) 945 368.
Agriturismo: Masseria S. Lucia,
Agnone, T: (0865) 77347.
Activities *Walking:* around
Frosolone and between
Pescopennataro and Capracotta.
Pony-trekking: Azienda I
Selvaggi, Strada Provinciale
Montesangrina, Loc. Stáffoli, T:
(0865) 77177. *Climbing:*
limestone walls at Colle
dell'Orso and Pescopennataro;
CAI Campobasso, Via Toscana
40, T: (0874) 66500. *Skiing:*
cross-country routes around
Capracotta.
Further information *Tourist
offices:* APT, Via Farinacci 9,
Isérnia, T: (0865) 3992 and
Piazza della Vittória 14,
Campobasso, T: (0874) 415 662.

CHAPTER 7

Lazio and Campania

Both Lazio and Campania were once wild and very beautiful regions. Both, in parts, still are, but each has to support a major Italian city, Rome and Naples respectively. Rome, of course, came forth from wilderness, from the wolf that suckled the twins Romulus and Remus. And Naples stands at the edge of the Campania *felix* of the Romans, the 'happy' region Pliny described as 'so blest with natural beauties and riches that it is clear that when nature formed it she took delight in accumulating all her blessings in one spot'.

Campania's privileged position in many ways has been its own downfall. Good climate, rich soils and seas have always made it prosperous. Today the region has Italy's highest population density. Naples has 80,000 people per square kilometre, a figure rivalled only by the likes of Cairo and Calcutta. The verve and spirit with which Neapolitans live elbow to elbow is legendary, but there is little in the city or its hinterland for anyone who relishes air and space.

Little save Vesuvius, which looms over Naples, ready one day to erupt and cover the city as it covered Pompeii and Herculaneum. Vesuvius is at the centre of a volcanic belt that runs behind the coasts of both Campania and Lazio. Other, less daunting dormant volcanoes emerge near Rome, in the Albani (or Frascati) hills to the south of the capital and the Tolfa hills and tufaceous lowlands of the Roman Campagna to the north, showing their presence in the old craters now filled with the lakes

The rock arch at Capo Palinuro on the Cilento coast has been carved by wind and waves.

of Bracciano, Vico and Bolsena.

I have sat and slept through several minor earthquakes in Rome, but nothing to compare with the events of 23 November 1980, when for about two minutes Italy shifted very slightly towards the Balkans. Seventeen towns were destroyed and 4,000 people killed in the earthquake, whose epicentre lay 30 kilometres (20 miles) below ground south of Naples.

To find Campania's natural highlights, you need to go beyond Vesuvius, putting Naples and its tectonic dangers firmly behind you. Travel south and you come to the Sorrento peninsula and the island of Capri, which have some of Europe's most fabled coastline, famed for its incandescent light and peacock-coloured seas. You will not find much in the way of wilderness here, but you will find tiny enclaves of rare fauna, lovely areas for walking and some of the most rapturous seascapes in Italy.

For the wind and the wet, and a last farewell to Naples, you must head further south to the shores of the Cilento, a mountainous area in Campania's south-east corner — as empty as Naples is full — and the first of the big southern massifs. By now you will have crossed the invisible border into the south, the 'other' Italy. Naples is its historical capital, but where the frontier lies is anyone's guess. The Milanese say Florence, the Florentines Rome, and the Romans, who do not really care, say the first petrol station south of Rome.

Inland from the Cilento lie the Apennines which run through both regions but, unlike the Abruzzese mountains further north, do not form high free-standing massifs. The wildest and most distinct heights here are the Picentini, raising a final green rampart before the worn hills and exhausted soils of Basilicata, the first of the

southern badlands that lie beyond. From the Picentini run short sharp rivers like the Sele, whose broad plain acts as one of the few refuges for birds migrating north up Italy's Tyrrhenian coast.

To find wild places north of Naples, take your cue from the birds. After leaving the oasis of the Sele plains, they put out to sea, likely as not to avoid Naples and, by way of the Pontine archipelago, reach the territory of southern Lazio. For many centuries this would have been as tempting a place as any for them to settle. Prime agricultural land until the end of the Roman Empire, this flat coastal strip fell into disuse and reverted to lake, marsh and woodland, a landscape that used to stretch virtually unbroken up the coasts of Campania and Lazio into the Maremma of southern Tuscany.

Much of this land was malarial, uncultivable and uninhabited. What little could be used provided meagre grazing for sheep and cattle. Until the 20th century it continued thus, with pastureland reaching up to, and often inside, the walls of Rome itself. This scene changed completely with the vast Fascist reclamation projects of the 1930s. All but a fragment of the area disappeared in Mussolini's Battle for Grain. What remains is the Circeo national park, a fascinating natural redoubt, as important as any of the mountain parks of the Alps or Abruzzo.

Southern Lazio's historical role as the empty quarter of the region has now largely been taken over by the area to the north of Rome. A complex succession of mountains, hills, basins and coastal lowlands, this stretch of country has been almost stripped of its population over the past 40 years or so by the lure of the capital, as southern Lazio had been before it by marsh and malarial mosquitoes. Northern Lazio is not at first sight promising scenically. The coast is drab indeed, relieved only by the Tolfa hills, the first of the low volcanic uplands whose gloomy lavas do so much to deaden the landscape.

But it would be a mistake to scuttle through it. Pockets of green are to be found, especially in the Tolfa's secret interior and in the sylvan hideaway that surrounds Lago di Vico. Moving eastwards across the Tiber valley, you cross the Sabine hills and push into the forgotten part of Lazio that stretches an arm into the Apennines. Here the region lays claim to its only mountains, the heights of Terminillo and the Simbruini and Ernici, the rocky gateway to the wilderness of the Abruzzo.

GETTING THERE
By air: numerous international flights go to Rome's Leonardo da Vinci airport (at Fiumicino, 1 hour from the centre by train), T: (06) 65951. Fewer go to Naples' Capodichino, T: (081) 789 6259. Charter flights go to Rome's Ciampino airport, T: (06) 794 0941.

By car: Rome is at the hub of central Italian communications. The A1, Italy's main arterial road, comes down from Milan and Florence and continues to Naples, where it becomes the A3 to Reggio di Calábria. The SS1 (Via Aurelia), slow and only part motorway, follows the coast from Genoa and Pisa. The A24 leads to L'Áquila, the Abruzzo, the Marche and Adriatic coast. The minor roads in Campania are generally slower and of inferior quality.

By rail: Rome and Naples are both on international routes from Paris, Vienna, Munich, Geneva and even Moscow. Both have trains to every corner of Italy. The Pendolino high-speed line links Rome–Florence–Milan; Rome–Pisa–Genoa, Rome–Pescara and Rome–Naples–Reggio–Palermo are the other main lines. In the south numerous minor routes run from Naples to Caserta, Benevento, the Cilento coast, Potenza, Bari, Brindisi and Reggio. Contact Ufficio Informazioni dei Treni, freephone T: (1478) 88088 within Italy, otherwise www.fs-on-line.it or www.trenitalia.com.

By bus: services run from Rome and Naples to all major cities and towns. Contact CO.TRA.L., Rome, freephone T: (800) 150 008 within Italy, and S.I.T.A., Naples, T: (081) 552 2176.

WHERE TO STAY
Hotels: try the English-speaking information service Enjoy Rome, Via Marghera 8, T: (06) 445 1843, www.enjoyrome.com; otherwise contact Informazioni Turistiche del Comune di Roma, T: (06) 3600 4399.

Agriturismo: contact Agenzia Agriturist, Corso V. Emanuele 101, Rome, T: (06) 685 2342 and Corso Lucci 137, Naples, T: (081) 285 243.

ACTIVITIES
Walking: accessible hills can be found in northern Lazio, such as the Tolfa and the Cimini, middling mountain ranges in both regions (Simbruini, Ernici, Picentini) and the isolated Alburni and Cilento massifs in southern Campania. Contact CAI, Rome, T: (06) 5728 7143 and Naples, T: (081) 668 128.

Caving: you can find caves in the Alburni mountains and marine caves both on the Cilento coast and around the Sorrento peninsula. Contact Gruppo Speleologico CAI, Castel dell'Ovo, Naples, or visit www.campania.speleo.it.

Hang-gliding: contact Federazione Italiana Volo Libero, Via Rosatelli, Rieti, T:

Although at first sight similar to many other wild roses, sweet briar (*Rosa rubiginosa*) is easily distinguished by the sticky russet glands beneath the leaves, which smell strongly of apples when crushed.

(0746) 203 138.

Skiing: resorts in Lazio are at Terminillo and, near Filettino, at Campo Staffi and Monte Livata; in Campania at Piano Laceno near Bagnoli Irpino. Visit www.mtnresorts.com.

FURTHER INFORMATION
Tourist offices: Via Parigi 5, Rome, T: (06) 4889 9253, www.regione.lazio.it; Piazza dei Martiri 58, Naples, T: (081) 405 311, www.regione.campania.it. **Ecology:** WWF, Via Po 25, Rome, T: (06) 844 971, www.wwf.lazio.it and Via A. da Salerno 13, Naples, T: (081) 560 7000.

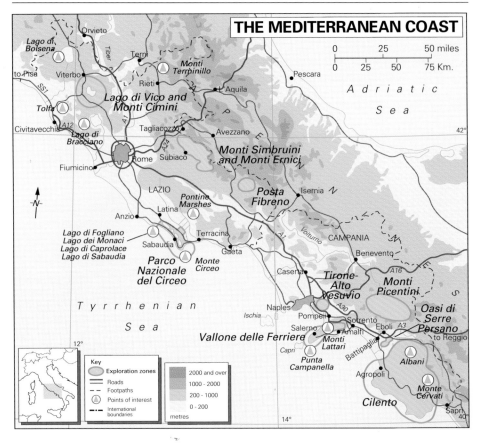

THE MEDITERRANEAN COAST

0   25   50 miles
0   25   50   75 Km.

Key
Exploration zones
Roads
Footpaths
Points of interest
International boundaries

2000 and over
1000 - 2000
200 - 1000
0 - 200
metres

Lago di Vico and Monti Cimini

Volcanic crater and lake in northern Lazio, 75 km (47 miles) from Rome; riserva naturale regionale 3,300 ha (8,150 acres) Includes ZPS

Imagine a secret lake ringed on three sides by steep wooded mountains, and you have Lago di Vico, the most beautiful of northern Lazio's volcanic lakes. Just 4 km (2 miles) wide, it is more intimate and more

rewarding than the nearby lakes of Bolsena and Bracciano.

None of the mountains — the Cimini — are high (1,053 m/3,455 ft at their summit) but they create a spectacular effect, forming a cone around the lake, whose perfect symmetry betrays its volcanic origins. Rising as a distinct blemish on their inner slopes is Monte Vénere, a newer volcanic outcrop that has pushed up through the skin of its parent.

The Cimini, like all Lazio's volcanic hills, were created during an eruptive, rather than explosive phase of the volcano-forming Quaternary period. Here, volcanoes burst into life with sudden, but quickly spent force, spreading lava floods

over a wide area, floods which then slumped into low elevations rather than building into the pyramid profiles of an Etna or a Fuji.

A misplaced snatch of spectacular scenery in an otherwise drab region, the reserve at Lago di Vico has largely resisted Rome's hunters and outdoor enthusiasts. The unspoiled woods above the lake shore — oak, beech and chestnut — are still wild and thick, a flourishing remnant of the mighty Cimina Silva, a forest so impenetrable that for years it held back the Roman advance into Tuscany and Umbria.

Soils round the shore, marshy

on its northern lee, are rich and acidic, a legacy of their volcanic origin. They support a luxuriant flora, from anemones in spring to cyclamen in autumn, alongside more unusual species such as the Gargano buttercup *(Ranunculus garganicus)* and the foxglove *Digitalis ferruginea*, a splendid plant with early yellow or reddish-brown flowers up to 3½ cm (1½ in) long.

In an area that is a desert for birds, the lake is an oasis. It supports up to 40 breeding pairs of great crested grebes, a touching sight in early summer when chicks can often be seen hitching a ride on their parents' backs, as well as pairs of kingfishers. Little bitterns skulk through the reeds in summer, their black and tan plumage and diminutive size distinguishing them from other European herons.

Black kites are the top avian predators from March to September, assisted by sparrow hawks which hunt all year; the marsh harrier and hen harrier pass through in winter. There are reports that long-eared owls may be nesting in the area, which also provides a winter refuge for a variety of wildfowl, including thousands of coot and pochard and the gadwall, which nests here. A careful search may reveal a few red-crested pochard, the bright red beaks and orange

heads of the males being instantly recognizable. Wild boar have been reintroduced to the surrounding woods.

The scenery beyond the inner ring of the Cimini is worth seeing, dominated by thousands of hazelnut trees and shallow, but steep-cut gorges which radiate from the crater in all directions.

Before you go *Maps:* IGM 1:25,000 Nos 355 II *Ronciglione* and 345 III *Viterbo*.

Getting there *By car:* A1 to Orte, then SS204 and SS2 (Via Cassia) for Viterbo and minor roads to the reserve; or SS2 from Rome to Sutri, then minor roads to Ronciglione. The scenic Via Cimina makes a circuit of the Cimini ridge.

By rail: infrequent trains on two rickety branch lines, with stations a long way from the villages they serve: Orte–Capránica (alight at Ronciglione) and Rome (S. Pietro)–Viterbo (alight at Capránica Scalo or Vertralla), T: (0761) 340 955.

By bus: CO.TRA.L. from Rome to most centres, and along the Via Cimina from Viterbo to Ronciglione, T: (0761) 226 592.

Where to stay *Hotels:* Bella Vénere (3-star) on south-east shore of lake, T: (0761) 612 342;

Il Farnese (2-star), Caprarola, T: (0761) 646 029; Leon D'Oro (3-star), Via della Cava 36, Viterbo, T: (0761) 344 444; Al Vecchio Mulino (3-star), Piazza Principe di Piemonte 1, Ronciglione, T: (0761) 625 011; and Dell'Eremo (3-star), Via S. Giorgio 26, Soriano nel Cimino, T: (0761) 748 844.

Agriturismo: La Vita, in the reserve, T: (0761) 612 077.

Outdoor living: no free camping, but there is a camp-site in the reserve, Camping Natura, Caprarola, T: (0761) 612 347.

Activities *Walking:* ascent of Vénere from Fontanile di Canale, reached by a lane on Vico's east shore from Punta del Lago, red waymarks (2 hrs). From the same departure point you can walk round the wooded northern rim of the crater on a medieval track, the Strada di Mezzo, finishing on the tarmac road at Fontanile della Vita (an area known as Le Pantanacce, 'the wretched bogs').

Further information *Tourist office:* Porta del Parco, Viterbo, T: (0761) 325 992. *Park office:* Via Regina Margherita 2, Caprarola, T: (0761) 647 444, www.riservavico.it.

Ecology: WWF, Via Ottusa 4, Viterbo, T: (0761) 345 784.

Limestone boulders litter the Camposecco, the aptly named 'dry field', one of several karstic plains dotted across the Monti Simbruini.

Monti Simbruini and Monti Ernici

Two outlying Apennine massifs known as the Scandinavia of Rome, on the border of Lazio and Abruzzo; partly protected by Parco Naturale Regionale dei Monti Simbruini (29,990 ha/74,105 acres) ZPS

Monti Simbruini and Monti Ernici

East of Rome, beyond Tívoli and Hadrian's Villa, rise the Simbruini and Ernici mountains, two broad chains which lie almost parallel along the Lazio and Abruzzo border. A foretaste of the high Apennines, and the first genuine wilderness close to Rome, they are often passed over in favour of the big Abruzzese massifs further to the east. Both have several peaks in excess of 2,000 metres (6,600 feet).

The Simbruini derive their name from the heavy rains (Latin *sub imbribus*) which all year round turn them into an area of gurgling streams and for centuries have provided Rome with water. These mountains are classic limestone creations of denuded slopes, beech forest and craggy ridges interspersed with karstic plains such as those at Campaegli near Cervara di Roma and Camposecco ('dry field') at Camerata Nuova. The Ernici, further south, are wilder, their slopes less rounded and their valleys more incised.

In the Aniene valley and on the flanks of the Pizzo Deta, the Ernici present you with the best chance of seeing the area's mammalian carnivores such as wildcats and badgers. Wolves, though rapidly declining in numbers because of hunting and logging, still haunt the woods. There may even be the occasional bear.

Where bears are thin on the ground, as in Italy and other parts of southern Europe, they do not form family groups. Instead the males lead a solitary existence, making long journeys in search of breeding partners. Research has shown that male bears can range over a phenomenal 2,700 square

kilometres (1,000 square miles) in the course of a year, mating with several females. Sporadic sightings of bears in the outlying Apennines can usually be attributed to the amatory wanderings of these lone males.

Both massifs offer forest walks as well as breezier excursions such as the traverse of the ridges between Monte Tarino, Monte Cotento and Monte Viglio in the Simbruini. Rock walls are scarce, with the exception of the Tagliata at Vallepietra, the 'valley of stone'. Valleys sometimes narrow into canyons, notably along the Aniene river between Jenne and Subiaco.

The caves that dot the hillsides, especially around Collepardo, are perfect haunts for foxes and showcases for the region's lush green flora. Fragrant bushes of sweet briar *(Rosa rubiginosa)*, rosemary and thyme guard the entrances. Clusters of maidenhair fern fall from ledges which are trimmed with tufts of *Campanula fragilis* and its bells of amethyst flowers. Out on the high meadows, spring flowers abound; around Fosso Fioio alone 20 species of orchid have been recorded.

The sparse beech forests in the higher reaches of the Simbruini and the Ernici provide an ideal habitat for white-backed woodpeckers, the largest of the black and white species in Europe, measuring 25 cm (10 in) from head to tail. Long-eared owls and occasional eagle owls also inhabit these woodlands, while the remote cliffs and ridges above the tree-line are home to a few pairs of peregrines and choughs.

BEFORE YOU GO

Maps: IGM 1:25,000 Nos 377 II *Balsorano*, 390 I *Sora*, 376 I *Vallepietra* and 376 IV *Subiaco*.

Guide-books: S. Ardito, *A piedi nel Lazio Vol. I* (Iter, 1994); for skiers, E. Ercolani, *Appennino Bianco* (Iter, 1988).

GETTING THERE

By car: take the A24 from Rome or L'Áquila and exit at Mandela, Carsóli or Tagliacozzo. For the southern Simbruini take the A25 to Avezzano and then the SS82; the Ernici are served by the A1 to Frosinone, then SS155 to Alatri and minor roads to Collepardo, Fiúggi and Subiaco. Attractive minor roads push north into the Simbruini, notably to Vallepietra in the middle of the regional park.

By rail: scenic but slow, the Avezzano–Sora line, T: (0776) 831 495, runs along the Liri valley parallel to both chains and has 5 convenient stations. The Rome–Avezzano line, T: (06) 484 403, has only 2 near the park, Mandela and Carsóli.

By bus: CO.TRA.L., T: (06) 57531, and A.R.P.A., T: (0863) 326 561, run buses to most centres from Rome, Frosinone and Avezzano.

WHERE TO STAY

Hotels: Miramonti (3-star), Via Variante 87, Tagliacozzo, T: (0863) 6581; Livata (3-star), Via dei Boschi 28, Subiaco, T: (0774) 826 031; Monte Viglio (2-star), Via Panoramica 18, Filettino, T: (0775) 581 814; Progress (3-star), Via Casilina km 81, Frosinone, T: (0775) 870 469.

Refuges: dotted over the hills, they include old shepherds' huts, mostly in a state of picturesque squalor. Contact CAI, Via Ferralli 34, Frosinone,

T: (0775) 852 103.

Outdoor living: camping is permitted throughout. Campsites include: Camping Luisiana, Via della Bandita 5, Monte Livata, T: (0774) 826 087; Camping Velino, Via Tiburtina Valeria km 100, Tagliacozzo, T: (0863) 610 253. There is also a camp-site at Collepardo.

ACTIVITIES

Walking: the best walk is up La Monna and Fanfalli from the huge abbey at Certosa di Trisulti (above Collepardo) via the Vado di Porca and the Vallone della Barca, yellow-red markings (5 hrs). Also try the ascent of Monte Viglio from Valico della Serra (4 hrs); to Monte Tarino from the Santuario della SS. Trinità church; or the traverse of the Valle d'Inferno from Trisulti. A perfect trek runs from Carsóli or Subiaco along the ridges of Tarino, Viglio and Monna, descending through the Pizzo Deta and Valle Roveto to finish in Villavallelonga. A recognized but unmarked trail runs from

Camerata Nuova to the Abruzzo national park via Balsorano (6 days); contact CAI at Frosinone (address above) or Via G. Marconi 8, Sora, T: (0776) 832 828.

Pony-trekking: Tagliacozzo is a major trekking centre, but there are clubs and stables throughout the area. Contact Azienda Agricola Colle Tocci, C.da Castagnola, Subiaco, T: (0774) 822 917.

Climbing: winter snow routes are found on Viglio and the Pizzo Deta; rock climbs around Tagliacozzo, Petrella Liri and Castellafiume.

Canoeing: in spring the runs down the Aniene between Trevi nel Lazio and Subiaco are the region's most renowned. Get details from the Canoanium Club, Via D. Alighiéri 34, Subiaco, T: (0774) 83419.

Skiing: the best cross-country skiing routes in central Italy start at Camporotondo, Pereto, Campaegli and Luco dei Marsi, with minor stations at Campocatino, Campo Staffi and Marsia Livata. Contact Società Montana Nuova,

The lanner falcon is the only member of its family known to attack flying birds head-on. Numbers in Europe are declining rapidly because young birds are taken from the nest by poachers, and pesticides in the food chain thin the shells of their eggs.

Marsia, T: (0863) 60128.
Bird-watching: for nature walks, courses and information, contact LIPU, Piazza Risorgimento 17, Sora, T: (0776) 832 038.

FURTHER INFORMATION
Tourist offices: Via V. Veneto 6, Tagliacozzo, T: (0863) 610 318; Via Cadorna 59, Subiaco, T: (0774) 822 013; Via Gorizia 4, Fiúggi Fonte, T: (0775) 515 446 (Apr–Nov only).
Park office: Jenne, T: (0774) 827 219.

Posta Fibreno

A soft sweet lake of limpid waters set in Lazio's pastoral hills, south of the Abruzzo and Ernici mountains; riserva naturale regionale
440 ha (1,087 acres)

Posta Fibreno is a haven for migrating winter birds and a pot-pourri of unusual natural phenomena. Fed by the icy-fresh meltwater from the mountains, which wells up after a 20-km (12-mile) journey underground, Fibreno is like a huge spring, augmented by nearby streams and waterfalls. Thanks to the volume and purity of its sources, this richly oxygenated lake is known for its crystal transparency and extraordinary red-green reflective tints. It is the only lake in Italy that has a visible underwater forest of algae and other water plants.

Apart from the Circeo, on the coast, Fibreno is one of the few undrained areas of the Pontine marshes, preserving a lush vegetation which has returned thickly to the lake shores where agricultural land

has been abandoned. It also contains strange floating islands mentioned by Pliny in his *Naturalis Historia*, beds of twisted and rotted undergrowth on which vegetation has taken root. Like emerald rafts, they drift aimless and windblown, moving gently under human weight like a listing boat.

Some 45 m (148 ft) deep below its deceptively placid surface, the lake harbours carp, eel, trout, tench and crayfish, a banquet for birds such as mallard, marsh harrier,

moorhen, teal, bittern, heron and kingfisher. Local people still fish in the traditional Pontine craft, flat punts known as *la nave*, 'the navy'. Once common all over Italy, those moored around Fibreno's tree-shaded inlets are the country's last; probably descendants of primitive boats hollowed from solid oak tree-trunks.
Before you go *Map:* IGM 1:25,000 No. 390 I *Sora.*
Getting there *By car:* A1 to Frosinone, then SS214 to Isola del Liri and Sora. Follow signs for Broccostella, then Madonna

An island of vegetation floats in the Fibreno lake, one of only a handful of refuges for birds on Italy's Tyrrhenian coast.

della Stella; village of Posta Fibreno is 3 km (2 miles) beyond. Avoid north-east point of lake between Carpello and Codigliano which is somewhat spoiled by tourist developments.
By rail: station at Sora (10 km/6 miles) on Roccasecca–Avezzano line (5 trains daily). CO.TRA.L. (see below) provide helpful local rail information.
By bus: CO.TRA.L. run to Sora and Posta Fibreno from Frosinone and Cassino, T: (0775) 83791.

Where to stay *Hotels:* Gardenia (3-star), Via Valcomperta 12, Sora, T: (0776) 891 313; Raffaello (3-star), Corso Galileo 11, Alvito, T: (0776) 510 949.
Agriturismo: try Il Casale (in the reserve), Loc. la Pesca 5, Posta Fibreno, T: (0776) 871 744.
Activities *Walking:* cultivated fields, marshes and occasional flooding can make walking difficult. Shore paths are busy in summer and at week-ends.

Bird-watching: contact Tenuta Ducale La Pesca (in the reserve), who run nature walks and bird-watching on the lake, T: (0776) 887 141.
Further information *Tourist office:* Via Aldo Moro 465, Frosinone, T: (0775) 83381.
Park office: Piazza C. Battisti, Posta Fibreno, T: (0776) 887 184.
Ecology: for guided visits to the reserve contact Lab-Ter, Via Fontana Carbone, Posta Fibreno, T: (0776) 887 184.

Circeo

*Stretch of unspoiled coast in Lazio,
midway between Rome and Naples;*
parco nazionale
8,622 ha (21,306 acres)
Includes Biosphere Reserve, ZPS

Posterity credits Mussolini with two things: he made the trains run on time and he drained the Pontine marshes. For centuries malaria-ridden and empty, today they are one of the most productive and intensely farmed pieces of land in Italy. New towns like Latina and Pontinia were designed on ugly grid-iron plans and plonked down in a landscape of flat and unimaginable tedium. It was from all this that the Circeo was salvaged in 1934.

As I set off from Rome one pristine morning, I was expecting the Circeo to be little more than a small and perfunctory relic. In the event it turned out to be a strange and beautiful place. At its centre is the town of Sabáudia. Different architects were given the task of designing new towns that would be the standard bearers of Fascist endeavour. Sabáudia was lucky. It escaped the grid-iron schemes of the others and was built as a garden town in keeping with its surroundings. It is the gateway to an exquisite piece of countryside.

Circeo's initial impression of compact uniformity is deceptive; it actually has many quite separate environments, and to explore them properly requires several days. You can choose between forests of Central European flavour, stands of dwarf palm and North African vegetation, four coastal lakes, 30 kilometres (20 miles) of dunes, swamps and *maquis*, 30 marine caves and, most strikingly, Monte Circeo, a knuckle of mountain (541 metres/1,775 feet) that overlooks the entire park.

If you like an overview of things, this is the best starting point. From the interminable plain to the south it resembles a figure reclining across the horizon. The profile is dominated by an abnormally large nose (though the locals' descriptions are a little more explicit). A mountain in level country inevitably attracts myth, the main one here being that it was the Isle of Circe in Homer's *Odyssey*. It is Circe's form, according to legend, that is sculpted into the mountain.

Either side of the central ridge are two contrasting environments. On the southerly sea-facing slopes, known as the Quarto Caldo — the 'hot side' — the mountain drops to the waves in rocky precipices. One, the Precipizio, plunges sheer for 200 metres (650 feet). *Maquis*, cistus and cedar cling to its ledges. In this warm Mediterranean world, whose chief glory is the dwarf fan palm, flowers attract chafer beetles, hummingbird hawk moths and butterflies such as cleopatras, green hair-streaks and long-tailed blues. Where the *maquis* grows under the cover of woodland, Sardinian warblers, subalpine warblers and woodchat shrikes are often found.

There are no such exotica on the north-facing Quarto Freddo, the 'cold side', where a thick forest predominates, mainly holm oak, deciduous oak and hornbeam. Here you might hear the fluty song of the golden oriole or glimpse great-spotted woodpeckers searching trunks and branches for insects.

The view from the summit of Monte Circeo is exceptional — turquoise seas, the distant island of Zannone, patchworks of canal-bordered fields and woods, and, most lovely of all, a sickle-shaped bay half lost in the haze of the far horizon. Along its curving shore lie four silver sun-dazzled lakes: Fogliano, Caprolace, Mónaci and Sabáudia. Filigree canals connect all four to the sea, allowing marine and freshwater species to co-exist.

The atmosphere of this littoral is sub-tropical, magical. How sad to think that the Tyrrhenian coast as far as Pisa was once like this. Forest creeps to the lakesides, umbrella pines elegantly shading the foreshore. The woods conceal old Roman remains, while on the infinite sandy crest of the dunes exists a world unto itself, the domain of bent grass, sea spray and constant wind.

All manner of birds prosper in this heady environment. Some 230 species have been recorded, many of them, even the rarest, remarkably easy to see. In autumn migrating flocks of woodcocks swarm over the lakes; spring brings turtle doves, cuckoos and quail, but there are also black-throated divers, glossy ibis, spoonbills, great white egrets, black storks, cormorants, ospreys and even the ludicrously long-legged 'knight of Italy', the black-winged stilt, or *Himantopus himantopus*, to give it its delightful Latin tag.

Behind the lakes lies the Selva di Terracina: 600 hectares (1,500 acres) of primeval forest and swamp that are vestiges of the ancient Pontine marshes and were recognized in 1977 as a Biosphere Reserve, a habitat of world-wide importance. When I first walked around this relict wood, I was distracted by fences, yellow signs and things ominously called 'didactic footpaths'. In time these petered out, and I even found the didactic notices telling me things that were a pleasure to know, such as that ivy can live for 500 years. Thereafter I was alone, and encountered not a soul in the course of a warm Friday afternoon. The most rewarding part of the day was being presented with all that I had been promised: the birds, boar, darting green lizards, macabre fungi, snakes, fallow deer and a huge range of trees.

Not everything in the park is perfect. Vipers abound, and you need to keep a wary eye open for them. Indian mongooses were introduced to keep them in check, but turned instead to less demanding prey such as birds and small mammals. As a result some of the smaller fauna are rather more scarce than they should be. In places, non-native pines and eucalyptus were planted (eucalyptus for its supposed anti-malarial properties), species which are at odds with Circeo's original oak forest. Nature is now putting things to rights, with slow recolonization by Turkey oak and European aspen (often the first trees to reclaim lost territory).

Peals of thunder and an almighty deluge cut short my walk, turning the forest into a percussion of dripping water and the paths into steaming, puddle-filled bogs. By this time I had come to the edge of the reserve. It was strange to walk to a fence where the wood suddenly stopped. Ahead, the rich soil, the odd tree, the cultivated fields fading away to the horizon had once all been wood, marsh and swamp. It was astonishing that anything as vigorous and fecund as the Circeo could have been trimmed so abruptly and irretrievably. Soaked as I was, I was rather thankful that the booming and crackling of the storm — nature at its most unbridled — had sent me scuttling for cover; a mere mortal, humbled, bedraggled and graceless.

BEFORE YOU GO

Maps: 1:40,000 and 1:25,000 sheets available at the park centre indicate trails, habitats and recommended areas for seeing particular birds and animals.

Guide-book: P. Sottoriva, *Parco Nazionale del Circeo* (De Agostini, 1982).

First aid: viper bites are serious; you should take serum within half an hour if bitten. It is available in most Italian pharmacies.

GETTING THERE

By car: from Rome, and its southern suburb EUR, take the SS148 (often called the most dangerous road in Italy) under the *anulare*, or ring road, towards Latina. South of the town follow the road to the coast at Capo Portiere and thence to Sabáudia (75 km/46 miles). From Naples and the south, use the A1, exit at Cassino, then SS630 to Formia and SS7 to Terracina.

By rail: frequent trains run on the nearby Rome–Naples Direttissima line via Formia, T: (081) 554 3188. Priverno station, T: (0773) 93060, is the nearest on the main line but is not connected by bus. Either change at Priverno for the branch line to Terracina (1 train daily) or alight at Latina Scalo (15 daily).

By bus: services from Latina sports stadium and Terracina run to Sabáudia and S. Felice Circeo. CO.TRA.L. buses go from Rome (EUR) to Latina, Sabáudia and S. Felice Circeo, T: (0773) 418 851.

WHERE TO STAY

Hotels: try Aragosta (3-star), Lungamare Pontino km 29, Sabáudia, T: (0773) 511 511, or Capo Circeo (3-star), Viale Europa 9, S. Felice Circeo, T: (0773) 540 403.

Outdoor living: camping is prohibited except at official sites which include S. Andrea, Sabáudia, T: (0773) 593 105, and Europa, Terracina, T: (0773) 726 523.

ACCESS

Some roads, such as the one between Fogliano and Caprolace

and the scenic Strada Mediana (SS148), are closed to cars. The wooded lake shores and dunes may be explored only on foot or by bicycle.

ACTIVITIES
Walking: routes are easy to plan using the park's own maps. The recommended ascent of Monte Circeo (2 hrs) starts from Torre Paola — after the bridge over the canal at the tip of Lago di Sabáudia; the path follows a knife-edge ridge and is well trodden. All other paths are very gentle.
Cycling: dune, forest and lakeside roads are all perfect for cycling, though head winds can make coastal routes hard going. Bikes are also permitted on most of the park's marked trails and can be hired from the Coop. Melacotogna (see below).
Climbing: the routes on the rock walls of Monte Circeo are the best in Lazio; the cream are on the Precipizio. Other itineraries (outside the park) exist on Monte Leano (676 m/2,218 ft), north-west of Terracina.
Boating: Co-op. Melacotogna runs trips on the lakes and around the Circeo promontory, T: (0773) 511 206.
Bird-watching: opportunities are excellent, with well-placed observation points. For information, nature walks, courses (spring and autumn) and summer cycling trips, contact LIPU, Corso Matteotti 169, Latina, T: (0773) 484 993.

FURTHER INFORMATION
Tourist offices: Pro Loco, Piazza del Comune 18, Sabáudia, T: (0773) 515 046 and Piazza Lanzuisi 4, S. Felice Circeo, T: (0773) 547 770.
Park office: Via Carlo Alberto 107, Sabáudia, T: (0773) 511 385, offers information, a small museum, even guides if required.

Monti Picentini

Limestone chain east of Salerno, some of the wildest mountains in Campania; parco naturale regionale
64,000 ha (158,150 acres)
ZPS

'Misty and rolling mountains, like clouds on the extreme horizon; solitary heights whipped by the wind', wrote Giustino Fortunato in 1879, one of the first Italian ramblers in the Abruzzo and Campania mountains.

Then, as now, the Picentini marked a divide between west and east. They were, wrote Carlo Levi in his famous novel, *Christ Stopped at Éboli*, the point at which Italian civilization ended. Though only a few kilometres inland from the Tyrrhenian coast, they are the last green hills before the barren interior of Basilicata, as well as the peninsular watershed, source of rivers such as the Sele and Tusciano.

Seeming taller than they really are as they rise from the broad Sele plain, the Picentini reach a high point at Monte Polverácchio (1,790 m/5,873 ft). Vast woods of beech and chestnut cloak their slopes and marvellous displays of wild flowers bring seasonal colour to the high meadows of Terminio and Montenero, the 'black mountain'. Here you might see foxes, wildcats, badgers and even wolves, just 50 km (30 miles) from Naples. The Picentini also support breeding black and red kites, peregrines, eagle owls and black woodpeckers.

My favourite mountain is the Accéllica. At 1,660 m (5,400 ft)

it is not the highest but, with twin peaks joined by a rocky crest, it is graced with the most elegant outline in the range. Conquering the modest summit provides the area's best walk.
Before you go *Maps:* IGM 1:25,000 Nos 449 II *Solofra* and 450 III *Montella.*
Guide-book: Alta Via dei Monti Picentini (Acerno Tourist Office, 1986).
Getting there *By car:* A3 (Battipáglia exit), and then the beautiful SS164 via Acerno to Bagnoli Irpino. From west use Avellino–Salerno motorway, exit at Serino and follow SS574.
By rail: station at Battipáglia on the main Naples–Salerno–Reggio di Calábria line.
Where to stay *Hotels:* Il Boschetto (2-star), Via Montella 48, Acerno, T: (089) 869 077; Belvedere (2-star), Via de Rogatis 37, Bagnoli Irpino, T: (0827) 62050.
Outdoor living: free camping allowed. Alternatively try Traiano Camper Club, Casalbore, T: (0825) 849 021.
Activities *Walking:* ascent of Accéllica from the Croci di Acerno (4 hrs). Alta Via dei Monti Picentini from Senérchia to Serino (3-5 days) in the south. Gentler walking in the Irpinia hills to the north; uncharted expeditions in the mountains east of the Picentini: Paratiello, Saracino, Eremita. *Skiing:* numerous forest tracks notably on and around Monte Cervialto and Polverácchio. Contact Consorzio Laceno, T: (0827) 68120, who also organize cycling and ponytrekking in summer.
Further information *Tourist offices:* Via Velia 15, Salerno, T: (089) 230 141; Via Duomo 47, Acerno, T: (089) 869 395.
Park office: c/o Comunità Montana Monti Picentini, Piazza Umberto I, T: (089) 866 160.
Ecology: WWF, Via S. Leonardo 103, Salerno, T: (089) 771 228.

Vesuvio

Snow comes early to the still autumnal Monti Picentini, a mountainous wilderness only a short distance from the urban clamour of Naples.

Europe's most famous volcano, overlooking Naples; parco nazionale 8,482 ha (20,960 acres) Includes Biosphere Reserve, Riserva Naturale Tirone-Alto Vesuvio (1,019 ha/2,518 acres)

Neither the largest — a midget next to Etna — nor the most dangerous of volcanoes, Vesuvius entered the history books with the apocalyptic eruption of AD 79. This two-day blast covered Italy in a thin layer of dust and buried the ancient cities of Pompeii and Herculaneum (today known as Pompei and Ercolano) under 20 m (70 ft) of mud and ash. 'Many a calamity has happened in the world, but never one that has caused so much entertainment to posterity as this one', wrote Goethe, on the destruction of Pompeii.

Magnificent Vesuvius may be, but wild — in the sense that the Monti Picentini are wild — unfortunately it is not. As Naples continues its chaotic spread, concrete advances on the volcano as remorselessly as lava. And yet, how hard to resist the primal allure of such a mountain!

The volcano divides into two parts: the looming profile that dominates the Bay of Naples is Monte Somma (1,132 m/3,713 ft), otherwise known as the *punta nasone*, 'big nose', named after the semi-circular remnant of an ancient crater blown to smithereens by the Pompeii eruption. Within this outer rim rises the Gran Cono, thrown up by the same eruption: a barren,

167

smooth-sided cone with a perfectly circular crater.

A strange solitary place, the crater is 300 m (1,000 ft) deep, 600 m (2,000 ft) across and quite breathtaking. The scale, silence and stillness are extraordinary. Ash and jagged rock are all. Sheer cliffs of pumice, dust and red-black lavas plunge to a chaos of scree, and only here and there do smoking fumaroles betray the life beneath the slumbering mountain.

This seemingly inert wilderness is what most people come to see, but for botanists, geologists and mineralogists, Vesuvius has other attractions. Nearly a thousand species of plants thrive on its fertile soils, among them pioneering varieties able to colonize the most inhospitable lava slopes — for example, the ash-coloured endemic lichen, *Stereocaulon vesuvianum*, which flourishes even on still-warm magma. On the southern slopes, oak, pine and birch woods have survived creeping urbanization,

particularly intrusive along the road that climbs from Boscotrecase. Foresters are replanting long-lost species such as willow, alder and black pine, as well as the greenweed *Genista aetnensis*, a native of Sicily and Sardinia, which will complement the common broom (currently the mountain's most widespread species). These and the other woods above Ercolano, in part protected by the small Tirone reserve, add up to an exhilarating area of green where you can pass a morning without meeting a soul.

Equally captivating is the valley between Somma and the Gran Cono, the Atrio del Cavallo, called more aptly the Valle d'Inferno, the 'valley of hell'. Here you can see the jet-black lava flows from the 1944 eruption and lava bombs of up to a metre (3 ft) across. The view is spectacular, embracing the Bay of Naples, the islands of Capri and Ischia, the Sorrento peninsula and much of the central Apennines to the south,

from the Monti Picentini to the Alburni.

Before you go *Map:* IGM 1:25,000 No. 447 III *Pozzuoli* — unnecessary for a casual visit. *Guide-book: Il Parco Nazionale del Vesuvio* (Regione Campania, 1999).

Getting there *By car:* A3 Naples–Salerno, exit at Ercolano or Torre del Greco. For Somma Vesuviana, take SS268 from Naples and follow signs for Comuni Vesuviani. *By rail:* a picturesque railway, the Circumvesuviana, encircles the volcano, stopping at every town in the park; frequent trains from Naples' central station, T: (081) 553 4188. *By bus:* Circumvesuviana run a special bus to the Osservatorio Vesuviano which leaves from Ercolano railway station, T: (081) 559 2582.

Where to stay *Hotels:* Augustus (4-star), Via Giovanni XXIII 61, Ottaviano, T: (081) 528 8455; Belvedere (2-star), Via Marittima 59, Ercolano, T: (081) 739 0744; and Parco dei Pini (3-star), Via E. De Nicola 34, Torre del Greco, T: (081) 849 2316.
Agriturismo: Bel Vesuvio Inn, T: (081) 771 1243; Il Cavaliere, T: (081) 574 3667.

Access: old Strada Matrone is closed to cars. Entry to Tirone reserve is by prior arrangement with Stazione Forestale Tre Case, T: (081) 537 2391. To visit the crater, you must hire a guide from the hut 1 km from the Osservatorio.

Activities *Walking:* only main paths are marked on park's map. To enter Tirone reserve, take first path off unclassified road from Ercolano. To visit crater, take the old Strada Matrone from Boscotrecase.
Further information *Park office:* Piazza Municipio 8, S. Sebastiano al Vesuvio, T: (081) 771 0911, or visit www.vesuviopark.it.

The elegant avocet, with its pied plumage and long bluish legs, is a common sight on the Tyrrhenian coast in winter. It feeds by scything its flattened upturned bill through shallow water, trapping small invertebrates between the mandibles.

Vallone delle Ferriere

Hidden valley on Campania's rugged Sorrento peninsula, with marvellous coastal views; includes riserva naturale (455 ha/1,124 acres) Includes ZPS

The otter requires specialized conditions, not least of which is clean water. Its numbers have been dropping all over Europe, but the decline in Italy has been particularly acute.

The Sorrento peninsula is not, at first glance, off Italy's beaten track. Yet it conceals a genuine patch of wilderness, all the better for being unexpected.

Leaving the terraces and plunging sea cliffs above Amalfi you climb to a high valley of ravines and exhilarating rock faces partially protected by the small Vallone (or Valle) delle Ferriere nature reserve. Pushing on, you emerge amongst the heights of the Monti Lattari, the peninsula's mountainous backbone.

Surprisingly rugged peaks, they are full of windswept walks and staggering panoramas. You might try the climbs at the western tip, best at sunset, from Termini to Monte San Costanzo (497 m/1,630 ft) and to the Punta Campanella. Views to Capri are unforgettable.

In the Ferriere valley specialized micro-climates support a lush panoply of wild flowers, some of them natives of Africa and Latin America. Maritime warming, south-facing slopes and the steepness of the valley sides (which slows water evaporation from the soil) all help reproduce tropical conditions. Rarities include the fern *Woodwardia radicans*, a pre-glacial relict of monstrous proportions with leaves up to 2½ m (8 ft) long. Discovered in 1710, it has declined to the

point where only ten plants remain. Almost as impressive are the ferns *Pteris vittata* and *cretica*, both capable of reaching a metre in length, the white-flowering grass of Parnassus (*Parnassia palustris*), the pink or pale blue butterwort *Pinguicola hirtiflora* and the scarce *Arisaurum proboscideum* of the arum-lily family.

Also enjoying the warmth are the diminutive Italian newt and the wonderfully named spectacled salamander, *Salamandrina terdigitata*. Only 7–11 cm (2½–4 in) long, the adult salamanders are unmistakable with their blackish backs and bright red undersides; the 'spectacles' take the form of a roughly triangular yellow-orange patch on the head which extends to the eyes. Kestrels, buzzards and peregrines haunt the crags and cliffs in large numbers.

Before you go *Maps:* IGM 1:25,000 Nos 466 II *Amalfi* and 466 I *Nocera Inferiore*. Kompass 1:50,000 No. 682 is excellent for the whole peninsula. *Guide-book:* Norman Douglas' *Siren Land*,

1988 (also on audio cassette), is a wonderful introduction to the Sorrento peninsula.
Access: to visit reserve in upper Ferriere valley you must contact Corpo Forestale dello Stato, T: (089) 873 043.
Getting there *By car:* A3 Naples–Salerno (Vietri exit) and SS163 to Amalfi. All roads in this region are beautifully scenic. *By rail:* Vietri is a stop on the Naples–Salerno line (trains hourly). Castellammare, on the north coast of the peninsula, is on the Naples–Sorrento line (trains every 30 mins). *By bus:* buses connect all main towns, most departing from Salerno's Corso Garibaldi; S.I.T.A., T: (089) 226 604.
Where to stay *Hotels:* Amalfi is the best base, but there are hotels all the way along the coast; booking recommended. Try Fiorenza (3-star), Via Trento 145, Salerno, T: (089) 338 800; Fontana (2-star), Piazza Duomo 7, Amalfi, T: (089) 871 530; Eden (3-star), Via Correale 25, Sorrento, T: (081) 878 1909. *Youth hostels:* Ostello Irno, Lungomare Marconi 34, Salerno, T: (089) 238 520;

Ostello Surriento, Via Capasso 5, Sorrento, T: (081) 878 1783; Ostello dei Galli, Via Capriglione, Véttica Maggiore, near Praiano, T: (089) 874 093. **Activities** *Walking:* plenty of short, sharp walks on the Lattari with marvellous views of Capri, Ischia and the Bay of Naples. You might try the Amalfi–Ferriere–Amalfi circuit (2 hrs), or the very popular hike from Monte Faito to Monte S. Angelo a Tre Pizzi (1,443 m/4,700 ft), highest point on the peninsula (3 hrs). A funicular runs from Castellammare to Faito. *Boating:* ferries link Naples, Capri, Ischia and peninsular towns; Alilauro, T: (081) 761 1004.

Further information *Tourist offices:* Corso Roma 27, Amalfi, T: (089) 871 107; Via Velia 15, Salerno, T: (089) 230 411; Via L. de Maio 35, Sorrento, T: (081) 807 4033.

Beyond fields lies the protected wetland of Serre-Persano, fringed by trees and backed by the distant ridges of the Monti Alburni.

Oasi di Serre-Persano

Wood-fringed lake in Campania; riserva naturale regionale e provinciale 4,000.ha (10,000 acres); includes WWF Oasi Persano (110 ha/272 acres)

Formed by the damming of the River Sele in 1934, the Serre-Persano's lake and marshland is a sanctuary of immense importance. It is one of the few protected wet habitats which provide resting places for birds on the Tyrrhenian migration route, between Circeo and the Vendicari marshes in Sicily.

The Sele itself is that rare thing in Italy, a clean river. Unpolluted in its short reach, it supports the last substantial colony of otters in Italy. It rises in the nearby Picentini, with the lake and lovely WWF oasis at the point where it breaks out on to the broad alluvial plain of the Piana del Sele.

Two paths thread through the oasis. The first, on the right bank, resembles a long shaded gallery, passing through thickets of willow and alder and winding past tree-laced streams. The second path, on the left bank, is more open, crossing vines, fields and *maquis*, and climbing a hill with views on to the lake and its emerald surroundings.

Virulent poaching threatened the reserve until 1977, and only ceased after pitched battles broke out between hunters and conservationists. The latter won.

Their reward is the arrival of thousands of wintering birds, and the first-time breeding here of species such as the black kite and great crested grebe. Mallard, pochard, tufted duck and teal are common visitors. Muddy islands harbour black-tailed godwit, ruff, snipe and wood sandpiper. Spring brings purple and grey, squacco and night herons, little egrets and cormorants. Among the reserve's rare visitors are ospreys, cranes, avocets and shelduck. The oasis is also home to badger, wild boar and weasel, as well as two or three of the local otters.

Getting there *By car:* from A3 Salerno–Reggio di Calábria, exit at Campagna and take short stretch of road to SS19.

Follow WWF panda signs to the oasis.
By rail: station at Campagna-Serre-Persano (4 km/2½ miles from oasis) on Battipaglia–Potenza–Taranto line.
By bus: from Salerno, S.I.T.A., T: (089) 405 145, run services to Serre; Mansi, T: (0828) 976 040, to Postiglione and Sicignano degli Alburni; and Pecori, T: (0828) 963 009, to Controne and Castelcivita. All stop at shelter on Via Falzia, 1 km from oasis.
Where to stay *Hotel:* Grazia at Éboli, T: (0828) 366 038, but the village is not pretty. *Outdoor living:* free camping prohibited. Try La Foce dei Tramonti camp-site at Paestum, T: (0828) 861 293.
Access: oasis open all year, Wed, Sat and Sun.

Activities *Bird-watching:* one of the finest sites in south Italy, equipped with hides, nature trails and observation platforms. If oasis is closed, sightings are possible all along River Sele and across Piana del Sele.
Further information *Ecology:* WWF, Via Falzia 13, Serre, T: (0828) 974 684, which also acts as park office.

Cilento

Alburni and Cilento massifs, tucked away in Campania's south-western reaches; part of Parco Nazionale del Cilento e Vallo di Diano
181,000 ha (450,000 acres)
Biosphere Reserve, World Heritage Site

🦃🦃🦃

Bounded to the east by the Diano valley and the black ribbon of the Autostrada del Sole, the Cilento region is Campania's loneliest corner, a little-known and rarely visited wilderness of quite astonishing richness. Its key areas are the Alburni mountains in the north, the less distinct and more extensive Cilento to the south, and the coastline in the west that marks the Cilento's dramatic drop to the Mediterranean.

The coastal section is the best known, climbing abruptly from the flat Piana del Sele at Agrópoli to a series of huge cliffs, green valleys, wind-twisted olive trees and gloomy wave-dashed promontories that stretch southwards for more than 100 kilometres (60 miles). Too much of this once desolate coast has been spoiled by tourism, though extensive tracts without road or village still await the lover of wild seascape.

Loneliest of these is the southernmost tip, the Punta degli Infreschi, a *parco blu*, or marine park. Peregrine falcons and sea-birds in their thousands inhabit its coves and ledges. Sandier reaches support woods of aleppo pine, *maquis* and dune plants, including an endemic primula, the deep-yellow-flowered Cilento (or Palinuro) primrose *(Primula palinuri)*. Coastal trails have been marked out, though the number of paths is small and those marked on maps are often overgrown. The best walking, with reasonably clear paths, is to the Punta degli Infreschi from Marina di Camerota, with the option of return by boat.

The Calore is one of few rivers to flow interrupted through the Monti Alburni. Many disappear into limestone sink-holes, re-emerging several miles away.

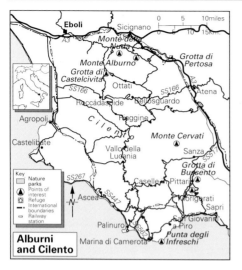

East from San Giovanni a Piro a track winds through the wild area known as the Ciolan- · dréa, climbing to the Vallone del Marcellino. Another walk from the village climbs to the colossal rock face of Monte Bulgheria (1,225 metres/4,019 feet), popular with climbers, and one of the most spectacular formations of its kind in the south.

Inland, the white limestone crests of the Alburni, spread on the horizon like an open fan, are as oxygen to a suffocating man after the murderous drive through the suburbs of Naples. A small range, some 20 kilometres (12 miles) from east to west, they are none-theless grand and imposing, rising from gentle, tree-lined slopes to a steep-sided serrated ridge at over 1,700 metres (5,600 feet). Like a row of worn-down teeth, at sun-set they take on a gorgeous amber hue the like of which you will otherwise find only in the Dolomites.

Close up, the mountains reveal pillars of fractured limestone, deep-riven gorges and fantastic rock pinnacles like the Figliolo ('little son'), 1,337 metres (4,386 feet) of dizzying verticality. Gigantic rock walls rear 400 metres (1,300 feet) high on the mountains' magnificent northern side, culminating in Monte Alburno (1,742 metres/5,715 feet), also known as Monte Panormo, famous for its sweeping views.

Thereafter the Alburni tail off in a different vein altogether, fading away to the south as a vast, sloping plateau famed for its cross-country and downhill skiing.

At their core the Alburni are a huge slab of Cretaceous limestone. For aeons of geological time — through the Oligocene — they were an island lashed by the sea. Today they have all the delightful quirks of limestone country: sink-holes, dry valleys, limestone pavements and some of the finest caves in southern Italy. The caverns here vary in size from little more than shadowy cracks to great amphitheatres that could shelter a whole town's population. Often remote, they have been animal shelters since time immemorial, rank from the presence of generations of goats brought to graze on the Alburni's rough pasture, their stone floors polished by the clattering of centuries of cloven hooves.

The most celebrated cavern is the Grotta dell'Angelo at Pertosa, studded with stalac-tites and plumbed by an underground lake of dark, numbingly cold water. The best of the caves open to the non-specialist is near Castelcivita. You might also want to see the huge sink-hole that swallows the Bussento river near Caselle in Pittari. The waters reap-pear at Morigerati. Experts could tackle the Grava di Fra Gentile, a daunting well 232 metres (761 feet) deep.

Anyone planning to spend any time in the Alburni, or the Appenines for that matter, is sooner or later going to have to make their minds up about limestone. Southern peasants call it *pietra viva*, 'living rock'. Sandstone, far more scarce in the southern Apennines, is dis-missed as *pietra morta*, 'dead rock'. D. H. Lawrence, for one, took them to task, seeing limestone as a lifeless rock that 'burns in the sun and withers'. The granites of Sardinia, by contrast, he thought glowered and glistened with 'a deep sparkle'.

South of the Alburni, a series of low hills intervenes, providing a respite of streams and valleys before the long, lateral ridges of the Cilento rear up beyond. This is some of the wildest, most abandoned territory in Italy — a huge area of few roads that ex-tends for almost 100 kilometres (60 miles). Some two-thirds of that distance you could trek without ever crossing tarmac. Paths and mule-tracks of utmost loneliness traverse a jumble of alternately steep and blunt nosed massifs, their summits ranging from about 1,000 metres (3,300 feet) in the west to the desolate Monte Cervati (1,899 metres/6,230 feet) towards the east. The domain only of wolf, fox and wildcat, this is fine, uncharted wilderness — truly a trekker's paradise — but one where you are alone and where care, equipment and experience are required in equal measure.

BEFORE YOU GO

Maps: IGM 1:25,000 Nos 487 I *Serre*, 488 IV *Polla*, 488 III *Sant' Arsénio* and 520 III *Camerota*.
Guide-book: A. Lopez, *Cilento e Vallo di Diano* (Mondadori, 1997).

GETTING THERE

By car: the Cilento is part-circled by the A3 motorway; take the exits at Sicignano, Polla or Petina for the Alburni mountains. The Atena Lucana exit leads to the SS166, which divides the Alburni and the Cilento, radiating glorious minor lanes into the hearts of both massifs. The Buonabitácolo-Padula exit feeds into the SS517 for Sanza, best base for the central Cilento peaks and the ascent of Monte Cervati. The SS517 also leads to the coast between Policastro and Marina di Camerota. The SS267, SS447 and SS562 run along the coast, forced inland just before the Punta degli Infreschi. The stretches south of Castellabate and around Palinuro are especially lovely.
By rail: the Naples–Reggio di Calábria line curves around the western and southern fringes of the Cilento promontory to useful stations at Pisciotta-Palinuro and Sapri.
By bus: services run from Salerno, Agrópoli and Sapri to most larger villages including S. Giovanni a Piro. Call S.I.T.A., T: (089) 226 604.

WHERE TO STAY

Hotels: there is a range of accommodation on the coast at Agrópoli, Castellabate, Palinuro and Sapri. La Pergola (1-star), Via Nazionale 17, S. Giovanni a Piro, T: (0974) 98317, is open all year and has a very good little restaurant used by people in the market.
Refuges: in the Alburni, the Panormo (1,233 m/4,045 ft) is reached by road from Ottati, a village 13 km (8 miles) south of the main ridge. Contact CAI, Via Trinità degli Spagnoli, Naples, T: (0339) 332 0588. At Treggiano try Rif. G.E.T., T: (080) 521 2747 (open all year).
Outdoor living: free camping is permitted, and in some places will be your only option. There are numerous year-round camp-sites on the coast, including Arco delle Rose at Agrópoli, T: (0974) 838 227; Baía del Silenzio at Caprioli, T: (0974) 976 079; Trezene at Castellabate, T: (0974) 965 004. Marina di Camerota on the Punta degli Infreschi has 3 camp-sites: Isola, T: (0974) 932 230; Mingrado, T: (0974) 931 391; and Sirene, T: (0974) 932 338.

ACTIVITIES

Walking: in the Alburni, start at Campo Farina (1,340 m/ 4,400ft). The main climb is to Monte della Nuda (1,704 m/ 5,590 ft) via Piano Manzerra and Palombella. The descent (to the starting point) is by way of Colle Marola (1,482 m/4,862 ft) and the Piano di Vallescura (4 hrs). Another fine walk strikes off north from Campo Farina for the Vuccolo dell'Arena (1,450 m/4,757 ft) and from there to the Alburni's main crest.
    Walks from the northern side include easy strolls around Petina, and steep but striking climbs to Monte della Nuda from Postiglione or Sicignano (5 hrs). These can be extended into 2-day treks by descending the ridge's southern flanks to Campo Farina.
Caving: Pertosa and Castelcivita caves are both open daily, except Mon, until 5.30 and 7.30 pm respectively. Serious spelunkers should contact CAI's Gruppo Grotte, Via Bonito 19, Naples, T: (081) 404 421; for guided visits contact Noitur, Agrópoli, T: (0974) 823 852.
Boating: boats can be rented from many villages, with or without crews, for diving, fishing, caving or casual trips along the coast. Contact the tourist office at Palinuro, or go direct to the Co-op. Pescatori on the harbour, T: (0974) 931 233.
Skin-diving: contact coastal tourist offices or Centro Subacqueo, S. Maria di Castellabate, T: (0974) 961 128; and Palinuro Sub Diving Centre, Palinuro, T: (0974) 938 509.

FURTHER INFORMATION

Tourist offices: Piazza Ferrovia, Salerno, T: (089) 231 432; Via S. Marco, Agrópoli, T: (0974) 824 855 — this office has the most comprehensive listings for the Cilento; Via Aquilia, Paestum, T: (0828) 811 016; Via Oberdan, Marina di Ascea, T: (0974) 971 230; Via Parrocchia 1, Palinuro, T: (0974) 931 147; Porto Piccolo, Marina di Camerota, T: (0974) 932 036.
Park office: Via F. Palumbo, Vallo della Lucania, T: (0974) 719 911, www.pncvd.it.
Ecology: WWF, Piazza Cavalieri, Albanelle, T: (0828) 781 713.

CHAPTER 8

The South of Italy

The Italian south is a world unto itself, the *mezzogiorno*, the 'land of the midday sun', a place bedevilled by a harsh natural regime and a history of poverty and emigration. Embracing the three regions of Puglia, Basilicata and Calábria, which occupy the heel and toe of Italy, it has long been the political stone in the Italian boot. Huge amounts of state aid have done something to lift it out of the social and economic doldrums in which it has laboured for centuries. Too often, however, changes have been cosmetic, failing to eradicate problems that are deeply rooted in the past and embedded in a contorted and intractable geography.

Over the whole area shines a quite unforgiving sun, bringing 'days of glistering summer heat', in the words of the traveller Norman Douglas, 'when the earth is burnt to cinders under a heavenly dome that glows like a brazier of molten copper'. Temperatures can reach 40°C (105°F). Further torment comes from the *scirocco*, a scorching North African wind that can blow for days on end. But it is important to know that this is not all some permanently parched Sahara. The forests of the Sila, and the spring green of the uplands, are so verdant they have been more than once compared to the Highlands of Scotland.

For the outdoor enthusiast, the varied landscapes of the south offer some of the finest and most unspoiled wilderness in the country. The Apennines continue their march down

Unspoiled shores still survive on the Gargano peninsula, an anomaly of white limestone up to 1,000 m (3,300 ft) high interrupting the uniform flatness of Italy's Adriatic coast.

the peninsula, becoming lower, but spreading range after range of middling hills in their wake. Occasionally they gather themselves for a flurry of high grandeur, as in the Pollino massif or, further south, the ranges of the Sila and Aspromonte. The rock-desert badlands of Basilicata have been talked of in the same breath as the Grand Canyon. Elsewhere the landscape is a typically Mediterranean ensemble of vines, olives and barren, sun-beaten slopes.

The south's eastern seaboard is Puglia, Italy's longest region, a fascinating area that includes the narrow stiletto of the Italian boot and more than 750 kilometres (500 miles) of the Adriatic coastline. The Roman poet Horace never mentioned Puglia without the epithet *siticulosa*, 'thirsty'. Not all is uniformly arid, however. It can be divided into four well-defined areas: the Tavoliere, Italy's largest area of plain after the Pianura Padana — wheat and monotony as far as the eye can see; the Gargano, a high wooded peninsula and the region's natural highlight; the Murge, a shimmering limestone jumble of hills and plateaux; and the Salento, the heel of the boot, cloaked in olive trees — another sun-baked summer cauldron. Puglia also scores well in its proximity to Greece, whence it enjoys stray species of birds.

West of Puglia lies Basilicata, once the glorious heartland of the Greek-colonized area known as Magna Graecia but in modern times a synonym for despair. Until well into the 20th century Basilicata was a mysterious land, sprawling and deserted, dotted with abandoned farms, 'hedged in by custom and sorrow, cut off from History and the State' in the words of the novelist Carlo Levi. Today things have begun to change for the better.

Ancient vineyards have been irrigated and brought back to life, and the Piana di Metaponto has become famous for its oats, barley, tangerines, apricots and almonds. Faithful to its ancient name of Lucania — derived from *lucus*, or wood — the region still has the highest percentage of tree cover in the country.

Basilicata's hills rise to about 1,000 metres (3,300 feet), their disparate sprawl collectively known as the Appennino Lucano. The most enticing prospect is the Pollino massif and its scattered siblings: mountain ramparts which fall as a mighty barrier across the region's southern border, almost severing Calábria, Italy's toe, from the rest of the country.

The mountains are another reason, if more were needed, for Calábria's historic destitution. Calábria used to be a byword for the south and its problems — emigration, crime, disease, illiteracy and malnutrition. Now not so poor, it suffers from new afflictions. Investment has raised living standards but impoverished the natural environment, particularly on the coast: once one of Calábria's glories, it is now blighted by ill-sited and ill-planned resorts.

Inland, however, Calábria preserves something of Italy's primeval heart: rolling hills, numerous streams, verdant pastures and vast woodlands. There are also pleasant surprises, charming antidotes to Calábria's poor popular image. The huge fields of jasmine, for instance: the region is among the world's largest exporters of the essential oil. And the bergamot, a golf-ball-sized orange that growers despair of producing in bulk anywhere but in southern Calábria. Its oil is one of the most powerful and precious known, a key ingredient of the world's finest scents, of Earl Grey tea and Eau de Cologne, which is an Italian invention.

GETTING THERE

By air: international flights go to Lamézia Terme, in Calábria, T: (0968) 411 032/414 111, and Bari, T: (080) 583 5200/04; internal flights to Bríndisi, T: (0831) 411 7208; Crotone, T: (0962) 794 388; Reggio di Calábria, T: (0965) 643 291.
By boat: several companies run ferries from Greece to Bríndisi including Appia Travel, T: (0831) 521 684, and Hellenica Mediterranean Lines, T: (0831) 528 531.
By car: the A14 motorway takes you to Puglia (Foggia–Bari–Táranto) and the A3 to Basilicata and Calábria (Salerno–Cosenza–Reggio di Calábria).
By rail: the Rome–Naples–Reggio di Calábria main line is the fastest, with connections from Naples to Foggia and Bari, and from Salerno to Potenza and Táranto. An inter-city line on the east coast connects all

the main cities in Puglia (Foggia, Bari, Bríndisi and Lecce). Scenic lines in Calábria include the Cosenza–S. Giovanni in Fiore and the Cosenza–Catanzaro. Contact Ufficio Informazioni dei Treni, freephone T: (1478) 88088 within Italy, otherwise visit www.fs-on-line.it or www.trenitalia.com.

WHERE TO STAY

Many new hotels have sprung up in the main towns and along the coasts, but elsewhere lodgings are difficult to find. Prices are mostly much lower than in the rest of the country. For *agriturismo* information contact Farm Holidays, T: (0564) 417 418, or visit www.vacanzeverdi.com.

ACTIVITIES

Walking: both regions have numerous hill and forest walks through some of Italy's least-

known countryside, but few marked long-distance trails.
Pony-trekking: for a list of stables, visit www.fise.it.
Fishing: contact FIPSAS, Via Michele di Pietro 17, Lecce, T: (0832) 242 812 or Via Rione Enel 6/a, Castellúccio Inferiore, T: (0973) 663 641.

FURTHER INFORMATION

Tourist offices: APT, Piazza Moro 33/a, Bari, T: (080) 524 2361, Via Cavour 15, Potenza, T: (0971) 411 839 and Via Roma 3, Reggio di Calábria, T: (0965) 21171.

FURTHER READING

La Puglia dei parchi (Regione Puglia Assessorato Ambiente, 2000); Carlo Levi, *Christ Stopped at Éboli* (Penguin, 2000); Norman Douglas, *Old Calabria* (Weidenfeld, 2001); and George Gissing, *By the Ionian Sea* (Northwestern University Press, 1996).

Gargano and Foresta Umbra

Limestone promontory at the north end of Puglia, a pronounced exception to the bas-relief of the Adriatic coastline; includes parco nazionale (121,118 ha/299,295 acres)
Includes ZPS

The Gargano is the spur of the Italian boot, a peninsula of alien limestone that extends 30 kilometres (20 miles) into the Adriatic. The Cónero promontory aside, it is the only piece of spectacular mountain scenery on the eastern seaboard between Venice and Otranto.

Rising sharply from the coastal plains, this rocky peninsula has a central plateau that undulates between 700 and 1,000

metres (2,300 and 3,300 feet). To the north are the salt lakes of Varano and Lésina, to the east the Foresta Umbra — the 'shady forest', 15,000 hectares (37,000 acres) of the most beautiful mixed woodland in Italy — and to the south the flat-lands of the Tavoliere. The coast is a partly unspoiled marine paradise of turquoise sea, wave-sculpted cliffs and sandy coves. In all senses but the literal, the Gargano is an island, bounded either by sea or by the un-compromising monotony of the Pugliese wheatlands.

Geologically, too, the Gargano is distinct, made up of a deformed limestone shield — 500 metres (1,600 feet) thick in places — hedged in on all sides by rift faults. Here the bedrock is of different origin from the limestones of the central Apennines. It has been called 'an island of Austrian stone stranded upon the beach of Italy', and in fact it is an outcrop of the Balkans, sheared off when two geological plates separated to form the Adriatic. Truly an island for millennia thereafter, it was eventually joined to

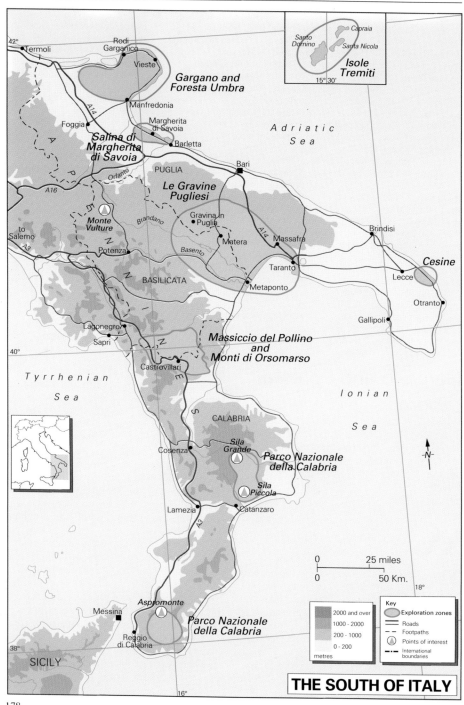

THE SOUTH OF ITALY

Remnants of the ancient Foresta Umbra still cover vast areas of the Gargano's hilly interior.

the mainland by the river-washed silt of the Ice Ages. Most of the terrain is karstic, riddled with more than 600 caves.

Lovers of cliffs and wild seas would be advised to avoid the areas around Vieste and the Báia delle Zágare, which have been blighted by mass tourism, and concentrate on the still gorgeous northern or southeastern headlands. Better still, they should try to come here in autumn and winter when the bathers have gone.

Most of the area's wilderness is now confined to the interior, where the Foresta Umbra offers solitude in high season as well as low. It is a primeval remnant of the Nemus Garganicum, the immense woodland that covered much of Puglia in antiquity. A natural museum, it has more than 2,000 species of plant, tree and shrub — 35 per cent of the Italian total — including 61 species of orchids, the highest concentration in Europe. The reasons for this profusion are various. Geographical remoteness has played its part, limiting human interference, as has the physical isolation from the Apennines, which has encouraged endemics. The local climate is by turns mild and severe, the topography both sheltered and exposed, the soils fertile. Conservation is strong — the central area of the forest has been state owned and protected since 1866.

Among the flowers are numerous species more typical of the Balkans than Italy, such as the bellflower *Campanula garganica* and the buttercup *Ranunculus garganicus*. The rare lilac-pink scabious *Scabiosa crenata* ssp. *dallaportae* can be seen only here and on the Greek island of Cephalonia. The best places to discover rare plants are the valleys around the hamlet of Santa Maria di Pulsano, a solitary and abandoned place that oozes mystery.

One of the most curious aspects of the Gargano's flora is the tendency of plants and trees to reach exaggerated proportions. Examples are the beeches of the Baracconi in the Foresta Umbra, the yews visible more or less everywhere and the holm oaks of the Bosco Quarto and the convent of the Cappuccini, near Vico del Gargano. The Gargano also claims Italy's two largest Aleppo pines, the older dominating the coast road between San Menáio and Péschici. Known as the Zappino dello Scorzone, this monster is 700 years old and has a girth of five metres (16 feet).

The forest fauna includes a rich variety of species common to the Apennines as well as 138 species that have been identified as 'transadriatic', distant ancestors of creatures that existed when Italy and the Balkans were joined during the Pleistocene epoch. The most famous inhabitant is the small roe-deer, *Capreolus capreolus*, one of the three remaining groups of the original pure-bred southern population. Wildcat and fox hunt here, and wild boar and fallow deer have been reintroduced. Among the 170 species of birds are goshawks and eagle owls, which relish the thick tree cover. Breeding birds include Egyptian vultures, honey buzzards, kestrels, sparrowhawks and a handful of short-toed eagles, peregrine falcons and lanner falcons as well as rare white-backed woodpeckers. Perhaps the loveliest bird is the stunning azure and turquoise roller, so called for its somersaulting courtship displays.

Stretched across the flat coastal margins in the north are the salt lakes of Varano and Lésina. Almost 30 kilometres (20 miles) in length, they are the largest lakes in the south and one of Italy's most important waterfowl sites. Plants suited to the unholy trinity of sand, sun and salt line the marshy banks, including the white-flowered *Cistus clusii*. Huge numbers of dippers and waders gather here, among them little egrets, purple and squacco herons, bittern and teal. You may also spot the black stork and the rare slender-billed curlew.

BEFORE YOU GO
Maps: IGM 1:50,000 Nos 383 *Sannicandro Gargánico*, 384 *Vico del Gargano*, 385 *Vieste*, 396 *San Severo*, 397 *Manfredónia* and 398 *Mattinata*.
Guide-book: G. Berthound, *Tutto Gargano 2000* (Camponozzi, 2000).

GETTING THERE
By car: the A14 from Pescara runs behind the Gargano. Exit at Póggio Imperiale for the north coast or at S. Severo to pick up SS272 across the central plateau. For the south, take the Foggia exit and SS89 to Manfredónia. A16 from Naples meets A14 nearby, at Canosa.
By rail: most trains on the east-coast main line stop at Foggia (change for Manfredónia) and some at S. Severo, junction for the north-coast branch to Péschici; contact Foggia, T: (0881) 771 984, or Ferrovie del Gargano, T: (0881) 772 491.
By bus: from Manfredónia, Foggia and Bari you can reach all the local towns with S.I.T.A., T: (0881) 773 117.

WHERE TO STAY
Hotels: try the D'Amato (4-star), Loc. Spiaggia, Péschici, T: (0884) 963 415; Sole (3-star), Loc. S. Menáio, Rodi Gargánico, T: (0884) 968 621.
Agriturismo: Parco Cimaglia, Vieste, T: (0884) 708 050/ 706 471; Parco dei Daini, Loc. Coppa Castellana, Péschici del Gargano, T: (0884) 963 055.
Outdoor living: Riviera, Cagnano Varano, T: (0884) 917 916, F: (0884) 550 028.

ACTIVITIES
Walking: recommended routes are Centro Visite Foresta Umbra to Monte Iacotenente (832 m/2,729 ft) via Coppa dei Prigionieri (4½ hrs); SS89 to Monte Sacro (874 m/2,867 ft, 3 hrs); coastal path from Mergoli to Vignanotica, near Báia delle Zágare (1¼ hrs).
Cycling: contact Comunità Montana del Gargano, T: (0884) 962 721.
Watersports: contact Windsurf Gargano, T: (0884) 646 735. 994 484.
Museum: Museo di Apricena, Corso Generale Torelli 108, Apricena, T: (0882) 646 735.

FURTHER INFORMATION
Tourist offices: Via Rossini, Laguna di Lésina, T: (0882) 992 727; Báia di Manacore, Péschici, T: (0884) 963 400; Corso Fazzini 8, Vieste, T: (0884) 707 495; Via E. Perrone 17, Foggia, T: (0881) 723 141.
Park office: Via S. Antonio Abate 121, Monte S. Angelo, T: (0884) 568 911; or visit www.parcogargano.it.
Visitor centres: Lésina, T: (0882) 99272; Foresta Umbra, T: (0884) 560 944; Monte S. Angelo, T: (0884) 565 444; Manfredónia, T: (0884) 571 009.

Gargano Peninsula

Isole Trémiti

Archipelago 22 km (14 miles) off the coast of Puglia, wild out of season; part of Parco Nazionale del Gargano, includes riserva marina *(1,509 ha/3,729 acres)*

The Trémiti probably take their name from Tre Monti, the 'three mountains' or three main islands that make up this tiny archipelago: San Dómino, San Nicola and Caprara. They are a miniature of all Puglia, graced with caves, bays, headlands, gorges, cliffs and dusty hinterlands of luminous skies and undulating hills. The limestone from which the islands are formed is thought to have been part of a natural bridge to the Balkan peninsula.

San Dómino is the largest island, described in tourist literature as the 'pearl of the Adriatic', which is a little generous, though there is real beauty in its cobalt sea and jutting coastline. The Ripa dei Falconi is its most dramatic feature, a 90-m (300-ft) cliff that was used as a backdrop for

the film *The Guns of Navarone* As its name suggests, the cliff was once famous for its birds of prey, particularly peregrines and Eleonora's falcons, but colonies have been depleted by nest-robbing and the seizing of the birds for falconry. Such birds as survive are now protected, and cling to the highest and most inaccessible parts of the cliff. Here they are accompanied by Manx and Cory's shearwaters, whose curious stiff-winged flight (or 'shearing' motion) can be observed as they skim the sea in search of fish.

Other features along this coast include the Architiello, an arch formed by marine erosion, rock pillars such as the Appicchio and the Pagliai, majestic pyramidal bluffs named after the traditional hayricks they resemble. Sea caves are numerous, the most famous being Bue Marino, the mauve-coloured Grotta delle Viole and Grotta delle Murene, a breeding ground for eels.

Long narrow San Nicola has a higher, slightly more uniform coast, though also pitted with caves and inlets. In spring a green carpet of *maquis* adds zest to the island, but by summer the treeless interior

takes on drier and more desolate tones. The crystal waters are rich in fish — giltheads, sea bass, red mullet and squid — and busy with fishermen and divers.

Caprara takes its name from the caper bushes that cover it almost entirely. It has just two sandy coves, and a series of curious rock bridges, strangely beautiful sculptures which, along with its emptiness, make this perhaps the most inviting of the Trémiti.

Pianosa, an isolated fourth island 40 km (25 miles) from the mainland, is inhabited by colonies of nesting gulls.

Getting there *By air:* daily helicopter to S. Dómino from Gino Lisa airport, Foggia, with Alidaunia, T: (0881) 617 916. *By sea:* to S. Dómino from Térmoli, with Adriatica di Navigazione, T: (0875) 705 343 (all year); also from Ortona, Vasto, Vieste and Manfredónia, T: (041) 781 861; from Rodi Gargánico and Péschici, Freccia Azzurra and Onda Azzurra, T: (0884) 964 234/964 919 (summer only). To S. Nicola and Caprara from S. Dómino, private boats.

When to go: population reaches 100,000 in summer, returning to 4,000 in winter.

Where to stay *Hotels:* Kyrie (3-star), T: (0882) 463 241, Al Faro (1-star), T: (0882) 463 424, both on S. Dómino. Also rooms in private houses (mainly on S. Dómino) through tourist offices. *Outdoor living:* Villaggio TCI on S. Dómino, T: (0882) 463 402 (open all year).

Access: most of S. Dómino, all of S. Nicola and parts of Caprara open for diving, sea-fishing and boating. Pianosa closed except to scientific expeditions and guided tours.

Activities *Diving:* Marlin Diving Center, T: (0882) 463 765.

Further information *Tourist office:* Piazza Kennedy, Vieste, T: (0884) 708 806.

Cory's shearwater is the largest tube-nosed water bird breeding in Europe, 45 cm (18 in) long. It can be identified by its large yellow bill and ashy brown upper parts.

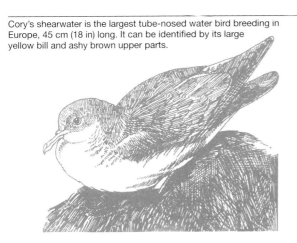

Saline di Margherita di Savóia

Salt-flats and relict coastal marsh on the southern edge of Puglia's Tavoliere plain; includes riserva naturale statale (3,871 ha/9,566 acres)
Includes Ramsar, ZPS

The Saline di Margherita di Savóia, named after Italy's first queen, are the largest and oldest salt-flats in Europe. This has been a salt-producing area since the 3rd century BC, and though the industrial element detracts — cranes and jetties are visible out at sea — it should not deter. Nor should the relief, which is monotonous, save for gleaming pyramids of salt and the Gargano's distant grey ridges. It is a perfect place to watch birds.

The flats are part of the coastal wetlands that run from Manfredónia to Margherita di Savóia. Until the drainage projects of 40 years ago this was a huge unbroken expanse of marshland. What remains today is but a tenth of the original. It still amounts to 75,000 ha (185,000 acres) of prime wetland, including not only the Saline but also the Alma Dannata lagoons, the basins of the Cervaro and Candelaro rivers and the reserves of Palude Frattarolo and Daunia Risi.

Thanks to its size, variety of salt- and freshwater habitats and availability of food, this stretch of coast is one of Europe's most important stopovers for migrating birds. The shallow salt-flats, with their invertebrate-rich sediments, are a marvellous food source for long-legged wading birds. They attract small flocks of spoonbills, unmistakable with

their snow-white plumage and broad-tipped, spatula-like beaks, as well as huge numbers of waterfowl.

Some birds even manage to breed in and around the less heavily worked salt-flats, which are fringed by specialized plants such as sea-blites and saltworts and surrounded in drier areas by a zone of Mediterranean *garrigue*. These shores are home to long-legged black-winged stilts, diminutive Kentish plovers and numerous little terns as well as a colony of 6,000 flamingoes, the biggest in mainland Italy.

In the freshwater and brackish marshes of the Palude Frattarolo and Daunia Risi, bird-watchers are treated to five species of breeding heron: bittern, night, purple, squacco and grey. Even more remarkable, a handful of nesting glossy ibis have made their home here; there is no mistaking these birds, half a metre (nearly two feet) in length, with long, down-curved beaks and purple-brown plumage tinged with metallic green.

Before you go *Maps:* IGM 1:50,000 Nos 409 *Zapponeta* and 410 *Torre Pietra*.
Getting there *By car:* A14 to Cerignola Est exit, then SS545 and 544. Coastal SS159 runs along north edge of flats. *By rail:* to Margherita di Savóia on Foggia–Bari main line; call F. S. Salinis, T: (0883) 651 588.
Where to stay *Hotels:* health-spa Grand Hotel Terme (4-star), Corso Garibaldi 1, T: (0883) 656 888, or Camporeale (2-star), Via Ariosto 25, T: (0883) 654 964, both in Margherita di Savóia. *Outdoor living:* Ranchmare, Via Manfredónia, Margherita di Savóia, T: (0883) 655 251 (summer only).
Access: entry to salt-flats only for scientific purposes, but good views with binoculars from perimeter; Palude Frattarolo

and Daunia Risi unrestricted.
Activities *Bird-watching:* call LIPU, Sezione Provinciale Foggia, T: (368) 737 9695, or Corpo Forestale dello Stato, T: (0884) 456 044.
Further information *Tourist offices:* Via Cirillo 2, Margherita di Savóia, T: (0883) 654 012. *Visitor centre:* Salpi observatory, contact Museo di Storia Naturale, Foggia, T: (0881) 663 972.

Cesine

Coastal lakes at the south end of Puglia, bordered by reed-beds, salt-marsh, scrub and woodland; riserva naturale statale
348 ha (860 acres)
Ramsar, WWF, ZPS

The Cesine are a pair of brackish lakes, Salapi and the larger Pantano Grande, that lie along a stretch of sandy coastline between Lecce and Otranto, part of an area called the Salento at the southernmost tip of the Italian heel.

One of the south's best bird-watching areas, the lakes appear as two glittering turquoise lagoons, separated from the Adriatic by a narrow fringe of dunes. Behind them the landscape is dry and solemn, dotted with white farmhouses and carpeted to the far distance with centuries-old olive trees providing one of Italy's best olive oils.

The succession of coastal habitats — beach, dune, swamp, *maquis*, lake and woodland — preserves, uniquely in Puglia, the classic profile of southern Mediterranean littorals. The name Cesine comes from the Latin *caedere*, 'to cut', a reference to the thinning and burning of woodland to promote new growth, and the lake shores are surrounded by a mantle of green that is in marked contrast to the sun-parched fields close by. Dunal *maquis*, blown into a tangled barrier and reinforced by the planting of pines, provides a wind-break for more delicate flora, allowing some 320 species to flourish here, covering huge areas with a perfumed carpet of flowers in spring. Among the many rare species are a number of orchids, including Bertoloni's ophrys, known locally as *pantofola di Vénere* ('Venus' slipper'), and the bug orchid *Orchis coriophora*, whose flowers supposedly smell of squashed bed-bugs — but who would know?

Between October and April the lakes are alive with frenzied wheeling and the flutter and beating of wings as up to 10,000 birds congregate during their autumn and spring migrations. The great white egret is an occasional visitor from Greece. Equally unusual is the black stork, rarely seen in western Europe except in south-west Spain where it breeds.
Before you go *Map:* IGM 1:25,000 No. 513 IV *San Foca*.
Getting there *By car:* SS543 from Lecce to S. Cataldo; SS611 from Otranto crosses the reserve. *By rail:* Lecce on main line from Foggia. *By bus:* hourly service from Lecce to S. Cataldo, S.G.M., T: (0832) 340 898.
Where to stay *Hotels:* Terra d'Otranto Village (3-star), S.Cataldo, T: (0832) 650 311; numerous in Lecce.
Access: unrestricted Sun before 10 am, otherwise guided tours; Co-op. Oasi, T: (0832) 892 264.
Further information *Tourist offices:* Via Vittório Emanuele 24, Lecce, T: (0832) 248 092; Pro Loco Vernole, T: (0832) 892 552. *Ecology:* WWF, Via Alessandria 2, Lecce, T: (0832) 392 300.

Le Gravine Pugliesi

Canyons on the Puglia-Basilicata border; includes parco archeologico storico naturale (6,628 ha/16,378 acres)
Includes World Heritage Site, ZPS

The Pugliesi *gravine* are some 25 gorges that run down to the coast between Metaponto and Táranto. Some are so small and thick with vegetation as to be inaccessible; others — seven or eight in all — are huge affairs, the most striking being Laterza, Castellaneta, Palagianello, Petruscio and Massafra.

Matera is the area's most westerly town and best base,

Bertoloni's ophrys is a remarkable orchid whose flowers produce insect-like scents. These heady aromas induce bees and wasps to try to copulate with it, enabling pollen to be transferred from one flower to another.

standing close to its own gorge, another of the more spectacular ones, 10 km (6 miles) long and up to 100 m (330 ft) deep. The canyon is riddled with *sassi*, 'stone' or cave dwellings, and Greek Orthodox crypts cut into the soft tufaceous rock that here supplants the prevailing limestone.

The first caves were probably dug in prehistory; some were added by anchorites and Eastern Orthodox Christians, others by peasants seeking shelter from Barbarian and later Moorish invaders. Many were inhabited until 1952 when they were condemned as unfit. More recently the *sassi*, some containing 10th-century frescoes, have been protected by UNESCO. The area has been designated a park in recognition of its unique qualities, Matera being the only town in Italy where you can see Egyptian vultures, peregrines, short-toed eagles, lanner falcons and rare lesser kestrels from your bedroom window.
Before you go *Maps:* IGM 1:50,000 Nos 472 *Matera*, 473 *Gioia del Colle*, 474 *Noci* and 493 *Táranto*.
Getting there *By car:* SS7 Matera–Massafra bisects many ravines. *By rail:* Matera on branch off Bari–Altamura–Potenza line; Castellaneta and Massafra on Bari–Táranto line; Apulo-Lucana, T: (0835) 332 861. *By bus:* from Matera and Táranto; S.I.T.A., T: (0835) 385 007.
Where to stay *Hotel:* Italia (3-star), Via Ridola 5, Matera, T: (0835) 333 561.
Activities *Walking:* best hikes in Matera, Laterza and Castellaneta gorges; Matera Turismo, T: (0835) 336 572.
Further information *Tourist office:* Via De Viti De Marco 9, Matera, T: (0835) 331 983. *Park office:* Via Sette Dolori 10, Matera, T: (0835) 336 166.

Massiccio del Pollino and dell'Orsomarso

Huge massifs cutting Calábria off from the rest of Italy, one of the ultimate European wildernesses; parco nazionale *192,565 ha (475,847 acres)*

ϟϟϟ

Pollino's colossal massif is the most impressive mountain region in the south, comparable in its empty grandeur only to the savage landscapes of Sardinia, Etna and the Abruzzo. Protected, with the neighbouring Orsomarso, as Italy's biggest national park, it is the highest point in southern Italy, and one of the most daunting and elemental ranges imaginable.

The heart of the chain, which straddles the border of Basilicata and Calábria, lies in the tormented ridge containing Monte Pollino itself. Though it lends its name to the massif, at 2,248 metres (7,375 feet) it is just lower than its neighbour, the 2,267-metre (7,437-feet) and quite inappropriately named Monte Dolcedorme, 'sweet slumber'. However, it is not so much Pollino's height that astounds as its sheer vastness. Words hardly begin to suggest the scale of the mountains that radiate from this central ridge. Figures, so much as they can, confirm the emptiness. The area has a population density of 60 people per square kilometre, one of the lowest in Italy. Most of them are lumped together in Castrovillari and the villages that line the twisting course of the A3, the only motorway that breaches this rocky rampart.

In typical Apennine fashion, Pollino's massifs present different faces to the world depending on whether your approach is from the north or the south. Overlooking the hilly expanses of Basilicata, the northern slopes are more gentle: a green, fresh-faced alternation of wood and water, containing some of the area's densest forests, notably the Bosco Magnano near San Severino Lucano and the Cugno dell'Acero above Terranova di Pollino. The south-facing slopes are more

Mediterranean, much steeper and more spectacular, an arid mixture of sun-bleached limestone and clinker-dry gorges, none more imposing than the Raganello, the south's greatest canyon, a Dantesque vision of rocky inhospitality that supports numerous birds of prey. Access is from the lonely village of San Lorenzo Bellizzi. Other hidden corners include the dizzying Bifurto abyss, an unbroken drop of 683 metres (2,240 feet); the water-carved Lao, Garavina and Barile gorges; and the Grotta delle Ninfe, a thermal spring famous since Roman times for its miracle-working waters.

Nowhere is the solemn, silent dignity of the mountains more keenly felt than on Dolcedorme. Its intimidating pyramidal shape seems to promise a stiff climb but, in the event, lets the walker off lightly. Most hikers start from the Rifugio De Gasperi on the Piano Ruggio and are rewarded in spring with breathtaking meadows of wild flowers, before the assault on the Canale di Malvento, 'the canyon of the bad winds'. A final haul to the summit provides one of Europe's finest panoramas. Three seas, the Ionian, Adriatic and Tyrrhenian, are visible on clear days, along with a huge swathe of southern Italy: the Calabrian plains of Sibari and Castrovillari; the distant dark humps of the Sila; and to their right, more distinct, the spine of the Catena Costiera, Calábria's coastal chain.

The Pollino marked the southernmost extent of the ice-sheet in Italy during the last period of glaciation. Faint reminders of this colder age remain in the summit snows — which in some years fail to melt even in summer, when temperatures on the Calabrian plains can reach 40° C (105 °F) — and in the vegetation. On the long climb to Dolcedorme's summit you can see the thick trunks and dense foliage of the majestic Bosnian pine, *Pinus leucodermis*. Symbol of the national park, the tree is a relic from prehistory that has its origins in the Balkans and no longer grows anywhere else in Italy. It can be found from 500 metres (1,500 feet) upwards, but prefers the sunniest, driest, rockiest heights. Resilient to strong winds, which often sculpt it into distinctive shapes, it survives in small groups or more often as

184

solitary sentinels, which can reach incredible ages: the so-called 'Patriarch' of the Bosco Pollinello is 920 years old.

Other strange flora inhabit the Pollino: the burning bush *Dictamnus albus*, for example, a mysterious plant which sometimes appears to shine in the dark; or the heavenly 'manna', made famous by the erroneous accounts of 19th-century travellers such as George Sandys, who said that 'it falls at night like dew on the mulberry leaves'. He was referring to the sugary resin that drips from the bark of the manna ash *Fraxinus ornus*, but this only happens when the bark is punctured. The tree is still commercially cultivated in Sicily, where the syrup obtained from the resin is used as a mild astringent.

Pollino's wildlife is that of an undisturbed high mountain habitat, with the two great symbols of such terrain, the wolf and the golden eagle, at the head of the list. Pollino offers probably your best chance in southern Italy of sighting wolves, if you have the patience and the sense of adventure these mountains demand. A few pairs of golden eagles are known to fly in the south of the range. In the east, you may see an Egyptian vulture, lanner falcon or black woodpecker; slightly more numerous are black and red kites, peregrines, Greek partridges, eagle owls and Cornish choughs.

The wildness of the place is confirmed by the presence of such shy creatures as otters, red squirrels, crested porcupines, rare wildcats and endemic roe-deer, which have vanished elsewhere in the south except

Pollino and Monti di Orsomarso

for the ancient nucleus that survives in the Gargano and the group that has been reintroduced in the Sila.

The wilderness of the Orsomarso, to the south-west, is nearly as immense as Pollino's. It contains almost no signs of human presence, apart from shepherds' huts that even shepherds have abandoned. Hardy and well-equipped walkers can make one of Italy's loneliest treks, the 45-kilometre (28-mile) journey along its main ridge, a succession of 12 rocky, almost Dolomitic summits over 1,700 metres (5,600 feet) high. Winter cross-country skiing is superb, as it is in much of the Pollino.

Many villages on and around the Pollino (Cívita, Eiánina, San Páolo Albanese) are peopled with the *arbëreshë* — inhabitants of Albanian descent who preserve customs and a way of life brought with them when the Turkish invasions of the 16th century forced them to flee to Italy. In dress, manner, food, language, music and religion, they can still be markedly different from neighbouring Italians, even after some 500 years.

BEFORE YOU GO
Maps: IGM 1:50,000 Nos 522 *Sense*, 533 *Maratea* and 534 *Castrovillari*. Potenza's tourist office issues a free map with walking and cross-country skiing itineraries.
Guide-books: M. Zanetti, *Escursioni nel Parco del Pollino* (Cierre, 2001); C. Pizzuti, *La grande attraversata del Pollino* (Editoriale Cosenza, 2000).

GETTING THERE
By car: come in on the A3. For

the Pollino, exit at Campotenese and take either of 2 lanes, both very scenic, to Rotonda or Rif. De Gasperi. For Raganello, leave at Frascineto-Castrovillari and take SS105 east, then SS92 north to Cerchiara and S. Lorenzo Bellizzi. For the Orsomarso, exit at Mormanno (then SS504) or Morano Cálabro (then SS105 southbound); there are no roads into the massif.
By rail: the nearest stations (not very near) are Sapri, T: (0973) 391

907, and Scalea, T: (0985) 20618, both on the Naples–Reggio di Calábria main line.
By bus: from Sapri take a bus to Lagonegro, and then another to either Rotonda or Castrovillari; contact S.L.A., Lagonegro, T: (0973) 210 116. From Scalea buses run to Castrovillari and Cosenza; contact S.A.I.M.A., Mormanno, T: (0981) 80267.

WHERE TO STAY
Hotels: try Viola (2-star), Via

185

The limestone uplands and hidden valleys of the Pollino massif are the haunt of wolves and golden eagles.

Convento, Terranova di Pollino, T: (0973) 93098; S. Elena (3-star), Via Scesa Laino, Mormanno, T: (0981) 81052.

Agriturismo: La Locanda del Parco, C.da Mazzicanino, T: (0981) 31304, and Le Fontanelle, C.da Mattinaza, T: (0981) 31656, both in Morano Cálabro; Parco Villa Elena, Mormanno, T: (0981) 80254, www.parcovillaelena.it.

Refuges: De Gasperi, T: (0973) 661 080; Fasanelli is in poor condition and only for use in emergencies.

Outdoor living: you can camp anywhere; alternatively try Camping Val Frida, Frazione Mezzana Salice, S. Severino Lucano, T: (0973) 570 204. The Orsomarso has many shepherds' huts suitable as bivouacs.

ACTIVITIES

Walking: although there are few marked routes, paths are often easy to follow because the

ground is open and barren. Distances are long and when snow is heavy from Nov onwards, the mountains require care and adequate equipment. The classic walk is the ascent of Pollino from the Colle dell'Impiso (1,573 m/5,160 ft, 5 hrs). Variations include a climb to the Serra del Prete (4 hrs) and a brief hike north to the Madonna del Pollino (1,537 m/5,042 ft, 3 hrs). The simplest stroll is up the Raganello gorge from S. Lorenzo Bellizzi (2 hrs). More strenuous walks include the mainly wooded trek from Casa del Conte to the Colle dell'Impiso via Piano del Pollino (12/13 hrs) and the long haul to Serra Dolcedorme from the car park at the Vaccaro springs above Cívita (16 hrs); most demanding is the coast-to-coast walk (7 days).

Mountain biking: routes through the Pollino are shown at www.itinerariitaliani.com/

bicibasilicata.htm.

Canoeing: the Lao rivér in the northern Orsomarso has one of southern Italy's best runs, from the bridge at Papasidero downstream to the SS18 coast road near Scalea (18 km/11 miles), Canoa Club Lao Pollino, T: (0981) 85673.

Skiing: contact APT Basilicata, T: (0971) 507 622, for cross-country routes.

FURTHER INFORMATION

Tourist offices: Via Cavour 15, Potenza, T: (0971) 448 601; Via Roma 6, Lagonegro, T: (0973) 21016; Viale del Lavoro 86, Castrovillari, T: (0981) 25208; www.aptbasilicata.it.

Park office: Palazzo Amato, Via Mordini 20, Rotonda, T: (0973) 661 692, www.parcopollino.it.

Visitor centre: Vico II Annunziata 11, Morano Cálabro, T: (0981) 30745.

Ecology: Ufficio Foreste Ecologia Basilicata, Potenza, T: (0971) 448 777; WWF, Via S. Aniceto 1, Castrovillari, T: (339) 769 7806, e-mail: wwfpollino@tin.it.

Sila

*Mountains and forests of central Calábria,
biggest wooded area in southern Italy;*
parco nazionale
ZPS
12,690 ha (31,360 acres)

Of all the ranges in the Apennines, the
Sila come closest to preserving the
primeval wooded appearance of southern
Italy before deforestation, cultivation and
the various depredations of man took their
toll. This timeless landscape belies the
popular sun-scorched image of the south,
unfolding instead lakes, torrents, forests,
deep valleys and frosted mountains.

The Sila cover most of the centre of
Calábria and are divided from north to
south into three ranges: the Sila Greca, the
Sila Grande and the Sila Piccola. Of similar
height, between 1,500 and 1,800 metres
(5,000 and 5,900 feet), they are often dis-
missed as high plateaux, a put-down that
does them little justice.

All three ranges manifest the belated
reappearance — after the Apennines' all
but unbroken chain of limestone — of
crystalline rocks in the Italian geological
picture. Granites start to appear south of
the Pollino, and in northern Calábria still
alternate with Triassic limestones, but from
the Sila southwards — with odd Tertiary
sandstones — they dominate completely.
Much older than the Appenines, the Sila
are the eroded summits of a range that
continues into the seas off southern Italy.

In places these crystalline bedrocks
crumble to form deep fertile soils, which in
turn support the huge forests from which
the Sila take their name (Latin *silva*,
'wood'). A valuable source of lumber, the
forests were felled from as early as the 9th
century, when Pope Gregory IV used their
timber to roof many of Rome's churches.
Later they were requisitioned for the
building of ships and railways.
Considerable replanting has since taken

place, and the virgin forests of the interior
are still so vast that the Sila are considered
one of Europe's most densely wooded
areas. Apennine wolves are more numerous
here than anywhere else in southern Italy, a
sure sign of wilderness. The principal tree
is the Calabrian pine, a localized speciality
with the long-winded title of *Pinus nigra*,
ssp. *laricio*, variety *calabrica*. In the Bosco
di Fallistro near Camigliatello Silano, you
can see the so-called *giganti della Sila*, 56
Calabrian pines thought to be nearly 400
years old, most more than 40 metres (130
feet) high, with trunks two metres (six feet)
in diameter.

As well as supporting a lush vegetation,
the impervious granite bedrock of the Sila
also provides an abundance of surface
water. The scores of rivers in Calábria are a
surprise and a relief after the wearing
aridity of much of the south. In partnership

Spring brings an all too brief mantle of green to the
Aspromonte, the 'rough mountain', before the long
dry summer sets in.

with the pines, the gurgling streams and waterfalls give the Sila a distinctly Nordic flavour, emphasized by three immense reservoirs built on their western flanks. All tend to enhance rather than disfigure this landscape. Of the three — Cecita, Arvo and Ampollino — the fjord-like Arvo is the most impressive. The Scandinavian simile can be continued through into the climate. The Sila may be close to Africa, but their winter is a bitingly cold and raw-winded affair. While summer plains burn under a Saharan sun, the winter slopes can be snow-covered for as many as four months of the year. During the bleakest weeks, the Sila are transformed into peninsular Italy's finest (and most severe) cross-country skiing area.

The grey wolf is the largest member of the dog family surviving in the wild, but at 75 cm (30 in) high to the shoulder, it is smaller than many people imagine.

BEFORE YOU GO

Maps: IGM 1:50,000 Nos 552 *Carigliano Calabro*, 560 *Spezzano della Sila* and 561 *San Giovanni in Fiore*. The park issues its own map of the Sila Grande: 1:25,000 *Carta della Fossiata* (useful only as a basic guide to paths).
Guide-book: A. Garcea, *Monumenti verdi in Sila Piccola e dintorni* (Abramo, 2002).

GETTING THERE

By car: take A3 to Cosenza Nord, then turn east on SS107, also known as Silana-Crotonese, which bisects the Grande and the Piccola. For Sila Greca take SS177 through Sila Grande to Longobucco; the Piccola is ringed by SS107 from Cosenza and SS109 from Catanzaro; SS179 and SS179 dir. enter the massif.
By rail: change at Páola on the Naples–Reggio di Calábria main line for Cosenza. A fantastic line runs from there to S. Giovanni in Fiore, offering gorgeous views *en route*; contact Naples station, T: (081) 553 4188.
By bus: all local services depart from Cosenza, and are run by S.I.M.E.T., T: (0984) 76908/ (0983) 520 315; for long-

distance routes, contact S.A.I., T: (0981) 500 331.

WHERE TO STAY

Hotels: Albergo Cozza (3-star), Via Roma 83, Camigliatello Silano, T: (0984) 578 034; della Posta (2-star), Villaggio Mancuso, T: (0961) 922 033.
Outdoor living: free camping is prohibited, but camp-sites can be found by Lago Cecita and near Lorica; call Opera Valorizzazione della Sila, Villaggio Racise, T: (0961) 922 009.

ACTIVITIES

Walking: there are many marked paths in both Sila Grande and Sila Piccola. The best base in the Grande is Camigliatello Silano; in the Piccola, Tirivolo or Villaggio Mancuso. Many walks also depart from S. Giovanni in Fiore, where three circular itineraries will take you to all the main ridges and the three lakes of Sila Grande. The paths are marked green (4 hrs), red (2 hrs) and yellow (2 hrs). For organized walks, contact Sila Trekking, Longobucco, T: (0983) 71317.
Skiing: Camigliatello Silano, T: (0984) 578 067, and Lorica, T:

(0984) 537 093, are first and foremost ski resorts. Trepidó Soprano and Villaggio Mancuso (lifts at Ciricillà) also have good pistes. Popular cross-country routes include the run from Monte Cúrcio to Monte Botte Donato and those around Croce di Magara and Silvana Mánsio.
Bird-watching: birds of prey, notably goshawks, peregrines and eagle owls, are best seen in the Boschi di Arnocampo between Lago di Cecita and the hamlet of Germano; contact LIPU, Rende, T: (0984) 447 092.
Ecology: the best place to look out for wolves is above the rangers' centre on Lago di Cecita. Pine and beech martens, badgers, otters, deer, wildcats and polecats may also be spotted, especially in the Sila Grande.

FURTHER INFORMATION

Tourist offices: Via Roma, Camigliatello Silano, T: (0984) 578 243; Via Spasari 3, Catanzaro, T: (0961) 741 764.
Park office: Viale della Repubblica 26, Cosenza, T: (0984) 76760.
Visitor centre: Villaggio Mancuso, T: (0961) 922 030.

Aspromonte

Rocky toe of the Italian boot, where Calábria ends and Sicily begins; parco nazionale
78,517 ha (194,023 acres)

There is a legend that until recently no one had ever crossed these mountains, indeed no one had ever wanted to, so wild and inhospitable were they. Latter-day bandits and kidnappers used to hide their victims in these trackless wastes, perhaps still do. To visit the area — and very few people bother — is to find the wild Italy of old, to discover a place where something of the country's soul can still be said to reside — where you can say, 'here is as it was'.

The Aspromonte, the 'rough mountain', occupies nearly the whole southern tip of the Italian peninsula. The last exuberant burst of Apennine wilderness, it shares some of the Sila's gifts of wood and water; where it differs, as its appellation suggests, is in its added ruggedness. Noble and charming under soft skies, the air clear and silky, more usually it is a harsh sun-beaten mixture of hill, valley and tormented mountains, its geology a chaos of different rocks — including lava — torn and contorted by weather and earthquakes into one of Italy's most inaccessible landscapes.

Making sense of this infernal topography is difficult. The sea is perhaps the best point of reference, enclosing the Aspromonte on three sides, and visible from most of its 22 peaks. The highest is Montalto (1,955 metres/6,414 feet), a vantage point which offers one of the great Italian views. To the west, Sicily stretches beyond the Straits of Messina, cloud-wreathed Etna clearly visible, and the Aeolian islands appear as small spots in the azure of the Tyrrhenian. Away to the east the Ionian Sea shines an equally vivid blue, lost only when mist — Aspromonte is also known as 'the cloud-gatherer' — wells up to shroud the summit.

There are few roads in the mountains, generally just empty valleys (known as *fiumare*) which radiate to the four points of the compass from the central massif. Most have water only in autumn and winter, when raging torrents replace summer's drought; in spring many of the dry beds are filled with wild flowers. This brief but rich flowering includes hare's-foot clover, Carthusian pinks, black bryony, long-spurred pansies, mountain cornflowers and sweet vernal-grass that contains coumarin and has the smell of new-mown hay. The tropical long-leaved fern *Woodwardia radicans* also thrives, a relic of a type of flora that was common in Europe 60 million years ago.

Another way to make sense of this tangled landscape is to compare the Aspromonte's contrasting flanks. The western slopes fall seawards in broad steps, creating a series of olive-covered plains and meadows in which the granite desolation is a touch more sweet and smiling. The eastern slopes, by contrast, are unashamedly barren: empty desert scenery, with fantastic rock formations and spectacular gorges that drop as much as 1,500 metres (5,000 feet) in their plunge to the sea.

Isolation has encouraged anomalies both animal and human. One of the Aspromonte's most famous residents is the *driomio*, a little dormouse. Usually found in the Alps, it is honoured here as the geographical subspecies *aspromontis*. A few pairs of rare Bonelli's eagles are among the 92 species of birds that nest here, hiding out on the most rugged and inaccessible cliffs of the Amendolea valley. No less remarkable is the survival of a Greek-speaking community, an outpost of Magna Graecia still holding out around the village of Bova.

Before you go *Maps:* IGM 1,50:000 Nos 589 *Palmi*, 590 *Taurianova* and 602 *Motta San Giovanni*.

Getting there *By car:* from north, leave A3 at Bagnara Cálabra, then SS112; from Reggio di Calábria, SS18 then SS184; from Mélito, SS183; all go to Gambárie, whence minor roads lead into massif, one to Montalto itself. *By rail:* Gióia Tauro and Reggio di Calábria on main line, T: (0965) 27120. *By bus:* Lirosi, T: (0966) 57552. **Where to stay** *Hotel:* Il Ritrovo (2-star), Via Garibaldi 15, Gambárie, T: (0965) 743 021. *Agriturismo:* Il Bergamotto, Loc. Amendolea, Condofuri, T: (0965) 727 213. *Outdoor living:* Villaggio del Pino, Scilla, T: (0965) 755 126; Al Boschetto, Condofuri, T: (0965) 784 100. **Activities** *Walking:* Sentiero del Brigante, from Gambárie to Serra S. Bruno (No. 206, 6–8 days); from Bova to Delianuova (No. 128, 3–4 days); from Roghudi to Butramo and Apóscipo canyons, Ferraina Falls and Amendolea valley (all 1 day); contact Gruppo Escursionistico Aspromonte, T: (0965) 332 822. For Englishman's Path (in footsteps of Edward Lear, 8 days), call Naturaliter, T: (0965) 626 840. *Skiing:* with sea views, Sci Club Gambárie, T: (0965) 743 061. **Further information** *Tourist offices:* Gambárie, T: (0965) 743 295 (summer/winter only); Via D. Tripepi 72, Reggio di Calábria, T: (0965) 898 496. *Park office:* Via Aurora, Gambárie, T: (0965) 743 060. *Ecology:* EOS Turismo Verde, Locri, T: (0964) 22526.

CHAPTER 9

Sicily and Sardinia

Sicily and Sardinia are the largest islands in the Mediterranean, mythical and mysterious places, and home to some of the wildest scenery. Both are lands apart, inhabited by peoples of fierce pride, and separated by history, culture and language not only from Italy, but also from anywhere else in Europe. D. H. Lawrence described Sicily as the place where 'Europe ends' and Sardinia as 'unlike any other place on earth' — 'inside the net of European civilization' but not yet 'dragged ashore to join the rest of Europe'. Visit both if you can, for to miss either, as Goethe said of Sicily, 'is not to have seen Italy at all'.

Sicily is the better known of the two. For all its Mafia associations, or the building that has ruined much of the coast, it is the most beautiful of islands, the charmed kingdom of Persephone, goddess of spring. It is the land of the lotus eaters, the shore Odysseus' weary crew saw as an earthly paradise and refused to leave. It is a haven of sun and golden fruits, the granary of the Roman Empire.

Sicily is transitional in every sense. It is the football forever being kicked towards Africa by the Italian boot, suspended at the edge of one continent, 150 kilometres (100 miles) from the other, exhibiting features of both. Its northern mountains evoke the woods and hills of central Europe; its desolate plains bring to mind the Spanish *meseta*; the olives and terracing of the

Dawn breaks over Lampedusa in the Pelágie islands, a remote archipelago lying between Sicily and the African coast.

east suggest Greece and the Aegean; the south's treeless hills and dunes foreshadow the deserts of North Africa. Only the constellation of offshore islands are unanchored to any obvious continental associations, drifting, sun-baked fragments in azure seas, timeless patches — for the most part — of wilderness all but lost to the world.

Besides the monumental presence of Mount Etna in the east, Sicily boasts only one genuinely mountainous region, the chain that runs for 150 kilometres (100 miles) along the northern coast. Its massifs, the Peloritani, Nébrodi and Madoníe, are a continuation of the mainland Apennines.

Western Sicily is geographically confusing, a mish-mash of limestone outcrops, undulating clay plateaux and eye-stretching carpets of vineyards and olives laid across the plains of Trápani and Marsala. The coast alternates between flat bays, low hills, headlands of outstanding beauty, such as Monte dello Zingaro, and lagoon-fringed dunes that form the first landfall for many birds migrating north from Africa in the spring. Over in the Etna-dominated east, the prosperous agricultural plains of Catania give way southwards to the Iblean mountains, a distinctive region of table-top uplands and steep-sided valleys.

Sicily's bare, desolate interior is what Giuseppe Tomasi di Lampedusa called 'the real Sicily' in his novel *The Leopard*: 'aridly undulating to the horizon in hill after hill, comfortless and irrational, with no lines that the mind could grasp, conceived apparently in a delirious moment of creation'. This is a sun-baked and monotonous landscape raked by barren valleys and bone-dry ravines, crossed by dusty white roads that stretch across burnt and exhausted soils to vanish in heat-shimmering horizons. Under an African sun, crickets make the only sound, plodding donkeys and women in black the only movement. Farms and trees are almost unknown, villages slumbering hilltop affairs whose poverty still reeks of Sicily's feudal heritage.

Sardinia can claim countryside still more extreme — so extreme, in fact, that many declare it the finest wilderness in all of western Europe. Only the luxury north-east coastal developments of the Aga Khan, the so-called Costa Smeralda, and the capital, Cagliari, show determined efforts to welcome the modern world. Although lesser entrepreneurs have followed the Aga Khan by trailing concrete in their wake, they have not made much progress. This is, of course, ironic good fortune for the landscape and its fauna. You can enjoy endless horizons of land unturned since the Romans, if ever, windswept uplands covered in dense scrub, vast forests of cork oak (accounting for three-quarters of Italy's cork production), ten offshore islands, lines of low hills and vast empty vistas of utter loneliness. It is almost fruitless to try to differentiate between one lonely spot in Sardinia and the next; most of the island will satisfy even the most exacting seeker of wilderness. Perhaps the loneliest, though, is the Gennargentu, a series of granite and limestone ranges that sprawls across most of the island's eastern side.

The landscape is of the most extraordinary variety, reflecting a geological complexity that leaves even dedicated studies floundering with descriptions like 'a mosaic of morphological areas'. What this fails to convey is that Sardinia contains Italy's oldest rocks and has been cut and thrust so often that its structure is an almost indecipherable jumble. Two thirds is granite, the rest a medley of almost any rock you care to mention. Most of the granite occurs in the east, but then so does most of the limestone; the answer is simply to try to enjoy the result.

As capricious as Sardinia's rocks are its rivers, meandering, ill-formed and hostage to summer droughts. The fluvial network, of leaf-skeleton complexity, fragments repeatedly. Few rivers keep one name for their entire course; some have as many as twelve names and many use the same name as others. All over the island, you will come across rivers named Mannu, which means 'big river'. Maps show 17 of these little 'big rivers', often no more than a generous trickle.

Water being too precious to be wasted, there are several reservoirs on the island but only one natural lake, Lago Baratz in the extreme north-west. There are, however, many natural *stagni* (salt lagoons) along the coast and those which have not been drained provide bases for most of the island's bird population. The most important are the lagoons at Cagliari, which support thousands of flamingoes despite being only a stone's throw from the city, and at Sínis on the western coast, one of the white-sand beach paradises that explain why half of Italy wishes to spend its annual summer holiday in Sardinia.

GETTING THERE

By air: to Sicily, you can fly from Europe to Palermo, T: (091) 702 0111, www.gesap.it, or to Catania, T: (095) 349 837/341 654. To Sardinia, international and domestic flights go to Ólbia, T: (0789) 68242, Cagliari, T: (070) 241 014, and Alghero, T: (079) 935 043.

By sea: timetables vary from month to month and company to company but services tend to be daily June–Sept. To Sicily, boats sail from Genoa, Livorno and Naples to Palermo; contact Grimaldi, T: (010) 589 331, or Tirrenia, T: (091) 602 1111. A car-ferry runs from Villa S. Giovanni to Messina (½ hr) all year round. Hydrofoils operate in summer between Naples and Trápani, Ustica Lines, T: (0923) 27 397. To Sardinia, the most popular ferries run from Civitavécchia to Ólbia (7 hrs), Arbatax (9 hrs) and Cagliari (12 hrs); others go from Genoa to Ólbia, Cagliari and Porto Tórres; Livorno and Piombino to Ólbia and Cagliari; Naples to Cagliari; and Palermo and Trápani to Cagliari. Contact Linea dei Golfi in Piombino,

T: (0565) 222 300; Sardinia Ferries in Golfo Aránci, T: (0789) 46780 or in Ólbia, T: (0789) 25200; and Tirrenia Navigazione in Ólbia, T: (0789) 24691 or in Cagliari, T: (070) 67901. For a railway-operated service from La Spézia to Golfo Aránci, contact Ufficio Informazioni dei Treni, freephone T: (1478) 88088 within Italy, otherwise visit www.fs-on-line.it or www.trenitalia.com.

WHEN TO GO

July and Aug are uncomfortably hot, hotels busy and prices high. Spring is best, when the almond is in blossom. Winter is mild, with frequent clear skies.

WHERE TO STAY

In Sicily, accommodation is ample in cities and coastal resorts, often scarce and poor in the interior. For the booklet *Sicilia Campeggi*, contact provincial tourist offices. Sardinia has many luxury hotels on the Costa Smeralda, but elsewhere little outside main towns. For *L'annuario degli alberghi e dei campeggi*, contact tourist offices. For

rural stays in both Sicily and Sardinia, contact Farm Holidays, T: (0564) 417 418, www.vacanzeverdi.com.

ACTIVITIES

Walking: in Sicily, there are only a few marked trails, mainly in the Madoníe mountains, but interesting walks can be had on Etna, in the Nébrodi and on the offshore islands, details from Club Alpino Siciliano (CAS), Via P. Paternostro 43, Palermo, T: (091) 581 323. Sardinia is pioneering country, with few recognized paths but many shepherds' tracks, CAI, Via Piccioni, Cagliari, T: (070) 667 877.

Caving: in Sicily, there are numerous caves, including the Addáura at Mondello, the Bue Marino at Filicudi and the Genovese on Levanzo; contact the Centro Speleologico Etneo, T: (095) 437 018. In Sardinia, you could explore Grotte Is Zuddas, T: (0781) 955 741, F: 955 772, or Grotte Su Mannau, T: (0781) 580 189/(347) 687 4748, both in Cagliari province; and Grotte di Nettuno, T: (079) 946 540, F: 974 881, near Alghero.

Fishing: in Sicily, approach FIPSAS, Via Terrasanta 49, Palermo, T: (091) 302 302 and Via Galermo 166/b, Catania, T: (095) 515 530; in Sardinia, FIPSAS, c/o Palestra Montemixi, Via dello Sport, Cagliari, T: (070) 304 723 (pm only).

Canoeing: in Sicily, embark at Graniti for a 9-km (6-mile) run down the Alcántara river, details from Acquaterra Adventure Club, Piazza Cavour 14, Catania, T: (095) 503 020, www.acquaterra.it; in Sardinia contact Canoa Club, Via dei Vigneti 7, Cagliari, T: (380) 887 7788, or Barbagia No Limits, Via

Cagliari 85, Gavoi, T: (0784) 529 016.

FURTHER INFORMATION
Tourist offices: in Sicily, Via Calábria 301, Messina, T: (090) 640 221; Via Cimarosa 10/12, Catania, T: (095) 730 6211/33; Via S. Sebastiano 43, Siracusa, T: (0931) 481 200; Viale Vittoria 255, Agrigento, T: (0922) 401 352; Piazza Castelnuovo 35, Palermo, T: (091) 583 847/605 8111. In Sardinia, Piazza Italia 19, Nuoro, T: (0784) 30083; Ente Provinciale per il Turismo, Piazza Deffenu 9, Cagliari, T: (070) 651 698; Via Cagliari 278, Oristano, T: (0783) 74191; Via

Caprera 36, Sássari, T: (079) 299 544/46.

FURTHER READING
For Sicily, M. Simeti's *On Persephone's Island* (Bantam, 2001) is fine and lyrical; G. Tomasi di Lampedusa's *The Leopard* (Panther Press, 1996) is one of Italy's greatest post-war novels. For Sardinia, try D. H. Lawrence, *Sea & Sardinia* (Penguin, 1999); Antonio Diego Manca, *The Woman of the Seven Springs* (Corbaccio, 1999); Neil Anderson, *The Lead Goat Veered Off: A Bicycling Adventure on Sardinia* (Cycle Logic Press, 2000).

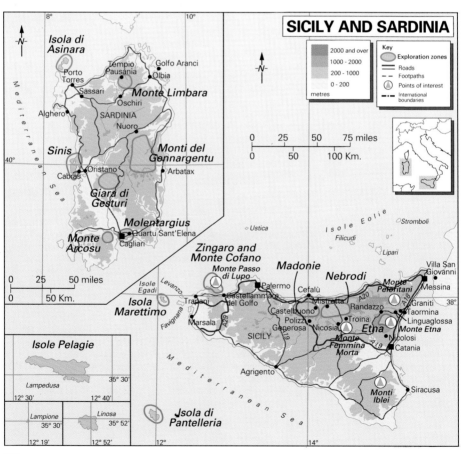

Etna

Europe's largest and most active volcano, rising like a pyramid on Sicily's east coast; parco naturale regionale *58,095 ha (143,560 acres)*

Fumes drift from the snowy summit of Mount Etna during one of the volcano's quieter periods.

Ancient navigators believed Etna to be the highest point on earth. The Arabs called it Jebel, from which derives its alternative name, Mongibello, the 'mountain of mountains'. Pindar described it as the column that supports the sky. Sicilians call it simply 'the mountain'. One of the greatest volcanoes in the world — 3,350 metres (10,990 feet) high and over 250 kilometres (150 miles) in circumference — it is probably the single most monumental land-form in the Mediterranean.

For all its majesty, it is a remarkably young volcano, perhaps only 60,000 years old, and it has some unusual characteristics. Here, in a rare configuration, magma wells up directly from the bowels of the earth, funnelled through a central crater which plunges 50 kilometres (30 miles), direct to the level at which continents drift. Another curiosity is Etna's tendency to split at the seams: eruptions frequently burst through its sides, a feature that has added more than 350 minor craters to the main cone over the millennia and lends the volcano a dangerous unpredictability.

The first recorded eruption was in 475 BC. There have been a countless number since — the most famous, perhaps, in 1329, 1669, 1928 and 1950-51, and the most recent in 2002. The 1971 eruption destroyed the early warning observatory; that of 1979 killed nine tourists; in 1983 the cable car was brought down; in 2001, emergency dams had to be built to divert lava flows from Rifugio Sapienza and Nicolosi. The most catastrophic outburst was that of 1669, when the mountain was rent apart leaving a chasm 25 kilometres (16 miles) long. Magma flowed for 122 days. Catania was engulfed and its castle surrounded by molten lava. The ash thrown up was carried for 100 kilometres (60 miles), and the lava took eight years to cool; peasants, we are told, continued to boil water on it long afterwards.

Today Etna is always at least smouldering, if not actively throwing out lava. This makes it a considerable tourist attraction. Jeeps and a summer procession of walkers make the pilgrimage as close to the main crater as the authorities or the volcano itself will allow. In late spring many make the so-called 'sea to ski' run — swimming in the Ionian sea and skiing on the upper slopes of Etna an hour later. Snow lingers from October through to June and was a source of local income, used to preserve food, until the advent of the refrigerator. Ninth-century Arabs used it to make ice-cream, introducing the inhabitants of the Italian peninsula to one of their great culinary glories.

Away from the people, however, in the surreal desolation of Etna's highest slopes, lies Europe's most extraordinary wilderness: 'Alone! — on this charr'd, blackened melancholy waste,' wrote Matthew Arnold. Everywhere seems an endless horizon of bare rock — not, to my mind, melancholy, but charged with the ethereal loveliness of desert landscapes. It is so beautiful, runs a local saying, that you need four eyes to take it all in. Views from the summit extend for 250 kilometres (150 miles), and Malta is visible on a clear day. Pumice and clinker strew the barren slopes of lava — red, grey, green or black, depending on their age. Shifting sands and powdered ash drift in wind-blown dunes, lunar and eerie; rivers of cooled lava lie like shrunken tentacles, black, with a hint of the obscene.

Ambivalent about the volcano's destructiveness, Sicilians continue to live on its flanks. It is not so much a relationship of love-hate, as that which exists between the sailor and the sea. Elemental and mysterious, turbulent and fickle, Etna takes but she also gives. After as little as a hundred years her lava can weather to a soil of untold fertility. Locals help it on its way by planting the prickly pear, whose powerful roots break up the rock, and follow up with hardy trees, like almond and pistachio. Eventually they plant vines. As a result, Etna's lower slopes are a Garden of Eden, and have one of the densest rural populations in Europe.

If you are lucky enough to climb to the main crater, following in the footsteps of the Emperor Hadrian among other notables, you will pass through a series of distinct changes in vegetation, remarkable for its almost tropical profusion and variety of species. Coastal *maquis* comes first, then a ring of fruit trees (orange, lemon, carob, fig, olive) and then, up to 300 metres (1,000 feet), a thick belt of vines that all but encircles the volcano.

Where cultivation peters out, holm oak, chestnut, beech and hazelnut trees flourish, along with the famous larch pines *(Pinus laricio)* which grow around Linguaglossa in the north-east. Predominant in the undergrowth and forest fringes is the greenweed *Genista aetnensis*, endemic to Sicily and Sardinia, which throws forth yellow-gold flowers with wanton abandon.

Etna's most prodigious plants are its high-mountain pioneering varieties, testament to nature's ingenuity in the face of adversity. Most hardy is *Stereocaulon vesuvianum*, a silver-grey lichen able to grow on lava that is still warm. Most extensive is the endemic legume *Astragalus siculus*, or *spino santo*, 'holy thorn', which covers huge areas of lava with its large hemispherical tussocks studded with delicate pink flowers. Other specialized plants include the barberry *Berberis aetnensis*, also found on mountains elsewhere in the central Mediterranean, the endemic Etna ragwort *Senecio aetnensis* and several species of violet, all adapted to life on lava beds at up to 2,400 metres (7,900 feet).

The volcano is famous for its venerable

individual trees, which botanists think may be some of the oldest in Europe. Best known is the Castagno dei Cento Cavalli, 'the chestnut of a hundred horses', named after the hundred horsemen who are said to have sheltered under its branches with Queen Joan I of Anjou. The circumference of its trunk is a mind-boggling 60 metres (200 feet), and its age is popularly claimed to be 3,000 to 4,000 years, a figure not disputed by botanists. It grows near Sant'Alfio, due east of Etna's summit. Elsewhere there are olive trees more than 2,000 years old.

The summit aside, the chief landmark is the Valle del Bove. A seven-kilometre (four-mile) gash on Etna's south-eastern flank, it is thought to be the remains of an earlier crater, the Trifoglietto, destroyed by the 1669 eruption. Lava walls plunge 1,000 metres (3,000 feet), their precipitous scarps pocked with small volcanic vents. You might also turn to side-shows further afield: the minor craters such as Monte Rosso (1669 eruption) and the Salto della Giumenta (1852); the organ-pipe columns of basalt at Gola dell'Alcántara; the *faraglioni* at Aci Castello near Catania, lava stacks which the Cyclops hurled at the escaping Odysseus in Homer's *Odyssey*; or the spring at Fiumefreddo, which gushes 2,000 litres (450 gallons) of water a second.

BEFORE YOU GO
Maps: TCI 1:50,000 *Carta del Parco dell'Etna*; IGM 1:50,000 Nos 612 *Randazzo*, 613 *Taormina*, 624 *Monte Etna* and 625 *Acireale*.
Guide-book: *Dentro il vulcano* (Parco dell'Etna, 1999).

GETTING THERE
By car: leave the A18 at Fiumefreddo or Giarre and follow minor roads to the east and north slopes, or at Acireale, and head for Nicolosi. SS120 and SS284 encircle the massif. 'Sea to snow' roads run up to Rif. Sapienza in the south, and to Rif. Citelli in the north-east.
By rail: alight at Riposto, Acireale or Catania (main-line station), T: (095) 730 6255, on the Messina–Siracusa line. A scenic 114-km (71-mile) private line, the Circumetnea, runs round the base of Etna from Catania (Borgo station) to Riposto, T: (095) 541 250/1.
By bus: you can leave Catania early am for Rif. Sapienza, returning late pm, A.S.T., T: (095) 723 0511; from the refuge (as well as from Piano Provenzana) a Jeep takes you as close to the crater as it is possible to go (Apr–Oct only).

WHERE TO STAY
Hotels: try the Scrivano (3-star), Via Bonaventura, Randazzo, T: (095) 921 126; Le Betulle (2-star), Loc. Piano Provenzana, Linguaglossa, T: (095) 643 430.
Agriturismo: try L'Antica Vigna, Loc. Montelaguardia, Randazzo, T: (095) 924 003, or Pulvirenti, Via G. Mameli 22, Trecastagni, T: (095) 780 7670 (both at the base of the volcano).
Refuges: choose between touristy Rif. Sapienza, T: (095) 911 062, or the more isolated Rif. Citelli, T: (095) 930 000.
Outdoor living: for stupendous dawns, try Camping Clan dei Ragazzi, Contrada Golfo

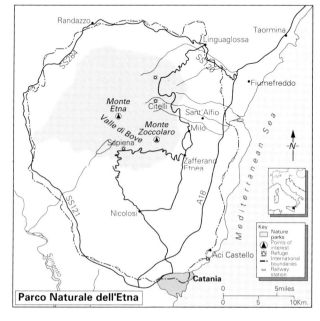

Parco Naturale dell'Etna

Monica, Linguaglossa, T: (095) 643 611, or Etna, Via Goethe, Nicolosi, T: (095) 914 309.

ACTIVITIES

Walking: the busiest ascent is from Rif. Sapienza using the track taken by Jeeps. To avoid crowds, climb from 1 km east of the refuge, following Schiena d'Asino to La Montagnola; from Rif. Citelli, via Serra delle Concazze; or from Zafferana Etnea, on a difficult path via Monte Zoccolaro and Valle del Bove (all 7 hrs). Take enough food and water, be prepared for snow and carry adequate equipment. Walk only in hiking boots; anything else the lava will cut to ribbons. A strong chill wind blows at all times, even in summer. For guides, contact Guide Alpine Etna Nord, T: (095) 647 833/647 592/643 430, or Guide Alpine Etna Sud, T: (095) 791 4755.

Skiing: there are fine cross-country routes, with runs at Linguaglossa and Nicolosi. Obtain ski passes from Funivie dell'Etna, T: (095) 911 158, or S.T.A.R., T: (095) 643 180.

Bird-watching: contact LIPU, Via Ventimiglia 84, Catania, T: (095) 535 935.

FURTHER INFORMATION

Tourist offices: Piazza S. Caterina, Taormina, T: (0942) 23243/4; Pro Loco, Piazza Annunziata 5, Linguaglossa, T: (095) 647 352/643 094; Via Garibaldi 65, Nicolosi, T: (095) 911 505/784; Via Cimarosa 10/12, Catania, T: (095) 730 6211.

Park office: Via Etnea 107/a, Nicolosi, T: (095) 821 111, www.parcoetna.ct.it.

Visitor centres: Randazzo, T: (095) 799 1611; Fornazzo di Milo, T: (095) 955 159.

Rugged limestone uplands such as these near Mezzojuso predominate in the Madoníe mountains, overlooking Sicily's north coast.

Monti Nébrodi

From the Greek nebros, *deer*

Extensive and heavily wooded mountains in northern Sicily; parco naturale regionale *85,600 ha (211,500 acres)*

The Nébrodi are one of the few places in Sicily to have retained their virgin appearance. Their clays and sandstones are still hidden under carpets of ancient forest, providing a green belt between the urban ugliness of the Tyrrhenian coast and the baked earth of the central plains.

The tracts of forest are huge, clothing steep river-cut slopes on the north and more rolling open country to the south. This is the kingdom of the beech, crowned by the centuries-old trees in the Monte Soro and Mangalaviti forests, with fiefdoms of ancient cork and holm oak interspersed on the lower slopes. Yew, a relict species in the Mediterranean, may be seen in the Tassita forest.

Foxes and wildcats prowl the thick undergrowth of the forest floor, and a wild variety of horse, the *sanfratello*, still roams the highest pastures. In spring and autumn migrating birds drop in to rest and refuel at the limpid lakes dotted among the woods, especially at Biviere di Cesarò and Urio Quattrocchi and at the reservoir at Ancipa to the south. Among the birds that breed in the mountains are the rare Sicilian rock partridge and several raptors, including lanner and peregrine falcons and golden eagles.

You can wander here for days without seeing a soul,

enjoying unexpected views, as the tree cover breaks, across to Mount Etna and the Aeolian islands. Summits average about 1,500 m (5,000 ft). A little lower than the Madonie to the west, these mountains are bulkier and, where sandstone predominates, softer in their contours.

Before you go: *Maps:* IGM 1:50,000 Nos 599 *Patti*, 611 *Mistretta* and 612 *Randazzo*.

Guide-book: *Il Parco dei Nébrodi* (Touring Club Italiano, 2001).

Getting there *By car:* from A20, exit at Brolo for Randazzo (SS116) or leave SS113 at S. Stéfano for Mistretta and Nicosia (SS117); from A19, exit at Enna for Nicosia (SS117). SS120 follows southern border of Nébrodi and SS289 crosses range. *By rail:* alight at stations on Messina–Palermo main line, or at Randazzo or Bronte on Circumetnea, T: (095) 921 156. *By bus:* Randazzo to Capo d'Orlando, S.A.I.S., T: (095) 536 168; for local connections, Bevacqua & Vitanza, T: (0941) 421 456/421 986/430 487.

Where to stay *Hotel:* Sicilia (1-star), Via Libertà 128, Mistretta, T: (0921) 81463. *Agriturismo:* Il Vignale, C.da Pado, Longi, T: (0941) 485 015. *Refuges:* contact park office (below) or CAI, Messina, T: (090) 693 196/292 2429.

Activities *Walking:* long haul from Mistretta to Portella Mitta near Floresta (4 days). *Bird-watching:* with Gino Fabbio, photographer, Via Industriale 78, Rocca di Capri Leone, e-mail: ginofabbio@tiscali.it.

Further information *Tourist offices:* Mistretta, T: (0921) 381 677/81035; Randazzo, T: (095) 799 0064. *Park office:* Via Ugo Foscolo 1, Alcara li Fusi, T: (0941) 793 904. *Visitor centres:* S. Stéfano di Camastra, T: (0921) 331 199; Tortorici, T: (0941) 423 1209; Cesarò, T: (095) 773 2061.

The cliffs and coastal margins of the Zingaro reserve, on Sicily's north-west cape, offer a foothold for dwarf palms and eyries for raptors.

Madoníe

Westernmost massif of Sicily's northern coastal chain; parco naturale regionale 39,972 ha (98,775 acres)

Sicily's highest and most impressive mountains after Etna, the Madoníe soar above the north coast, crowned with bare and atmospheric summits and jacketed with woods of pine, beech and chestnut. Exhibiting classic limestone characteristics, they sport fine canyons like those of Pollina (known as Tiberius' gorges), towering crags, such as those at Monte Quacella and Piano Zucchi, and huge *quarare* or sink-holes typical of the mainland Apennines.

Though lofty — the highest point is Pizzo Carbonara (1,979 m/6,493 ft) — and undeniably wild, they have not escaped the taint of tourism. Proximity to Palermo and lingering summit snows have been their downfall. Over the last 30 years skiers, day-trippers and villas have all crowded in, brought by roads like the one from Petralia Sottana to the Piano Battaglia, carried on looping viaducts across some of the Madoníe's most beautiful valleys.

Blemished though they may be, the mountains host more than half the 2,600 plant species found in Sicily, most of them endemics. The most densely wooded areas clustering around Castelbuono, Monte Quacella and the Piano Battaglia are a natural botanical garden. The Vallone della Madonna degli Angeli, near Polizzi Generosa, is the last redoubt of an endemic fir, *Abies nebrodensis*, which was once widespread in the Sicilian mountains. A mere 29 examples survive.

The long-distance path across the Nébrodi to Etna, the Alta Via dei Monti di Sicilia, starts in the Madoníe, and it offers many rewards to walkers. The chances of spotting birds of prey such as Egyptian vultures, peregrines and golden and Bonelli's eagles are good. In high summer the dark purple petals of the violet *Viola nebrodensis* contrast beautifully with the pale limestone bedrock. Views, too, are wonderful, spreading out to the Aeolian islands, Etna and the immensity of the Sicilian interior.

Before you go *Maps:* IGM 1:50,000 Nos 609 *Termini Imerese*, 610 *Castelbuono*. *Guidebook:* F. Alaimo, *Parco delle Madoníe* (Fabio Orlando, 1997).
Getting there *By car:* from A19, exit at Tre Monzelli, Scillato or Buonfornello; from A20, at Castelbuono or Cefalù. Well-signed minor roads from Collesano to Piano Zucchi (15 km/9 miles) and Piano Battaglia (25 km/16 miles). *By rail:* Cefalù on Messina–Palermo main line, T: (0921) 923 147. *By bus:* S.A.I.S., T: (091) 616 6028; A.S.T., T: (091) 681 6002.
Where to stay *Hotel:* La Sabbia d'Oro (3-star), C.da S. Lucia, Cefalù, T: (0921) 421 565.
Refuges: Francesco Crispi, Loc. Piano Sempria, T: (0921) 672 279; 200

Marini, Piano della Battaglia, T: (0921) 649 994. *Outdoor living:* Costa Ponente, T: (0921) 420 085 (open all year) and Plaja degli Uccelli, T: (0921) 999 068 (open May–Sept), both in Cefalù.
Activities *Walking:* from Piano Zucchi to Rif. Marini (3 hrs), to Pizzo Carbonara (2 hrs), with optional circuit to Pizzo Antenna Grande (add 2 hrs) and Monte dei Cervi (another 2 hrs). *Skiing:* cross-country and alpine on Piano Battaglia, CAI, Petralia Sottana, T: (0921) 641 028. *Birdwatching:* LIPU, Via Houel 7, Palermo; T: (091) 320 506.
Further information *Tourist offices:* Cefalù, T: (0921) 421 050; Castelbuono, T: (0921) 671 124. *Park office:* Corso P. Agliata 16, Petralia Sottana, T: (0921) 684 011, or visit www.parcodellemadonie.it.

Zingaro and Monte Cófano

Cliffs and bays on Sicily's north-west coast, with rugged mountainous hinterland; includes two riserve naturali regionali orientate (2,138 ha/5,283 acres)
ZPS

Oases of solitude and silence, the neighbouring headlands of Zingaro and Cófano, between Castellammare and Trápani, owe their survival to perhaps the bravest battle against developers in Italy's history. A mass demonstration in May 1980 halted a road-building scheme and led to the formation of the Zingaro reserve a year later — the first on Sicily. It also prompted the creation of three parks and a further 47 reserves elsewhere, affording protection

to some 9 per cent of the island.

The Zingaro reserve covers just 7 km (4 miles) of coast north of Castellammare, but the abandonment of the coastal road has in effect saved the whole headland. Beyond Scopello, vertiginous limestone cliffs rise from a rugged shoreline pitted with bays and shingle beaches. Behind, mountains tumble seaward, culminating in Monte Passo del Lupo and, at the northern extremity, Monte Mónaco. Dominating the next headland to the west is the miniature Dolomite of Monte Cófano, now also protected by a reserve.

The rocks, caves and thick vegetation along these stretches of coast are well suited to birds, present in ever-increasing number and variety since the creation of the reserves; 40 species have been sighted, including raptors which used to be traded to Arab markets as hunting birds but are now largely safe, among them peregrines, kestrels, lanner falcons and, on occasion, Egyptian vultures. Several pairs of Bonelli's eagles breed here, although they remain at risk from poachers. The best spot for a sighting is on Monte Mónaco, where Europe's smallest sea-bird, the storm petrel, can also be found.

Tracts of dwarf fan palm take pride of place among the Zingaro reserve's 325 plant species, this being the one area in Italy where Europe's only indigenous palm can be said to form woods. The trees reach heights of about 2 m (7 ft) and with the other dominant cover — maquis, bay laurel, wild fennel, caper — add a hint of North Africa to the coast of Sicily.
Before you go *Maps:* IGM 1:50,000 No 593 *Custonaci*.
Getting there *By car:* A29 from Palermo to Castellammare del Golfo, then SS187 and minor road to Scopello. From Trápani, minor roads via Custonaci to S. Vito lo Capo. *By rail:*

Castellammare, on Palermo–Trápani line, T: (0924) 597 240.
By bus: from Palermo, Russo, T: (0924) 31364; from Trápani, A.S.T., T: (0923) 21021.
Where to stay *Hotels:* La Tavernetta (1-star), Scopello, T: (0924) 541 129; Capo S. Vito (3-star), S. Vito lo Capo, T: (0923) 972 284. *Outdoor living:* try Báia di Giudaloca at Castellammare, T: (0924) 541 262 (Apr–Sept).
Access: no camping, boats banned from 300-m (1,000-ft) exclusion zone along shoreline. Zingaro reserve severely damaged by fire, summer 2003.
Activities *Walking:* 3 main walks within Zingaro reserve; within Cófano reserve, ascent of Monte Cófano from Golfo di Cófano (2 hrs). Elsewhere, possibilities include S. Vito lo Capo to Castelluzzo (3 hrs); Castelluzzo to Báia di Cófano (1 hr). *Bird-watching:* LIPU, Via Giovanna d'Arco 2, Alcamo, T: (0924) 597 821.
Further information *Tourist offices:* IAT, Via Savoia, S. Vito lo Capo, T: (0923) 972 464 (summer only). *Park offices:* Riserva dello Zingaro, T: (0924) 35108; Riserva di Monte Cófano, T: (0923) 807 111.

Bonelli's eagle, with its long-tailed silhouette and dashing flight, is also known as the partridge eagle after its favoured prey.

Isola Maréttimo

Most distant island of the Égadi archipelago, off western Sicily; part of Isole Égadi riserva naturale regionale *and* area marina protetta *(52,300 ha/129,200 acres)* ZPS

Maréttimo, closed to cars and largely inaccessible even by boat, is spared the hordes that clamber over its rocky neighbours, Lévanzo and Favignana. Elongated, rugged and sacred to the ancient Greeks, the island is by far the most spectacular off Sicily and, some say, the wildest in the Mediterranean.

A couple of little-used and vegetation-choked paths straggle to the hinterland, climbing the rock-strewn heights of Monte Falcone (686 m/2,251 ft), a lovely vantage point, especially on clear winter days. Caves stud the landscape, the most famous being Tuono, Presepe and Cammello. Most occur along the shoreline, while others scatter the steep hills of the interior, scoured into the limestone that makes up most of the island.

The coast is captivating, all white shimmering cliffs and wave-gnawed headlands, dolomitic in places. Punta Tróia's rocky cape is especially grand, though best observed from a safe distance offshore. On the western coast, you can explore numerous tiny bays, the most secluded being those at Cala Bianca and Cala Nera.

Other islands in the archipelago were once linked to the mainland; Maréttimo has always enjoyed isolation, to the benefit of its native species. Rosemary-dominated *garrigue* and stunted *maquis* are the predominant plant cover. By Sicilian standards water is abundant and vegetation comparatively luxuriant. Although only one patch of ancient woodland has survived — a stand of aleppo pines at Fonte Pegna — 515 lesser plant species grow on the island. Some have developed strains that are found nowhere else, including the large carnation-like thorow-wax *Bupleurum dianthifolium*, a member of the carrot family. Many of the endemic species survive on high rock ledges known locally as *orru*, where they are out of reach of nibbling goats.

An attractive stopping place for many thousands of migrating birds, the island is also a nesting ground for storm petrels, extremely rare in Sicily but here forming a colony of up to 400 pairs.
Before you go *Map:* IGM 1:50,000 No. 604 *Isola di Maréttimo.*
Getting there *By sea:* ferry (2½ hrs) and hydrofoil (1 hr) from Trápani daily in summer, calling at Favignana and Lévanzo, Siremar, T: (0923) 545 455.
Where to stay *Hotel:* only 1, Residence Maréttimo, T: (0923) 923 202 (summer only). For

rooms (and excursions) try Rosa dei Venti, T: (0923) 923 249.
Outdoor living: prohibited on Maréttimo; on Favignana, Egád, T: (0923) 921 555 (summer only).
Activities *Walking:* two coastal paths from Maréttimo port, north to Punta Tróia, south to lighthouse passing Cala Sarde and Cala Nera (both 1 ¼ hrs). Also track from port to Monte Falcone (3 hrs). *Climbing:* many limestone routes, particularly on west side. *Fishing:* to accompany local fishermen, call Co-op. S. Giuseppe, T: (0923) 923 290.
Further information *Tourist offices:* Maréttimo, T: (0923) 923 000/233 (summer only); Favignana, T: (0923) 921 647.

Isola di Pantelleria

Fourth largest of the Italian islands, an unspoiled hideaway in the Sicilian Channel; riserva naturale regionale
2,560 ha (6,330 acres)
ZPS

Early Phoenician settlers on Pantelleria called it Hiranini, the 'island of birds', after the migrating flocks that still cross from Tunisia, which at its nearest point lies just 70 km (45 miles) to the west. The present name derives from the Arabic for 'daughter of the winds', after a constant maddening breeze that relents only in high summer. In Roman times it was a place of banishment.

Volcanic in origin, Pantelleria is still a hotbed of fiery activity. Although the last eruption was in 1891 and the original crater at Monte Gibelè (700 m/2,296 ft) is extinct, the

island hisses and steams from 24 minor craters, known as *cúddie* in local dialect, and from blow holes called *favare* or *mofete*. The most impressive of these are the Grotta del Bagno Asciutto, which you pass on the climb to the old crater from Sibà, and the Stufa ('oven') di Khazén, in the north-west of the island. They form famous natural saunas where you can sit and sweat in dark caves; take a towel and expect to last about 10 minutes.

Elsewhere you might explore the hot springs that boil into the sea at Sataria or the thermal pools at Gadir. Lovely, too, is the Spécchio di Vénere, 'Venus's mirror', a half-clear, half-volcanic sludge of a lake that sits — constantly warmed — in an old crater.

Some of Pantelleria is bleakly volcanic in appearance, like the obsidian-black coastline and other points where the underlying basalts show through, such as gloomy Monte Gibelè.

Walks are lonely affairs, through sparse and darkened landscapes scorched by the sun and whipped by the incessant salt-filled wind. A lot of the island is eerily deserted, especially in the south-east, the Dietro Isola, the 'back of the island'. The prevailing vegetation is the *maquis* whose chief components are holm oak, juniper, myrtle, strawberry tree and broom. In places pine woods creep up the mountainsides, especially at Montagna Grande, the island's highest peak (836 m/2,743 ft). The tang of herbs — mint, sage and oregano — fills the misty-edged air.

Occasionally you come across white houses which are Arab in appearance, the traditional *dammusi*, dwellings that date back to Neolithic times, topped with domes whose function is to collect

rain-water. You may also see the mysterious *sesi*, 20 giant funeral mounds made from rough-hewn volcanic blocks.

Some of the land is fertile and supports caper bushes, dwarf olive groves with trees barely 50 cm (18 in) high and the special Zibibbo vines, which have been planted for centuries on small ridges to catch what little rain falls on the parched island. Orange and lemon groves, protected from the wind by cone-shaped walls, are another example of the islanders' ingenuity in husbanding scarce resources. Known as the Giardini Panteschi, these little oases may be tiny, sometimes containing just a single tree, and they dot the landscape like so many miniature keeps.
Before you go *Map:* IGM 1:25,000 No. 256 III *Isola di Pantelleria.*
Getting there *By air:* flights once daily from Palermo and 3 times daily from Trápani to Pantelleria airport, T: (0923) 912 462; weekends from Milan (June–Oct) and more frequently from Rome (June–Sept). *By sea:* 1 boat (5 hrs, May–Sept), 1 hydrofoil (2 hrs, June–Oct) daily from Trápani; Siremar, T: (0923) 545 555, or Ustica Lines, T: (0923) 222 000.
Where to stay *Hotels:* often expensive and closed in winter. Miryam (2-star), Corso Umberto 1, Pantelleria, T: (0923) 911 374, is open all year. To rent a *dammuso* house, contact Call Tour, T: (0923) 911 065.
Activities *Walking:* 21 paths, marked 1–14 and A–G. Good map from G.A.L. Leader Ulixes, Via Salibi, Pantelleria, T: (0923) 911 251. *Bird-watching:* observatory at Spécchio di Vénere.
Further information *Tourist offices:* Piazza Cavour 1, Pantelleria, T: (0923) 911 838/ 695 011; Piazza Saturno, Trápani, T: (0923) 29000 (open summer only).

Isole Pelágie

From the Greek pelagia, *out at sea*

Islands of Lampedusa, Linosa and Lampione, Italy's remotest outposts; includes riserva naturale regionale *on Lampedusa (360 ha/890 acres) Includes two ZPSs*

The three islands of the Pelágie archipelago, arid and sparsely populated, are some of the most primitive and isolated in Europe. The most southerly points of Italy, they are closer to Africa — in latitude and appearance — than to the Italian mainland.

All three lie south of Tunis. Geologically, Lampedusa and Lampione form part of the Dark Continent, sitting on a limestone platform never deeper than 100 m (330 ft), the continental shelf that links them to Tunisia. Lampedusa, thanks to its proximity to Tunisian ports, has become a favourite landfall for boat people desperate to reach European shores. Linosa, further out to sea, is the last gasp of a volcanic chain that extends south from Vesuvius and the Pontine islands.

All are neglected spots, lost to the sea and the four winds. Long deforested, they are little but dust-bowl and scrub. On Lampedusa people joke about the island's 'national park': two trees withered by lack of water and incessant wind (there is no park). A long way to go for little reward? The pleasures are utter solitude and some of the cleanest water in the Mediterranean.

Lampedusa is mainly bare rock and low whitish limestone hills. Cliffs form its ramparts, especially in the north, full of ragged precipices and fish-teeming grottos. Gentler inlets on the south coast are host to sardines, sponges and corals.

Linosa has three craters to explore and a few lavic beaches. It is as far from civilization as you get, at least in western Europe. The ashen soil, strewn with coke-like boulders, is dry and black, adding to the cauldron effect which, in summer, makes the island one of the hottest places in Italy. Prickly pears, lentisk and fig form the scant vegetation. Paths thread the interior, leading to caves which provide nesting sites for hundreds of Cory's shearwaters. The little cucureddu owl, which almost died out here, is now protected.

Lampione is the smallest island. Like the others it is populated by numerous reptiles, including western whip snakes and geckoes. Sub-aqua opportunities are particularly good here. The sea-bed slopes gently and the fish grow to huge proportions.

The Pelágie archipelago lies athwart the bird migration route between Africa and Europe. In early autumn small groups of resident Eleonora's falcons form offshore and launch some of nature's most organized hunting expeditions, trapping young migratory birds as they cross the Mediterranean to Africa.

On Isolotto dei Conigli ('little rabbit island') next to Lampedusa, and occasionally on Linosa, sea-turtles come ashore early in summer to lay their eggs in the fine sands of the islands' beaches.

Before you go *Map:* IGM 1:25,000 No. 265 II *Isola di Lampedusa, Isola di Linosa, Isola Lampione.*

Getting there *By air:* 2 daily flights from Palermo to Lampedusa airport, T: (0922) 970 006; 1 daily from Milan and Rome (July–Sept), Alitalia, T: (0922) 970 229.

By sea: daily ferry from Porto Empédocle (hourly buses from Agrigento station) to Linosa (7 hrs) and Lampedusa (9 hrs); daily hydrofoil (4 hrs, July–Sept); tickets from Siremar in Agrigento and Porto Empédocle, T: (0922) 636 683, Lampedusa, T: (0922) 970 003, or Linosa, T: (0922) 972 062.

Where to stay *Hotels:* on Lampedusa, Belvedere (2-star), Piazza Marconi 4/6, T: (0922) 970 188, and Medusa (3-star), Via Rialto Medusa 5, T: (0922) 970 126 (all year); on Linosa, for hotels (few) and rooms, call tourist office.

Outdoor living: La Roccia, C.da Cala Greca, Lampedusa, T: (0922) 970 055 (summer only).

Access: on Isolotto dei Conigli, restricted to path in north of island; contact Legambiente, Via V. Emanuele, Lampedusa, T: (0922) 971 611.

Activities *Pony-trekking:* call tourist offices. *Skin-diving:* on Lampedusa, Lo Verde, T: (0922) 971 986, Mediterraneo, T: (0922) 971 526; on Linosa, Mare Nostrum, T: (0922) 972 042.

Further Information *Tourist office:* Via V. Emanuele, Lampedusa, T: (0922) 971 390. *Park office:* Via V. Emanuele, Lampedusa, T (0922) 971 812.

The carob or locust tree has thick leathery pods which contain 55 per cent sugar and may be used as animal fodder and a chocolate substitute.

Monti del Gennargentu

Extreme mountain wilderness occupying most of east-central Sardinia, with the Gennargentu at its heart; includes parco nazionale *(71,000 ha/175,450 acres)*

No invaders, not even the Romans, have ever succeeded in penetrating the remote heights of the Gennargentu. No Christian voices were heard in its pagan desolation for seven centuries. Today it is crossed by just two main roads and is still virtually uninhabited. Some parts are so untouched by man that they have never been named. Such shepherds as dwell on its lonely slopes are people of fierce dignity, sustained by proud and ancient traditions. This is the true Sardinia, say the Sards, its customs, language and super-stitions intact, its people the pure-bred stocky islanders of antiquity, untainted by the 'continentals' — the Phoenicians, Romans, Spaniards, or worse, the Italians.

The Gennargentu is the highest and gentlest of the mountain landscapes on Sardinia's eastern coast, a granite dome which rises to the island's summit, the Punta la Mármora (1,834 metres/6,017 feet). Some say the Gennargentu's literal translation, 'silver gate', refers to the reflection of the sun on its winter snows; others that it owes its name to the silvery colour of its rocks. Whatever the origin, it is a soft and slightly melancholy place which preserves a rounded dignity. It is encircled by far-rippling outer ranges which, if inferior in altitude, are richer in scenic drama. In a great curtain wall curving clockwise from south to west rise the Barbágia, varied in composition and divided into four bastions — Seúlo, Belvì, Mandrolisai and Ollolai — and to the north the famous limestone mountains of the Sopramonte. Where these fall sheer to the sea in the Golfo di Orosei, they create a coastline considered by many to be without equal in Europe.

The sea has always been the way of the invader, and for centuries the islanders retreated from it simply to be free of danger. Moving inland from the east, however, they found only poor winter grazing and so continued with their flocks to the richer pastures of the west. The mountains, uneconomic and inhospitable, were left largely as the islanders had found them — solemn and deserted.

Some of the most distinctive scenery lies in the Barbágia, particularly in the Barbágia Seúlo and Belvì to the south. Here, among the steep valleys and sweeping forests of oak, rise the so-called *tacchi* or *toneri*, high limestone tors that erupt, isolated and splintered, from the schists and granites of the surrounding

The Mediterranean monk seal has a world population of less than 500. The seals used to breed in Sardinian waters, but are thought to have stopped since tourism encroached on their birthing beaches.

hills. The most impressive are the Tacchi d'Ogliastra, such as Punta Corongiu near Jerzu, Santu Orgi near Ulássai and Monte Tónneri near Seui. Other fine examples, Texili and Tonara, are found near Aritzo. The most famous is the mighty obelisk of Perda 'e Liana (1,293 metres/4,242 feet), which dominates the whole of the Ogliastra region and is visible from a great distance.

The sturdy rustic villages of shepherds in the Barbágia are a joy to behold after the monotony of the urban eyesores on the Sardinian plains. Though many appear as single settlements on the map, historically they are made up of different hamlets, each founded as the headquarters of a different clan. Désulo, for example, in the Mandrolisai range, consists of three hamlets: Asuai, Issiria and Ovolaccio, each founded by a separate family. One bred cattle, a second pigs and the third, sheep.

The Sopramonte, by contrast, have had no urban tradition since prehistoric times. Silent and sun-beaten, with griffon vultures circling on high, this is a vast empty waste of dazzling heat-shimmering limestone, crossed by hidden and difficult paths. Roamed by taciturn and weather-beaten shepherds, it is still the haunt of bandits whose sense of honour usually — but don't count on it — forbids the seizing of foreigners. At the heart of this rough white-rocked wilderness lie unforgettable sights for the determined walker, such as the remote prehistoric rock village under Monte Tiscali; the Su Gorropu canyons, the grandest in Italy, 500 metres (1,500 feet) deep, whose relict woods contain yews many hundreds of years old; and the so-called *codule* of Luna and Sisine, only slightly smaller gorges, oleander-filled and surrounded by some of the Mediterranean's largest oak forests. Elsewhere are caves such as the Su Sterru, the karstic plateaux of Doinanicoro and the sink-hole at Su Suercone, 200 metres (650 feet) deep.

In places spring rains nurture waving fields of foxgloves and red peonies, as well as endemics such as the redcurrant, *Ribes sardoum*, and the sea-thrift, *Armeria sardoa*. Each mountain range yields its own indigenous plant types. The Gennargentu boasts a crucifer, *Iberis pruitii*, and a caraway-scented thyme, *Thymus herba-barona*, which perfumes its scrubby summer pastures. The Mandrolisai are blanketed with verdant swathes of cork oak and chestnut, while the Sopramonte have virgin forests of holm oak, a comparatively rare tree since the building of the Sardinian railways. Closer to the sea, olive, carob and lentisk testify to the hot arid conditions. Walkers everywhere will learn to rue the thickets of spurge and dense tangle of *maquis*.

Wherever man is scarce, you may hope to find rare animals, and these mountains are no exception, especially the desolate Sopramonte, where a population of about 1,500 mouflon hold out in wooded areas like the Foresta Demaniale di Montarbu. This lovely animal, the male distinguished by scimitar-curved horns, is related to the Asiatic wild sheep and has been present on the island since classical times.

Bearded and black vultures, once seen in Sardinian skies, are now extinct, but among the 100 or so species of birds in the mountains are 24 pairs of griffon vultures. Five pairs of Bonelli's eagles compete for carrion with 20 pairs of golden eagles and numerous colonies of goshawks (60–80 pairs) and peregrines (150 pairs). Audouin's gulls and Eleonora's falcons breed on the lonely cliff edges of the Golfo di Orosei.

205

BEFORE YOU GO

Maps: IGM 1:25,000 Nos 499 I *Nuoro Ovest* and 499 II *Orani*, 500 II *Dorgali* and 500 III *Oliena*, 501 IV *Orosei*, 517 I *Cantoniera Genna Silana*, 517 II *Baunei*, 517 III *Talána*, 517 IV *Funtana Bona*, 518 III *Capo di Monte Santu* and 518 IV *Punta'e Lattone*.
Guide-book: M. Oviglia, *Gennargentu ultimo paradiso* (Soredit, 1998).

GETTING THERE

By car: take SS131/128 via Monastir from Cagliari and the south, SS125/131 from Ólbia and the north; exit at Nuoro, then follow SS389. Especially lovely stretches of road are Désulo–Fonni (highest village in Sardinia), Oliena–Dorgali and Dorgali–Baunei.
By rail: historic *trenini verdi*, 'green trains', operate on various routes June–Oct and stop frequently at 19th-century country stations. The spectacular Mandas–Arbatax line and the Cagliari–Isili–Sórgono line serve the south and west respectively; the Macomér–Nuoro branch the north. Book through Servizio Commerciale/Marketing Ferrovie dello Stato, T: (070) 580 246, or visit www.treninoverde.com.
By bus: services run to bigger villages from Ólbia and Nuoro; A.R.S.T., T: (0784) 32201, freephone T: (800) 865 042.

WHERE TO STAY

Hotels: Il Portico (2-star), Via Mannu 26, Nuoro, T: (0784) 37535; Bue Marino (1-star), Cala Gonone, T: (0784) 93130; except in Nuoro, most hotels are closed Oct–Mar.
Agriturismo: Guthiddai, Oliena, T: (0784) 286 017; Padrus Ebbas, Fonni, T: (0784) 58354; L'Edera, Belvi, T: (0784) 629 898; S'Orroali, Villanova Strisaili, T: (0782) 30067.
Refuges: Sa Oche, Via Carmine 7,

Oliena, T: (0784) 287 107; Gorropu, Loc. Ortunule, Dorgali, T: (0784) 94897 (June–Dec).
Outdoor living: free camping is permitted, but take plenty of water; organized sites include Iscrixedda, Via Is Orrosas, Lotzorai, T: (0784) 93696 (mid-May–Oct), and Orrì, Loc. Spiaggia Orrì, Tortolì, T: (0782) 624 927 (Jun–Sept only).

ACCESS

Unless accompanied by someone who knows the area, do not stray from marked routes or you could be kidnapped.

ACTIVITIES

Walking: paths are few, navigation difficult and water scarce, but the rewards are huge. Fine routes are from Fonni to Bruncu Spina (1,829 m/6,001 ft); from the Su Cologone spring (signposted from the Oliena–Dorgali road) along the Lanaitto valley to Tiscali, returning down the parallel Doloverre di Surtana (4 hrs, some blue markings); and along the coast from Cala Gonone to Cala di Luna (8 hrs/3 hrs with return by boat, summer only, check times); or from Cala Gonone to Baunei (4 days). For guides, call Centro Escursioni Sardegna, Cala Gonone, T: (0784) 920 025/(349) 672 7750.
Climbing: there are superlative routes on the coastal cliffs and the Sopramonte limestone,

The basalt plateau of the Giara di Gésturi provides a belvedere for views across Sardinia's harsh interior.

including Punta Cusidore (Olíena); Su Gorropu and Doloverre di Surtana canyons (Dorgali); and Monte Irveri (Cala Gonone).

Pony-trekking: for treks from Olíena to Orosei (4 days) and Cala Gonone across the island to Capo Mannu (12 days), call CAI, Cagliari (see below).

FURTHER INFORMATION
Tourist offices: APT, Piazza d'Italia 19, Nuoro, T: (0784) 30083; Pro Loco, Via Lamarmora 181, Dorgali, T: (0784) 96243 and Piazza Chiesa, Sádali, T: (0782) 59094.
Ecology: WWF, Cagliari, T: (070) 670 308 and Nuoro, T: (0784) 32888; CAI, Cagliari, T: (070) 667 877.

Giara di Gésturi

High, isolated plateau in south-central Sardinia
Includes Ramsar, ZPS

The Gésturi is a singular basalt plateau, or *giara*, that rears up 550 m (1,800 ft) above the surrounding plains and pastoral hill country. It is also known as La Giara Grande or, in Sard language, Sa Jara Manna. From afar the 12-km (7-mile) wide,

steep-sided plateau appears unexceptional. On its top, however, spreads one of Sardinia's oddest landscapes, as eerie and mysterious as *The Lost World* of Conan Doyle, especially on damp foggy days.

Herb and *maquis*-covered plains stretch to infinity, dotted with outcrops of pinky-black basalt and vast woods of cork oak. Prehistoric settlements, the *nuraghi*, add to the feeling of otherworldliness. So, too, do the wild horses that roam the heathland, shy and tiny creatures like Shetland ponies.

Trickling streams and areas

of marsh form on the plateau after rain, rich in spring flowers and host to occasional migrating birds. The biggest areas of marsh are Paúli Maiori and Paúli Minori, where numerous invertebrates have lived unchanged for 200 million years.

The little bustard is in evidence, along with the buzzard and the endemic barbary partridge. Other animals you may see, especially close to the Giara's wooded springs, or *mitzas*, are foxes and a distinct Sardinian variety of wildcat, *Felis silvestris lybica*. **Before you go** *Maps:* IGM 1:25,000 Nos 529 II *Usellus*, 530 III *Láconi*, 539 I *Tuili*, 540 IV *Isili*.

Getting there *By car:* from SS131, branch on to SS197 south of Sanluri, heading for Barúmini. Gésturi village is 5 km (3 miles) beyond, with road running final 5 km to plateau. *By rail:* Sanluri, on Cagliari–Oristano main line, T: (070) 491 304. *By bus:* Sanluri to Gésturi, A.R.S.T., T: (070) 409 8324.

Where to stay *Hotel:* Sa Lolla (3-star), Via Cavour 49, Barúmini, T: (070) 936 8419. *Agriturismo:* Co-op. Sa Jara Manna, Barúmini, T: (070) 936 8170/9116, www.sajaramanna.it. *Outdoor living:* free camping permitted, or Sennisceddu, Pau, T: (0783) 939 281.

Activities *Walking:* for round trip from Tuili (1 day), take road west to Turri and north to Setzu; continue north to plateau. Follow path to *nuraghe* at Nuracciassu and to shepherds' huts at Cuili di Aggiu, then north to marshes of S'Ala de Mengianu and Paúli Maiori, and on to Morisia botanical gardens. Turn south to archaeological site of S. Luisa and back to Tuili. *Outdoor sports:* contact Co-op. Sa Jara Manna (above). **Further information:** Comune di Gésturi, T: (070) 936 9341.

Molentargius

Flamingo breeding ground on the outskirts of Cagliari, Sardinia's capital; parco naturale regionale 1,622 ha (4,008 acres) Ramsar, ZPS

The salt-marsh of Molentargius is among the biggest in Europe, and one of the continent's finest bird-watching areas. A third of all European species (180) have been recorded here, among them the huge flocks of flamingoes that bring the marsh its fame. Continuing a centuries-old tradition, noted in medieval records, the flamingoes congregate in their thousands. They are an unforgettable sight, whether flying or simply feeding in shallow water, heads dipping, necks gracefully curved, the ordered pink ranks living up to their local name: *sa genti arrúbia*, the 'red people'. Since 1993 they have been breeding here — a first in Italy and, in an urban setting, anywhere in the Mediterranean.

Molentargius is an ecological paradox. Only one km (⅔ mile) east of Cagliari, a busy and growing city, it is threatened by pollution, arson and land reclamation. None of this seems to put off the flamingoes or the numerous other residents, including the cattle egrets and glossy ibis which have been breeding in these brackish marshes since 1985. Perversely, environmental pollution has been to their advantage, since it encourages the growth of reeds, which are where the birds nest.

The thousands of birds which stop off here are locked on to one of the Mediterranean's key migration routes, which passes over the

Cape Bon promontory in Tunisia and divides, one branch passing over Sardinia and the other over Sicily. In spite of apparently massive disincentives, the birds' natural instincts continue to bring them to the edge of one of Italy's major cities. **Before you go** *Maps:* IGM 1:25,000 Nos 557 II *Quartu Sant'Élena* and III *Cagliari*. **Getting there** *By car:* head for Quartu S. Élena or take road parallel to Stagno di Quartu. *By rail:* Cagliari main station. *By bus:* Nos 30/31 (circular lines) skirt north side of reserve. **Where to stay** *Hotel:* Jolly (3-star), Circ. Pirri 626, Cagliari, T: (070) 485 861. *Outdoor living:* Pini e Mare, Loc. Capitana, Quartu S. Élena, T: (070) 803 103. **Access:** guided visits only, Legambiente, Cagliari, T: (070) 671 003.

Activities *Bird-watching:* LIPU, Via Cilea 79, Quartu S. Élena, T: (070) 837 458.

Further Information *Tourist office:* Piazza Deffenu 9, Cagliari, T: (070) 651 698. *Ecology:* Associazione Parco Molentargius, Via Garibaldi 5, Cagliari, T: (070) 671 003.

Monte Arcosu

Virgin wilderness in Sulcis mountains of south-west Sardinia; includes riserva naturale statale, oasi WWF (2,900 ha/7,160 acres) Includes ZPS

Arcosu occupies a place in conservation folklore, having been bought with 600 million Lira (300,000 Euros) raised almost entirely by public subscription. Italy's largest WWF oasis, it was founded in 1985 chiefly to ensure the

The diminutive Corsican red deer has been saved from extinction and now thrives in three separate areas in Sardinia.

survival of the Corsican red deer, *Cervus elaphus corsicanus*. This dark and compact creature, little more than 90 cm (3 ft) tall, is a distinct subspecies of the European red deer. It was once common all over Corsica and Sardinia but by 1985 it was extinct in the French island and nearly so in the Italian. Thanks to the conservation efforts, it now numbers a healthy 3,000 in Sardinia and has been reintroduced to Corsica.

The reserve is in a mountain environment of exquisite beauty, tucked into a corner of the Sulcis massif. At its heart is the Guttureddu valley, whose crystal-clear river sparkles over polished granite pebbles and glides through shadowy, tree-lined pools. At dawn and dusk, the deer come down to drink, gathering around tiny beaches of brilliant white sand.

Above the river rises a vast area of *maquis* and woodland, a mix of vicious thorny scrub and classic Sardinian forest: cork and holm oak, oleander, carob and alder. Here and there are modest meadows, dotted in spring with a timid first flowering of 23 different species of orchids. At the valley head rises a spectacular ring of dark schist peaks, silhouetted against the surrounding white granite mountains. Splintered tors and crags are the seat of peregrines, goshawks and majestic Bonelli's eagles.

Before you go *Map:* IGM 1:25,000 No. 565 I *Capoterra*.

Getting there *By car:* from Cagliari, take SS195 towards Pula, turn off to Capoterra, go through village and past S. Lucia church. Right at fork.

When to go: autumn for mushrooms, mating of deer and vegetation refreshed by rains; mid-Apr–early June for wild flowers and breeding birds.

Access: open Sat, Sun and public holidays all year; on weekday or in group, must book through WWF Sardegna, T: (070) 968 714, or Co-op. Il Caprifoglio, Via Umberto I 15, Uta, T: (070) 968 714, www.il-caprifoglio.it.

Where to stay *Hotel:* Rosa (3-star), Via Venezia 47, Capoterra, T: (070) 722 016. *Refuge:* Foresteria Sa Canna, contact Co-op. Il Caprifoglio (above).

Outdoor living: Flumendosa, Loc. S. Margherita, Pula, T: (070) 920 8364 (July–Sept).

Activities *Walking:* 20 km (12 miles) of paths.

Further information *Tourist office:* Piazza Deffenu 9, Cagliari, T: (070) 651 698.

The shore of the Sínis peninsula *(overleaf)* is strewn with a curious shingle made of seaweed. Strands of the alga *Posidonia oceanica* are brought to land and formed into pebble-like balls by the action of the waves.

Sínis

Vast dunes, lagoons and spectacular cliff scenery along Sardinia's west coast; area marina protetta Includes Ramsar, ZPS

Western Sardinia's wildest stretch of coast has the Sínis peninsula at its centre. To the south lie the Oristano gulf, the Arburese mountains and what is unofficially known as the Costa Verde: towering cliffs and inlets unspoiled by roads or villages. To the north, as far as Bosa, extends yet more pristine coastline.

Sínis itself, with its pools and lagoons, marshes and estuary, is an escapist's dream. It is probably the ultimate sea and sand experience in Italy, a Caribbean wilderness of white sand and turquoise water.

It is also one of the country's chief bird-watching areas, on a par with Orbetello and the Po Delta, and has become another of Sardinia's flamingo stopovers. Sale Porcus, one of the main lagoons, attracts up to 8,000 birds in the winter. In summer it dries up, leaving a crust of salt behind. Other lagoons, such as Cábras, Místras, Seu and the more southerly S'Ena Arrúbia, are home to vast numbers of crustaceans that provide food for the flamingoes and account for their pink colouring. All the lagoons are immensely rich in fish, eels, grey mullet, bass and giltheads among them.

In these wetlands you will find two of Europe's most threatened birds, the white-headed duck and Audouin's gull. The oasis at Seu is the only place in Europe where you can glimpse the endangered Barbary partridge, which breeds here. You should also see birds only a little less rare, such as the garganey, red-crested pochard, purple gallinule, purple heron, bittern, black-winged stilt, osprey, little bustard and marsh harrier.

Before the summer sun turns Sínis into a scorched and shimmering miasma, the dunes are carpeted in a tapestry of scented *maquis* and flowers, including violets, the endemic sea-lavender *Limonium lausianum*, rock-roses and the splendid barbary nut *Iris sisyrinchium*, whose blue flowers mirror the azure of sea and sky.

Before you go *Maps:* IGM 1:25,000 Nos 514 III *Capo Mannu*, 528 III *Capo San Marco* and 528 IV *San Salvatore*.
Getting there *By car:* SS131 to Oristano, then SS292 and web of minor roads. *By rail:* Oristano, on Cagliari–Ólbia line, T: (0783) 72270. *By bus:* Oristano to Cábras, A.R.S.T., T: (0783) 71776.
When to go: mid-Apr–early June for flowering of orchids and *maquis*, winter for flamingoes.

Where to stay *Hotel:* Mistral (3-star), Via Martiri di Belfiore, Oristano, T: (0783) 212 505. *Outdoor living:* Is Arénas, T: (0783) 52284 (summer only), and Nurapolis, T: (0783) 52283 (all year), both in pine woods near Narbolia, north of Sinis peninsula. *Agriturismo:* Bentu e Soi, Oristano, T: (0783) 212 533; Sa Ruda, Cábras, T: (0783) 391 800; Sa Zenti Arrúbia, S. Vero Milis, T: (0783) 58010.
Activities *Pony-trekking:* Guide Equestri Ambientali, Oasi di Sale Porcus, T: (0783) 528 100. *Watersports:* Diving Club Putzu Idu, T: (0783) 53747; Simbula Giovanni, Cábras, T: (0783) 290 634. *Bird-watching:* for tours to Sale Porcus, contact LIPU, Quartu S. Élena, Cagliari, T: (070) 837 458.
Further information *Tourist offices:* Pro Loco, Oristano, T: (0783) 74191; S. Vero Milis, T: (0783) 53453. *Park office:* Via Tharros, Cábras, T: (0783) 290 071, or visit the web-site, www.areamarinasinis.it. *Visitor centre:* S. Vero Milis, T: (0783) 52200.

The night heron can be identified by its hunched silhouette when stalking fish and amphibians and its erratic moth-like flight when disturbed.

Isola di Asinara

Rugged island off Sardinia's north-west cape; parco nazionale
5,192 ha (12,830 acres)

Tourism has a tendency to cluster: off the north-east cape of Sardinia it has turned the Maddalena archipelago into a busy holiday resort, while to the north-west it has left the island of Asinara all but untouched.

Lying at the tip of a finger-like peninsula, Asinara has always been difficult of access. Depopulated in 1885, it became a penal colony in World War I and a high-security prison in the 1970s. It is still a closely guarded, isolated place and virtually uninhabited. Rocky, narrowing at its waist to a long thin isthmus, the island is covered in craggy hills which culminate in Punta di Scomúnica (408 m/1,339 ft). The coast is cut by bays and sandy creeks, with large reefs of pink coral just offshore. Civilized comforts are absent, but the lap of waves and the sun-beaten seascape are their own reward.

Thanks to its long isolation, Asinara is home to 687 species of flora (almost a third of the Sardinian total), 11 reptiles and numerous mammals. Its most characteristic inhabitants are the endemic white donkeys, which are found nowhere else in the Mediterranean. Standing barely 90 cm (3 ft) tall, they are thought to be the descendants of animals imported from Egypt by the Duke of Asinara in 1800 and abandoned when the island's population departed. Their white coats (and pink eyes) are probably explained by a form of

incomplete albinism. Now roaming wild, they are most likely to be seen near Santa Maria and Trabuccato.
Before you go *Maps:* IGM 1:25,000 425 II *Isola Asinara* and 440 I *Stintino*. **Getting there** *By sea:* twice daily from Porto Tórres, call Golia, T: (0332) 902 521, and Stintino, call Ogliastra, T: (0337) 756 945. *By car:* SS131 or SS200 to Porto Tórres, minor roads to Stintino. *By rail:* Porto Tórres, T: (079) 299 544. **Where to stay** *Hotel:* Tórres (3-star), Via Sássari 75, Porto Tórres, T: (079) 501 604. *Agriturismo:* Gavina Salinas, Porto Tórres, T: (079) 516 183. *Youth hostel:* Balai, Porto Tórres, T: (079) 502 761. **Access:** only with guide. Must leave on last boat, 7 pm. Tickets, freephone T: (800) 561 166 within Italy, or www.parcoasinarastore.it. **Activities** *Cycling:* bikes for hire at Fornelli, la Reale and Cala d'Oliva. *Boating:* for glass-bottomed boat trips, contact park office. *Watersports:* Asinara Diving Center, Stintino, T/F: (079) 527 000. **Further information** *Tourist office:* Pro Loco, Via XX Settembre, Porto Tórres, T: (079) 515 000. *Park office:* Via Iosto 7, Porto Tórres, T: (079) 503 388, www.parcoasinara.it.

Monte Limbara

Pink-granite mountains of northern Sardinia, dominated by Monte Limbara

Monte Limbara distinguishes itself from the rolling wilderness of northern Sardinia by virtue of its height, reaching 1,359 m (4,459 ft) at Punta Balistreri. It is an empty and forbidding

massif, raked by long rocky ridges and broad boulder-strewn valleys. Stretching away on all sides are retinues of lower ranges and plateaux, similar in character.

Throughout the area, but especially on the plateau above Aggius, to the north of Limbara, stand high granite tors, wind-sculpted into fantastic shapes. Many are covered in gorgeous golden lichens, dazzling against the underlying granite, which here in the north is pink or grey.

This is classic territory for birds of prey on the look-out for quarry such as the blue rock thrush, known in Italian as the 'solitary sparrow'. Peregrines are much in evidence. Goshawks and golden eagles can also be seen, along with ravens, alpine swifts and crag martins.

Patches of Corsican pine, holm and cork oak push through the scrubby vegetation, and in the south farmers scratch a living from odd patches of cultivated land, following the pattern of isolated farms, or *stazzi*, adopted by Corsican settlers over the centuries. Otherwise all is emptiness and silence.
Before you go *Maps:* IGM 1:25,000 Nos 443 I *Calangianus,* II *Monti* and IV *Témpio Pausánia.* **Getting there** *By car:* SS127 from Ólbia to Témpio Pausánia, then minor roads into hills. *By rail:* Témpio Pausánia, on Sássari–Palau line; T: (079) 241 301. *By bus:* Ólbia to Témpio Pausánia and local villages, A.R.S.T., T: (0789) 24979. **Where to stay** *Hotel:* Petit Hotel (3-star), Témpio Pausánia, T: (079) 631 134. *Agriturismo:* Muto di Gallura, Aggius, T: (079) 620 559. **Activities** *Walking:* routes from Cammina Limbara, Témpio Pausánia, T: (079) 670 704. **Further information** *Tourist office:* Piazza Gallura 2, Témpio Pausánia, T: (079) 631 273.

GLOSSARY

Agriturismo, an increasingly popular accommodation option allowing you to spend the night in a rural setting, usually on a working farm. Most landlords offer good home cooking and a range of outdoor activities, predominantly pony-trekking. Prices are low. Most regional and local tourist offices have lists of *agriturist* operators.
Alte Vie, marked long-distance paths found mainly in the mountains of northern Italy.
APT, Azienda di Promozione Turistica, tourist organization responsible for each region or town.
Autostrade, motorways, e.g. A1, for which tolls are normally charged.
Biosphere Reserve, a site included in the UNESCO Man and the Biosphere (MAB) programme, which aims to develop reserves of sustainable biodiversity and promote interdisciplinary research and training. This conservation project began in 1971.
Bivacco, bivouac, smaller than a refuge, a rather spartan mountain hostel. Unmanned.
CAI, Club Alpino Italiano, primarily a climbing organization, but takes a strong interest in all issues affecting the mountains (see p14).
Cammino dell'Alleanza, the Italian section of European Trail E1, running from Lombardy to Sicily.
Contrada (C.da), an appellation used for a group of streets close together that share a name.
ENIT, Ente Nazionale Italiano per il Turismo, Italian Government Tourist Office.
European Diploma, European Council Diploma for Conservation. A prestigious if little-known award, given for the good management of protected areas.
FIPSAS, Federazione Italiana Pesca Sportiva e Attività Subacquee, national body devoted originally to fishing but now also to sub-aqua water sports.
FISE, Federazione Italiana Sport Equestri, chiefly concerned with equestrian events, but its branch offices also provide information on pony-trekking and recognized riding stables.
Frazione (Fraz.), a small borough within a town.
FS, Ferrovie dello Stato, the state railways.
GEA, Grande Escursione Appenninica, path crossing the Apennines from Tuscany to Umbria.
GHRV, Grande Haute Route Valdotaine, long-distance route for Alpine skiers.
GTA, Grande Traversata delle Alpi, long-distance path running through the Piedmont section of the Alps.
IAT, Informazione e Accoglienza Turistica, subsidiary branches of the APT.
IGC, Istituto Geografico Centrale, produces a series of 24 contour maps covering north-west Italy.
IGM, Istituto Geografico Militare, produces military maps covering the whole of Italy.
Italia Nostra, one of the longest-established and most highly respected of Italy's pressure groups, originally concerned with urban conservation but now also with outdoor environmental issues.
Kompass, series of contour maps covering most of northern Italy, usually on a scale of 1:50,000.
Legambiente, one of the youngest and most dynamic environmental pressure groups, initially concerned with pollution and anti-nuclear campaigns but now increasingly with wildlife conservation.
LIPU, Lega Italiana per la Protezione degli Uccelli, Italy's leading society for the protection of birds. Most towns have a branch office, many of which organize working parties or bird-watching trips.
Località (Loc.), an appellation designed to clarify the location of a remote address where no street or road names exist. Used for areas outside villages or in parks, often on dirt tracks.
Oasi Naturali, nature oases, by far the smallest of Italy's wild places and a fairly new environmental initiative. Most are run, and often owned, by private bodies, notably WWF (which manages 134), LIPU (32) and Legambiente (38).
Parchi Nazionali, national parks, of which Italy has 21. They are administered by the state and mostly embrace large mountainous regions.
Parchi Naturali Regionali, regional nature parks, numbering 138, administered by one or other of Italy's 20 regions.
Pro Loco, tourist information offices run by APT in smaller towns.
Ramsar, wildlife designation providing protection under international law for wetlands, in particular those used by wintering wildfowl and wading birds. Sites world-wide provide a network of areas for migrating birds. Ramsar is the Iranian town where this convention was adopted in 1971.
Rifugio, refuge, a mountain hostel normally open Jun–Sept. Most are run by CAI.
Riserve Naturali Regionali, regional nature reserves. Regions have widely differing

numbers of parks and reserves: Lombardy has 81 and Sicily 43; Marche, Umbria, Puglia and Calábria have barely a handful between them.
Riserve Naturali Statali, state nature reserves, numbering 146, usually tiny and covering areas of outstanding natural interest. Many are contained within larger protected areas, such as national parks.
SIC, Siti di Importanza Comunitaria, special areas of conservation, of which Italy has 132, covered by the 1992 EU Habitats Directive.
SS, Strade Statali, national main roads, e.g. SS1.
Superstrade, toll-free motorways.
Tabacco, two series of contour maps covering the Dolomites and the north-eastern Alps.
TCI, Touring Club Italiano, a private organization founded in 1894 to disseminate travel literature.
Transboundary Protected Areas, areas administered by park authorities who co-operate across national borders: Stélvio and Engadina parks (with Switzerland), Alpi Maríttime and Mercantour (France) and Gran Paradiso and Vanoise (France).
World Heritage Sites, sites listed as being of cultural or natural importance by UNESCO.
WWF, World Wide Fund for Nature (formerly World Wildlife Fund). The Italian branch was established in 1966.
Zone di Tutela Biologica Marina, coastal marine reserves, of which Italy has 20, also referred to as Riserve Naturali Marine or Aree Protette Marine.
ZPS, Zone di Protezione Speciale, special protection areas, of which Italy has 72, established in response to the 1979 EC Birds Directive.

USEFUL ADDRESSES

Alleanza Assicurazioni, Viale Rubettino 51, 88049 Soveria Mannelli (CZ), T (0968) 666 806, www.alleanza assicurazioni.it.

Associazione Italiana del Turismo Responsabile (AITR), Via Breda 54, 20216 Milan, T: (02) 2578 5763, F: (02) 255 2270, e-mail: info@aitr.org, www.aitr.org.

Autostrade International S.p.A, Via Bergamini 50, 00159 Rome, Italy, T: (06) 4363 2121, F: (06) 4363 2131, e-mail: info@autostrade.it, www.autostrade.it.

Edizioni Multigraphic, Via Campani 64, 50127 Florence, T: (055) 412 908.

Ente Nazionale Italiano per il Turismo (ENIT), Via Marghera 2-6, 00185 Rome, T: (06) 49711, F: (06) 446 3379/446 9907, e-mail: sedecentrale@ enit.it, www.enit.it.

ENIT (UK), 1 Princes Street, London W1B 2AY, T: (020) 7408 1254, F: (020) 7399 3567, e-mail: italy@italiantourist board.co.uk.

ENIT (USA), 630 Fifth Avenue, Suite 1565, New York, NY-10111, T: (212) 245 4822, F: (212) 586 9249, e-mail: enitny@italiantourism.com.

Ferrovie dello Stato (Italian State Railways), national rail enquiries line, Ufficio dei Treni, T: (1478) 88088, freephone within Italy, e-mail: info@fs-on-line.it, www.fs-on-line.com, www.trenitalia.com.

Istituto Geografico Centrale (IGC), Via Prati 2, 10121 Turin, T/F: (011) 534 850.
Istituto Geografico Militare (IGM), Viale Strozzi 10, 50129 Florence, T: (055) 489 867, F: (055) 489 743, www.igmi.org.

Kompass, Loc. Ghiaie di Gardolo 166/d, 38014 Gardolo (TN), T: (0461) 961 217.

Società Geografica Italiana, Via della Navicella 12, 00184 Rome, T: (06) 700 8279, F: (06) 7707 9518.

Tabacco, Via E. Fermi 78, 33010 Tavagnecco (UD), T: (0432) 573 822.

The Map Shop, 15 High Street, Upton upon Severn, Worcestershire, WR8 0HJ, freephone T: (0800) 085 4080 (from UK only), T: (01684) 593 146, F: (01684) 594 559, www.themapshop.co.uk.

Touring Club Italiano (TCI), Corso Italia 10, 20122 Milan, T: (02) 85261, F: (02) 852 6320, e-mail: relest@touringclub.it, www.touringclub.it.

ACCOMMODATION

Associazione Italiana Alberghi della Gioventù (AIG), Via Cavour 44, 00184 Rome, T: (06) 487 1152, F: (06) 488 0492, e-mail: aig@uni.net.

Associazione Nazionale per l'Agriturismo, l'Ambiente e il Territorio (AGRITURIST), Corso Vittorio Emanuele 101, 00186 Rome, T: (06) 685 2342, F: (06) 685 2424, www.acli.it.

Associazione Nazionale Bed & Breakfast e Affitta Camere (ANBBA), Via Istria 12, 30126 Lido di Venezia (VE), T: (041) 731 429, F: (041) 276 9546, e-mail: info@sleepingitaly.com.

NATURE AND ECO-TOURISM

Associazione Italiana Wilderness (AIW), Via Bonetti 71, 17013 Murialdo (SV), T: (019) 53545, e-mail: wilderness.italia@libero.it, www.wilderness.it.

Associazione Verde Ambiente e Società (VAS), Via Flaminia 53, 00196 Rome, T: (06) 360 8181, F: (06) 3608 1827, e-mail: vas@vasonline.it, www.vasonline.it.

Earth Fund, Via C. Battisti 58 bis, 21043 Castiglione Olona (VA), T: (0331) 858 051, e-mail: info@fondoperlaterra. org, www.fondoperlaterra.org.

Fare Verde, Via Iside 8, 00184 Rome, T: (06) 700 5726, www.fareverde.it.

Federazione Italiana Parchi e Riserve Naturali, Via Cristoforo Colombo 149, 00147 Rome, T: (06) 5160 4940, F: (06) 5143 0472, e-mail: segreteria.federparchi @parks.it, www.parks.it.

Federazione Nazionale Pro Natura, Via Pastrengo 13, 10128 Turin, T: (011) 509 6618, F: (011) 503 155, e-mail: info@pro-natura.it, www.pro-natura.it.

Friends of the Earth, Via di Torre Argentina 18, 00186 Rome, T: (06) 686 8289, F: (06) 6830 8610, e-mail: amiterra@ amicidellaterra.it, www.amicidellaterra.it.

Greenpeace, Viale Manlio Gelsomini 28, 00153 Rome, T: (06) 572 9991, F: (06) 578 3531, e-mail: staff@ greenpeace.it, www. greenpeace.it.

Italia Nostra, Via N. Porpora 22, 00198 Rome, T: (06) 844 0631, F: (06) 884 4634, e-mail: info@italianostra.org, www.italianostra.org.

Lega Italiana dei Diritti dell'Animale (LIDA), Via di Piazza Vascella 7, 01037 Ronciglione (VT), T: (0761) 612 075, e-mail: info@lida.it, www.lida.it.

Lega Italiana per la Protezione degli Uccelli (LIPU), Via Trento 49, 43100 Parma, T: (0521) 273 043, F: (0521) 273 419, e-mail: info@lipu.it, www.lipu.it.

Legambiente, Via Salaria 403, 00199 Rome, T: (06) 862 681, F: (06) 8621 8474, e-mail: legambiente@legambiente.com, www.legambiente.com.

Marevivo, Scalo de Pinedo, 00196 Rome, T: (06) 320 2949/322 2565, F: (06) 322 2564, e-mail: marevivo@ marevivo.it, www.marevivo.it.

Nimpha, Via Benedetto Croce 42, 00142 Rome, T: (06) 5960 6523, e-mail: info@ nimphaonlus.it, www.nimphaonlus.it.

Terranostra, Via XXIV Maggio 43, 00187 Rome, T: (06) 468 2368, www.terranostra.it.

World Wide Fund for Nature (WWF), Via Po 25/c, 00198 Rome, T: (06) 844 971, F: (06) 855 4410, e-mail: posta@ wwf.it, www.wwf.it.

SPORT

Associazione Italiana Guide Ambientali Escursionistiche (GAE), Borgata Capoluogo 15, 10080 Ceresole Reale (TO), T: (0124) 953 115, e-mail: infogenerali@gae.it, www.gae.it.

Club Alpino Italiano (CAI), Via Petrella 19, 20124 Milan, T: (02) 205 7231, F: (02) 205 723 201, e-mail: segreteria. generale@cai.it, www.cai.it.

Federazione Arrampicata Sportiva Italiana (FASI), Via del Pilastro 8, 40127 Bologna, T: (051) 633 3357, www.federclimb.it.

Federazione Italiana Canoa e Kayak (FICK), Viale Tiziano 70, 00196 Rome, T: (06) 3685 8188, e-mail: federcanoa@ federcanoa.it, www. federcanoa.it.

Federazione Italiana Canottaggio (FIC), Viale Tiziano 70, 00196 Rome, T: (06) 3685 8650, e-mail: info@canottaggio.org, www.canottaggio.org.

Federazione Italiana Pesca Sportiva e Attività Subacquee (FIPSAS), Viale Tiziano 70, 00196 Rome, T: (06) 3685 8365, e-mail: segreteria@ fipsas.it, www.fipsas.it.

Federazione Italiana Sport Equestri (FISE), Viale Tiziano 74, 00196 Rome, T: (06) 3685 8326, e-mail: news@fise.it, www.fise.it.

Federazione Italiana Sport Invernali (FISI), Via Piranesi 44, 20137 Milan, T: (02) 75731, F: (02) 738 0624.

Federazione Italiana Vela (FIV), Viale Brigata Bisagno 2/17, 16129 Genoa, T: (010) 565 083, F: (010) 592 864.

INDEX

PICTURE CREDITS

Front Cover – FLPA/Marka, J. Cleare, Mountain Camera. 10/11 – T. Jepson. 18/19 – FLPA/Marka. 22/23 – FLPA/Marka. 27 – T. Jepson. 30 – T. Jepson. 34/35 – FLPA/Marka. 38/39 – Woolverton Picture Library. 46/47 – T. Jepson. 51 – FLPA/Marka. 54 – FLPA/Marka. 58 – V. Tomaselli, Panda Photo. 59 – FLPA/Marka. 62/63 – G. Cappelli, Panda Photo. 71 – FLPA/Marka. 74/75 – FLPA/Marka. 68/69 – R. Mattio, Panda Photo. 79 – R. Ricci, Panda Photo. 82/83 – D. Walsh. 90/91 – FLPA/Marka. 94 – T. Jepson. 98 – FLPA/Marka. 99 – FLPA/Marka. 102/103 – D. Walsh. 106/107 – J. Cleare, Mountain Camera. 111 – T. Jepson. 114/115 – FLPA/Marka. 118 – J. Cleare, Mountain Camera. 122 – S. Benn. 126/127 – FLPA/Marka. 130/131 – FLPA/Marka. 138 – Italian Tourist Office. 142/143 – E. Parker, Hutchinson Library. 146 – J. Sutherland, Nature Photographers Ltd. 147 – FLPA/Marka. 150 – Sheldrake. 154/155 – FLPA/Marka. 159 – A. Mongiu, Panda Photo. 162/163 – A. Mongiu, Panda Photo. 167 – A. Nadri, Panda Photo. 170 – A. Nadri, Panda Photo. 171 – A. Nadri, Panda Photo. 174/175 – FLPA/Marka. 179 – S.Benn. 186 – FLPA/Marka. 187 – N. Birch. 190/191 – FLPA/Marka. 195 – N. Birch. 198 – R. Francis, Hutchinson Library. 199 – FLPA/Marka. 206/207 – FLPA/Marka. 210/211 – FLPA/Marka.

ACKNOWLEDGEMENTS

The contributors and editors wish to extend their grateful thanks to the following people: Nigel Bradley, Piers Burnett, John Burton, Julia Farino, IUCN, Jane Judd, David Stubbs.